LEADERSHIP

Sixth Edition

To Laurel, Scott, Lisa, and Madison

LEADERSHIP

Theory and Practice • Sixth Edition

PETER G. NORTHOUSE

Western Michigan University

Los Angeles | London | New Delhi
Singapore | Washington DC

Los Angeles | London | New Delhi
Singapore | Washington DC

FOR INFORMATION:

SAGE Publications, Inc.
2455 Teller Road
Thousand Oaks, California 91320
E-mail: order@sagepub.com

SAGE Publications Ltd.
1 Oliver's Yard
55 City Road
London EC1Y 1SP
United Kingdom

SAGE Publications India Pvt. Ltd.
B 1/I 1 Mohan Cooperative Industrial Area
Mathura Road, New Delhi 110 044
India

SAGE Publications Asia-Pacific Pte. Ltd.
33 Pekin Street #02-01
Far East Square
Singapore 048763

Acquiring Editor: Lisa Cuevas Shaw and
                    Patricia Quinlin
Associate Editor: Maggie Stanley
Editorial Assistant: Mayan N. White
Assistant Editor: MaryAnn Vail
Project Editor: Eric Garner
Copy Editor: Melinda Masson
Typesetter: C&M Digitals (P) Ltd.
Proofreader: Susan Schon
Indexer: Judy Hunt
Cover Designer: Gail Buschman
Marketing Manager: Helen Salmon/Liz Thorton
Permissions Editor: Karen Ehrmann

Printed in the United States of America

Library of Congress Cataloging-in-Publication Data

Northouse, Peter Guy.

Leadership : theory and practice / Peter G. Northouse. – 6th ed.

p. cm.
Includes bibliographical references and index.

ISBN 978-1-4522-0340-9 (pbk.)

1. Leadership. 2. Leadership–Case studies. I. Title.

HM1261.N67 2013
303.3'4–dc23   2011049043

12 13 14 15 16 10 9 8 7 6 5 4 3 2 1

Contents

Preface

This sixth edition of *Leadership: Theory and Practice* is written with the objective of bridging the gap between the often-simplistic popular approaches to leadership and the more abstract theoretical approaches. Like the previous editions, this edition reviews and analyzes a selected number of leadership theories, giving special attention to how each theoretical approach can be applied in real-world organizations. In essence, my purpose is to explore how leadership theory can inform and direct the way leadership is practiced.

New to this volume is a chapter on *servant leadership*, which examines the nature of servant leadership, its underpinnings, and how it works. The chapter presents both a definition and a new evidence-based model of servant leadership. In addition, the strengths and weaknesses of the servant leadership approach are examined, and a questionnaire to help readers assess their own levels of servant leadership is provided. Three case studies illustrating servant leadership are presented at the end of the chapter.

This edition retains many special features from previous editions but has been updated to include new research findings, figures and tables, and everyday applications for many leadership topics including leader–member exchange theory, transformational and authentic leadership, team leadership, the labyrinth of women's leadership, and historical definitions of leadership. The format of this edition parallels the format used in earlier editions. As with previous editions, the overall goal of *Leadership: Theory and Practice* is to advance our understanding of the many different approaches to leadership and ways to practice it more effectively.

SPECIAL FEATURES ─────────────────────────────

Although this text presents and analyzes a wide range of leadership research, every attempt has been made to present the material in a clear, concise, and interesting manner. Reviewers of the book have consistently commented that clarity is one of its major strengths. In addition to the writing style, several other features of the book help make it user-friendly.

- Each chapter follows the same format: It is structured to include first theory and then practice.
- Every chapter contains a discussion of the strengths and criticisms of the approach under consideration, and assists the reader in determining the relative merits of each approach.
- Each chapter includes an application section that discusses the practical aspects of the approach and how it could be used in today's organizational settings.
- Three case studies are provided in each chapter to illustrate common leadership issues and dilemmas. Thought-provoking questions follow each case study, helping readers to interpret the case.
- A questionnaire is provided in each of the chapters to help the reader apply the approach to his or her own leadership style or setting.
- Figures and tables illustrate the content of the theory and make the ideas more meaningful.

Through these special features, every effort has been made to make this text substantive, understandable, and practical.

AUDIENCE ─────────────────────────────

This book provides both an in-depth presentation of leadership theory and a discussion of how it applies to real-life situations. Thus, it is intended for undergraduate and graduate classes in management, leadership studies, business, educational leadership, public administration, nursing and allied health, social work, criminal justice, industrial and organizational psychology, communication, religion, agricultural education, political and military science, and training and development. It is particularly well suited as a supplementary text for core organizational behavior courses or as an overview text within MBA curricula. This book would also be useful as a text in student activities, continuing education, in-service training, and other leadership-development programs.

Instructor Teaching Site

Instructor Resources are available on the password-protected section of the book's companion website. Test banks include multiple choice and true/false questions to test comprehension of fundamental material, as well as essay questions that ask students to apply the material. An electronic testbank, compatible with PCs and Macs through Diploma software, is also available. Chapter-specific resources include PowerPoint slides, study and discussion questions, suggested exercises, full-text journal articles, video links, audio links, and full-text reference articles. General resources include course-long projects, sample syllabi, and film resources. Printable PDF versions of the questionnaires from the text are included for instructors to print and distribute for classroom use. The companion site also features information on how to use social media with *Leadership*, 6th edition, including instructions for creating wikis, blogs, and Twitter feeds to accompany the text and specific topics to discuss using these different technologies. Go to www.sagepub.com/northouse6e to access the companion site.

Student Study Site

To maximize students' comprehension of this material, student resources are available on the open-access portion of the book's companion website. Resources include web quizzes, SAGE journal articles with discussion questions, video links, audio links, handbook and encyclopedia articles, and other study aides and resources. Students can go to www.sagepub.com/northouse6e to access the site.

Media Icons

Icons appearing at the bottom of the page will direct you to online media such as videos, audio links, journal articles, and reference articles that correspond with key chapter concepts. Visit the Student Study Site at www.sagepub.com/northouse6e to access this media.

 Video Icon

 Audio Icon

 Journal Icon

Reference Article Icon

Acknowledgments

Many people directly or indirectly contributed to the development of the sixth edition of *Leadership: Theory and Practice*. First, I would like to acknowledge my editor, Lisa Shaw, and her talented team at SAGE Publications (Mayan, MaryAnn, Helen, Sarah, and Maggie) who have contributed significantly to the quality of this edition and ensured its success. For their very capable work during the production phase, I would like to thank copy editor Melinda Masson, and senior project editor Eric Garner. In his or her own unique way, each of these people made valuable contributions to the sixth edition.

For comprehensive reviews of the sixth edition, I would like to thank the following reviewers:

Meera Alagaraja, *University of Louisville*

S. Todd Deal, *Georgia Southern University*

Carol McMillan, *New School University*

Keeok Park, *University of La Verne*

Harriet L. Schwartz, *Carlow University*

Kelli K. Smith, *University of Nebraska-Lincoln*

Danny L. Talbot, *Washington State University*

Robert L. Taylor, *University of Louisville*

John Tummons, *University of Missouri*

David E. Williams, *Texas Tech University*

Sharon A. Wulf, *Worcester Polytechnic Institute School of Business*

For their exceptional work creating content for the leadership profile tool that accompanies the interactive eBook version of this text, I would like to thank John Baker (Western Kentucky University), Isolde Anderson (Hope College), and Eleanor Dombrowski (University of Toledo).

I would also like to thank the following people, who updated and created the excellent resources that appear on the Instructor Teaching Site and the Student Study Site:

Isolde Anderson, Hope College

Andrea Markowitz, Write for Your Business

Lizz Mathews, Western Michigan University

Mary Mathews, Western Michigan University

Rebecca G. McBride, Old Dominion University

Trey Patrick Mitchell, Western Michigan University

Lisa J. Northouse, Western Michigan University

Anita Pankake, University of Texas–Pan American

A special acknowledgment goes to Laurel Northouse for her insightful critiques and ongoing support. In addition, I am grateful to Marie Lee, for her exceptional editing and guidance throughout this project. For his review of and comments on the servant leadership chapter, I am indebted to Robert Liden (University of Illinois at Chicago).

Finally, I would like to thank the many undergraduate and graduate students whom I have taught through the years. Their ongoing feedback has helped clarify my thinking about leadership and encouraged me to make plain the practical implications of leadership theories.

Introduction

L eadership is a highly sought-after and highly valued commodity. In the 15 years since the first edition of this book was published, the public has become increasingly captivated by the idea of leadership. People continue to ask themselves and others what makes good leaders. As individuals, they seek more information on how to become effective leaders. As a result, bookstore shelves are filled with popular books about leaders and advice on how to be a leader. Many people believe that leadership is a way to improve their personal, social, and professional lives. Corporations seek those with leadership ability because they believe they bring special assets to their organizations and, ultimately, improve the bottom line. Academic institutions throughout the country have responded by providing programs in leadership studies.

In addition, leadership has gained the attention of researchers worldwide. A review of the scholarly studies on leadership shows that there is a wide variety of different theoretical approaches to explain the complexities of the leadership process (e.g., Bass, 1990; Bryman, 1992; Bryman, Collinson, Grint, Jackson & Uhl-Bien, 2011; Day & Antonakis, 2012; Gardner, 1990; Hickman, 2009; Mumford, 2006; Rost, 1991). Some researchers conceptualize leadership as a trait or as a behavior, whereas others view leadership from an information-processing perspective or relational standpoint. Leadership has been studied using both qualitative and quantitative methods in many contexts, including small groups, therapeutic groups, and large organizations. Collectively, the research findings on leadership from all of these areas provide a picture of a process that is far more sophisticated and complex than the often-simplistic view presented in some of the popular books on leadership.

This book treats leadership as a complex process having multiple dimensions. Based on the research literature, this text provides an in-depth description and application of many different approaches to leadership. Our emphasis is on how theory can inform the practice of leadership. In this book, we describe each theory and then explain how the theory can be used in real situations.

LEADERSHIP DEFINED

There are many ways to finish the sentence, "Leadership is. . . ." In fact, as Stogdill (1974, p. 7) pointed out in a review of leadership research, there are almost as many different definitions of *leadership* as there are people who have tried to define it. It is much like the words *democracy, love,* and *peace.* Although each of us intuitively knows what we mean by such words, the words can have different meanings for different people. As Box 1.1 shows, scholars and practitioners have attempted to define leadership for more than a century without universal consensus.

Box 1.1 The Evolution of Leadership Definitions

While many have a gut-level grasp of what leadership is, putting a definition to the term has proved to be a challenging endeavor for scholars and practitioners alike. More than a century has lapsed since leadership became a topic of academic introspection, and definitions have evolved continuously during that period. These definitions have been influenced by many factors from world affairs and politics to the perspectives of the discipline in which the topic is being studied. In a seminal work, Rost (1991) analyzed materials written from 1900 to 1990, finding more than 200 different definitions for leadership. His analysis provides a succinct history of how leadership has been defined through the last century:

1900–1929

Definitions of leadership appearing in the first three decades of the 20th century emphasized control and centralization of power with a common theme of domination. For example, at a conference on leadership in 1927, leadership was defined as "the ability to impress the will of the leader on those led and induce obedience, respect, loyalty, and coopera- tion" (Moore, 1927, p. 124).

1930s

Traits became the focus of defining leadership, with an emerging view of leadership as influence rather than domination. Leadership is also identified as the interaction of an individual's specific personality traits with those of a group, noting that while the attitudes and activities of the many are changed by the one, the many may also influence a leader.

1940s

The group approach came into the forefront with leadership being defined as the behavior of an individual while involved in directing group activities (Hemphill, 1949). At the same time, leadership by persuasion is distinguished from "drivership" or leadership by coercion (Copeland, 1942).

1950s

Three themes dominated leadership definitions during this decade:
- **continuance of group theory,** which framed leadership as what leaders do in groups;
- **leadership as a relationship that develops shared goals,** which defined leadership based on behavior of the leader; and
- **effectiveness,** in which leadership is defined by the ability to influence overall group effectiveness.

1960s

Although a tumultuous time for world affairs, the 1960s saw harmony amongst leadership scholars. The prevailing definition of leadership as *behavior* that influences people toward shared goals was underscored by Seeman (1960) who described leadership as "acts by persons which influence other persons in a shared direction" (p. 53).

1970s

The group focus gave way to the organizational behavior approach, where leadership became viewed as "initiating and maintaining groups or organizations to accomplish group or organizational goals" (Rost, 1991, p. 59). Burns's (1978) definition, however, is the most important concept of leadership to emerge: "Leadership is the reciprocal process of mobilizing by persons with certain motives and values, various economic, political, and other resources, in a context of competition and conflict, in order to realize goals independently or mutually held by both leaders and followers" (p. 425).

(Continued)

 1.3 Perspectives of Leadership   **1.4** Followership

(Continued)

1980s

This decade exploded with scholarly and popular works on the nature of leadership, bringing the topic to the apex of the academic and public consciousnesses. As a result, the number of definitions for leadership became a prolific stew with several persevering themes:

- **Do as the leader wishes.** Leadership definitions still predominantly deliver the message that leadership is getting followers to do what the leader wants done.
- **Influence.** Probably the most often used word in leadership definitions of the 1980s, *influence* is examined from every angle. In an effort to distinguish leadership from management, however, scholars insist that leadership is *noncoercive* influence.
- **Traits.** Spurred by the national bestseller *In Search of Excellence* (Peters & Waterman, 1982), the leadership-as-excellence movement brought leader traits back to the spotlight. As a result, many people's understanding of leadership is based on a trait orientation.
- **Transformation.** Burns (1978) is credited for initiating a movement defining leadership as a transformational process, stating that leadership occurs "when one or more persons engage with others in such a way that leaders and followers raise one another to higher levels of motivation and morality" (p. 83).

Into the 21st Century

After decades of dissonance, leadership scholars agree on one thing: They can't come up with a common definition for leadership. Debate continues as to whether leadership and management are separate processes, while others emphasize the trait, skill, or relational aspects of leadership. Because of such factors as growing global influences and generational differences, leadership will continue to have different meanings for different people. The bottom line is that leadership is a complex concept for which a determined definition may long be in flux.

SOURCE: Adapted from *Leadership for the Twenty-First Century,* by J. C. Rost, 1991, New York: Praeger.

Ways of Conceptualizing Leadership

In the past 60 years, as many as 65 different classification systems have been developed to define the dimensions of leadership (Fleishman et al., 1991). One such classification system, directly related to our discussion, is

 1.1 Leadership and Power   **1.5** Leadership in Organizations

the scheme proposed by Bass (1990, pp. 11–20). He suggested that some definitions view leadership as the *focus of group processes*. From this perspective, the leader is at the center of group change and activity and embodies the will of the group. Another set of definitions conceptualizes leadership from a *personality perspective*, which suggests that leadership is a combination of special traits or characteristics that some individuals possess. These traits enable those individuals to induce others to accomplish tasks. Other approaches to leadership define it as an *act* or a *behavior*—the things leaders do to bring about change in a group.

In addition, some define leadership in terms of the *power relationship* that exists between leaders and followers. From this viewpoint, leaders have power that they wield to effect change in others. Others view leadership as a *transformational* process that moves followers to accomplish more than is usually expected of them. Finally, some scholars address leadership from a *skills perspective*. This viewpoint stresses the capabilities (knowledge and skills) that make effective leadership possible.

Definition and Components

Despite the multitude of ways in which leadership has been conceptualized, the following components can be identified as central to the phenomenon: (a) Leadership is a process, (b) leadership involves influence, (c) leadership occurs in groups, and (d) leadership involves common goals. Based on these components, the following definition of leadership is used in this text:

✳ **Leadership** is a process whereby an individual influences a group of individuals to achieve a common goal.

Defining leadership as a *process* means that it is not a trait or characteristic that resides in the leader, but rather a transactional event that occurs between the leader and the followers. *Process* implies that a leader affects and is affected by followers. It emphasizes that leadership is not a linear, one-way event, but rather an interactive event. When leadership is defined in this manner, it becomes available to everyone. It is not restricted to the formally designated leader in a group.

Leadership involves *influence*. It is concerned with how the leader affects followers. Influence is the sine qua non of leadership. Without influence, leadership does not exist.

Leadership occurs in *groups*. Groups are the context in which leadership takes place. Leadership involves influencing a group of individuals who have

 **1.2** Role of Leadership   **1.2** Working Across Generations

a common purpose. This can be a small task group, a community group, or a large group encompassing an entire organization. Leadership is about one individual influencing a group of others to accomplish common goals. Others (a group) are required for leadership to occur. Leadership training programs that teach people to lead themselves are not considered a part of leadership within the definition that is set forth in this discussion.

Leadership includes attention to *common goals*. Leaders direct their energies toward individuals who are trying to achieve something together. By *common*, we mean that the leaders and followers have a mutual purpose. Attention to common goals gives leadership an ethical overtone because it stresses the need for leaders to work with followers to achieve selected goals. Stressing mutuality lessens the possibility that leaders might act toward followers in ways that are forced or unethical. It also increases the possibility that leaders and followers will work together toward a common good (Rost, 1991).

Throughout this text, the people who engage in leadership will be called *leaders*, and those toward whom leadership is directed will be called *followers*. Both leaders and followers are involved together in the leadership process. Leaders need followers, and followers need leaders (Burns, 1978; Heller & Van Til, 1983; Hollander, 1992; Jago, 1982). Although leaders and followers are closely linked, it is the leader who often initiates the relationship, creates the communication linkages, and carries the burden for maintaining the relationship.

In our discussion of leaders and followers, attention will be directed toward follower issues as well as leader issues. Leaders have an ethical responsibility to attend to the needs and concerns of followers. As Burns (1978) pointed out, discussions of leadership sometimes are viewed as elitist because of the implied power and importance often ascribed to leaders in the leader-follower relationship. Leaders are not above or better than followers. Leaders and followers must be understood in relation to each other (Hollander, 1992) and collectively (Burns, 1978). They are in the leadership relationship together—and are two sides of the same coin (Rost, 1991).

LEADERSHIP DESCRIBED

In addition to definitional issues, it is also important to discuss several other questions pertaining to the nature of leadership. In the following section, we will address questions such as how leadership as a trait differs from leadership as a process; how appointed leadership differs from emergent leadership; and how the concepts of power, coercion, and management differ from leadership.

Trait Versus Process Leadership

We have all heard statements such as "He is born to be a leader" or "She is a natural leader." These statements are commonly expressed by people who take a trait perspective toward leadership. The trait perspective suggests that certain individuals have special innate or inborn characteristics or qualities that make them leaders, and that it is these qualities that differentiate them from nonleaders. Some of the personal qualities used to identify leaders include unique physical factors (e.g., height), personality features (e.g., extraversion), and other characteristics (e.g., intelligence and fluency; Bryman, 1992). In Chapter 2, we will discuss a large body of research that has examined these personal qualities.

To describe leadership as a trait is quite different from describing it as a process (Figure 1.1). The trait viewpoint conceptualizes leadership as a property or set of properties possessed in varying degrees by different people (Jago, 1982). This suggests that it resides *in* select people and restricts leadership to those who are believed to have special, usually inborn, talents.

Figure 1.1   The Different Views of Leadership

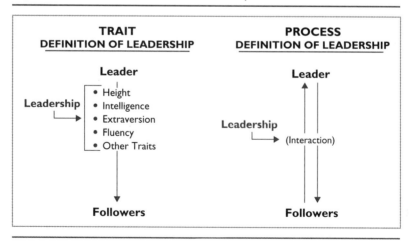

SOURCE: Adapted from *A Force for Change: How Leadership Differs From Management* (pp. 3–8), by J. P. Kotter, 1990, New York: Free Press.

The process viewpoint suggests that leadership is a phenomenon that resides in the context of the interactions between leaders and followers and makes leadership available to everyone. As a process, leadership can be observed in leader behaviors (Jago, 1982), and can be learned. The process definition of leadership is consistent with the definition of leadership that we have set forth in this chapter.

Assigned Versus Emergent Leadership

Some people are leaders because of their formal position in an organization, whereas others are leaders because of the way other group members respond to them. These two common forms of leadership are called *assigned leadership* and *emergent leadership*. Leadership that is based on occupying a position in an organization is assigned leadership. Team leaders, plant managers, department heads, directors, and administrators are all examples of assigned leadership.

Yet the person assigned to a leadership position does not always become the real leader in a particular setting. When others perceive an individual as the most influential member of a group or an organization, regardless of the individual's title, the person is exhibiting emergent leadership. The individual acquires emergent leadership through other people in the organization who support and accept that individual's behavior. This type of leadership is not assigned by position; rather, it emerges over a period through communication. Some of the positive communication behaviors that account for successful leader emergence include *being verbally involved, being informed, seeking others' opinions, initiating new ideas,* and *being firm but not rigid* (Fisher, 1974).

In addition to communication behaviors, researchers have found that personality plays a role in leadership emergence. For example, Smith and Foti (1998) found that certain personality traits were related to leadership emergence in a sample of 160 male college students. The individuals who were more dominant, more intelligent, and more confident about their own performance (general self-efficacy) were more likely to be identified as leaders by other members of their task group. Although it is uncertain whether these findings apply to women as well, Smith and Foti suggested that these three traits could be used to identify individuals perceived to be emergent leaders.

✳ Leadership emergence may also be affected by gender-biased perceptions. In a study of 40 mixed-sex college groups, Watson and Hoffman (2004)

1.3 Effective Leadership

found that women who were urged to persuade their task groups to adopt high-quality decisions succeeded with the same frequency as men with identical instructions. Although women were equally influential leaders in their groups, they were rated significantly lower than comparable men were on leadership. Furthermore, these influential women were also rated as significantly less likable than comparably influential men were. These results suggest that there continue to be barriers to women's emergence as leaders in some settings.

A unique perspective on leadership emergence is provided by social identity theory (Hogg, 2001). From this perspective, leadership emergence is the degree to which a person fits with the identity of the group as a whole. As groups develop over time, a group prototype also develops. Individuals emerge as leaders in the group when they become most like the group prototype. Being similar to the prototype makes leaders attractive to the group and gives them influence with the group.

The leadership approaches we discuss in the subsequent chapters of this book apply equally to assigned leadership and emergent leadership. When a person is engaged in leadership, that person is a leader, whether leadership was assigned or emerged. This book focuses on the leadership process that occurs when any individual is engaged in influencing other group members in their efforts to reach a common goal.

Leadership and Power

The concept of power is related to leadership because it is part of the influence process. Power is the capacity or potential to influence. People have power when they have the ability to affect others' beliefs, attitudes, and courses of action. Ministers, doctors, coaches, and teachers are all examples of people who have the potential to influence us. When they do, they are using their power, the resource they draw on to effect change in us.

The most widely cited research on power is French and Raven's (1959) work on the bases of social power. In their work, they conceptualized power from the framework of a dyadic relationship that included both the person influencing and the person being influenced. French and Raven identified five common and important bases of power: referent, expert, legitimate, reward, and coercive (Table 1.1). Each of these bases of power increases a leader's capacity to influence the attitudes, values, or behaviors of others.

1.3 Nursing Roles in Heathcare   **1.1** Power and Leadership

Table 1.1 Five Bases of Power

Referent Power	Based on followers' identification and liking for the leader. A teacher who is adored by students has referent power.
Expert Power	Based on followers' perceptions of the leader's competence. A tour guide who is knowledgeable about a foreign country has expert power.
Legitimate Power	Associated with having status or formal job authority. A judge who administers sentences in the courtroom exhibits legitimate power.
Reward Power	Derived from having the capacity to provide rewards to others. A supervisor who gives rewards to employees who work hard is using reward power.
Coercive Power	Derived from having the capacity to penalize or punish others. A coach who sits players on the bench for being late to practice is using coercive power.

SOURCE: Adapted from "The Bases of Social Power," by J. R. French Jr. and B. Raven, 1962, in D. Cartwright (Ed.), *Group Dynamics: Research and Theory* (pp. 259–269), New York: Harper & Row.

In organizations, there are two major kinds of power: position power and personal power. *Position power* is the power a person derives from a particular office or rank in a formal organizational system. It is the influence capacity a leader derives from having higher status than the followers have. Vice presidents and department heads have more power than staff personnel do because of the positions they hold in the organization. Position power includes legitimate, reward, and coercive power (Table 1.2).

Personal power is the influence capacity a leader derives from being seen by followers as likable and knowledgeable. When leaders act in ways that are important to followers, it gives leaders power. For example, some managers have power because their subordinates consider them to be good role models. Others have power because their subordinates view them as highly competent or considerate. In both cases, these managers' power is ascribed to them by others, based on how they are seen in their relationships with others. Personal power includes referent and expert power (see Table 1.2).

In discussions of leadership, it is not unusual for leaders to be described as wielders of power, as individuals who dominate others. In these instances, power is conceptualized as a tool that leaders use to achieve

Table 1.2   Types and Bases of Power

Position Power	Personal Power
Legitimate	Referent
Reward	Expert
Coercive	

SOURCE: Adapted from *A Force for Change: How Leadership Differs From Management* (pp. 3–8), by J. P. Kotter, 1990, New York: Free Press.

their own ends. Contrary to this view of power, Burns (1978) emphasized power from a relationship standpoint. For Burns, power is not an entity that leaders use over others to achieve their own ends; instead, power occurs in relationships. It should be used by leaders and followers to promote their collective goals.

In this text, our discussions of leadership treat power as a relational concern for both leaders and followers. We pay attention to how leaders work with followers to reach common goals.

Leadership and Coercion

Coercive power is one of the specific kinds of power available to leaders. Coercion involves the use of force to effect change. *To coerce* means to influence others to do something against their will and may include manipulating penalties and rewards in their work environment. Coercion often involves the use of threats, punishment, and negative reward schedules. Classic examples of coercive leaders are Adolf Hitler in Germany, the Taliban leaders in Afghanistan, Jim Jones in Guyana, and North Korea's Supreme Leader Kim Jong-il, each of whom has used power and restraint to force followers to engage in extreme behaviors.

It is important to distinguish between coercion and leadership because it allows us to separate out from our examples of leadership the behaviors of individuals such as Hitler, the Taliban, and Jones. In our discussions of leadership, coercive people are not used as models of ideal leadership. Our definition suggests that leadership is reserved for those who influence a group of individuals toward a common goal. Leaders who use coercion are interested in their own goals and seldom are interested in the wants and needs of subordinates. Using coercion runs counter to working *with* followers to achieve a common goal.

1.4 Leadership and Coercion   1.2 Leadership Defined

Leadership and Management

Leadership is a process that is similar to management in many ways. Leadership involves influence, as does management. Leadership entails working with people, which management entails as well. Leadership is concerned with effective goal accomplishment, and so is management. In general, many of the functions of management are activities that are consistent with the definition of leadership we set forth at the beginning of this chapter.

But leadership is also different from management. Whereas the study of leadership can be traced back to Aristotle, management emerged around the turn of the 20th century with the advent of our industrialized society. Management was created as a way to reduce chaos in organizations, to make them run more effectively and efficiently. The primary functions of management, as first identified by Fayol (1916), were planning, organizing, staffing, and controlling. These functions are still representative of the field of management today.

In a book that compared the functions of management with the functions of leadership, Kotter (1990) argued that the functions of the two are quite dissimilar (Figure 1.2). The overriding function of management is to

Figure 1.2   Functions of Management and Leadership

Management Produces Order and Consistency	Leadership Produces Change and Movement
Planning and Budgeting	Establishing Direction
• Establish agendas	• Create a vision
• Set timetables	• Clarify big picture
• Allocate resources	• Set strategies
Organizing and Staffing	Aligning People
• Provide structure	• Communicate goals
• Make job placements	• Seek commitment
• Establish rules and procedures	• Build teams and coalitions
Controlling and Problem Solving	Motivating and Inspiring
• Develop incentives	• Inspire and energize
• Generate creative solutions	• Empower subordinates
• Take corrective action	• Satisfy unmet needs

SOURCE: Adapted from *A Force for Change: How Leadership Differs From Management* (pp. 3–8), by J. P. Kotter, 1990, New York: Free Press.

provide order and consistency to organizations, whereas the primary function of leadership is to produce change and movement. Management is about seeking order and stability; leadership is about seeking adaptive and constructive change.

As illustrated in Figure 1.2, the major activities of management are played out differently than the activities of leadership. Although they are different in scope, Kotter (1990, pp. 7–8) contended that both management and leadership are essential if an organization is to prosper. For example, if an organization has strong management without leadership, the outcome can be stifling and bureaucratic. Conversely, if an organization has strong leadership without management, the outcome can be meaningless or misdirected change for change's sake. To be effective, organizations need to nourish both competent management and skilled leadership.

Many scholars, in addition to Kotter (1990), argue that leadership and management are distinct constructs. For example, Bennis and Nanus (1985) maintained that there is a significant difference between the two. *To manage* means to accomplish activities and master routines, whereas *to lead* means to influence others and create visions for change. Bennis and Nanus made the distinction very clear in their frequently quoted sentence, "Managers are people who do things right and leaders are people who do the right thing" (p. 221).

Rost (1991) has also been a proponent of distinguishing between leadership and management. He contended that leadership is a multidirectional influence relationship and management is a unidirectional authority relationship. Whereas leadership is concerned with the process of developing mutual purposes, management is directed toward coordinating activities in order to get a job done. Leaders and followers work together to create real change, whereas managers and subordinates join forces to sell goods and services (Rost, 1991, pp. 149–152).

Approaching the issue from a narrower viewpoint, Zaleznik (1977) went so far as to argue that leaders and managers themselves are distinct, and that they are basically different types of people. He contended that managers are reactive and prefer to work with people to solve problems but do so with low emotional involvement. They act to limit choices. Zaleznik suggested that leaders, on the other hand, are emotionally active and involved. They seek to shape ideas instead of responding to them and act to expand the available options to solve long-standing problems. Leaders change the way people think about what is possible.

Although there are clear differences between management and leadership, the two constructs overlap. When managers are involved in influencing a group to meet its goals, they are involved in leadership. When leaders are involved in planning, organizing, staffing, and controlling, they are involved in management. Both processes involve influencing a group of individuals toward goal attainment. For purposes of our discussion in this book, we focus on the leadership process. In our examples and case studies, we treat the roles of managers and leaders similarly and do not emphasize the differences between them.

PLAN OF THE BOOK

This book is user-friendly. It is based on substantive theories but is written to emphasize practice and application. Each chapter in the book follows the same format. The first section of each chapter briefly describes the leadership approach and discusses various research studies applicable to the approach. The second section of each chapter evaluates the approach, highlighting its strengths and criticisms. Special attention is given to how the approach contributes or fails to contribute to an overall understanding of the leadership process. The next section uses case studies to prompt discussion of how the approach can be applied in ongoing organizations. Finally, each chapter provides a leadership questionnaire along with a discussion of how the questionnaire measures the reader's leadership style. Each chapter ends with a summary and references.

SUMMARY

Leadership is a topic with universal appeal; in the popular press and academic research literature, much has been written about leadership. Despite the abundance of writing on the topic, leadership has presented a major challenge to practitioners and researchers interested in understanding the nature of leadership. It is a highly valued phenomenon that is very complex.

Through the years, leadership has been defined and conceptualized in many ways. The component common to nearly all classifications is that leadership is an influence process that assists groups of individuals toward goal attainment. Specifically, in this book leadership is defined as a process whereby an individual influences a group of individuals to achieve a common goal.

Because both leaders and followers are part of the leadership process, it is important to address issues that confront followers as well as issues that confront leaders. Leaders and followers should be understood in relation to each other.

In prior research, many studies have focused on leadership as a trait. The trait perspective suggests that certain people in our society have special inborn qualities that make them leaders. This view restricts leadership to those who are believed to have special characteristics. In contrast, the approach in this text suggests that leadership is a process that can be learned, and that it is available to everyone.

Two common forms of leadership are *assigned* and *emergent. Assigned leadership* is based on a formal title or position in an organization. *Emergent leadership* results from what one does and how one acquires support from followers. Leadership, as a process, applies to individuals in both assigned roles and emergent roles.

Related to leadership is the concept of power, the potential to influence. There are two major kinds of power: position and personal. Position power, which is much like assigned leadership, is the power an individual derives from having a title in a formal organizational system. It includes legitimate, reward, and coercive power. Personal power comes from followers and includes referent and expert power. Followers give it to leaders because followers believe leaders have something of value. Treating power as a shared resource is important because it deemphasizes the idea that leaders are power wielders.

While coercion has been a common power brought to bear by many individuals in charge, it should not be viewed as ideal leadership. Our definition of leadership stresses *using influence* to bring individuals toward a common goal, while coercion involves the use of threats and punishment to *induce change* in followers for the sake of the leaders. Coercion runs counter to leadership because it does not treat leadership as a process that emphasizes working *with* followers to achieve shared objectives.

Leadership and management are different concepts that overlap. They are different in that management traditionally focuses on the activities of planning, organizing, staffing, and controlling, whereas leadership emphasizes the general influence process. According to some researchers, management is concerned with creating order and stability, whereas leadership is about adaptation and constructive change. Other researchers go so far as to argue that managers and leaders are different types of people, with managers being more reactive and less emotionally involved and leaders being more proactive and more emotionally involved. The overlap between leadership and management is centered on how both involve influencing a group of individuals in goal attainment.

In this book, we discuss leadership as a complex process. Based on the research literature, we describe selected approaches to leadership and assess how they can be used to improve leadership in real situations.

Visit the Student Study Site at **www.sagepub.com/northouse6e** for web quizzes, leadership questionnaires, and media links represented by the icons.

REFERENCES

Bass, B. M. (1990). *Bass and Stogdill's handbook of leadership: A survey of theory and research.* New York: Free Press.

Bennis, W. G., & Nanus, B. (1985). *Leaders: The strategies for taking charge.* New York: Harper & Row.

Bryman, A. (1992). *Charisma and leadership in organizations.* London: Sage.

Bryman, A., Collinson, D., Grint, K., Jackson, G., Uhl-Bien, M. (Eds.). (2011). *The SAGE handbook of leadership.* London, UK: Sage.

Burns, J. M. (1978). *Leadership.* New York: Harper & Row.

Copeland, N. (1942). *Psychology and the soldier.* Harrisburg, PA: Military Service Publications.

Day, D. V., & Antonakis, J. (Eds.). (2012). *The nature of leadership* (2nd ed.). Thousand Oaks, CA: Sage.

Fayol, H. (1916). *General and industrial management.* London: Pitman.

Fisher, B. A. (1974). *Small group decision making: Communication and the group process.* New York: McGraw-Hill.

Fleishman, E. A., Mumford, M. D., Zaccaro, S. J., Levin, K. Y., Korotkin, A. L., & Hein, M. B. (1991). Taxonomic efforts in the description of leader behavior: A synthesis and functional interpretation. *Leadership Quarterly, 2*(4), 245–287.

French, J. R., Jr., & Raven, B. (1959). The bases of social power. In D. Cartwright (Ed.), *Studies in social power* (pp. 259–269). Ann Arbor, MI: Institute for Social Research.

Gardner, J. W. (1990). *On leadership.* New York: Free Press.

Heller, T., & Van Til, J. (1983). Leadership and followership: Some summary propositions. *Journal of Applied Behavioral Science, 18*, 405–414.

Hemphill, J. K. (1949). *Situational factors in leadership.* Columbus: Ohio State University, Bureau of Educational Research.

Hickman, G. R. (Ed.). (2009). *Leading organizations: Perspectives for a new era* (2nd ed.). Thousand Oaks, CA: Sage.

Hogg, M. A. (2001). A social identity theory of leadership. *Personality and Social Psychology Review, 5*, 184–200.

Hollander, E. P. (1992). Leadership, followership, self, and others. *Leadership Quarterly, 3*(1), 43–54.

Jago, A. G. (1982). Leadership: Perspectives in theory and research. *Management Science, 28*(3), 315–336.

Kotter, J. P. (1990). *A force for change: How leadership differs from management.* New York: Free Press.

Moore, B. V. (1927). The May conference on leadership. *Personnel Journal, 6*, 124–128.

Mumford, M. D. (2006). *Pathways to outstanding leadership: A comparative analysis of charismatic, ideological, and pragmatic leaders.* Mahwah, NJ: Lawrence Erlbaum.

Peters, T. J., & Waterman, R. H. (1982). *In search of excellence: Lessons from America's best-run companies.* New York: Warner Books.

Rost, J. C. (1991). *Leadership for the twenty-first century.* New York: Praeger.

Seeman, M. (1960). *Social status and leadership.* Columbus: Ohio State University, Bureau of Educational Research.

Smith, J. A., & Foti, R. J. (1998). A pattern approach to the study of leader emergence. *Leadership Quarterly, 9*(2), 147–160.

Stogdill, R. M. (1974). *Handbook of leadership: A survey of theory and research.* New York: Free Press.

Watson, C., & Hoffman, L. R. (2004). The role of task-related behavior in the emergence of leaders. *Group & Organization Management, 29*(6), 659–685.

Zaleznik, A. (1977, May–June). Managers and leaders: Are they different? *Harvard Business Review, 55*, 67–78.

2

Trait Approach

DESCRIPTION

Of interest to scholars throughout the 20th century, the trait approach was one of the first systematic attempts to study leadership. In the early 20th century, leadership traits were studied to determine what made certain people great leaders. The theories that were developed were called "great man" theories because they focused on identifying the innate qualities and characteristics possessed by great social, political, and military leaders (e.g., Catherine the Great, Mohandas Gandhi, Indira Gandhi, Abraham Lincoln, Joan of Arc, and Napoleon Bonaparte). It was believed that people were born with these traits, and that only the "great" people possessed them. During this time, research concentrated on determining the specific traits that clearly differentiated leaders from followers (Bass, 1990; Jago, 1982).

In the mid-20th century, the trait approach was challenged by research that questioned the universality of leadership traits. In a major review, Stogdill (1948) suggested that no consistent set of traits differentiated leaders from nonleaders across a variety of situations. An individual with leadership traits who was a leader in one situation might not be a leader in another situation. Rather than being a quality that individuals possess, leadership was reconceptualized as a relationship between people in a social situation. Personal factors related to leadership continued to be important, but researchers contended that these factors were to be considered as relative to the requirements of the situation.

The trait approach has generated much interest among researchers for its explanation of how traits influence leadership (Bryman, 1992). For example, an analysis of much of the previous trait research by Lord, DeVader, and Alliger (1986) found that personality traits were strongly associated with individuals' perceptions of leadership. Similarly, Kirkpatrick and Locke (1991) went so far as to claim that effective leaders are actually distinct types of people in several key respects.

The trait approach has earned new interest through the current emphasis given by many researchers to visionary and charismatic leadership (see Bass, 1990; Bennis & Nanus, 1985; Nadler & Tushman, 1989; Zaccaro, 2007; Zaleznik, 1977). Charismatic leadership catapulted to the forefront of public attention with the 2008 election of the United States' first African American president, Barack Obama, who is charismatic, among many other attributes. In a study to determine what distinguishes charismatic leaders from others, Jung and Sosik (2006) found that charismatic leaders consistently possess traits of self-monitoring, engagement in impression management, motivation to attain social power, and motivation to attain self-actualization. In short, the trait approach is alive and well. It began with an emphasis on identifying the qualities of great persons, shifted to include the impact of situations on leadership, and, currently, has shifted back to reemphasize the critical role of traits in effective leadership.

Although the research on traits spanned the entire 20th century, a good overview of this approach is found in two surveys completed by Stogdill (1948, 1974). In his first survey, Stogdill analyzed and synthesized more than 124 trait studies conducted between 1904 and 1947. In his second study, he analyzed another 163 studies completed between 1948 and 1970. By taking a closer look at each of these reviews, we can obtain a clearer picture of how individuals' traits contribute to the leadership process.

Stogdill's first survey identified a group of important leadership traits that were related to how individuals in various groups became leaders. His results showed that the average individual in the leadership role is different from an average group member with regard to the following eight traits: intelligence, alertness, insight, responsibility, initiative, persistence, self-confidence, and sociability.

The findings of Stogdill's first survey also indicated that an individual does not become a leader solely because that individual possesses certain traits. Rather, the traits that leaders possess must be relevant to situations in which the leader is functioning. As stated earlier, leaders in one situation may not necessarily be leaders in another situation. Findings showed that leadership was not a passive state but resulted from a working relationship between the leader and other group members. This research marked the beginning of a new approach to leadership research that focused on leadership behaviors and leadership situations.

 2.2 Role of Consultant Nurses   **2.1** Trait Leadership

Stogdill's second survey, published in 1974, analyzed 163 new studies and compared the findings of these studies to the findings he had reported in his first survey. The second survey was more balanced in its description of the role of traits and leadership. Whereas the first survey implied that leadership is determined principally by situational factors and not personality factors, the second survey argued more moderately that both personality and situational factors were determinants of leadership. In essence, the second survey validated the original trait idea that a leader's characteristics are indeed a part of leadership.

Similar to the first survey, Stogdill's second survey also identified traits that were positively associated with leadership. The list included the following 10 characteristics:

1. drive for responsibility and task completion;

2. vigor and persistence in pursuit of goals;

3. risk taking and originality in problem solving;

4. drive to exercise initiative in social situations;

5. self-confidence and sense of personal identity;

6. willingness to accept consequences of decision and action;

7. readiness to absorb interpersonal stress;

8. willingness to tolerate frustration and delay;

9. ability to influence other people's behavior; and

10. capacity to structure social interaction systems to the purpose at hand.

Mann (1959) conducted a similar study that examined more than 1,400 findings regarding personality and leadership in small groups, but he placed less emphasis on how situational factors influenced leadership. Although tentative in his conclusions, Mann suggested that personality traits could be used to distinguish leaders from nonleaders. His results identified leaders as strong in the following six traits: intelligence, masculinity, adjustment, dominance, extraversion, and conservatism.

Lord et al. (1986) reassessed Mann's (1959) findings using a more sophisticated procedure called meta-analysis. Lord et al. found that intelligence, masculinity, and dominance were significantly related to how individuals perceived leaders. From their findings, the authors argued

2.1 Great Man Theory

strongly that personality traits could be used to make discriminations consistently across situations between leaders and nonleaders.

Both of these studies were conducted during periods in American history where male leadership was prevalent in most aspects of business and society. In Chapter 14, we explore more contemporary research regarding the role of gender in leadership, and we look at whether traits such as masculinity and dominance still bear out as important factors in distinguishing between leaders and nonleaders.

Yet another review argues for the importance of leadership traits: Kirkpatrick and Locke (1991, p. 59) contended that "it is unequivocally clear that leaders are not like other people." From a qualitative synthesis of earlier research, Kirkpatrick and Locke postulated that leaders differ from nonleaders on six traits: drive, motivation, integrity, confidence, cognitive ability, and task knowledge. According to these writers, individuals can be born with these traits, they can learn them, or both. It is these six traits that make up the "right stuff" for leaders. Kirkpatrick and Locke contended that leadership traits make some people different from others, and this difference should be recognized as an important part of the leadership process.

In the 1990s, researchers began to investigate the leadership traits associated with "social intelligence," characterized as those abilities to understand one's own and others' feelings, behaviors, and thoughts and to act appropriately (Marlowe, 1986). Zaccaro (2002) defined social intelligence as having such capacities as social awareness, social acumen, self-monitoring, and the ability to select and enact the best response given the contingencies of the situation and social environment. A number of empirical studies showed these capacities to be a key trait for effective leaders. Zaccaro, Kemp, and Bader (2004) included such social abilities in the categories of leadership traits they outlined as important leadership attributes (see Table 2.1).

Table 2.1 provides a summary of the traits and characteristics that were identified by researchers from the trait approach. It illustrates clearly the breadth of traits related to leadership. Table 2.1 also shows how difficult it is to select certain traits as definitive leadership traits; some of the traits appear in several of the survey studies, whereas others appear in only one or two studies. Regardless of the lack of precision in Table 2.1, however, it represents a general convergence of research regarding which traits are leadership traits.

2.3 Importance of Leadership Traits

Table 2.1   Studies of Leadership Traits and Characteristics

Stogdill (1948)	Mann (1959)	Stogdill (1974)	Lord, DeVader, and Alliger (1986)	Kirkpatrick and Locke (1991)	Zaccaro, Kemp, and Bader (2004)
intelligence	intelligence	achievement	intelligence	drive	cognitive abilities
alertness	masculinity	persistence	masculinity	motivation	extraversion
insight	adjustment	insight	dominance	integrity	conscientiousness
responsibility	dominance	initiative		confidence	emotional stability
initiative	extraversion	self-confidence		cognitive ability	openness
persistence	conservatism	responsibility		task knowledge	agreeableness
self-confidence		cooperativeness			motivation
sociability		tolerance			social intelligence
		influence			self-monitoring
		sociability			emotional intelligence
					problem solving

SOURCES: Adapted from "The Bases of Social Power," by J. R. P. French, Jr., and B. Raven, 1962, in D. Cartwright (Ed.), *Group Dynamics: Research and Theory* (pp. 259–269), New York: Harper and Row; Zaccaro, Kemp, & Bader (2004).

What, then, can be said about trait research? What has a century of research on the trait approach given us that is useful? The answer is an extended list of traits that individuals might hope to possess or wish to cultivate if they want to be perceived by others as leaders. Some of the traits that are central to this list include intelligence, self-confidence, determination, integrity, and sociability (Table 2.2).

Table 2.2   Major Leadership Traits

- Intelligence
- Self-confidence
- Determination
- Integrity
- Sociability

Intelligence

Intelligence or intellectual ability is positively related to leadership. Based on their analysis of a series of recent studies on intelligence and

2.2 Essence of Leadership

various indices of leadership, Zaccaro et al. (2004) found support for the finding that leaders tend to have higher intelligence than nonleaders. Having strong verbal ability, perceptual ability, and reasoning appears to make one a better leader. Although it is good to be bright, the research also indicates that a leader's intellectual ability should not differ too much from that of the subordinates. If the leader's IQ is very different from that of the followers, it can have a counterproductive impact on leadership. Leaders with higher abilities may have difficulty communicating with followers because they are preoccupied or because their ideas are too advanced for their followers to accept.

An example of a leader for whom intelligence was a key trait was Steve Jobs, founder and CEO of Apple Computers. Jobs once said, "I have this really incredible product inside me and I have to get it out" (Sculley, 2011, p. 27). Those visionary products, first the Apple II and Macintosh computers and then iMac, iPod, iPhone, and iPad, have revolutionized the personal computer and electronic device industry, changing the way people play and work.

In the next chapter of this text, which addresses leadership from a skills perspective, intelligence is identified as a trait that significantly contributes to a leader's acquisition of complex problem-solving skills and social judgment skills. Intelligence is described as having a positive impact on an individual's capacity for effective leadership.

Self-Confidence

Self-confidence is another trait that helps one to be a leader. Self-confidence is the ability to be certain about one's competencies and skills. It includes a sense of self-esteem and self-assurance and the belief that one can make a difference. Leadership involves influencing others, and self-confidence allows the leader to feel assured that his or her attempts to influence others are appropriate and right.

Again, Steve Jobs is a good example of a self-confident leader. When Jobs described the devices he wanted to create, many people said they weren't possible. But Jobs never doubted his products would change the world, and, despite resistance, he did things the way he thought best. "Jobs was one of those CEOs who ran the company like he wanted to. He believed he knew more about it than anyone else, and he probably did," said a colleague (Stone, 2011).

2.2 Steve Jobs

Determination

Many leaders also exhibit determination. Determination is the desire to get the job done and includes characteristics such as initiative, persistence, dominance, and drive. People with determination are willing to assert themselves, are proactive, and have the capacity to persevere in the face of obstacles. Being determined includes showing dominance at times and in situations where followers need to be directed.

Lance Armstrong has shown determination in a number of ways. The seven-time Tour de France champion has shown his determination as a cyclist, but also in his efforts to battle cancer. A cancer survivor, Armstrong founded the Livestrong organization, an organization that champions cancer awareness and support for survivors. His aim is "to guide people through the cancer experience, bring them together to fight cancer—and work for a world in which our fight is no longer necessary" (Livestrong, 2011).

Integrity

Integrity is another of the important leadership traits. Integrity is the quality of honesty and trustworthiness. People who adhere to a strong set of principles and take responsibility for their actions are exhibiting integrity. Leaders with integrity inspire confidence in others because they can be trusted to do what they say they are going to do. They are loyal, dependable, and not deceptive. Basically, integrity makes a leader believable and worthy of our trust.

In our society, integrity has received a great deal of attention in recent years. For example, as a result of two situations—the position taken by President George W. Bush regarding Iraq's alleged weapons of mass destruction and the impeachment proceedings during the Clinton presidency—people are demanding more honesty of their public officials. Similarly, scandals in the corporate world (e.g., Enron and WorldCom), have led people to become skeptical of leaders who are not highly ethical. In the educational arena, new K–12 curricula are being developed to teach character, values, and ethical leadership. (For instance, see the Character Counts! program developed by the Josephson Institute of Ethics in California at http://www.charactercounts.org, and the Pillars of Leadership program taught at the J. W. Fanning Institute for Leadership in Georgia at http://www.fanning.uga.edu.) In short, society is demanding greater integrity of character in its leaders.

2.4 Leadership in Nursing

Sociability

A final trait that is important for leaders is sociability. Sociability is a leader's inclination to seek out pleasant social relationships. Leaders who show sociability are friendly, outgoing, courteous, tactful, and diplomatic. They are sensitive to others' needs and show concern for their well-being. Social leaders have good interpersonal skills and create cooperative relationships with their followers.

An example of a leader with great sociability skills is Michael Hughes, a university president. Hughes prefers to walk to all his meetings because it gets him out on campus where he greets students, staff, and faculty. He has lunch in the dorm cafeterias or student union and will often ask a table of strangers if he can sit with them. Students rate him as very approachable, while faculty say he has an open-door policy. In addition, he takes time to write personal notes to faculty, staff, and students to congratulate them on their successes.

Although our discussion of leadership traits has focused on five major traits (i.e., intelligence, self-confidence, determination, integrity, and sociability), this list is not all-inclusive. While other traits indicated in Table 2.1 are associated with effective leadership, the five traits we have identified contribute substantially to one's capacity to be a leader.

Until recently, most reviews of leadership traits have been qualitative. In addition, they have lacked a common organizing framework. However, the research described in the following section provides a quantitative assessment of leadership traits that is conceptually framed around the five-factor model of personality. It describes how five major personality traits are related to leadership.

Five-Factor Personality Model and Leadership

Over the past 25 years, a consensus has emerged among researchers regarding the basic factors that make up what we call personality (Goldberg, 1990; McCrae & Costa, 1987). These factors, commonly called the *Big Five*, are neuroticism, extraversion (surgency), openness (intellect), agreeableness, and conscientiousness (dependability). (See Table 2.3.)

To assess the links between the Big Five and leadership, Judge, Bono, Ilies, and Gerhardt (2002) conducted a major meta-analysis of 78 leadership and personality studies published between 1967 and 1998. In general,

2.2 Impression Management

Table 2.3 Big Five Personality Factors

Neuroticism	The tendency to be depressed, anxious, insecure, vulnerable, and hostile
Extraversion	The tendency to be sociable and assertive and to have positive energy
Openness	The tendency to be informed, creative, insightful, and curious
Agreeableness	The tendency to be accepting, conforming, trusting, and nurturing
Conscientiousness	The tendency to be thorough, organized, controlled, dependable, and decisive

SOURCE: Goldberg, L. R. (1990). An alternative "description of personality": The big-five factor structure. *Journal of Personality and Social Psychology, 59,* 1216–1229.

Judge et al. found a strong relationship between the Big Five traits and leadership. It appears that having certain personality traits is associated with being an effective leader.

Specifically, in their study, *extraversion* was the factor most strongly associated with leadership. It is the most important trait of effective leaders. Extraversion was followed, in order, by *conscientiousness, openness,* and *low neuroticism.* The last factor, *agreeableness,* was found to be only weakly associated with leadership.

Emotional Intelligence

Another way of assessing the impact of traits on leadership is through the concept of emotional intelligence, which emerged in the 1990s as an important area of study in psychology. It has been widely studied by researchers, and has captured the attention of many practitioners (Caruso & Wolfe, 2004; Goleman, 1995, 1998; Mayer & Salovey, 1995, 1997; Mayer, Salovey, & Caruso, 2000; Shankman & Allen, 2008).

As the two words suggest, emotional intelligence has to do with our emotions (affective domain) and thinking (cognitive domain), and the interplay between the two. Whereas *intelligence* is concerned with our ability to learn *information* and apply it to life tasks, *emotional intelligence* is concerned with our ability to understand *emotions* and apply this understanding to life's tasks. Specifically, *emotional intelligence* can be defined as the ability to perceive and express emotions, to use emotions to facilitate thinking, to understand and reason with emotions, and to effectively

2.3 Emotional and Other Intelligences   2.5 Effective and Ineffective Leaders

manage emotions within oneself and in relationships with others (Mayer, Salovey, & Caruso, 2000).

There are different ways to measure emotional intelligence. One scale is the Mayer-Salovey-Caruso Emotional Intelligence Test (MSCEIT; Mayer, Caruso, & Salovey, 2000). The MSCEIT measures emotional intelligence as a set of mental abilities, including the abilities to perceive, facilitate, understand, and manage emotion.

Goleman (1995, 1998) takes a broader approach to emotional intelligence, suggesting that it consists of a set of personal and social competencies. Personal competence consists of self-awareness, confidence, self-regulation, conscientiousness, and motivation. Social competence consists of empathy and social skills such as communication and conflict management.

Shankman and Allen (2008) developed a practice-oriented model of emotionally intelligent leadership, which suggests that leaders must be conscious of three fundamental facets of leadership: context, self, and others. In the model, emotionally intelligent leaders are defined by 21 capacities to which a leader should pay attention, including group savvy, optimism, initiative, and teamwork.

There is a debate in the field regarding how big a role emotional intelligence plays in helping people be successful in life. Some researchers, such as Goleman (1995), suggested that emotional intelligence plays a major role in whether people are successful at school, home, and work. Others, such as Mayer, Salovey, and Caruso (2000), made softer claims for the significance of emotional intelligence in meeting life's challenges.

As a leadership ability or trait, emotional intelligence appears to be an important construct. The underlying premise suggested by this framework is that people who are more sensitive to their emotions and the impact of their emotions on others will be leaders who are more effective. As more research is conducted on emotional intelligence, the intricacies of how emotional intelligence relates to leadership will be better understood.

HOW DOES THE TRAIT APPROACH WORK? ————

The trait approach is very different from the other approaches discussed in subsequent chapters because it focuses exclusively on the leader, not on

 2.3 Emotional Intelligence   ▶ 2.3 Emotional Intelligence

the followers or the situation. This makes the trait approach theoretically more straightforward than other approaches. In essence, the trait approach is concerned with what traits leaders exhibit and who has these traits.

The trait approach does not lay out a set of hypotheses or principles about what kind of leader is needed in a certain situation or what a leader should do, given a particular set of circumstances. Instead, this approach emphasizes that having a leader with a certain set of traits is crucial to having effective leadership. It is the leader and the leader's personality that are central to the leadership process.

The trait approach suggests that organizations will work better if the people in managerial positions have designated leadership profiles. To find the right people, it is common for organizations to use personality assessment instruments. The assumption behind these procedures is that selecting the right people will increase organizational effectiveness. Organizations can specify the characteristics or traits that are important to them for particular positions and then use personality assessment measures to determine whether an individual fits their needs.

The trait approach is also used for personal awareness and development. By analyzing their own traits, managers can gain an idea of their strengths and weaknesses, and can get a feel for how others in the organization see them. A trait assessment can help managers determine whether they have the qualities to move up or to move to other positions in the company.

A trait assessment gives individuals a clearer picture of who they are as leaders and how they fit into the organizational hierarchy. In areas where their traits are lacking, leaders can try to make changes in what they do or where they work to increase their traits' potential impact.

Near the end of the chapter, a leadership instrument is provided that you can use to assess your leadership traits. This instrument is typical of the kind of personality tests that companies use to assess individuals' leadership potential. As you will discover by completing this instrument, trait measures are a good way to assess your own characteristics.

STRENGTHS

The trait approach has several identifiable strengths. First, the trait approach is intuitively appealing. It fits clearly with our notion that leaders are the individuals who are out front and leading the way in our society. The image in the popular press and community at large is that leaders are a special kind of people—people with gifts who can do extraordinary things. The trait approach is consistent with this perception because it is built on the premise that leaders are different, and their difference resides in the special traits they possess. People have a need to see their leaders as gifted people, and the trait approach fulfills this need.

A second strength of the trait approach is that it has a century of research to back it up. No other theory can boast of the breadth and depth of studies conducted on the trait approach. The strength and longevity of this line of research give the trait approach a measure of credibility that other approaches lack. Out of this abundance of research has emerged a body of data that points to the important role of various personality traits in the leadership process.

Another strength, more conceptual in nature, results from the way the trait approach highlights the leader component in the leadership process. Leadership is composed of leaders, followers, and situations, but the trait approach is devoted to only the first of these—leaders. Although this is also a potential weakness, by focusing exclusively on the role of the leader in leadership the trait approach has been able to provide us with a deeper and more intricate understanding of how the leader and the leader's personality are related to the leadership process.

Last, the trait approach has given us some benchmarks for what we need to look for if we want to be leaders. It identifies what traits we should have and whether the traits we do have are the best traits for leadership. Based on the findings of this approach, personality and assessment procedures can be used to offer invaluable information to supervisors and managers about their strengths and weaknesses and ways to improve their overall leadership effectiveness.

CRITICISMS

In addition to its strengths, the trait approach has several weaknesses. First and foremost is the failure of the trait approach to delimit a definitive list of leadership traits. Although an enormous number of studies have been conducted over the past 100 years, the findings from these studies have been ambiguous and uncertain at times. Furthermore, the list of traits that has emerged appears endless. This is obvious from Table 2.1, which lists a multitude of traits. In fact, these are only a sample of the many leadership traits that were studied.

Another criticism is that the trait approach has failed to take situations into account. As Stogdill (1948) pointed out more than 50 years ago, it is difficult to isolate a set of traits that are characteristic of leaders without also factoring situational effects into the equation. People who possess certain traits that make them leaders in one situation may not be leaders in another situation. Some people may have the traits that help them emerge as leaders but not the traits that allow them to maintain their leadership over time. In other words, the situation influences leadership. It is therefore difficult to identify a universal set of leadership traits in isolation from the context in which the leadership occurs.

A third criticism, derived from the prior two criticisms, is that this approach has resulted in highly subjective determinations of the most important leadership traits. Because the findings on traits have been so extensive and broad, there has been much subjective interpretation of the meaning of the data. This subjectivity is readily apparent in the many self-help, practice-oriented management books. For example, one author might identify ambition and creativity as crucial leadership traits; another might identify empathy and calmness. In both cases, it is the author's subjective experience and observations that are the basis for the identified leadership traits. These books may be helpful to readers because they identify and describe important leadership traits, but the methods used to generate these lists of traits are weak. To respond to people's need for a set of definitive traits of leaders, authors have set forth lists of traits, even if the origins of these lists are not grounded in strong, reliable research.

Research on traits can also be criticized for failing to look at traits in relationship to leadership outcomes. This research has emphasized the identification of traits, but has not addressed how leadership traits affect group members and their work. In trying to ascertain universal leadership traits, researchers have focused on the link between specific traits and leader emergence, but they have not tried to link leader traits with other outcomes such as productivity or employee satisfaction. For example, trait research does not provide data on whether leaders who might have high intelligence and strong integrity have better results than leaders without these traits. The trait approach is weak in describing how leaders' traits affect the outcomes of groups and teams in organizational settings.

A final criticism of the trait approach is that it is not a useful approach for training and development for leadership. Even if definitive traits could be identified, teaching new traits is not an easy process because traits are not easily changed. For example, it is not reasonable to send managers to a training program to raise their IQ or to train them to become extroverted. The point is that traits are largely fixed psychological structures, and this limits the value of teaching and leadership training.

APPLICATION

Despite its shortcomings, the trait approach provides valuable information about leadership. It can be applied by individuals at all levels and in all types of organizations. Although the trait approach does not provide a definitive set of traits, it does provide direction regarding which traits are good to have if one aspires to a leadership position. By taking personality tests and other similar questionnaires, people can gain insight into whether they have certain traits deemed important for leadership, and they can pinpoint their strengths and weaknesses with regard to leadership.

As we discussed previously, managers can use information from the trait approach to assess where they stand in their organization and what they need to do to strengthen their position. Trait information can suggest areas in which their personal characteristics are very beneficial to the company and areas in which they may want to get more training to enhance their overall approach. Using trait information, managers can develop a deeper understanding of who they are and how they will affect others in the organization.

CASE STUDIES

In this section, three case studies (Cases 2.1, 2.2, and 2.3) are provided to illustrate the trait approach and to help you understand how the trait approach can be used in making decisions in organizational settings. The settings of the cases are diverse—directing a research department, running an office supply business, and being head of recruitment for a large bank—but all of the cases deal with trait leadership. At the end of each case, you will find questions that will help in analyzing the cases.

CASE 2.1

Choosing a New Director of Research

Sandra Coke is vice president for research and development at Great Lakes Foods (GLF), a large snack food company that has approximately 1,000 employees. As a result of a recent reorganization, Sandra must choose the new director of research. The director will report directly to Sandra and will be responsible for developing and testing new products. The research division of GLF employs about 200 people. The choice of directors is important because Sandra is receiving pressure from the president and board of GLF to improve the company's overall growth and productivity.

Sandra has identified three candidates for the position. Each candidate is at the same managerial level. She is having difficulty choosing one of them because each has very strong credentials. Alexa Smith is a longtime employee of GLF who started part-time in the mailroom while in high school. After finishing school, Alexa worked in as many as 10 different positions throughout the company to become manager of new product marketing. Performance reviews of Alexa's work have repeatedly described her as being very creative and insightful. In her tenure at GLF, Alexa has developed and brought to market four new product lines. Alexa is also known throughout GLF as being very persistent about her work: When she starts a project, she stays with it until it is finished. It is probably this quality that accounts for the success of each of the four new products with which she has been involved.

A second candidate for the new position is Kelsey Metts, who has been with GLF for 5 years and is manager of quality control for established products. Kelsey has a reputation of being very bright. Before joining GLF, she received her MBA at Harvard, graduating at the top of her class. People talk about Kelsey as the kind of person who will be president of her own company someday. Kelsey is also very personable. On all her performance reviews, she received extra-high scores on sociability and human relations. There isn't a supervisor in the company who doesn't have positive things to say about how comfortable it is to work with Kelsey. Since joining GLF, Kelsey has been instrumental in bringing two new product lines to market.

Thomas Santiago, the third candidate, has been with GLF for 10 years and is often consulted by upper management regarding strategic planning and corporate direction setting. Thomas has been very involved in establishing

(Continued)

(Continued)

the vision for GLF and is a company person all the way. He believes in the values of GLF, and actively promotes its mission. The two qualities that stand out above the rest in Thomas's performance reviews are his honesty and integrity. Employees who have worked under his supervision consistently report that they feel they can trust Thomas to be fair and consistent. Thomas is highly respected at GLF. In his tenure at the company, Thomas has been involved in some capacity with the development of three new product lines.

The challenge confronting Sandra is to choose the best person for the newly established director's position. Because of the pressure she feels from upper management, Sandra knows she must select the best leader for the new position.

Questions

1. Based on the information provided about the trait approach in Tables 2.1 and 2.2, if you were Sandra, who would you select?

2. In what ways is the trait approach helpful in this type of selection?

3. In what ways are the weaknesses of the trait approach highlighted in this case?

CASE 2.2

A Remarkable Turnaround

Carol Baines was married for 20 years to the owner of the Baines Company until he died in a car accident. After his death, Carol decided not to sell the business but to try to run it herself. Before the accident, her only involvement in the business was in informal discussions with her husband over dinner, although she has a college degree in business, with a major in management.

Baines Company was one of three office supply stores in a city with a population of 200,000 people. The other two stores were owned by national chains. Baines was not a large company, and employed only five people. Baines had stable sales of about $200,000 a year, serving mostly the smaller companies in the city. The firm had not grown in a number of years and was beginning to feel the pressure of the advertising and lower prices of the national chains.

For the first 6 months, Carol spent her time familiarizing herself with the employees and the operations of the company. Next, she did a city-wide analysis of companies that had reason to purchase office supplies. Based on her understanding of the company's capabilities and her assessment of the potential market for their products and services, Carol developed a specific set of short-term and long-term goals for the company. Behind all of her planning, Carol had a vision that Baines could be a viable, healthy, and competitive company. She wanted to carry on the business that her husband had started, but more than that she wanted it to grow.

Over the first 5 years, Carol invested significant amounts of money in advertising, sales, and services. These efforts were well spent because the company began to show rapid growth immediately. Because of the growth, the company hired another 20 people.

The expansion at Baines was particularly remarkable because of another major hardship Carol had to confront. Carol was diagnosed with breast cancer a year after her husband died. The treatment for her cancer included 2 months of radiation therapy and 6 months of strong chemotherapy. Although the side effects included hair loss and fatigue, Carol continued to manage the company throughout the ordeal. Despite her difficulties, Carol was successful. Under the strength of her leadership, the growth at Baines continued for 10 consecutive years.

Interviews with new and old employees at Baines revealed much about Carol's leadership. Employees said that Carol was a very solid person. She cared deeply about others and was fair and considerate. They said she created a family-like atmosphere at Baines. Few employees had quit Baines since Carol took over. Carol was devoted to all the employees, and she supported their interests. For example, the company sponsored a softball team in the summer and a basketball team in the winter. Others described Carol as a strong person. Even though she had cancer, she continued to be positive and interested in them. She did not get depressed about the cancer and its side effects, even though coping with cancer was difficult. Employees said she was a model of strength, goodness, and quality.

At age 55, Carol turned the business over to her two sons. She continues to act as the president but does not supervise the day-to-day operations. The company is doing more than $3.1 million in sales, and it outpaces the other two chain stores in the city.

(Continued)

(Continued)

Questions

1. How would you describe Carol's leadership traits?

2. How big a part did Carol's traits play in the expansion of the company?

3. Would Carol be a leader in other business contexts?

CASE 2.3

Recruiting for the Bank

Pat Nelson is the assistant director of human resources in charge of recruitment for Central Bank, a large, full-service banking institution. One of Pat's major responsibilities each spring is to visit as many college campuses as he can to interview graduating seniors for credit analyst positions in the commercial lending area at Central Bank. Although the number varies, he usually ends up hiring about 20 new people, most of whom come from the same schools, year after year.

Pat has been doing recruitment for the bank for more than 10 years, and he enjoys it very much. However, for the upcoming spring he is feeling increased pressure from management to be particularly discriminating about whom he recommends hiring. Management is concerned about the retention rate at the bank because in recent years as many as 25% of the new hires have left. Departures after the first year have meant lost training dollars and strain on the staff who remain. Although management understands that some new hires always leave, the executives are not comfortable with the present rate, and they have begun to question the recruitment and hiring procedures.

The bank wants to hire people who can be groomed for higher-level leadership positions. Although certain competencies are required of entry-level credit analysts, the bank is equally interested in skills that will allow individuals to advance to upper management positions as their careers progress.

In the recruitment process, Pat always looks for several characteristics. First, applicants need to have strong interpersonal skills, they need to be confident, and they need to show poise and initiative. Next, because banking involves fiduciary responsibilities, applicants need to have proper ethics, including a strong sense of the importance of confidentiality. In addition, to do the work in the bank, they need to have strong analytical and technical skills, and experience in working with computers. Last, applicants need to exhibit a good work ethic, and they need to show commitment and a willingness to do their job even in difficult circumstances.

Pat is fairly certain that he has been selecting the right people to be leaders at Central Bank, yet upper management is telling him to reassess his hiring criteria. Although he feels that he has been doing the right thing, he is starting to question himself and his recruitment practices.

Questions

1. Based on ideas described in the trait approach, do you think Pat is looking for the right characteristics in the people he hires?

2. Could it be that the retention problem raised by upper management is unrelated to Pat's recruitment criteria?

3. If you were Pat, would you change your approach to recruiting?

LEADERSHIP INSTRUMENT

Organizations use a wide variety of questionnaires to measure individuals' personality characteristics. In many organizations, it is common practice to use standard personality measures such as the Minnesota Multiphasic Personality Inventory or the Myers-Briggs Type Indicator®. These measures provide valuable information to the individual and the organization about the individual's unique attributes for leadership and where the individual could best serve the organization.

In this section, the Leadership Trait Questionnaire (LTQ) is provided as an example of a measure that can be used to assess your personal leadership characteristics. The LTQ quantifies the perceptions of the individual leader and selected observers, such as subordinates or peers. It measures an individual's traits and points the individual to the areas in which that individual may have special strengths or weaknesses.

By taking the LTQ, you can gain an understanding of how trait measures are used for leadership assessment. You can also assess your own leadership traits.

Leadership Trait Questionnaire (LTQ)

Instructions: The purpose of this questionnaire is to measure personal characteristics of leadership. The questionnaire should be completed by the leader and five people who are familiar with the leader. Make five copies of this questionnaire. This questionnaire should be completed by you and five people you know (e.g., roommates, coworkers, relatives, friends).

Using the following scale, have each individual indicate the degree to which he or she agrees or disagrees with each of the 14 statements below. Do not forget to complete one for yourself.

_____ (leader's name) is

Key: 1 = Strongly   2 = Disagree   3 = Neutral   4 = Agree   5 = Strongly
           disagree   agree

1.	**Articulate**: Communicates effectively with others	1 2 3 4 5
2.	**Perceptive**: Is discerning and insightful	1 2 3 4 5
3.	**Self-confident**: Believes in himself/herself and his/her ability	1 2 3 4 5
4.	**Self-assured**: Is secure with self, free of doubts	1 2 3 4 5
5.	**Persistent**: Stays fixed on the goals, despite interference	1 2 3 4 5
6.	**Determined**: Takes a firm stand, acts with certainty	1 2 3 4 5
7.	**Trustworthy**: Is authentic and inspires confidence	1 2 3 4 5
8.	**Dependable**: Is consistent and reliable	1 2 3 4 5
9.	**Friendly**: Shows kindness and warmth	1 2 3 4 5
10.	**Outgoing**: Talks freely, gets along well with others	1 2 3 4 5
11.	**Conscientious**: Is thorough, organized, and controlled	1 2 3 4 5
12.	**Diligent**: Is persistent, hardworking	1 2 3 4 5
13.	**Sensitive**: Shows tolerance, is tactful and sympathetic	1 2 3 4 5
14.	**Empathic**: Understands others, identifies with others	1 2 3 4 5

Scoring

1. Enter the responses for Raters 1, 2, 3, 4, and 5 in the appropriate columns as shown in Example 2.1. The example provides hypothetical ratings to help explain how the questionnaire can be used.

2. For each of the 14 items, compute the average for the five raters and place that number in the "average rating" column.

3. Place your own scores in the "self-rating" column.

Example 2.1 Leadership Traits Questionnaire Ratings

	Rater 1	Rater 2	Rater 3	Rater 4	Rater 5	Average rating	Self-rating
1. Articulate	4	4	3	2	4	3.4	4
2. Perceptive	2	5	3	4	4	3.6	5
3. Self-confident	4	4	5	5	4	4.4	4
4. Self-assured	5	5	5	5	5	5	5
5. Persistent	4	4	3	3	3	3.4	3
6. Determined	4	4	4	4	4	4	4
7. Trustworthy	5	5	5	5	5	5	5
8. Dependable	4	5	4	5	4	4.4	4
9. Friendly	5	5	5	5	5	5	5
10. Outgoing	5	4	5	4	5	4.6	4
11. Conscientious	2	3	2	3	3	2.6	4
12. Diligent	3	3	3	3	3	3	4
13. Sensitive	4	4	5	5	5	4.6	3
14. Empathic	5	5	4	5	4	4.6	3

Scoring Interpretation

The scores you received on the LTQ provide information about how you see yourself and how others see you as a leader. The chart allows you to see where your perceptions are the same as those of others and where they differ.

The example ratings show how the leader self-rated higher than the observers did on the characteristic *articulate*. On the second characteristic, *perceptive*, the leader self-rated substantially higher than others. On the *self-confident* characteristic, the leader self-rated quite close to others' ratings but lower. There are no best ratings on this questionnaire. The purpose of the instrument is to give you a way to assess your strengths and weaknesses and to evaluate areas where your perceptions are congruent with those of others and where there are discrepancies.

SUMMARY

The trait approach has its roots in leadership theory that suggested that certain people were born with special traits that made them great leaders. Because it was believed that leaders and nonleaders could be differentiated by a universal set of traits, throughout the 20th century researchers were challenged to identify the definitive traits of leaders.

Around the mid-20th century, several major studies questioned the basic premise that a unique set of traits defined leadership. As a result, attention shifted to incorporating the impact of situations and of followers on leadership. Researchers began to study the interactions between leaders and their context instead of focusing only on leaders' traits. More recently, there have been signs that trait research has come full circle, with a renewed interest in focusing directly on the critical traits of leaders.

From the multitude of studies conducted through the years on personal characteristics, it is clear that many traits contribute to leadership. Some of the important traits that are consistently identified in many of these studies are intelligence, self-confidence, determination, integrity, and sociability. In addition, researchers have found a strong relationship between leadership and the traits described by the *five-factor personality model*. *Extraversion* was the trait most strongly associated with leadership, followed by *conscientiousness, openness, low neuroticism,* and *agreeableness.* Another recent line of research has focused on *emotional intelligence* and its relationship to leadership. This research suggests that leaders who are sensitive to their emotions and to the impact of their emotions on others may be leaders who are more effective.

On a practical level, the trait approach is concerned with which traits leaders exhibit and who has these traits. Organizations use personality assessment instruments to identify how individuals will fit within their organizations. The trait approach is also used for personal awareness and development because it allows managers to analyze their strengths and weaknesses and to gain a clearer understanding of how they should try to change to enhance their leadership.

There are several advantages to viewing leadership from the trait approach. First, it is intuitively appealing because it fits clearly into the popular idea that leaders are special people who are out front, leading the way in society. Second, a great deal of research validates the basis of this perspective. Third, by focusing exclusively on the leader, the trait approach provides an in-depth understanding of the leader component in the leadership process. Last, it has provided some benchmarks against which individuals can evaluate their own personal leadership attributes.

On the negative side, the trait approach has failed to provide a definitive list of leadership traits. In analyzing the traits of leaders, the approach has failed to take into account the impact of situations. In addition, the approach has resulted in subjective lists of the most important leadership traits, which are not necessarily grounded in strong, reliable research.

Furthermore, the trait approach has not adequately linked the traits of leaders with other outcomes such as group and team performance. Last, this approach is not particularly useful for training and development for leadership because individuals' personal attributes are largely stable and fixed, and their traits are not amenable to change.

Visit the Student Study Site at **www.sagepub.com/northouse6e** for web quizzes, leadership questionnaires, and media links represented by the icons.

REFERENCES

Bass, B. M. (1990). *Bass and Stogdill's handbook of leadership: A survey of theory and research.* New York: Free Press.

Bennis, W. G., & Nanus, B. (1985). *Leaders: The strategies for taking charge.* New York: Harper & Row.

Bryman, A. (1992). *Charisma and leadership in organizations.* London: Sage.

Caruso, D. R., & Wolfe, C. J. (2004). Emotional intelligence and leadership development. In D. V. Day, S. J. Zaccaro, & S. M. Halpin (Eds.), *Leader development for transforming organizations: Growing leaders for tomorrow* (pp. 237–266). Mahwah, NJ: Lawrence Erlbaum.

Goldberg, L. R. (1990). An alternative "description of personality": The big-five factor structure. *Journal of Personality and Social Psychology, 59,* 1216–1229.

Goleman, D. (1995). *Emotional intelligence.* New York: Bantam.

Goleman, D. (1998). *Working with emotional intelligence.* New York: Bantam.

Jago, A. G. (1982). Leadership: Perspectives in theory and research. *Management Science, 28*(3), 315–336.

· Judge, T. A., Bono, J. E., Ilies, R., & Gerhardt, M. W. (2002). Personality and leadership: A qualitative and quantitative review. *Journal of Applied Psychology, 87,* 765–780.

Jung, D., & Sosik, J. J. (2006). Who are the spellbinders? Identifying personal attributes of charismatic leaders. *Journal of Leadership & Organizational Studies, 12,* 12–27.

2.4 Chapter Summary

Kirkpatrick, S. A., & Locke, E. A. (1991). Leadership: Do traits matter? *The Executive, 5,* 48–60.

Livestrong. (2011). *Who we are.* Retrieved October 11, 2011, from http://www .livestrong.org/Who-We-Are

Lord, R. G., DeVader, C. L., & Alliger, G. M. (1986). A meta-analysis of the relation between personality traits and leadership perceptions: An application of validity generalization procedures. *Journal of Applied Psychology, 71,* 402–410.

Mann, R. D. (1959). A review of the relationship between personality and performance in small groups. *Psychological Bulletin, 56,* 241–270.

Marlowe, H. A. (1986). Social intelligence: Evidence for multidimensionality and construct independence. *Journal of Educational Psychology, 78,* 52–58.

Mayer, J. D., Caruso, D. R., & Salovey, P. (2000). Selecting a measure of emotional intelligence: The case for ability scales. In R. Bar-On & J. D. A. Parker (Eds.), *The handbook of emotional intelligence* (pp. 320–342). New York: Jossey-Bass.

Mayer, J. D., & Salovey, P. (1995). Emotional intelligence and the construction and regulation of feelings. *Applied & Preventive Psychology, 4,* 197–208.

Mayer, J. D., & Salovey, P. (1997). What is emotional intelligence? In P. Salovey & D. Sluyter (Eds.), *Emotional development and emotional intelligence: Implications for educators* (pp. 3–31). New York: Basic Books.

Mayer, J. D., Salovey, P., & Caruso, D. R. (2000). Models of emotional intelligence. In R. J. Sternberg (Ed.), *Handbook of intelligence* (pp. 396–420). Cambridge: Cambridge University Press.

McCrae, R. R., & Costa, P. T. (1987). Validation of the five-factor model of personality across instruments and observers. *Journal of Personality and Social Psychology, 52,* 81–90.

Nadler, D. A., & Tushman, M. L. (1989). What makes for magic leadership? In W. E. Rosenbach & R. L. Taylor (Eds.), *Contemporary issues in leadership* (pp. 135–139). Boulder, CO: Westview.

Sculley, J. (2011, October 10). No bozos. Ever. *Bloomberg Businessweek, 4249,* p. 27.

Shankman, M. L., & Allen, S. J. (2008). *Emotionally intelligent leadership: A guide for college students.* San Francisco, CA: Jossey-Bass.

Stogdill, R. M. (1948). Personal factors associated with leadership: A survey of the literature. *Journal of Psychology, 25,* 35–71.

Stogdill, R. M. (1974). *Handbook of leadership: A survey of theory and research.* New York: Free Press.

Stone, B. (2011, October 10). The Return. *Bloomberg Businessweek, 4249,* p. 40.

Zaccaro, S. J. (2002). Organizational leadership and social intelligence. In R. Riggio (Ed.), *Multiple intelligence and leadership* (pp. 29–54). Mahwah, NJ: Lawrence Erlbaum.

Zaccaro, S. J. (2007). Trait-based perspectives of leadership. *American Psychologist, 62,* 6–16.

Zaccaro, S. J., Kemp, C., & Bader, P. (2004). Leader traits and attributes. In J. Antonakis, A. T. Cianciolo, & R. J. Sternberg (Eds.), *The nature of leadership* (pp. 101–124). Thousand Oaks, CA: Sage.

Zaleznik, A. (1977, May–June). Managers and leaders: Are they different? *Harvard Business Review, 55,* 67–78.

3

Skills Approach

DESCRIPTION

Like the trait approach we discussed in Chapter 2, the skills approach takes a leader-centered perspective on leadership. However, in the skills approach we shift our thinking from a focus on personality characteristics, which usually are viewed as innate and largely fixed, to an emphasis on skills and abilities that can be learned and developed. Although personality certainly plays an integral role in leadership, the skills approach suggests that knowledge and abilities are needed for effective leadership.

Researchers have studied leadership skills directly or indirectly for a number of years (see Bass, 1990, pp. 97–109). However, the impetus for research on skills was a classic article published by Robert Katz in the *Harvard Business Review* in 1955, titled "Skills of an Effective Administrator." Katz's article appeared at a time when researchers were trying to identify a definitive set of leadership traits. Katz's approach was an attempt to transcend the trait problem by addressing leadership as a set of developable *skills*. More recently, a revitalized interest in the skills approach has emerged. Beginning in the early 1990s, a multitude of studies have been published that contend that a leader's effectiveness depends on the leader's ability to solve complex organizational problems. This research has resulted in a comprehensive skill-based model of leadership that was advanced by Mumford and his colleagues (Mumford, Zaccaro, Harding, Jacobs, & Fleishman, 2000; Yammarino, 2000).

In this chapter, our discussion of the skills approach is divided into two parts. First, we discuss the general ideas set forth by Katz regarding three basic administrative skills: technical, human, and conceptual. Second, we discuss the recent work of Mumford and colleagues that has resulted in a new skills-based model of organizational leadership.

Three-Skill Approach

Based on field research in administration and his own firsthand observations of executives in the workplace, Katz (1955, p. 34) suggested that effective administration (i.e., leadership) depends on three basic personal skills: technical, human, and conceptual. Katz argued that these skills are quite different from traits or qualities of leaders. *Skills* are what leaders *can accomplish*, whereas *traits* are who leaders *are* (i.e., their innate characteristics). Leadership skills are defined in this chapter as the ability to use one's knowledge and competencies to accomplish a set of goals or objectives. This chapter shows that these leadership skills can be acquired and leaders can be trained to develop them.

Technical Skill

Technical skill is knowledge about and proficiency in a specific type of work or activity. It includes competencies in a specialized area, analytical ability, and the ability to use appropriate tools and techniques (Katz, 1955). For example, in a computer software company, technical skill might include knowing software language and programming, the company's software products, and how to make these products function for clients. Similarly, in an accounting firm, technical skill might include understanding and having the ability to apply generally accepted accounting principles to a client's audit. In both these examples, technical skills involve a hands-on activity with a basic product or process within an organization. Technical skills play an essential role in producing the actual products a company is designed to produce.

As illustrated in Figure 3.1, technical skill is most important at lower and middle levels of management and less important in upper management. For leaders at the highest level, such as chief executive officers (CEOs), presidents, and senior officers, technical competencies are not as essential. Individuals at the top level depend on skilled subordinates to handle technical issues of the physical operation.

Human Skill

Human skill is knowledge about and ability to work with *people*. It is quite different from technical skill, which has to do with working with *things* (Katz, 1955). Human skills are "people skills." They are the abilities that help a leader to work effectively with subordinates, peers, and superiors

3.1 Evidence-Based Practice   3.2 Colin Powell

to accomplish the organization's goals. Human skills allow a leader to assist group members in working cooperatively as a group to achieve common goals. For Katz, it means being aware of one's own perspective on issues and, at the same time, being aware of the perspective of others. Leaders with human skills adapt their own ideas to those of others. Furthermore, they create an atmosphere of trust where employees can feel comfortable and secure and where they can feel encouraged to become involved in the planning of things that will affect them. Being a leader with human skills means being sensitive to the needs and motivations of others and taking into account others' needs in one's decision making. In short, human skill is the capacity to get along with others as you go about your work.

In Figure 3.1, human skills are important in all three levels of management. Although managers at lower levels may communicate with a far

Figure 3.1   Management Skills Necessary at Various Levels of an Organization

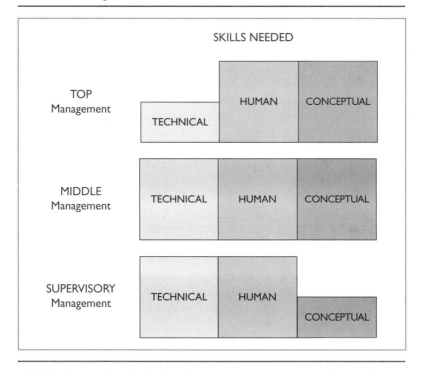

SOURCE: Adapted from "Skills of an Effective Administrator," by R. L. Katz, 1955, *Harvard Business Review*, 33(1), pp. 33–42.

greater number of employees, human skills are equally important at middle and upper levels.

Conceptual Skill

Broadly speaking, conceptual skills are the ability to work with ideas and concepts. Whereas technical skills deal with *things* and human skills deal with *people*, conceptual skills involve the ability to work with *ideas*. A leader with conceptual skills is comfortable talking about the ideas that shape an organization and the intricacies involved. He or she is good at putting the company's goals into words and can understand and express the economic principles that affect the company. A leader with conceptual skills works easily with abstractions and hypothetical notions.

Conceptual skills are central to creating a vision and strategic plan for an organization. For example, it would take conceptual skills for a CEO in a struggling manufacturing company to articulate a vision for a line of new products that would steer the company into profitability. Similarly, it would take conceptual skill for the director of a nonprofit health organization to create a strategic plan that could compete successfully with for-profit health organizations in a market with scarce resources. The point of these examples is that conceptual skill has to do with the mental work of shaping the meaning of organizational or policy issues—understanding what a company stands for and where it is or should be going.

In Figure 3.1, conceptual skill is most important at the top management levels. In fact, when upper-level managers do not have strong conceptual skills, they can jeopardize the whole organization. Conceptual skills are also important in middle management; as we move down to lower management levels, conceptual skills become less important.

Summary of the Three-Skill Approach

To summarize, the three-skill approach includes technical, human, and conceptual skills. It is important for leaders to have all three skills; depending on where they are in the management structure, however, some skills are more important than others are.

Katz's work in the mid-1950s set the stage for conceptualizing leadership in terms of skills, but it was not until the mid-1990s that an empirically-based skills approach received recognition in leadership research. In the next section, the comprehensive skill-based model of leadership is presented.

Skills Model

Beginning in the early 1990s, a group of researchers, with funding from the U.S. Army and Department of Defense, set out to test and develop a comprehensive theory of leadership based on problem-solving skills in organizations. The studies were conducted over a number of years using a sample of more than 1,800 Army officers, representing six grade levels, from second lieutenant to colonel. The project used a variety of new measures and tools to assess the skills of these officers, their experiences, and the situations in which they worked.

The researchers' main goal was to explain the underlying elements of effective performance. They addressed questions such as these: What accounts for why some leaders are good problem solvers and others are not? What specific skills do high-performing leaders exhibit? How do leaders' individual characteristics, career experiences, and environmental influences affect their job performance? As a whole, researchers wanted to identify the leadership factors that create exemplary job performance in an actual organization.

Based on the extensive findings from the project, Mumford and colleagues formulated a skill-based model of leadership. The model is characterized as a *capability* model because it examines the relationship between a leader's knowledge and skills (i.e., capabilities) and the leader's performance (Mumford, Zaccaro, Harding, et al., 2000, p. 12). Leadership capabilities can be developed over time through education and experience. Unlike the "great man" approach (discussed in this text, Chapter 2), which implies that leadership is reserved for only the gifted few, the skills approach suggests that many people have the potential for leadership. If people are capable of learning from their experiences, they can acquire leadership. The skills approach can also be distinguished from the leadership approaches we will discuss in subsequent chapters, which focus on behavioral patterns of leaders (e.g., the style approach, transformational leadership, or leader–member exchange theory). Rather than emphasizing *what leaders do*, the skills approach frames leadership as *the capabilities (knowledge and skills) that make effective leadership possible* (Mumford, Zaccaro, Harding, et al., 2000, p. 12).

3.1 Conceptualizations of Skill   **3.2** Leadership Development

The skill-based model of Mumford's group has five components: competencies, individual attributes, leadership outcomes, career experiences, and environmental influences. A portion of the model, illustrating three of these components, appears in Figure 3.2. This portion of the model is essential to understanding the overall skill-based leadership model.

Figure 3.2 Three Components of the Skills Model

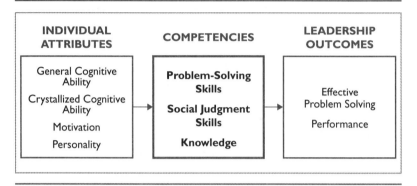

SOURCE: Adapted from "Leadership Skills for a Changing World: Solving Complex Social Problems," by M. D. Mumford, S. J. Zaccaro, F. D. Harding, T. O. Jacobs, and E. A. Fleishman, 2000, *Leadership Quarterly*, *11*(1), 23.

Competencies

As can be observed in the middle box in Figure 3.2, problem-solving skills, social judgment skills, and knowledge are at the heart of the skills model. These three competencies are the key factors that account for effective performance.

Problem-Solving Skills. What are problem-solving skills? According to Mumford, Zaccaro, Harding, et al. (2000), problem-solving skills are a leader's creative ability to solve new and unusual, ill-defined organizational problems. The skills include being able to define significant problems, gather problem information, formulate new understandings about the problem, and generate prototype plans for problem solutions. These skills do not function in a vacuum, but are carried out in an organizational context. Problem-solving skills demand that leaders understand their own leadership capacities as they apply possible solutions to the unique problems in their organization (Mumford, Zaccaro, Connelly, & Marks, 2000).

3.2 Problem-Solving Approaches   3.3 Decision Making

Being able to construct solutions plays a special role in problem solving. In considering solutions to organizational problems, skilled leaders need to attend to the time frame for constructing and implementing a solution, short-term and long-term goals, career goals and organizational goals, and external issues, all of which could influence the solution (Mumford, Zaccaro, Harding, et al., 2000, p. 15).

To clarify what is meant by problem-solving skills, consider the following hypothetical situation. Imagine that you are the director of human resources for a medium-sized company and you have been informed by the president that you have to develop a plan to reduce the company's health care costs. In deciding what you will do, you could demonstrate problem-solving skills in the following ways. First, you identify the full ramifications for employees of changing their health insurance coverage. What is the impact going to be? Second, you gather information about how benefits can be scaled back. What other companies have attempted a similar change, and what were their results? Third, you find a way to teach and inform the employees about the needed change. How can you frame the change in such a way that it is clearly understood? Fourth, you create possible scenarios for how the changes will be instituted. How will the plan be described? Fifth, you look closely at the solution itself. How will implementing this change affect the company's mission and your own career? Last, are there issues in the organization (e.g., union rules) that may affect the implementation of these changes?

As illustrated by this example, the process of dealing with novel, ill-defined organizational problems is complex and demanding for leaders. In many ways, it is like a puzzle to be solved. For leaders to solve such puzzles, the skill-based model suggests that problem-solving skills are essential.

Social Judgment Skills. In addition to problem-solving skills, effective leadership performance also requires social judgment skills (see Figure 3.2). In general, social judgment skills are the capacity to understand people and social systems (Zaccaro, Mumford, Connelly, Marks, & Gilbert, 2000, p. 46). They enable leaders to *work with others* to solve problems and to marshal support to implement change within an organization. Social judgment skills are the people skills that are necessary to solve unique organizational problems.

Conceptually, social judgment skills are similar to Katz's (1955) early work on the role of human skills in management. In contrast to Katz's work, Mumford and colleagues have delineated social judgment skills into

3.4 Flexibility

the following: perspective taking, social perceptiveness, behavioral flexibility, and social performance.

Perspective taking means understanding the attitudes that *others* have toward a particular problem or solution. It is empathy applied to problem solving. Perspective taking means being sensitive to other people's perspectives and goals—being able to understand their point of view on different issues. Included in perspective taking is knowing how different constituencies in an organization view a problem and possible solutions. According to Zaccaro, Gilbert, Thor, and Mumford (1991), perspective-taking skills can be likened to *social intelligence*. These skills are concerned with knowledge about people, the social fabric of organizations, and the interrelatedness of each of them.

Social perceptiveness is insight and awareness into how others in the organization function. What is important to others? What motivates them? What problems do they face, and how do they react to change? Social perceptiveness means understanding the unique needs, goals, and demands of different organizational constituencies (Zaccaro et al., 1991). A leader with social perceptiveness has a keen sense of how employees will respond to any proposed change in the organization. In a sense, you could say it allows the leader to know the pulse of employees on any issue at any time.

In addition to understanding others accurately, social judgment skills also involve reacting to others with flexibility. *Behavioral flexibility* is the capacity to change and adapt one's behavior in light of an understanding of others' perspectives in the organization. Being flexible means one is not locked into a singular approach to a problem. One is not dogmatic but rather maintains an openness and willingness to change. As the circumstances of a situation change, a flexible leader changes to meet the new demands.

Social performance includes a wide range of leadership competencies. Based on an understanding of employees' perspectives, leaders need to be able to communicate their own vision to others. Skill in persuasion and communicating change is essential to do this. When there is resistance to change or interpersonal conflict about change, leaders need to function as mediators. To this end, skill in conflict resolution is an important aspect of social performance competency. In addition, social performance sometimes requires that leaders coach subordinates, giving them direction and support as they move toward selected organizational goals. In all, social performance includes many related skills that may come under the umbrella of communication.

3.3 Managerial Leadership

To review, social judgment skills are about being sensitive to how your ideas fit in with others. Can you understand others' perspectives and their unique needs and motivations? Are you flexible, and can you adapt your own ideas to others? Can you work with others even when there is resistance and conflict? Social judgment skills are the people skills needed to advance change in an organization.

Knowledge. As shown in the model (see Figure 3.2), the third aspect of competencies is knowledge. Knowledge is inextricably related to the application and implementation of problem-solving skills in organizations. It directly influences a leader's capacity to define complex organizational problems and to attempt to solve them (Mumford, Zaccaro, Harding, et al., 2000). *Knowledge* is the accumulation of information and the mental structures used to organize that information. Such a mental structure is called a *schema* (a summary, a diagrammatic representation, or an outline). Knowledge results from having developed an assortment of complex schemata for learning and organizing data.

For example, all of us take various kinds of facts and information into our minds. As we organize that information into categories or schemata, the information becomes more meaningful. Knowledge emerges from the facts *and* the organizational structures we apply to them. People with a lot of knowledge have more complex organizing structures than those with less knowledge. These knowledgeable people are called *experts*.

Consider the following baseball example. A baseball expert knows a lot of facts about the game; the expert knows the rules, strategies, equipment, players, and much, much more. The expert's knowledge about baseball includes the facts, but it also includes the complex mental structures used in organizing and structuring those facts. That person knows not only the season and lifetime statistics for each player, but also that player's quirks and injuries, the personality of the manager, the strengths and weaknesses of available substitutes, and so on. The expert knows baseball because she or he comprehends the complexities and nuances of the game. The same is true for leadership in organizations. Leaders with knowledge know much about the products, the tasks, the people, the organization, and all the different ways these elements are related to each other. A knowledgeable leader has many mental structures with which to organize the facts of organizational life.

Knowledge has a positive impact on how leaders engage in problem solving. It is knowledge and expertise that make it possible for people to

3.5 Motivation and Leadership Styles

think about complex system issues and identify possible strategies for appropriate change. Furthermore, this capacity allows people to use prior cases and incidents in order to plan for needed change. It is knowledge that allows people to use the past to constructively confront the future.

To summarize, the skills model consists of three competencies: problem-solving skills, social judgment skills, and knowledge. Collectively, these three components are positively related to effective leadership performance (see Figure 3.2).

Individual Attributes

Returning to Figure 3.2, the box on the left identifies four individual attributes that have an impact on leadership skills and knowledge: general cognitive ability, crystallized cognitive ability, motivation, and personality. These attributes play important roles in the skills model. Complex problem solving is a very difficult process and becomes more difficult as people move up in the organization. These attributes support people as they apply their leadership competencies.

General Cognitive Ability. General cognitive ability can be thought of as a person's intelligence. It includes perceptual processing, information processing, general reasoning skills, creative and divergent thinking capacities, and memory skills. General cognitive ability is linked to biology, not to experience.

General cognitive ability is sometimes described as fluid intelligence, a type of intelligence that usually grows and expands up through early adulthood and then declines with age. In the skills model, intelligence is described as having a positive impact on the leader's acquisition of complex problem-solving skills and the leader's knowledge.

Crystallized Cognitive Ability. Crystallized cognitive ability is intellectual ability that is learned or acquired over time. It is the store of knowledge we acquire through experience. We learn and increase our capacities over a lifetime, increasing our leadership potential (e.g., problem-solving skills, conceptual ability, and social judgment skills). In normally functioning adults, this type of cognitive ability grows continuously and typically does not fall off in adulthood. It includes being able to comprehend complex information and learn new skills and information, as well as being able to communicate to others in oral and written forms (Connelly

3.1 Global Leaders

et al., 2000, p. 71). Stated another way, crystallized cognitive ability is acquired intelligence: the ideas and mental abilities people learn through experience. Because it stays fairly stable over time, this type of intelligence is not diminished as people get older.

Motivation. Motivation is listed as the third attribute in the model. Although the model does not purport to explain the many ways in which motivation may affect leadership, it does suggest three aspects of motivation that are essential to developing leadership skills (Mumford, Zaccaro, Harding, et al., 2000, p. 22): First, leaders must be *willing* to tackle complex organizational problems. This first step is critical. For leadership to occur, a person wants to lead. Second, leaders must be willing to express *dominance*—to exert their influence, as we discussed in Chapter 2. In influencing others, the leader must take on the responsibility of dominance because the influence component of leadership is inextricably bound to dominance. Third, leaders must be committed to the *social good* of the organization. The *social good* is a broad term that can refer to a host of outcomes. However, in the skills model it refers to the leader's willingness to take on the responsibility of trying to advance the overall human good and value of the organization. Taken together, these three aspects of motivation (willingness, dominance, and social good) prepare people to become leaders.

Personality. Personality is the fourth individual attribute in the skills model. Placed where it is in the model, this attribute reminds us that our personality has an impact on the development of our leadership skills. For example, openness, tolerance for ambiguity, and curiosity may affect a leader's motivation to try to solve some organizational problem. Or, in conflict situations, traits such as confidence and adaptability may be beneficial to a leader's performance. The skills model hypothesizes that any personality characteristic that helps people to cope with complex organizational situations probably is related to leader performance (Mumford, Zaccaro, Harding, et al., 2000).

Leadership Outcomes

In the right-hand box in Figure 3.2, effective problem solving and performance are the outcomes of leadership. These outcomes are strongly influenced by the leader's competencies (i.e., problem-solving skills, social judgment skills, and knowledge). When leaders exhibit these competencies, they increase their chances of problem solving and overall performance.

 3.3 Mentoring and Coaching

Effective Problem Solving. As we discussed earlier, the skills model is a *capability model*, designed to explain why some leaders are good problem solvers and others are not. Problem solving is the keystone in the skills approach. In the model (see Figure 3.2), problem-solving skills, as competencies, lead to effective problem solving as a leadership outcome. The criteria for good problem solving are determined by the originality and the quality of expressed solutions to problems. Good problem solving involves creating solutions that are logical, effective, and unique, and that go beyond given information (Zaccaro et al., 2000).

Performance. In the model, performance outcomes reflect how well the leader has done her or his job. To measure performance, standard external criteria are used. If the leader has done well and been successful, the leader's evaluations will be positive. Leaders who are effective receive good annual performance reviews, get merit raises, and are recognized by superiors and subordinates as competent leaders. In the end, performance is the degree to which a leader has successfully performed the assigned duties.

Taken together, effective problem solving and performance are the two ways to assess leadership effectiveness using the skills model. Furthermore, good problem solving and good performance go hand in hand. A full depiction of the comprehensive skills model appears in Figure 3.3. It contains two other components, not depicted in Figure 3.2, that contribute to overall leadership performance: career experiences and environmental influences.

Career Experiences

As you can see in Figure 3.3, career experiences have an impact on the characteristics and competencies of leaders. The skills model suggests that the experiences acquired in the course of leaders' careers influence their knowledge and skills to solve complex problems. Mumford, Zaccaro, Harding, et al. (2000, p. 24) pointed out that leaders can be helped through challenging job assignments, mentoring, appropriate training, and hands-on experience in solving new and unusual problems. In addition, the authors think that career experiences can positively affect the individual characteristics of leaders. For example, certain on-the-job assignments could enhance a leader's motivation or intellectual ability.

In the first section of this chapter, we discussed Katz's (1955) work, which notes that conceptual skills are essential for upper-level administrators. This

3.4 Role of Emotions

Figure 3.3   Skills Model of Leadership

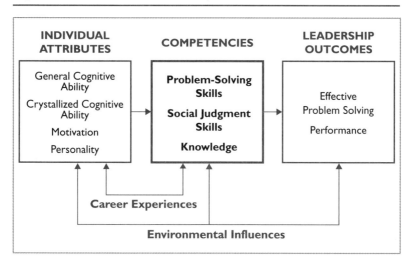

SOURCE: Adapted from "Leadership Skills for a Changing World: Solving Complex Social Problems," by M. D. Mumford, S. J. Zaccaro, F. D. Harding, T. O. Jacobs, and E. A. Fleishman, 2000, *Leadership Quarterly, 11*(1), 23.

is consistent with Mumford, Zaccaro, Harding, et al.'s (2000) skills model, which contends that leaders develop competencies over time. Career experience helps leaders to improve their skills and knowledge over time. Leaders learn and develop higher levels of conceptual capacity if the kinds of problems they confront are progressively more complex and more long term as they ascend the organizational hierarchy (Mumford, Zaccaro, Connelly, et al., 2000). Similarly, upper-level leaders, as opposed to first-line supervisors, develop new competencies because they are required to address problems that are more novel, that are more poorly defined, and that demand more human interaction. As these people move through their careers, higher levels of problem-solving and social judgment skills become increasingly important (Mumford & Connelly, 1991).

So the skills and knowledge of leaders are shaped by their career experiences as they address increasingly complex problems in the organization. This notion of developing leadership skills is unique and quite different from other leadership perspectives. If we say, "Leaders are shaped by their experiences," then it means leaders are not born to be leaders (Mumford, Zaccaro, Harding, et al., 2000). Leaders can develop their abilities through experience, according to the skills model.

Environmental Influences

The final component of the skills model is environmental influences, which is illustrated at the bottom of Figure 3.3. Environmental influences represent factors that lie outside the leader's competencies, characteristics, and experiences. These environmental influences can be *internal* and *external*.

Internal environmental influences affecting leadership performance can include such factors as technology, facilities, expertise of subordinates, and communication. For example, an aging factory or one lacking in high-speed technology could have a major impact on the nature of problem-solving activities. Another example might be the skill levels of subordinates: If a leader's subordinates are highly competent, they will definitely improve the group's problem solving and performance. Similarly, if a task is particularly complex or a group's communication poor, the leader's performance will be affected.

External environmental influences, including economic, political, and social issues, as well as natural disasters, can provide unique challenges to leaders. In March 2011, a massive earthquake and tsunami devastated large parts of Japan, crippling that nation's automobile manufacturing industry. Toyota Motor Corp. alone had more than 650 of its suppliers and component manufacturers wiped out, halting worldwide production of Toyota vehicles and devastating the company's sales. At the same time, this disaster was a boon to American carmakers who increased shipments and began outselling Toyota, which had dominated the market. Leaders of these automobile companies, both Japanese and American, had to respond to unique challenges posed by external forces completely beyond their control.

The skills model does not provide an inventory of specific environmental influences. Instead, it acknowledges the existence of these factors and recognizes that they are indeed influences that can affect a leader's performance. In other words, environmental influences are a part of the skills model but not usually under the control of the leader.

Summary of the Skills Model

In summary, the skills model frames leadership by describing five components of leader performance. At the heart of the model are three

3.4 Leadership Methodology   3.2 Veterans and Leadership Skills competencies: *problem-solving skills, social judgment skills,* and *knowledge.* These three competencies are the central determinants of effective problem solving and performance, although individual attributes, career experiences, and environmental influences all have impacts on leader competencies. Through job experience and training, leaders can become better problem solvers and more effective leaders.

HOW DOES THE SKILLS APPROACH WORK?

The skills approach is primarily descriptive: It *describes* leadership from a skills perspective. Rather than providing prescriptions for success in leadership, the skills approach provides a structure for understanding the nature of effective leadership. In the previous sections, we discussed the skills perspective based on the work of Katz (1955) and Mumford, Zaccaro, Harding, et al. (2000). What does each of these bodies of work suggest about the structure and functions of leadership?

The three-skill approach of Katz suggests that the importance of certain leadership skills varies depending on where leaders are in a management hierarchy. For leaders operating at lower levels of management, technical and human skills are most important. When leaders move into middle management, it becomes important that they have all three skills: technical, human, and conceptual. At the upper management levels, it is paramount for leaders to exhibit conceptual and human skills.

This approach was reinforced in a 2007 study that examined the skills needed by executives at different levels of management. The researchers used a four-skill model, similar to Katz's approach, to assess cognitive skills, interpersonal skills, business skills, and strategic skills of 1,000 managers at the junior, middle, and senior levels of an organization. The results showed that interpersonal and cognitive skills were required more than business and strategic skills for those on the lower levels of management. As one climbed the career ladder, however, the execution of higher levels of all four of these leadership skills became necessary (Mumford, Campion, & Morgeson, 2007).

In their skills model, Mumford, Zaccaro, Harding, et al. (2000) provided a more complex picture of how skills relate to the manifestation of effective leadership. Their skills model contends that leadership outcomes are the direct result of a leader's competencies in problem-solving skills, social judgment skills, and knowledge. Each of these competencies includes a large repertoire of abilities, and each can be learned and developed. In addition, the model illustrates how individual attributes such as general cognitive ability, crystallized cognitive ability, motivation, and personality influence the leader's competencies. And finally, the model describes how career experiences and environmental influences play a direct or indirect role in leadership performance.

The skills approach works by providing a *map* for how to reach effective leadership in an organization: Leaders need to have problem-solving skills, social judgment skills, and knowledge. Workers can improve their capabilities in these areas through training and experience. Although each leader's personal attributes affect his or her skills, it is the leader's *skills* themselves that are most important in addressing organizational problems.

STRENGTHS

In several ways, the skills approach contributes positively to our understanding about leadership. First, it is a leader-centered model that stresses the importance of developing particular leadership skills. It is the first approach to conceptualize and create a structure of the process of leadership around *skills*. Whereas the early research on skills highlighted the importance of skills and the value of skills across different management levels, the later work placed learned skills at the center of effective leadership performance at *all* management levels.

Second, the skills approach is intuitively appealing. To describe leadership in terms of skills makes leadership available to everyone. Unlike personality traits, skills are competencies that people can learn or develop. It is like playing a sport such as tennis or golf. Even without natural ability in these sports, people can improve their games with practice and instruction. The same is true with leadership. When leadership is framed as a set of skills, it becomes a process that people can study and practice to become better at performing their jobs.

Third, the skills approach provides an expansive view of leadership that incorporates a wide variety of components, including problem-solving skills, social judgment skills, knowledge, individual attributes, career experiences, and environmental influences. Each of these components can

3.5 Leadership Skill Development

further be subdivided into several subcomponents. The result is a picture of leadership that encompasses a multitude of factors. Because it includes so many variables, the skills approach can capture many of the intricacies and complexities of leadership not found in other models.

Last, the skills approach provides a structure that is very consistent with the curricula of most leadership education programs. Leadership education programs throughout the country have traditionally taught classes in creative problem solving, conflict resolution, listening, and teamwork, to name a few. The content of these classes closely mirrors many of the components in the skills model. Clearly, the skills approach provides a structure that helps to frame the curricula of leadership education and development programs.

CRITICISMS

Like all other approaches to leadership, the skills approach also has certain weaknesses. First, the breadth of the skills approach seems to extend beyond the boundaries of leadership. For example, by including motivation, critical thinking, personality, and conflict resolution, the skills approach addresses more than just leadership. Another example of the model's breadth is its inclusion of two types of intelligence (i.e., general cognitive ability and crystallized cognitive ability). Although both areas are studied widely in the field of cognitive psychology, they are seldom addressed in leadership research. By including so many components, the skills model of Mumford and others becomes more general and less precise in explaining leadership performance.

Second, related to the first criticism, the skills model is weak in predictive value. It does not explain specifically how variations in social judgment skills and problem-solving skills affect performance. The model suggests that these components are related, but it does not describe with any precision just how that works. In short, the model can be faulted because it does not explain *how* skills lead to effective leadership performance.

In addition, the skills approach can be criticized for claiming *not* to be a trait model when, in fact, a major component in the model includes individual attributes, which are trait-like. Although Mumford and colleagues describe cognitive abilities, motivation, and personality variables as factors contributing to competencies, these are also factors that are typically considered to be trait variables. The point is that the individual attributes component of the skills model is trait driven, and that shifts the model away from being strictly a skills approach to leadership.

The final criticism of the skills approach is that it may not be suitably or appropriately applied to other contexts of leadership. The skills model was constructed by using a large sample of military personnel and observing their performance in the armed services. This raises an obvious question: Can the results be generalized to other populations or organizational settings? Although some research suggests that these Army findings can be generalized to other groups (Mumford, Zaccaro, Connelly, et al., 2000), more research is needed to address this criticism.

APPLICATION

Despite its appeal to theorists and academics, the skills approach has not been widely used in applied leadership settings. For example, there are no training packages designed specifically to teach people leadership skills from this approach. Although many programs have been designed to teach leadership skills from a general self-help orientation, few of these programs are based on the conceptual frameworks set forth in this chapter.

Despite the lack of formal training programs, the skills approach offers valuable information about leadership. The approach provides a way to delineate the skills of the leader, and leaders at all levels in an organization can use it. In addition, this approach helps us to identify our strengths and weaknesses in regard to these technical, human, and conceptual skills. By taking a skills inventory such as the one provided at the end of this chapter, people can gain further insight into their own leadership competencies. Their scores allow them to learn about areas in which they may want to seek further training to enhance their overall contributions to their organization.

From a wider perspective, the skills approach may be used in the future as a template for the design of extensive leadership development programs. This approach provides the evidence for teaching leaders the important aspects of listening, creative problem solving, conflict resolution skills, and much more.

▶ **3.6** Skills and Business Intelligence

CASE STUDIES

The following three case studies (Cases 3.1, 3.2, and 3.3) describe leadership situations that can be analyzed and evaluated from the skills perspective. The first case involves the principal investigator of a federally funded research grant. The second case takes place in a military setting and describes how a lieutenant colonel handles the downsizing of a military base. In the third case, we learn about how the owner of an Italian restaurant has created his own recipe for success.

As you read each case, try to apply the principles of the skills approach to the leaders and their situations. At the end of each case are questions that will assist you in analyzing the case.

CASE 3.1

A Strained Research Team

Dr. Adam Wood is the principal investigator on a 3-year, $1 million federally funded research grant to study health education programs for older populations, called the Elder Care Project. Unlike previous projects, in which Dr. Wood worked alone or with one or two other investigators, on this project Dr. Wood has 11 colleagues. His project team is made up of two co-investigators (with PhDs), four intervention staff (with MAs), and five general staff members (with BAs). One year into the project, it has become apparent to Dr. Wood and the team that the project is underbudgeted and has too few resources. Team members are spending 20%–30% more time on the project than has been budgeted to pay them. Regardless of the resource strain, all team members are committed to the project; they believe in its goals and the importance of its outcomes. Dr. Wood is known throughout the country as the foremost scholar in this area of health education research. He is often asked to serve on national review and advisory boards. His publication record is second to none. In addition, his colleagues in the university know Dr. Wood as a very competent researcher. People come to Dr. Wood for advice on research design and methodology questions. They also come to him for questions about theoretical formulations. He has a reputation as someone who can see the big picture on research projects.

Despite his research competence, there are problems on Dr. Wood's research team. Dr. Wood worries there is a great deal of work to be

(Continued)

(Continued)

done but that the members of the team are not devoting sufficient time to the Elder Care Project. He is frustrated because many of the day-to-day research tasks of the project are falling into his lap. He enters a research meeting, throws his notebook down on the table, and says, "I wish I'd never taken this project on. It's taking way too much of my time. The rest of you aren't pulling your fair share." Team members feel exasperated at Dr. Wood's comments. Although they respect his competence, they find his leadership style frustrating. His negative comments at staff meetings are having a demoralizing effect on the research team. Despite their hard work and devotion to the project, Dr. Wood seldom compliments or praises their efforts. Team members believe that they have spent more time than anticipated on the project and have received less pay or credit than expected. The project is sucking away a lot of staff energy, yet Dr. Wood does not seem to understand the pressures confronting his staff.

The research staff is starting to feel burned out, but members realize they need to keep trying because they are under time constraints from the federal government to do the work promised. The team needs to develop a pamphlet for the participants in the Elder Care Project, but the pamphlet costs are significantly more than budgeted in the grant. Dr. Wood has been very adept at finding out where they might find small pockets of money to help cover those costs.

Although team members are pleased that he is able to obtain the money, they are sure he will use this as just another example of how he was the one doing most of the work on the project.

Questions

1. Based on the skills approach, how would you assess Dr. Wood's leadership and his relationship to the members of the Elder Care Project team? Will the project be successful?

2. Does Dr. Wood have the skills necessary to be an effective leader of this research team?

3. The skills model describes three important competencies for leaders: problem-solving skills, social judgment skills, and knowledge. If you were to coach Dr. Wood using this model, what competencies would you address with him? What changes would you suggest that he make in his leadership?

CASE 3.2

A Shift for Lieutenant Colonel Adams

Lt. Col. John Adams was an aeronautical engineer in the Air Force who was recognized as an accomplished officer; he rose quickly through the ranks of lieutenant, captain, and major. In addition, he successfully completed a number of professional development courses in the Air Force and received a master's degree in engineering. In the earlier part of his service, his career assignments required overseeing 15- to 20-person shifts that were responsible for routine maintenance schedules for squadron and base aircraft. As he progressed in rank, he moved to engineering projects, which were supported by small technical staffs.

Based on his strong performance, Major Adams was promoted to lieutenant colonel earlier than his peers. Instead of moving him into another engineering position, the personnel bureau and his assignment officer decided that Lieutenant Colonel Adams would benefit from a tour in which he could expand his professional background and experience. Consequently, he was assigned to Base X as the commanding officer of the administration branch. Base X was an airbase with approximately 5,000 military and civilian personnel.

As the administration officer, Adams was the senior human resource officer and the principal adviser to the base commander on all human resource issues. Adams and his staff of 135 civilian and military personnel were responsible for personnel issues, food services, recreation, family support, and medical services. In addition, Lieutenant Colonel Adams was assigned to chair the Labor–Management Relations Committee for the base.

At the end of the Cold War, as part of the declared peace dividend, the government decided to reduce its defense budget. In February, barely 6 months after Adams took over command of the administration branch, the federal government announced a significant reduction in the size of the military and the closure of many bases. Base X was to be closed as an air base and reassigned to the Army. The closure was to take place within 1 year, and the base was to be prepared for the arrival of the first Army troops in 2 years. As part of the reduction program, the federal government initiated voluntary retirement programs for civilian and military personnel. Those wanting to retire had until April 1 to decide.

(Continued)

(Continued)

Orders for the conversion of the airbase included the following:

- The base will continue normal operations for 6 months.
- The squadrons—complete with aircrews, equipment, and families (1,000)—must be relocated to their new bases and operational by August 1.
- The remaining base personnel strength, both civilian and military, must be reduced by 30%.
- The base must continue to provide personnel for operational missions.
- The reduction of personnel must be consistent with federal voluntary early-retirement programs.
- The base must be prepared with a support structure to accept 2,000 new soldiers, expected to arrive in 2 years.

Adams was assigned to develop a human resource plan that would meet the imposed staff levels for the entire base while ensuring that the base was still able to perform the operational tasks it had been given. Faced with this daunting task, Adams conducted an extensive review of all of the relevant orders concerning the base transformation, and he familiarized himself with all of the rules concerning the early-retirement program. After a series of initial meetings with the other base branch chiefs, he laid out a plan that could be accomplished by the established deadlines. At the same time, he chaired a number of meetings with his own staff about how to meet the mandated reductions within his own branch.

After considering the target figures for the early-retirement program, it was clear that the mandated numbers could not be reached. Simply allowing everyone who had applied for early retirement to leave was not considered an option because doing so would devastate entire sections of the base. More job cuts were required, and choices had to be made as to who would stay, why, and in what areas. Adams met stiff resistance in the meetings to determine what sections would bear the brunt of the additional cutbacks.

Adams conducted his own independent analysis of his own branch before consulting with his staff. Based on his thorough examination of the data, he mandated further reductions in his sections. Specifically targeted were personnel in base housing, single-person accommodations, family services, and recreational sections. He also mandated a further 10% cut of military positions in his sections.

After meeting the mandated reduction targets, Lieutenant Colonel Adams was informed that the federal government would accept all personnel who applied for early retirement, which was an unexpected decision. When superimposed on the already mandated reductions, this move caused critical shortages in key areas. Within weeks of implementation of the plan, the base commander was receiving mounting complaints from both civilian and military members over the implementation of the plan.

Incidents of stress, frustration, and discontent rose dramatically. Families trying to move found support services cut back or nonexistent. The transition staff was forced to work evenings and weekends. Family support services were swamped and asking for additional help.

Despite spending a large amount of overtime trying to address the diverse issues both basewide and within his branch, Adams found himself struggling to keep his head above water. To make matters worse, the base was having difficulty meeting its operational mission, and vital sections were critically understaffed. The base commander wanted answers. When pressed, Adams stated that his plan met all of the required deadlines and targets, and the plan conformed to all of the guidelines of the early retirement programs. "Maybe so," replied the base commander, "but you forgot about the bigger picture."

Questions

1. Based on the skills model, how would you assess Lt. Col. John Adams's ability to meet the challenges of the base administration position?

2. How would you assess his ability to meet the additional tasks he faced regarding the conversion of the base?

3. If you were to coach Adams on how he could improve his leadership, what would you tell him?

CASE 3.3

Andy's Recipe

Andy Garafallo owns an Italian restaurant that sits in the middle of a cornfield near a large Midwestern city. On the restaurant's far wall is an elaborate mural of the canals of Venice. A gondola hangs on the opposite wall, up by the ceiling. Along another wall is a row of real potted lemon

(Continued)

(Continued)

trees. "My ancestors are from Sicily," says Andy. "In fact, I can remember seeing my grandfather take a bite out of a lemon, just like the ones hanging on those trees."

Andy is very confident about his approach to this restaurant, and he should be, because the restaurant is celebrating its 25th anniversary. "I'm darned sure of what I want to do. I'm not trying different fads to get people to come here. People come here because they know they will get great food. They also want to support someone with whom they can connect. This is my approach. Nothing more, nothing less." Although other restaurants have folded, Andy seems to have found a recipe for success.

Since opening his restaurant, Andy has had a number of managers. Currently, he has three: Kelly, Danielle, and Patrick. Kelly is a kitchen (food prep) manager who is known as very honest and dependable. She loves her work, and is efficient, good with ordering, and good with preparation. Andy really likes Kelly but is frustrated with her because she has such difficulty getting along with the salespeople, delivery people, and waitstaff.

Danielle, who works out front in the restaurant, has been with Andy the longest, 6 years. Danielle likes working at Garafallo's—she lives and breathes the place. She fully buys into Andy's approach of putting customers first. In fact, Andy says she has a knack for knowing what customers need even before they ask. Although she is very hospitable, Andy says she is lousy with numbers. She just doesn't seem to catch on to that side of the business.

Patrick, who has been with Andy for 4 years, usually works out front but can work in the kitchen as well. Although Patrick has a strong work ethic and is great with numbers, he is weak on the people side. For some reason, Patrick treats customers as if they are faceless, coming across as very unemotional. In addition, Patrick tends to approach problems with an either–or perspective. This has gotten him into trouble on more than one occasion. Andy wishes that Patrick would learn to lighten up. "He's a good manager, but he needs to recognize that some things just aren't that important," says Andy.

Andy's approach to his managers is that of a teacher and coach. He is always trying to help them improve. He sees part of his responsibility as teaching them every aspect of the restaurant business. Andy's stated goal is that he wants his managers to be "A" players when they leave his business to take on jobs elsewhere. Helping people to become the best they can be is Andy's goal for his restaurant employees.

Although Andy works 12 hours a day, he spends little time analyzing the numbers. He does not think about ways to improve his profit margin by cutting corners, raising an item price here, or cutting quality there. Andy says, "It's like this: The other night I got a call from someone who said they wanted to come in with a group and wondered if they could bring along a cake. I said 'yes' with one stipulation....I get a piece! Well the people came and spent a lot of money. Then they told me that they had actually wanted to go to another restaurant but the other place would not allow them to bring in their own cake." Andy believes very strongly in his approach. "You get business by being what you should be." Compared with other restaurants, his restaurant is doing quite well. Although many places are happy to net 5%–7% profit, Andy's Italian restaurant nets 30% profit, year in and year out.

Questions

1. What accounts for Andy's success in the restaurant business?

2. From a skills perspective, how would you describe the three managers, Kelly, Danielle, and Patrick? What does each of them need to do to improve his or her skills?

3. How would you describe Andy's competencies? Does Andy's leadership suggest that one does not need all three skills in order to be effective?

LEADERSHIP INSTRUMENT

Many questionnaires assess an individual's skills for leadership. A quick search of the Internet provides a host of these questionnaires. Almost all of them are designed to be used in training and development to give people a feel for their leadership abilities. Surveys have been used for years to help people understand and improve their leadership style, but most questionnaires are not used in research because they have not been tested for reliability and validity. Nevertheless, they are useful as self-help instruments because they provide specific information to people about their leadership skills.

In this chapter, we present a comprehensive skills model that is based on many empirical studies of leaders' skills. Although the questionnaires used in these studies are highly reliable and are valid instruments, they are not suitable for our more pragmatic discussion of leadership in this text. In essence, they are too complex and involved. For example, Mumford, Zaccaro, Harding, et al. (2000) used measures that included open-ended responses and very sophisticated scoring procedures. Though critically important for validating the model, these complicated measures are less valuable as self-instruction questionnaires.

A skills inventory is provided in the next section to assist you in understanding how leadership skills are measured and what your own skills might be. Your scores on the inventory will give you a sense of your own leadership competencies. You may be strong in all three skills, or you may be stronger in some skills than in others. The questionnaire will give you a sense of your own skills profile. If you are stronger in one skill and weaker in another, this may help you determine where you want to improve in the future.

Skills Inventory

Instructions: Read each item carefully and decide whether the item describes you as a person. Indicate your response to each item by circling one of the five numbers to the right of each item.

Key: 1 = Not   2 = Seldom   3 = Occasionally   4 = Somewhat   5 = Very
      true   true   true   true   true

1. I enjoy getting into the details of how things work.   1 2 3 4 5
2. As a rule, adapting ideas to people's needs is   1 2 3 4 5
   easy for me.
3. I enjoy working with abstract ideas.   1 2 3 4 5
4. Technical things fascinate me.   1 2 3 4 5
5. Being able to understand others is the most important   1 2 3 4 5
   part of my work.
6. Seeing the big picture comes easy for me.   1 2 3 4 5
7. One of my skills is being good at making things work.   1 2 3 4 5
8. My main concern is to have a supportive   1 2 3 4 5
   communication climate.
9. I am intrigued by complex organizational problems.   1 2 3 4 5
10. Following directions and filling out forms comes easily   1 2 3 4 5
    for me.
11. Understanding the social fabric of the organization   1 2 3 4 5
    is important to me.
12. I would enjoy working out strategies for my   1 2 3 4 5
    organization's growth.
13. I am good at completing the things I've been   1 2 3 4 5
    assigned to do.
14. Getting all parties to work together is a challenge   1 2 3 4 5
    I enjoy.
15. Creating a mission statement is rewarding work.   1 2 3 4 5
16. I understand how to do the basic things required   1 2 3 4 5
    of me.
17. I am concerned with how my decisions affect the   1 2 3 4 5
    lives of others.
18. Thinking about organizational values and philosophy   1 2 3 4 5
    appeals to me.

Scoring

The skills inventory is designed to measure three broad types of leadership skills: technical, human, and conceptual. Score the questionnaire by doing the following. First, sum the responses on items 1, 4, 7, 10, 13, and 16. This is your technical skill score. Second, sum the responses on items 2, 5, 8, 11, 14, and 17. This is your human skill score. Third, sum the responses on items 3, 6, 9, 12, 15, and 18. This is your conceptual skill score.

Total scores: Technical skill _____ Human skill _____ Conceptual skill _____

Scoring Interpretation

23–30 High Range

14–22 Moderate Range

6–13 Low Range

The scores you received on the skills inventory provide information about your leadership skills in three areas. By comparing the differences between your scores, you can determine where you have leadership strengths and where you have leadership weaknesses. Your scores also point toward the level of management for which you might be most suited.

SUMMARY

The skills approach is a leader-centered perspective that emphasizes the competencies of leaders. It is best represented in the early work of Katz (1955) on the *three-skill approach* and the more recent work of Mumford and his colleagues (Mumford, Zaccaro, Harding, et al., 2000), who initiated the development of a comprehensive *skills model of leadership*.

In the three-skill approach, effective leadership depends on three basic personal skills: technical, human, and conceptual. Although all three skills are important for leaders, the importance of each skill varies between management levels. At lower management levels, technical and human skills are most important. For middle managers, the three different skills are equally important. At upper management levels, conceptual and human skills are most important, and technical skills become less important. Leaders are more effective when their skills match their management level.

In the 1990s, the skills model was developed to explain the capabilities (knowledge and skills) that make effective leadership possible. Far more complex than Katz's paradigm, this model delineated five components of effective leader performance: competencies, individual attributes, leadership outcomes, career experiences, and environmental influences. The leader competencies at the heart of the model are problem-solving skills, social judgment skills, and knowledge. These competencies are directly affected by the leader's individual attributes, which include the leader's general cognitive ability, crystallized cognitive ability, motivation, and personality. The leader's competencies are also affected by his or her career experiences and the environment. The model postulates that effective problem solving and performance can be explained by the leader's basic competencies and that these competencies are in turn affected by the leader's attributes, experience, and environment.

There are several strengths in conceptualizing leadership from a skills perspective. First, it is a leader-centered model that stresses the importance of the leader's abilities, and it places learned skills at the center of effective leadership performance. Second, the skills approach describes leadership in such a way that it makes it available to everyone. Skills are competencies that we all can learn to develop and improve. Third, the skills approach provides a sophisticated map that explains how effective leadership performance can be achieved. Based on the model, researchers can develop complex plans for studying the leadership process. Last, this approach provides a structure for leadership education and development programs that include creative problem solving, conflict resolution, listening, and teamwork.

In addition to the positive features, there are also some negative aspects to the skills approach. First, the breadth of the model seems to extend beyond the boundaries of leadership, including, for example, conflict management, critical thinking, motivation theory, and personality theory. Second, the skills model is weak in predictive value. It does not explain how a person's competencies lead to effective leadership performance.

Third, the skills model claims not to be a trait approach; nevertheless, individual traits such as cognitive abilities, motivation, and personality play a large role in the model. Finally, the skills model is weak in general application because it was constructed using data only from military personnel. Until the model has been tested with other populations, such as small and large organizations and businesses, its basic tenets must still be questioned.

Visit the Student Study Site at **www.sagepub.com/northouse6e** for web quizzes, leadership questionnaires, and media links represented by the icons.

REFERENCES

Bass, B. M. (1990). *Bass & Stogdill's handbook of leadership: Theory, research, and managerial application* (3rd ed.). New York: Free Press.

Connelly, M. S., Gilbert, J. A., Zaccaro, S. J., Threlfall, K. V., Marks, M. A., & Mumford, M. D. (2000). Exploring the relationship of leadership skills and knowledge to leader performance. *Leadership Quarterly, 11*(1), 65–86.

Katz, R. L. (1955). Skills of an effective administrator. *Harvard Business Review, 33*(1), 33–42.

Mumford, M. D., & Connelly, M. S. (1991). Leaders as creators: Leader performance and problem solving in ill-defined domains. *Leadership Quarterly, 2,* 289–315.

Mumford, M. D., Zaccaro, S. J., Connelly, M. S., & Marks, M. A. (2000). Leadership skills: Conclusions and future directions. *Leadership Quarterly, 11*(1), 155–170.

Mumford, M. D., Zaccaro, S. J., Harding, F. D., Jacobs, T. O., & Fleishman, E. A. (2000). Leadership skills for a changing world: Solving complex social problems. *Leadership Quarterly, 11*(1), 11–35.

Mumford, T. V., Campion, M. A., & Morgeson, F. P. (2007). The leadership skills strataplex: Leadership skill requirements across organizational levels. *Leadership Quarterly, 18,* 154–166.

Yammarino, F. J. (2000). Leadership skills: Introduction and overview. *Leadership Quarterly, 11*(1), 5–9.

Zaccaro, S. J., Gilbert, J., Thor, K. K., & Mumford, M. D. (1991). Leadership and social intelligence: Linking social perceptiveness and behavioral flexibility to leader effectiveness. *Leadership Quarterly, 2,* 317–331.

Zaccaro, S. J., Mumford, M. D., Connelly, M. S., Marks, M. A., & Gilbert, J. A. (2000). Assessment of leader problem-solving capabilities. *Leadership Quarterly, 11*(1), 37–64.

Style Approach

DESCRIPTION

The style approach emphasizes the behavior of the leader. This distinguishes it from the trait approach (Chapter 2), which emphasizes the personality characteristics of the leader, and the skills approach (Chapter 3), which emphasizes the leader's capabilities. The style approach focuses exclusively on what leaders do and how they act. In shifting the study of leadership to leader style or behaviors, the style approach expanded the study of leadership to include the actions of leaders toward subordinates in various contexts.

Researchers studying the style approach determined that leadership is composed of two general kinds of behaviors: *task behaviors* and *relationship behaviors*. Task behaviors facilitate goal accomplishment: They help group members to achieve their objectives. Relationship behaviors help subordinates feel comfortable with themselves, with each other, and with the situation in which they find themselves. The central purpose of the style approach is to explain how leaders combine these two kinds of behaviors to influence subordinates in their efforts to reach a goal.

Many studies have been conducted to investigate the style approach. Some of the first studies to be done were conducted at The Ohio State University in the late 1940s, based on the findings of Stogdill's (1948) work, which pointed to the importance of considering more than leaders' traits in leadership research. At about the same time, another group of researchers at the University of Michigan was conducting a series of studies that explored how leadership functioned in small groups. A third line of research was begun by Blake and Mouton in the early 1960s; it explored how managers used task and relationship behaviors in the organizational setting.

Although many research studies could be categorized under the heading of the style approach, the Ohio State studies, the Michigan studies, and the studies by Blake and Mouton (1964, 1978, 1985) are strongly representative of the ideas in this approach. By looking closely at each of these groups of studies, we can draw a clearer picture of the underpinnings and implications of the style approach.

The Ohio State Studies

A group of researchers at Ohio State believed that the results of studying leadership as a personality trait seemed fruitless and decided to analyze how individuals *acted* when they were leading a group or an organization. This analysis was conducted by having subordinates complete questionnaires about their leaders. On the questionnaires, subordinates had to identify the number of times their leaders engaged in certain types of behaviors.

The original questionnaire used in these studies was constructed from a list of more than 1,800 items describing different aspects of leader behavior. From this long list of items, a questionnaire composed of 150 questions was formulated; it was called the Leader Behavior Description Questionnaire (LBDQ; Hemphill & Coons, 1957). The LBDQ was given to hundreds of people in educational, military, and industrial settings, and the results showed that certain clusters of behaviors were typical of leaders. Six years later, Stogdill (1963) published a shortened version of the LBDQ. The new form, which was called the LBDQ-XII, became the most widely used instrument in leadership research. A style questionnaire similar to the LBDQ appears later in this chapter. You can use this questionnaire to assess your own leadership behavior.

Researchers found that subordinates' responses on the questionnaire clustered around two general types of leader behaviors: *initiating structure* and *consideration* (Stogdill, 1974). Initiating structure behaviors are essentially task behaviors, including such acts as organizing work, giving structure to the work context, defining role responsibilities, and scheduling work activities. Consideration behaviors are essentially relationship behaviors and include building camaraderie, respect, trust, and liking between leaders and followers.

The two types of behaviors identified by the LBDQ-XII represent the core of the style approach and are central to what leaders do: Leaders provide

 4.1 Different Leadership Styles   **4.2** Leadership Behavior

structure for subordinates, and they nurture them. The Ohio State studies viewed these two behaviors as distinct and independent. They were thought of not as two points along a single continuum, but as two different continua. For example, a leader can be high in initiating structure and high or low in task behavior. Similarly, a leader can be low in setting structure and low or high in consideration behavior. The degree to which a leader exhibits one behavior is not related to the degree to which she or he exhibits the other behavior.

Many studies have been done to determine which style of leadership is most effective in a particular situation. In some contexts, high consideration has been found to be most effective, but in other situations, high initiating structure is most effective. Some research has shown that being high on both behaviors is the best form of leadership. Determining how a leader optimally mixes task and relationship behaviors has been the central task for researchers from the style approach. The path–goal approach, which is discussed in Chapter 7, exemplifies a leadership theory that attempts to explain how leaders should integrate consideration and structure into the leader's style.

The University of Michigan Studies

Whereas researchers at Ohio State were developing the LBDQ, researchers at the University of Michigan were also exploring leadership behavior, giving special attention to the impact of leaders' behaviors on the performance of small groups (Cartwright & Zander, 1960; Katz & Kahn, 1951; Likert, 1961, 1967).

The program of research at Michigan identified two types of leadership behaviors: *employee orientation* and *production orientation*. Employee orientation is the behavior of leaders who approach subordinates with a strong human relations emphasis. They take an interest in workers as human beings, value their individuality, and give special attention to their personal needs (Bowers & Seashore, 1966). Employee orientation is very similar to the cluster of behaviors identified as consideration in the Ohio State studies.

Production orientation consists of leadership behaviors that stress the technical and production aspects of a job. From this orientation, workers are viewed as a means for getting work accomplished (Bowers & Seashore, 1966). Production orientation parallels the initiating structure cluster found in the Ohio State studies.

Unlike the Ohio State researchers, the Michigan researchers, in their initial studies, conceptualized employee and production orientations as opposite ends of a single continuum. This suggested that leaders who were oriented toward production were less oriented toward employees, and those who were employee oriented were less production oriented. As more studies were completed, however, the researchers reconceptualized the two constructs, as in the Ohio State studies, as two independent leadership orientations (Kahn, 1956). When the two behaviors are treated as independent orientations, leaders are seen as being able to be oriented toward both production and employees at the same time.

In the 1950s and 1960s, a multitude of studies were conducted by researchers from both Ohio State and the University of Michigan to determine how leaders could best combine their task and relationship behaviors to maximize the impact of these behaviors on the satisfaction and performance of followers. In essence, the researchers were looking for a universal theory of leadership that would explain leadership effectiveness in every situation. The results that emerged from this large body of literature were contradictory and unclear (Yukl, 1994). Although some of the findings pointed to the value of a leader being both highly task oriented and highly relationship oriented in all situations (Misumi, 1985), the preponderance of research in this area was inconclusive.

Blake and Mouton's Managerial (Leadership) Grid

Perhaps the best known model of managerial behavior is the Managerial Grid®, which first appeared in the early 1960s and has been refined and revised several times (Blake & McCanse, 1991; Blake & Mouton, 1964, 1978, 1985). It is a model that has been used extensively in organizational training and development. The Managerial Grid, which has been renamed the Leadership Grid®, was designed to explain how leaders help organizations to reach their purposes through two factors: *concern for production* and *concern for people*. Although these factors are described as leadership orientations in the model, they closely parallel the task and relationship leadership behaviors we have been discussing throughout this chapter.

Concern for production refers to how a leader is concerned with achieving organizational tasks. It involves a wide range of activities, including attention to policy decisions, new product development, process issues, workload, and sales volume, to name a few. Not limited to an organization's manufactured product or service, concern for production can refer to whatever the organization is seeking to accomplish (Blake & Mouton, 1964).

Concern for people refers to how a leader attends to the people in the organization who are trying to achieve its goals. This concern includes building organizational commitment and trust, promoting the personal worth of employees, providing good working conditions, maintaining a fair salary structure, and promoting good social relations (Blake & Mouton, 1964).

The Leadership (Managerial) Grid joins concern for production and concern for people in a model that has two intersecting axes (Figure 4.1). The horizontal axis represents the leader's concern for results, and the vertical axis represents the leader's concern for people. Each of the axes is drawn as a 9-point scale on which a score of 1 represents *minimum concern* and 9 represents *maximum concern*. By plotting scores from each of the axes, various leadership styles can be illustrated. The Leadership Grid portrays five major leadership styles: authority–compliance (9,1), country-club management (1,9), impoverished management (1,1), middle-of-the-road management (5,5), and team management (9,9).

Authority–Compliance (9,1)

The 9,1 style of leadership places heavy emphasis on task and job requirements, and less emphasis on people, except to the extent that people are tools for getting the job done. Communicating with subordinates is not emphasized except for the purpose of giving instructions about the task. This style is result driven, and people are regarded as tools to that end. The 9,1 leader is often seen as controlling, demanding, hard driving, and overpowering.

Country-Club Management (1,9)

The 1,9 style represents a low concern for task accomplishment coupled with a high concern for interpersonal relationships. Deemphasizing production, 1,9 leaders stress the attitudes and feelings of people, making sure the personal and social needs of followers are met. They try to create a positive climate by being agreeable, eager to help, comforting, and uncontroversial.

Figure 4.1 The Leadership Grid

Impoverished Management (1,1)

The 1,1 style is representative of a leader who is unconcerned with both the task and interpersonal relationships. This type of leader goes through the motions of being a leader but acts uninvolved and withdrawn. The 1,1 leader often has little contact with followers and could be described as indifferent, noncommittal, resigned, and apathetic.

▶ **4.2** Transformational Leadership   ▶ **4.3** Managerial Grid Theory

Middle-of-the-Road Management (5,5)

The 5,5 style describes leaders who are compromisers, who have an intermediate concern for the task and an intermediate concern for the people who do the task. They find a balance between taking people into account and still emphasizing the work requirements. Their compromising style gives up some of the push for production and some of the attention to employee needs. To arrive at an equilibrium, the 5,5 leader avoids conflict and emphasizes moderate levels of production and interpersonal relationships. This type of leader often is described as one who is expedient, prefers the middle ground, soft-pedals disagreement, and swallows convictions in the interest of "progress."

Team Management (9,9)

The 9,9 style places a strong emphasis on both tasks and interpersonal relationships. It promotes a high degree of participation and teamwork in the organization and satisfies a basic need in employees to be involved and committed to their work. The following are some of the phrases that could be used to describe the 9,9 leader: *stimulates participation, acts determined, gets issues into the open, makes priorities clear, follows through, behaves open-mindedly*, and *enjoys working*.

In addition to the five major styles described in the Leadership Grid, Blake and his colleagues have identified two other styles that incorporate multiple aspects of the grid.

Paternalism/Maternalism

Paternalism/maternalism refers to a leader who uses both 1,9 and 9,1 styles but does not integrate the two (Figure 4.2). This is the "benevolent dictator" who acts graciously but does so for the purpose of goal accomplishment. In essence, the paternalistic/maternalistic style treats people as if they were dissociated from the task. Paternalistic/maternalistic leaders are often described as "fatherly" or "motherly" toward their followers; regard the organization as a "family"; make most of the key decisions; and reward loyalty and obedience while punishing noncompliance.

Figure 4.2   Paternalism/Maternalism

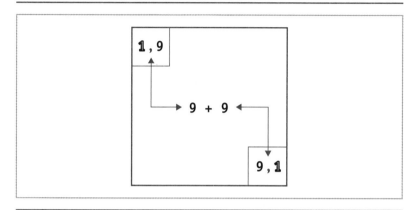

SOURCE: The Leadership Grid© figure, Paternalism figure, and Opportunism figure from *Leadership Dilemmas—Grid Solutions,* by Robert R. Blake and Anne Adams McCanse. (Formerly the Managerial Grid by Robert R. Blake and Jane S. Mouton). Houston: Gulf Publishing Company (Grid figure: p. 29, Paternalism figure: p. 30, Opportunism figure: p. 31). Copyright 1991 by Scientific Methods, Inc. Reproduced by permission of the owners.

Opportunism

Opportunism refers to a leader who uses any combination of the basic five styles for the purpose of personal advancement (Figure 4.3). An opportunistic leader will adapt and shift his or her leadership style to gain personal advantage, putting self-interest ahead of other priorities. Both the performance and the effort of the leader are to realize personal gain. Some phrases used to describe this style of leadership include *ruthless, cunning,* and *self-motivated,* while some could argue that these types of leaders are *adaptable* and *strategic.*

Blake and Mouton (1985) indicated that people usually have a dominant grid style (which they use in most situations) and a backup style. The backup style is what the leader reverts to when under pressure, when the usual way of accomplishing things does not work.

In summary, the Leadership Grid is an example of a practical model of leadership that is based on the two major leadership behaviors: task and relationship. It closely parallels the ideas and findings that emerged in the Ohio State and University of Michigan studies. It is used in consulting for organizational development throughout the world.

4.3 Opportunism and Business Ethics   **4.1** Charisma

Figure 4.3   Opportunism

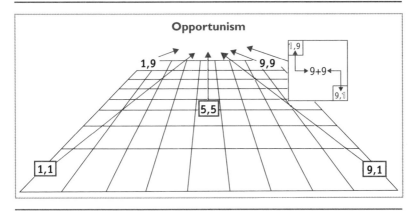

SOURCE: The Leadership Grid© figure, Paternalism figure, and Opportunism figure from *Leadership Dilemmas—Grid Solutions*, by Robert R. Blake and Anne Adams McCanse. (Formerly the Managerial Grid by Robert R. Blake and Jane S. Mouton). Houston: Gulf Publishing Company (Grid figure: p. 29, Paternalism figure: p. 30, Opportunism figure: p. 31). Copyright 1991 by Scientific Methods, Inc. Reproduced by permission of the owners.

HOW DOES THE STYLE APPROACH WORK?

Unlike many of the other approaches discussed in the book, the style approach is not a refined theory that provides a neatly organized set of prescriptions for effective leadership behavior. Rather, the style approach provides a framework for assessing leadership in a broad way, as behavior with a task and relationship dimension. The style approach works not by telling leaders how to behave, but by describing the major components of their behavior.

The style approach reminds leaders that their actions toward others occur on a task level and a relationship level. In some situations, leaders need to be more task oriented, whereas in others they need to be more relationship oriented. Similarly, some subordinates need leaders who provide a lot of direction, whereas others need leaders who can show them a great deal of nurturance and support. The style approach gives the leader a way to look at his or her own behavior by subdividing it into two dimensions.

An example may help explain how the style approach works. Imagine two college classrooms on the first day of class and two professors with

▶ **4.4** Personal Leadership Style

entirely different styles. Professor Smith comes to class, introduces herself, takes attendance, goes over the syllabus, explains the first assignment, and dismisses the class. Professor Jones comes to class and, after introducing herself and handing out the syllabus, tries to help the students to get to know one another by having each of the students describe a little about themselves, their majors, and their favorite nonacademic activities. The leadership styles of professors Smith and Jones are quite different. The preponderance of what Professor Smith does could be labeled task behavior, and the majority of what Professor Jones does could be labeled relationship behavior. The style approach provides a way to inform the professors about the differences in their behaviors. Depending on the response of the students to their style, the professors may want to change their behavior to improve their teaching on the first day of class.

Overall, the style approach offers a means of assessing in a general way the behaviors of leaders. It reminds leaders that their impact on others occurs through the tasks they perform as well as in the relationships they create.

STRENGTHS

The style approach makes several positive contributions to our understanding of the leadership process. First, the style approach marked a major shift in the general focus of leadership research. Before the inception of the style approach, researchers treated leadership exclusively as a personality trait (see Chapter 2). The style approach broadened the scope of leadership research to include the behaviors of leaders and what they do in various situations. No longer was the focus of leadership on the personal characteristics of leaders: It was expanded to include what leaders did and how they acted.

Second, a wide range of studies on leadership style validates and gives credibility to the basic tenets of the approach. First formulated and reported by researchers from The Ohio State University and the University of Michigan, and subsequently reported in the works of Blake and Mouton (1964, 1978, 1985) and Blake and McCanse (1991), the style approach is substantiated by a multitude of research studies that offer a viable approach to understanding the leadership process.

Third, on a conceptual level, researchers from the style approach have ascertained that a leader's style consists primarily of two major types of behaviors: task and relationship. The significance of this idea is not to be understated. Whenever leadership occurs, the leader is acting out both task and relationship behaviors; the key to being an effective leader often rests on how the leader balances these two behaviors. Together they form the core of the leadership process.

Fourth, the style approach is heuristic. It provides us with a broad conceptual map that is worthwhile to use in our attempts to understand the complexities of leadership. Leaders can learn a lot about themselves and how they come across to others by trying to see their behaviors in light of the task and relationship dimensions. Based on the style approach, leaders can assess their actions and determine how they may want to change to improve their leadership style.

CRITICISMS

Along with its strengths, the style approach also has several weaknesses. First, the research on styles has not adequately shown how leaders' styles are associated with performance outcomes (Bryman, 1992; Yukl, 1994). Researchers have not been able to establish a consistent link between task and relationship behaviors and outcomes such as morale, job satisfaction, and productivity. According to Yukl (1994, p. 75), the "results from this massive research effort have been mostly contradictory and inconclusive." He further pointed out that the only strong finding about leadership styles is that leaders who are considerate have followers who are more satisfied.

Another criticism is that this approach has failed to find a universal style of leadership that could be effective in almost every situation. The overarching goal for researchers studying the style approach appeared to be the identification of a universal set of leadership behaviors that would consistently result in effective outcomes. Because of inconsistencies in the research findings, this goal was never reached. Similar to the trait approach, which was unable to identify the definitive personal characteristics of leaders, the style approach has been unable to identify the universal behaviors that are associated with effective leadership.

A final criticism of the style approach is that it implies that the most effective leadership style is the high–high style (i.e., high task and high relationship). Although some researchers (e.g., Blake & McCanse, 1991; Misumi, 1985) suggested that high–high managers are most effective, that

4.3 Aesthetic Leadership

may not be the case in all situations. In fact, the full range of research find-ings provides only limited support for a universal high–high style (Yukl, 1994). Certain situations may require different leadership styles; some may be complex and require high-task behavior, and others may be simple and require supportive behavior. At this point in the development of research on the style approach, it remains unclear whether the high–high style is the best style of leadership.

APPLICATION

The style approach can be applied easily in ongoing leadership settings. At all levels in all types of organizations, managers are continually engaged in task and relationship behaviors. By assessing their own style, managers can determine how they are coming across to others and how they could change their behaviors to be more effective. In essence, the style approach provides a mirror for managers that is helpful in answering the frequently asked question, "How am I doing as a leader?"

Many leadership training and development programs throughout the country are structured along the lines of the style approach. Almost all are designed similarly and include giving managers questionnaires that assess in some way their task and relationship behaviors toward subordinates. Par-ticipants use these assessments to improve their overall leadership styles.

An example of a training and development program that deals exclu-sively with leader styles is Blake and Mouton's Leadership Grid (formerly Managerial Grid) seminar. Grid seminars are about increasing productiv-ity, improving morale, and gaining employee commitment. They are offered by Grid International, an international organization development company (http://www.gridinternational.com). At grid seminars, self-assessments, small-group experiences, and candid critiques allow manag-ers to learn how to define effective leadership, how to manage for optimal results, and how to identify and change ineffective leadership behaviors. The conceptual framework around which the grid seminars are structured is the style approach to leadership.

In short, the style approach applies to nearly everything a leader does. It is an approach that is used as a model by many training and develop-ment companies to teach managers how to improve their effectiveness and organizational productivity.

4.4 Leadership Trust | 4.5 Negative Leadership

————————— **CASE STUDIES** —————————

In this section, you will find three case studies (Cases 4.1, 4.2, and 4.3) that describe the leadership styles of three different managers, each of whom is working in a different organizational setting. The first case is about a maintenance director in a large hospital, the second deals with a supervisor in a small sporting goods store, and the third is concerned with the director of marketing and communications at a college. At the end of each case are questions that will help you to analyze the case from the perspective of the style approach.

CASE 4.1

A Drill Sergeant at First

Mark Young is the head of the painting department in a large hospital; 20 union employees report to him. Before coming on board at the hospital, he had worked as an independent contractor. At the hospital, he took a position that was newly created because the hospital believed change was needed in how painting services were provided.

Upon beginning his job, Mark did a 4-month analysis of the direct and indirect costs of painting services. His findings supported the perceptions of his administrators that painting services were inefficient and costly. As a result, Mark completely reorganized the department, designed a new scheduling procedure, and redefined the expected standards of performance.

Mark says that when he started out in his new job he was "all task," like a drill sergeant who didn't seek any input from his subordinates. From Mark's point of view, the hospital environment did not leave much room for errors, so he needed to be strict about getting painters to do a good job within the constraints of the hospital environment.

As time went along, Mark relaxed his style and was less demanding. He delegated some responsibilities to two crew leaders who reported to him, but he always stayed in close touch with each of the employees. On a weekly basis, Mark was known to take small groups of workers to the local sports bar for burgers on the house. He loved to banter with the employees and could take it as well as dish it out.

(Continued)

(Continued)

Mark is very proud of his department. He says he always wanted to be a coach, and that's how he feels about running his department. He enjoys working with people; in particular, he says he likes to see the glint in their eyes when they realize that they've done a good job and they have done it on their own.

Because of Mark's leadership, the painting department has improved substantially and is now seen by workers in other departments as the most productive department in hospital maintenance. Painting services received a customer rating of 92%, which is the highest of any service in the hospital.

Questions

1. From the style perspective, how would you describe Mark's leadership?

2. How did his style change over time?

3. In general, do you think he is more task oriented or more relationship oriented?

4. What score do you think he would get on Blake and Mouton's grid?

CASE 4.2

Eating Lunch Standing Up

Susan Parks is the part-owner and manager of Marathon Sports, an athletic equipment store that specializes in running shoes and accessories. The store employs about 10 people, most of whom are college students who work part-time during the week and full-time on weekends. Marathon Sports is the only store of its kind in a college town with a population of 125,000. The annual sales figures for the store have shown 15% growth each year.

Susan has a lot invested in the store, and she works very hard to make sure the store continues to maintain its reputation and pattern of growth. She works 50 hours a week at the store, where she wears many hats, including those of buyer, scheduler, trainer, planner, and salesperson. There is never a moment when Susan is not doing something. Rumor has it that she eats her lunch standing up.

Employees' reactions to Susan are strong and varied. Some people like her style, and others do not. Those who like her style talk about how organized and efficient the store is when she is in charge. Susan makes the tasks and goals for everyone very clear. She keeps everyone busy; when they go home at night, they feel as if they have accomplished something. They like to work for Susan because she knows what she is doing. Those who do not like her style complain that she is too driven. It seems that her sole purpose for being at the store is to get the job done. She seldom, if ever, takes a break or just hangs out with the staff. These people say Susan is pretty hard to relate to, and as a result it is not much fun working at Marathon Sports.

Susan is beginning to sense that employees have a mixed reaction to her leadership style. This bothers her, but she does not know what to do about it. In addition to her work at the store, Susan struggles hard to be a good spouse and mother of three children.

Questions

1. According to the style approach, how would you describe Susan's leadership?

2. Why does her leadership style create such a pronounced reaction from her subordinates?

3. Do you think she should change her style?

4. Would she be effective if she changed?

CASE 4.3

We Are Family

Betsy Moore has been hired as the director of marketing and communications for a medium-sized college in the Midwest. With a long history of success as a marketing and public relations professional, she

(Continued)

(Continued)

was the unanimous choice of the hiring committee. Betsy is excited to be working for Marianne, the vice president of college advancement, who comes from a similar background to Betsy's. In a meeting with Marianne, Betsy is told the college needs an aggressive plan to revamp and energize the school's marketing and communications efforts. Betsy and Marianne seem in perfect sync with the direction they believe is right for the college's program. Marianne also explains that she has established a departmental culture of teamwork and empowerment and that she is a strong advocate of being a mentor to her subordinates rather than a manager.

Betsy has four direct reports: two writers, Bridget and Suzanne, who are young women in their 20s; and Carol and Francine, graphic designers who are in their 50s. In her first month, Betsy puts together a meeting with her direct reports to develop a new communications plan for the college, presenting the desired goals to the team and asking for their ideas on initiatives and improvements to meet those goals. Bridget and Suzanne provide little in the way of suggested changes, with Bridget asking pointedly, "Why do we need to change anything?"

In her weekly meeting with the vice president, Betsy talks about the resistance to change she encountered from the team. Marianne nods, saying she heard some of the team members' concerns when she went to lunch with them earlier in the week. When Betsy looks surprised, Marianne gives her a knowing smile. "We are like a family here; we have close relationships outside of work. I go to lunch or the movies with Suzanne and Bridget at least once a week. But don't worry; I am only a sounding board for them, and encourage them to come to you to resolve their issues. They know you are their boss."

But they don't come to Betsy. Soon, Bridget stops coming to work at 8 a.m., showing up at 10 a.m. daily. As a result, she misses the weekly planning meetings. When Betsy approaches her about it, Bridget tells her, "It's OK with Marianne; she says as long as I am using the time to exercise and improve my health she supports it."

Betsy meets with Suzanne to implement some changes to Suzanne's pet project, the internal newsletter. Suzanne gets blustery and tearful, accusing Betsy of insulting her work. Later, Betsy watches Suzanne and Marianne leave the office together for lunch. A few hours later, Marianne comes into Betsy's office and tells her, "Go easy on the newsletter changes. Suzanne is an insecure person, and she is feeling criticized and put down by you right now."

Betsy's relationship with the other two staff members is better. Neither seems to have the close contact with Marianne that the younger team members have. They seem enthusiastic and supportive of the new direction Betsy wants to take the program in.

As the weeks go by, Marianne begins having regular "Mentor Meetings" with Bridget and Suzanne, going to lunch with both women at least twice a week. After watching the three walk out together one day, Francine asks Betsy if it troubles her. Betsy replies, as calmly as she can, "It is part of Marianne's mentoring program."

Francine rolls her eyes and says, "Marianne's not mentoring anyone; she just wants someone to go to lunch with every day."

After 4 months on the job, Betsy goes to Marianne and outlines the challenges that the vice president's close relationships with Bridget and Suzanne have presented to the progress of the marketing and communications program. She asks her directly, "Please stop."

Marianne gives her the knowing, motherly smile again. "I see a lot of potential in Bridget and Suzanne and want to help foster that," she explains. "They are still young in their careers, and my relationship with them is important because I can provide the mentoring and guidance to develop their abilities."

"But it's creating problems between them and me," Betsy points out. "I can't manage them if they can circumvent me every time they disagree with me. We aren't getting any work done. You and I have to be on the same team."

Marianne shakes her head. "The problem is that we have very different leadership styles. I like to empower people, and you like to boss them around."

Questions

1. Marianne and Betsy do indeed have different leadership styles. What style would you ascribe to Betsy? To Marianne?

2. Does Betsy need to change her leadership style to improve the situation with Bridget and Suzanne? Does Marianne need to change her style of leadership?

3. How can Marianne and Betsy work together?

LEADERSHIP INSTRUMENT ————————————————

Researchers and practitioners alike have used many different instruments to assess the styles of leaders. The two most commonly used measures have been the LBDQ (Stogdill, 1963) and the Leadership Grid (Blake & McCanse, 1991). Both of these measures provide information about the degree to which a leader acts task directed or people directed. The LBDQ was designed primarily for research and has been used extensively since the 1960s. The Leadership Grid was designed primarily for training and development; it continues to be used today for training managers and supervisors in the leadership process.

To assist you in developing a better understanding of how leadership style is measured and what your own style might be, a leadership style questionnaire is included in this section. This questionnaire is made up of 20 items that assess two orientations: *task* and *relationship*. By scoring the style questionnaire, you can obtain a general profile of your leadership behavior.

Style Questionnaire

Instructions: Read each item carefully and think about how often you (or the person you are evaluating) engage in the described behavior. Indicate your response to each item by circling one of the five numbers to the right of each item.

Key: 1 = Never   2 = Seldom   3 = Occasionally   4 = Often   5 = Always

1.	Tells group members what they are supposed to do.	1	2	3	4	5
2.	Acts friendly with members of the group.	1	2	3	4	5
3.	Sets standards of performance for group members.	1	2	3	4	5
4.	Helps others in the group feel comfortable.	1	2	3	4	5
5.	Makes suggestions about how to solve problems.	1	2	3	4	5
6.	Responds favorably to suggestions made by others.	1	2	3	4	5
7.	Makes his or her perspective clear to others.	1	2	3	4	5
8.	Treats others fairly.	1	2	3	4	5
9.	Develops a plan of action for the group.	1	2	3	4	5
10.	Behaves in a predictable manner toward group members.	1	2	3	4	5
11.	Defines role responsibilities for each group member.	1	2	3	4	5
12.	Communicates actively with group members.	1	2	3	4	5
13.	Clarifies his or her own role within the group.	1	2	3	4	5
14.	Shows concern for the well-being of others.	1	2	3	4	5
15.	Provides a plan for how the work is to be done.	1	2	3	4	5
16.	Shows flexibility in making decisions.	1	2	3	4	5
17.	Provides criteria for what is expected of the group.	1	2	3	4	5
18.	Discloses thoughts and feelings to group members.	1	2	3	4	5
19.	Encourages group members to do high-quality work.	1	2	3	4	5
20.	Helps group members get along with each other.	1	2	3	4	5

Scoring

The style questionnaire is designed to measure two major types of leadership behaviors: task and relationship. Score the questionnaire by doing the following: First, sum the responses on the odd-numbered items. This is your task score. Second, sum the responses on the even-numbered items. This is your relationship score.

Total scores: Task _____ Relationship _____

Scoring Interpretation

45–50	Very high range
40–44	High range
35–39	Moderately high range
30–34	Moderately low range
25–29	Low range
10–24	Very low range

The score you receive for task refers to the degree to which you help others by defining their roles and letting them know what is expected of them. This factor describes your tendencies to be task directed toward others when you are in a leadership position. The score you receive for relationship is a measure of the degree to which you try to make subordinates feel comfortable with themselves, each other, and the group itself. It represents a measure of how people oriented you are.

Your results on the style questionnaire give you data about your task orientation and people orientation. What do your scores suggest about your leadership style? Are you more likely to lead with an emphasis on task or with an emphasis on relationship? As you interpret your responses to the style questionnaire, ask yourself if there are ways you could change your style to shift the emphasis you give to tasks and relationships. To gain more information about your style, you may want to have four or five of your coworkers fill out the questionnaire based on their perceptions of you as a leader. This will give you additional data to compare and contrast to your own scores about yourself.

SUMMARY

The style approach is strikingly different from the trait and skills approaches to leadership because the style approach focuses on what leaders do rather than who leaders are. It suggests that leaders engage in two primary types of behaviors: task behaviors and relationship behaviors. How leaders combine these two types of behaviors to influence others is the central focus of the style approach.

The style approach originated from three different lines of research: the Ohio State studies, the University of Michigan studies, and the work of Blake and Mouton on the Managerial Grid.

Researchers at Ohio State developed a leadership questionnaire called the Leader Behavior Description Questionnaire (LBDQ), which identified *initiation of structure* and *consideration* as the core leadership behaviors. The Michigan studies provided similar findings but called the leader behaviors *production orientation* and *employee orientation*.

Using the Ohio State and Michigan studies as a basis, much research has been carried out to find the best way for leaders to combine task and relationship behaviors. The goal has been to find a universal set of leadership behaviors capable of explaining leadership effectiveness in every situation. The results from these efforts have not been conclusive, however. Researchers have had difficulty identifying one best style of leadership.

Blake and Mouton developed a practical model for training managers that described leadership behaviors along a grid with two axes: concern for results and concern for people. How leaders combine these orientations results in five major leadership styles: authority–compliance (9,1), country-club management (1,9), impoverished management (1,1), middle-of-the-road management (5,5), and team management (9,9).

The style approach has several strengths and weaknesses. On the positive side, it has broadened the scope of leadership research to include the study of the behaviors of leaders rather than only their personal traits or characteristics. Second, it is a reliable approach because it is supported by a wide range of studies. Third, the style approach is valuable because it underscores the importance of the two core dimensions of leadership behavior: task and relationship. Fourth, it has heuristic value in that it provides us with a broad conceptual map that is useful in gaining an understanding of our own leadership behaviors. On the negative side, researchers have not been able to associate the behaviors of leaders (task and relationship) with outcomes such as morale, job satisfaction, and productivity. In addition, researchers from the style approach have not been able to identify a universal set of leadership behaviors that would consistently result in effective leadership. Last, the style approach implies but fails to support fully the idea that the most effective leadership style is a high–high style (i.e., high task and high relationship).

Overall, the style approach is not a refined theory that provides a neatly organized set of prescriptions for effective leadership behavior. Rather, the style approach provides a valuable framework for assessing leadership in a broad way as assessing behavior with task and relationship dimensions. Finally, the style approach reminds leaders that their impact on others occurs along both dimensions.

Visit the Student Study Site at **www.sagepub.com/northouse6e** for web quizzes, leadership questionnaires, and media links represented by the icons.

REFERENCES

Blake, R. R., & McCanse, A. A. (1991). *Leadership dilemmas: Grid solutions.* Houston, TX. Gulf Publishing Company.

Blake, R. R., & Mouton, J. S. (1964). *The managerial grid.* Houston, TX: Gulf Publishing Company.

Blake, R. R., & Mouton, J. S. (1978). *The new managerial grid.* Houston, TX: Gulf Publishing Company.

Blake, R. R., & Mouton, J. S. (1985). *The managerial grid III.* Houston, TX: Gulf Publishing Company.

Bowers, D. G., & Seashore, S. E. (1966). Predicting organizational effectiveness with a four-factor theory of leadership. *Administrative Science Quarterly, 11,* 238–263.

Bryman, A. (1992). *Charisma and leadership in organizations.* London: Sage.

Cartwright, D., & Zander, A. (1960). *Group dynamics research and theory.* Evanston, IL: Row, Peterson.

Hemphill, J. K., & Coons, A. E. (1957). Development of the Leader Behavior Description Questionnaire. In R. M. Stogdill & A. E. Coons (Eds.), *Leader behavior: Its description and measurement* (Research Monograph No. 88). Columbus: Ohio State University, Bureau of Business Research.

Kahn, R. L. (1956). The prediction of productivity. *Journal of Social Issues, 12*, 41–49.

Katz, D., & Kahn, R. L. (1951). Human organization and worker motivation. In L. R. Tripp (Ed.), *Industrial productivity* (pp. 146–171). Madison, WI: Industrial Relations Research Association.

Likert, R. (1961). *New patterns of management.* New York: McGraw-Hill.

Likert, R. (1967). *The human organization: Its management and value.* New York: McGraw-Hill.

Misumi, J. (1985). *The behavioral science of leadership: An interdisciplinary Japanese research program.* Ann Arbor: University of Michigan Press.

Stogdill, R. M. (1948). Personal factors associated with leadership: A survey of the literature. *Journal of Psychology, 25*, 35–71.

Stogdill, R. M. (1963). *Manual for the Leader Behavior Description Questionnaire form XII.* Columbus: Ohio State University, Bureau of Business Research.

Stogdill, R. M. (1974). *Handbook of leadership: A survey of theory and research.* New York: Free Press.

Yukl, G. (1994). *Leadership in organizations* (3rd ed.). Englewood Cliffs, NJ: Prentice Hall.

5

Situational Approach

DESCRIPTION

One of the more widely recognized approaches to leadership is the situational approach, which was developed by Hersey and Blanchard (1969a) based on Reddin's (1967) 3-D management style theory. The situational approach has been refined and revised several times since its inception (see Blanchard, Zigarmi, & Nelson, 1993; Blanchard, Zigarmi, & Zigarmi, 1985; Hersey & Blanchard, 1977, 1988), and it has been used extensively in organizational leadership training and development.

As the name of the approach implies, situational leadership focuses on leadership in situations. The premise of the theory is that different situations demand different kinds of leadership. From this perspective, to be an effective leader requires that a person adapt his or her style to the demands of different situations.

Situational leadership stresses that leadership is composed of both a directive and a supportive dimension, and that each has to be applied appropriately in a given situation. To determine what is needed in a particular situation, a leader must evaluate her or his employees and assess how competent and committed they are to perform a given task. Based on the assumption that employees' skills and motivation vary over time, situational leadership suggests that leaders should change the degree to which they are directive or supportive to meet the changing needs of subordinates.

In brief, the essence of situational leadership demands that leaders match their style to the competence and commitment of the subordinates.

Effective leaders are those who can recognize what employees need and then adapt their own style to meet those needs.

The situational approach is illustrated in the model developed by Blanchard (1985) and Blanchard et al. (1985), called the Situational Leadership II (SLII) model (Figure 5.1). The model is an extension and refinement of the original situational leadership model developed by Hersey and Blanchard (1969a).

The dynamics of situational leadership are best understood when we separate the SLII model into two parts: *leadership style* and *development level of subordinates*.

Figure 5.1 Situational Leadership II

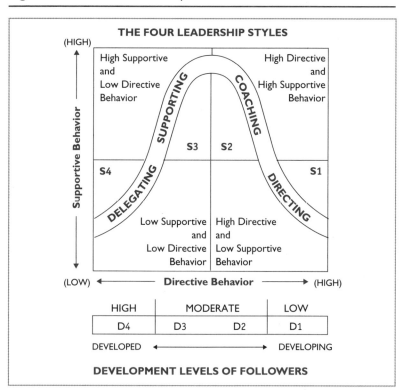

SOURCE: From *Leadership and the One Minute Manager: Increasing Effectiveness Through Situational Leadership,* by K. Blanchard, P. Zigarmi, and D. Zigarmi, 1985, New York: William Morrow. Used with permission.

5.1 Creating a Compelling Vision

Leadership Styles

Leadership style consists of the behavior pattern of a person who attempts to influence others. It includes both *directive (task) behaviors* and *supportive (relationship) behaviors*. Directive behaviors help group members accomplish goals by giving directions, establishing goals and methods of evaluation, setting time lines, defining roles, and showing how the goals are to be achieved. Directive behaviors clarify, often with one-way communication, what is to be done, how it is to be done, and who is responsible for doing it. Supportive behaviors help group members feel comfortable about themselves, their coworkers, and the situation. Supportive behaviors involve two-way communication and responses that show social and emotional support to others. Examples of supportive behaviors include asking for input, solving problems, praising, sharing information about oneself, and listening. Supportive behaviors are mostly job related.

Leadership styles can be classified further into four distinct categories of directive and supportive behaviors (see Figure 5.1). The first style (S1) is a *high directive–low supportive* style, which is also called a *directing* style. In this approach, the leader focuses communication on goal achievement, and spends a smaller amount of time using supportive behaviors. Using this style, a leader gives instructions about what and how goals are to be achieved by the subordinates and then supervises them carefully.

The second style (S2) is called a *coaching* approach and is a *high directive–high supportive* style. In this approach, the leader focuses communication on both achieving goals and meeting subordinates' socioemotional needs. The coaching style requires that the leader involve himself or herself with subordinates by giving encouragement and soliciting subordinate input. However, coaching is an extension of S1 in that it still requires that the leader make the final decision on the *what* and *how* of goal accomplishment.

Style 3 (S3) is a *supporting* approach that requires that the leader take a *high supportive–low directive* style. In this approach, the leader does not focus exclusively on goals but uses supportive behaviors that bring out the employees' skills around the task to be accomplished. The supportive style includes listening, praising, asking for input, and giving feedback. A leader using this style gives subordinates control of day-to-day decisions but remains available to facilitate problem solving. An S3 leader is quick to give recognition and social support to subordinates.

 5.2 Ken Blanchard   **5.3** Global Leadership

Last, S4 is called the *low supportive–low directive* style, or a *delegating* approach. In this approach, the leader offers less task input and social support, facilitating employees' confidence and motivation in reference to the task. The delegative leader lessens involvement in planning, control of details, and goal clarification. After the group agrees on what it is to do, this style lets subordinates take responsibility for getting the job done the way they see fit. A leader using S4 gives control to subordinates and refrains from intervening with unnecessary social support.

The SLII model (see Figure 5.1) illustrates how directive and supportive leadership behaviors combine for each of the four different leadership styles. As shown by the arrows on the bottom and left side of the model, directive behaviors are high in the S1 and S2 quadrants and low in S3 and S4, whereas supportive behaviors are high in S2 and S3 and low in S1 and S4.

Development Levels

A second major part of the situational leadership model concerns the development level of subordinates. Development level is the degree to which subordinates have the competence and commitment necessary to accomplish a given task or activity (Blanchard et al., 1985). Stated another way, it indicates whether a person has mastered the skills to do a specific task and whether a person has developed a positive attitude regarding the task (Blanchard et al., 1993). Employees are at a high development level if they are interested and confident in their work and know how to do the task. Employees are at a low development level if they have little skill for the task at hand but believe that they have the motivation or confidence to get the job done.

The levels of development are illustrated in the lower portion of the diagram in Figure 5.1. The levels describe various combinations of commitment and competence for employees on a given task. They are intended to be task specific and are not intended to be used for the purpose of labeling followers.

On a particular task, employees can be classified into four categories: D1, D2, D3, and D4, from low development to high development. Specifically, D1 employees are low in competence and high in commitment. They are new to a task and do not know exactly how to do it, but they are excited about the challenge of it. D2 employees are described as having some competence but low commitment. They have started to learn a job, but they also have

5.1 Development Levels

lost some of their initial motivation about the job. D3 represents employees who have moderate to high competence but may lack commitment. They have essentially developed the skills for the job, but they are uncertain as to whether they can accomplish the task by themselves. Finally, D4 employees are the highest in development, having both a high degree of competence and a high degree of commitment to getting the job done. They have the skills to do the job and the motivation to get it done.

HOW DOES THE SITUATIONAL APPROACH WORK?

The situational approach is constructed around the idea that employees move forward and backward along the developmental continuum, which represents the relative competence and commitment of subordinates. For leaders to be effective, it is essential that they determine where subordinates are on the developmental continuum and adapt their leadership styles so they directly match their style to that development level.

In a given situation, the first task for a leader is to determine the nature of the situation. Questions such as the following must be addressed: What task are subordinates being asked to perform? How complex is the task? Are the subordinates sufficiently skilled to accomplish the task? Do they have the desire to complete the job once they start it? Answers to these questions will help leaders to identify correctly the specific developmental level at which their subordinates are functioning. For example, new employees who are very excited but lack understanding of job requirements would be identified as D1-level employees. Conversely, seasoned workers with proven abilities and great devotion to a company would be identified as functioning at the D4 level.

Having identified the correct development level, the second task for the leader is to adapt his or her style to the prescribed leadership style represented in the SLII model. There is a one-to-one relationship between the development level of subordinates (D1, D2, etc.) and the leader's style (S1, S2, etc.). For example, if subordinates are at the first level of development, D1, the leader needs to adopt a high-directive and low-supportive leadership style (S1, or directing). If subordinates are more advanced and at the second development level, D2, the leader needs to adopt a high directive–high supportive leadership style (S2, or coaching). For each level of development, there is a specific style of leadership that the leader should adopt.

▶ **5.2** Lessons on Leadership

An example of this would be Rene Martinez, who owns a house paint-ing business. Rene specializes in restoration of old homes and over 30 years has acquired extensive knowledge of the specialized abilities required including understanding old construction and painting materials and tech-niques, plaster repair, carpentry, and window glazing. Rene has three employees: Ashley, who has worked for him for seven years and whom he trained from the beginning of her career; Levi, who worked for a commer-cial painter for four years before being hired by Rene two years ago; and Anton, who is just starting out.

Because of Ashley's years of experience and training, Rene would clas-sify her as a D3 employee. She is very competent, but still seeks Rene's insight on some tasks. She is completely comfortable prepping surfaces for painting and directing the others, but has some reluctance to taking on jobs that involve carpentry. Depending on the work he assigns Ashley, Rene moves between S3 (supporting) and S4 (delegating) leadership behaviors.

When it comes to painting, Levi is a D4 needing little direction or sup-port from Rene. But Levi has to be trained in many other aspects of home restoration, making him a D1 or D2 in those skills. Levi is a quick learner, and Rene finds he only needs to be shown or told how to do something once before he is able to complete it easily. In most situations, Rene uses an S2 (coaching) leadership behavior with Levi. If the task is more com-plicated and requires detailed training, Rene moves back into the S1 (directing) behavior with Levi.

Anton is completely new to this field, coming in at the D1 level of development. What he lacks in experience he more than makes up for in energy. He is always willing to jump in and do whatever he's asked to do. He is not as careful as he needs to be, however, often neglecting the proper prepping techniques and cleanup about which Rene is a stickler. Rene finds that not only he, but also Ashley, uses an S1 (directing) behavior with Anton. Because Levi is also fairly new, he finds it difficult to be directive with Anton, but likes to give him help when he seems unsure of himself, falling in to the S3 (supporting) behavior.

This example illustrates how subordinates can move back and forth along the development continuum, requiring leaders to be flexible in their leadership behavior. Subordinates may move from one development level to another rather quickly over a short period (e.g., a day or a week), or more slowly on tasks that proceed over much longer periods of time

5.2 Leader Effectiveness

(e.g., a month). Leaders cannot use the same style in all contexts; rather, they need to adapt their style to subordinates and their unique situations. Unlike the trait and contingency approaches, which advocate a fixed style for leaders, the situational approach demands that leaders demonstrate a high degree of flexibility.

STRENGTHS

The situational approach to leadership has several strengths, particularly for practitioners. The first strength is that it has stood the test of time in the marketplace. Situational leadership is well known and frequently used for training leaders within organizations. Hersey and Blanchard (1993) reported that it has been a factor in training programs of more than 400 of the Fortune 500 companies. It is perceived by corporations as offering a credible model for training people to become effective leaders.

A second strength of situational leadership is its practicality. Situational leadership is easy to understand, intuitively sensible, and easily applied in a variety of settings. Whereas some leadership approaches provide complex and sophisticated ways to assess your own leadership behavior (e.g., the decision-making approach in Vroom & Yetton, 1973), situational leadership provides a straightforward approach that is easily used. Because it is described at an abstract level that is easily grasped, the ideas behind the approach are quickly acquired. In addition, the principles suggested by situational leadership are easy to apply across a variety of settings, including work, school, and family.

Closely akin to the strength of practicality is a third strength of situational leadership: its prescriptive value. Whereas many theories of leadership are descriptive in nature, the situational approach is prescriptive. It tells you what you should and should not do in various contexts. For example, if your subordinates are very low in competence, situational leadership prescribes a directing style for you as the leader. On the other hand, if your employees appear to be competent but lack confidence, the situational approach suggests that you lead with a supporting style. These prescriptions provide leaders with a valuable set of guidelines that can facilitate and enhance leadership.

A fourth strength of situational leadership is that it emphasizes leader flexibility (Graeff, 1983; Yukl, 1989). Situational leadership stresses that

5.2 Creative Leadership

leaders need to find out about their subordinates' needs and then adapt their leadership style accordingly. Leaders cannot lead using a single style: They must be willing to change their style to meet the requirements of the situation. Situational leadership recognizes that employees act differently when doing different tasks, and that they may act differently during different stages of the same task. Effective leaders are those who can change their own style based on the task requirements and the subordinates' needs, even in the middle of a project.

Finally, situational leadership reminds us to treat each subordinate differently based on the task at hand and to seek opportunities to help subordinates learn new skills and become more confident in their work (Fernandez & Vecchio, 1997; Yukl, 1998). Overall, this approach underscores that subordinates have unique needs and deserve our help in trying to become better at doing their work.

CRITICISMS

Despite its extensive use in leadership training and development, situational leadership does have some limitations. The following criticisms point out several weaknesses in situational leadership and help to provide a more balanced picture of the general utility of this approach in studying and practicing leadership.

The first criticism of situational leadership is that only a few research studies have been conducted to justify the assumptions and propositions set forth by the approach. Although many doctoral dissertations address dimensions of situational leadership, most of these research studies have not been published. The lack of a strong body of research on situational leadership raises questions about the theoretical basis of the approach (Fernandez & Vecchio, 1997; Graeff, 1997; Vecchio & Boatwright, 2002; Vecchio, Bullis, & Brazil, 2006). Can we be sure it is a valid approach? Is it certain that this approach does indeed improve performance? Does this approach compare favorably with other leadership approaches in its impact on subordinates? It is difficult to give firm answers to these questions when the testing of this approach has not resulted in a significant amount of published research findings.

A second criticism that can be directed at situational leadership concerns the ambiguous conceptualization in the model of subordinates' development levels. The authors of the model do not make clear how commitment is combined with competence to form four distinct levels of development (Graeff, 1997; Yukl, 1989). In one of the earliest versions of the model, Hersey and Blanchard (1969b) defined the four levels of commitment (maturity) as unwilling and unable (Level 1), willing and unable (Level 2), unwilling and able (Level 3), and willing and able (Level 4). In a more recent version, represented by the SLII model, development level is described as high commitment and low competence in D1, low commitment and some competence in D2, variable commitment and high competence in D3, and high commitment and high competence in D4.

The authors of situational leadership do not explain the theoretical basis for these changes in the composition of each of the development levels. Furthermore, they do not explain how competence and commitment are weighted across different development levels. As pointed out by Blanchard et al. (1993), there is a need for further research to establish how competence and commitment are conceptualized for each development level. Closely related to the general criticism of ambiguity about subordinates' development levels is a concern with how commitment itself is conceptualized in the model. For example, Graeff (1997) suggested the conceptualization is very unclear. Blanchard et al. (1985) stated that subordinates' commitment is composed of confidence and motivation, but it is not clear how confidence and motivation combine to define commitment. According to the SLII model, commitment starts out high in D1, moves down in D2, becomes variable in D3, and rises again in D4. Intuitively, it appears more logical to describe subordinate commitment as existing on a continuum moving from low to moderate to high.

The argument provided by Blanchard et al. (1993) for how commitment varies in the SLII model is that subordinates usually start out motivated and eager to learn, and then they may become discouraged and disillusioned. Next, they may begin to lack confidence or motivation, or both, and last they become highly confident and motivated. But why is this so? Why do subordinates who learn a task become less committed? Why is there a decrease in commitment at Development Levels 2 and 3? Without research findings to substantiate the way subordinate commitment is conceptualized, this dimension of situational leadership remains unclear.

A fourth criticism of situational leadership has to do with how the model matches leader style with subordinate development levels—the prescriptions of the model. To determine the validity of the prescriptions suggested by the Hersey and Blanchard approach, Vecchio (1987) conducted a study

5.4 Impact of Power

of more than 300 high school teachers and their principals. He found that newly hired teachers were more satisfied and performed better under principals who had highly structured leadership styles, but that the performance of more experienced and mature teachers was unrelated to the style their principals exhibited.

Vecchio and his colleagues have replicated this study twice: first in 1997, using university employees (Fernandez & Vecchio, 1997), and most recently in 2006, studying more than 800 U.S. Military Academy cadets (Vecchio et al., 2006). Both studies failed to find strong evidence to support the basic prescriptions suggested in the situational leadership model.

A fifth criticism of situational leadership is that it fails to account for how certain demographic characteristics (e.g., education, experience, age, and gender) influence the leader–subordinate prescriptions of the model. For example, a study conducted by Vecchio and Boatwright (2002) showed that level of education and job experience were inversely related to directive leadership and were not related to supportive leadership. In other words, employees with more education and more work experience desired less structure. An interesting finding is that age was positively related to desire for structure: The older employees desired more structure than the younger employees did. In addition, their findings indicated that female and male employees had different preferences for styles of leadership. Female employees expressed a stronger preference for supportive leadership, whereas male employees had a stronger desire for directive leadership. These findings indicate that demographic characteristics may affect employees' preferences for a particular leadership style. However, these characteristics are not considered in the situational leadership model.

Situational leadership can also be criticized from a practical standpoint because it does not fully address the issue of one-to-one versus group leadership in an organizational setting. For example, should a leader with a group of 20 employees lead by matching her or his style to the overall development level of the group or to the development level of individual members of the group? Carew, Parisi-Carew, and Blanchard (1990) suggested that groups go through development stages that are similar to individuals', and that therefore leaders should try to match their styles to the group's development level. However, if the leader matches her or his style to the mean development level of a group, how will this affect the individuals whose development levels are quite different from those of their colleagues? Existing research on situational leadership does not answer this question. More research is needed to explain how leaders can adapt

5.4 Practice of Corporate Hiring   5.3 Task Leadership

their styles simultaneously to the development levels of individual group members and to the group as a whole.

A final criticism of situational leadership can be directed at the leadership questionnaires that accompany the model. Questionnaires on situational leadership typically ask respondents to analyze various work situations and select the best leadership style for each situation. The questionnaires are constructed to force respondents to describe leadership style in terms of the specific parameters of situational leadership (i.e., directing, coaching, supporting, and delegating) rather than in terms of other leadership behaviors. Because the best answers available to respondents have been predetermined, the questionnaires are biased in favor of situational leadership (Graeff, 1983; Yukl, 1989).

APPLICATION

As we discussed earlier in this chapter, situational leadership is used in consulting because it is an approach that is easy to conceptualize and apply. The straightforward nature of situational leadership makes it practical for managers to use.

The principles of this approach can be applied at many different levels in an organization. They can apply to how a chief executive officer (CEO) of a large corporation works with a board of directors, and they can also apply to how a crew chief in an assembly plant leads a small group of production workers. Middle managers can use situational leadership to direct staff meetings, and heads of departments can use this approach in planning structural changes within an organization. There is no shortage of opportunities for using situational leadership.

Situational leadership applies during the initial stages of a project, when idea formation is important, and during the various subsequent phases of a project, when implementation issues are important. The fluid nature of situational leadership makes it ideal for applying to subordinates as they move forward or go backward (regress) on various projects. Because situational leadership stresses adapting to followers, it is ideal for use with followers whose commitment and competence change over the course of a project.

Given the breadth of the situational approach, it is applicable in almost any type of organization, at any level, for nearly all types of tasks. It is an encompassing model with a wide range of applications.

———————————— **CASE STUDIES** ————————————

To see how situational leadership can be applied in different organizational settings, you may want to assess Cases 5.1, 5.2, and 5.3. For each of these cases, ask yourself what you would do if you found yourself in a similar situation. At the end of each case, there are questions that will help you analyze the context from the perspective of situational leadership.

CASE 5.1

What Style Do I Use?

Bruce Cannon is the owner of a 5-year-old small plastics company that employs about 20 people. The company consists of three areas: engineering, sales, and production. For each of these areas, there is a single manager.

Rick Nakano heads the engineering crew. He is a seasoned engineer and is the oldest employee in the company (he is 55 years old). Rick was hired because of his engineering ability and experience.

Before joining the company, Rick worked for 20 years as an engineer for Ford Motor Company. His coworkers perceive him as very competent, even-tempered, and interested in the company.

Rick has been spending most of his time in recent weeks on developing a long-range plan for the company. His goal is to develop a creative model for making decisions about future expenditures for materials, equipment, plant development, and personnel. Rick feels good about the way upper management has reacted to the first drafts of his plans.

Beth Edwards heads the sales force, which is the smallest unit in the company. Beth is the most recent hire in the company and has 15 years of sales experience in a different product area. Beth's peers see her as highly motivated but not too knowledgeable about the company's products. Beth's goal is to increase the company's annual sales by 30%. However, the first quarter sales figures indicate the rate of growth to be only 2%.

Although Beth has been upbeat since the day she arrived, in recent weeks there have been problems in her department. Her sales staff talks about how little she knows about the plastics industry. In discussions about new products, Beth often is confused. In addition, she has difficulty describing the company's capabilities to customers because she does not understand fully how a plastics company of this type functions.

Steve Lynch is the manager of production and has been with the company since its inception. Steve started out with the company just out of high school, working on the line, and moved up in the company as a result of his hard work. His goal is to streamline production and decrease costs by 10%. He knows production backward and forward but is a bit apprehensive about his new role as production manager. In fact, Steve is afraid he might fail as manager. He does not know whether he is ready to have others depend on him when he has always been the one depending on others. The owner, Bruce, has great faith in Steve and has had several meetings with him to clarify his role and reassure him that he can do the work. He is certain that Steve will be an outstanding production manager.

Bruce meets weekly with each of his managers to talk about how their groups are fitting in with the overall company goals. In his upcoming weekly conference, he wants to discuss with them what new procedures they could implement within their departments to improve their long-term performance. Bruce is wondering how he should approach each of his managers.

Questions

1. According to the basic assumptions of situational leadership, where would you place the three managers in regard to levels of development in the SLII model (see Figure 5.1)?

2. If you were Bruce, would you act the same toward each of the three managers?

3. Which conference would be the hardest for you, and which would be the easiest? Why?

CASE 5.2

Why Aren't They Listening?

Jim Anderson is a training specialist in the human resource department of a large pharmaceutical company. In response to a recent companywide survey, Jim specifically designed a 6-week training program on listening and communication skills to encourage effective management in the company.

(Continued)

(Continued)

Jim's goals for the seminar are twofold: for participants to learn new communication behaviors and for participants to enjoy the seminar so they will want to attend future seminars.

The first group to be offered the program was middle-level managers in research and development. This group consisted of about 25 people, nearly all of whom had advanced degrees. Most of this group had attended several in-house training programs in the past, so they had a sense of how the seminar would be designed and run. Because the previous seminars had not always been very productive, many of the managers felt a little disillusioned about coming to the seminar. As one of the managers said, "Here we go again: a fancy in-house training program from which we will gain nothing."

Because Jim recognized that the managers were very experienced, he did not put many restrictions on attendance and participation. He used a variety of presentation methods and actively solicited involvement from the managers in the seminar. Throughout the first two sessions, he went out of his way to be friendly with the group. He gave them frequent coffee breaks during the sessions; during these breaks, he promoted socializing and networking.

During the third session, Jim became aware of some difficulties with the seminar. Rather than the full complement of 25 managers, attendance had dropped to about only 15 managers. Although the starting time was established at 8:30, attendees had been arriving as late as 10:00. During the afternoon sessions, some of the managers were leaving the sessions to return to their offices at the company.

As he approached the fourth session, Jim was apprehensive about why things had been going poorly. He had become quite uncertain about how he should approach the group. Many questions were running through his mind: Had he treated the managers in the wrong way? Had he been too easy regarding attendance at the sessions? Should he have said something about the managers skipping out in the afternoon? Were the participants taking the seminar seriously? Jim was certain that the content of the seminars was innovative and substantive, but he could not figure out what he could change to make the program more successful. He sensed that his style was not working for this group, but he didn't have a clue as to how he should change what he was doing to make the sessions better.

Questions

1. According to the SLII model (see Figure 5.1), what style of leadership is Jim using to run the seminars?

2. At what level are the managers?

3. From a leadership perspective, what is Jim doing wrong?

4. What specific changes could Jim implement to improve the seminars?

CASE 5.3

Getting the Message Across

Ann Caldera is the program director of a college campus radio station (WCBA) that is supported by the university. WCBA has a long history and is viewed favorably by students, faculty, the board of trustees, and the people in the community.

Ann does not have a problem getting students to work at WCBA. In fact, it is one of the most sought-after university-related activities. The few students who are accepted to work at WCBA are always highly motivated because they value the opportunity to get hands-on media experience. In addition, those who are accepted tend to be highly confident (sometimes naïvely so) of their own radio ability. Despite their eagerness, most of them lack a full understanding of the legal responsibilities of being on the air.

One of the biggest problems that confronts Ann every semester is how to train new students to follow the rules and procedures of WCBA when they are doing on-air announcing for news, sports, music, and other radio programs. It seems as if every semester numerous incidents arise in which an announcer violates in no small way the FCC rules for appropriate airtime communication. For example, rumor has it that one year a first-year student disc jockey on the evening shift announced that a new band was playing in town, the cover was $10, and everyone should go to hear the group. Making an announcement such as this is a clear violation of FCC rules: It is illegal.

Ann is frustrated with her predicament but cannot seem to figure out why it keeps occurring. She puts a lot of time and effort into helping new DJs,

(Continued)

(Continued)

but they just do not seem to get the message that working at WCBA is a serious job and that obeying the FCC rules is an absolute necessity. Ann wonders whether her leadership style is missing the mark.

Each semester, Ann gives the students a very complete handout on policies and procedures. In addition, she tries to get to know each of the new students personally. Because she wants everybody to be happy at WCBA, she tries very hard to build a relational climate at the station. Repeatedly, students say that Ann is the nicest adviser on campus. Because she recognizes the quality of her students, Ann mostly lets them do what they want at the station.

Questions

1. What's the problem at WCBA?

2. Using SLII as a basis, what would you advise Ann to do differently at the station?

3. Based on situational leadership, what creative schemes could Ann use to reduce FCC infractions at WCBA?

LEADERSHIP INSTRUMENT

Although different versions of instruments have been developed to measure situational leadership, nearly all of them are constructed similarly. As a rule, the questionnaires provide 12 to 20 work-related situations and ask respondents to select their preferred style for each situation from four alternatives. The situations and styles are written to directly represent the leadership styles of the four quadrants in the model. Questionnaire responses are scored to give respondents information about their primary and secondary leadership styles, their flexibility, and their leadership effectiveness.

The brief questionnaire provided in this section illustrates how leadership style is measured in questionnaires of situational leadership. For each situation on the questionnaire, you have to identify the development level of the employees in the situation and then select one of the four response alternatives that indicate the style of leadership you would use in that situation.

Expanded versions of the brief questionnaire give respondents an over-all profile of their leadership style. By analyzing the alternatives a respondent makes on the questionnaire, one can determine that respondent's primary and secondary leadership styles. By analyzing the range of choices a respondent makes, one can determine that respondent's leadership flexibility. Leadership effectiveness and diagnostic ability can be measured by analyzing the number of times the respondent made accurate assessments of a preferred leadership style.

In addition to these self-scored questionnaires, situational leadership uses similar forms to tap the concurrent perceptions that bosses, associates, and followers have of a person's leadership style. These questionnaires give respondents a wide range of feedback on their leadership styles and the opportunity to compare their own views of leadership with the way others view them in a leadership role.

Situational Leadership

Instructions: Look at the following four leadership situations and indicate what the development level is in each situation, which leadership style each response represents, and which leadership style is needed in the situation (i.e., action A, B, C, or D).

Situation 1

Because of budget restrictions imposed on your department, it is necessary to consolidate. You are thinking of asking a highly capable and experienced member of your department to take charge of the consolidation. This person has worked in all areas of your department and has the trust and respect of most of the staff. She is very willing to help with the consolidation.

A. Assign the project to her and let her determine how to accomplish it.

B. Assign the task to her, indicate to her precisely what must be done, and supervise her work closely.

C. Assign the task to her and provide support and encouragement as needed.

D. Assign the task to her and indicate to her precisely what needs to be done but make sure you incorporate her suggestions.

Development level _____ Action _____

Situation 2

You have recently been made a department head of the new regional office. In getting to know your departmental staff, you have noticed that one of your inexperienced employees is not following through on assigned tasks. She is enthusiastic about her new job and wants to get ahead in the organization.

A. Discuss the lack of follow-through with her and explore the alternative ways this problem can be solved.

B. Specify what she must do to complete the tasks but incorporate any suggestions she may have.

C. Define the steps necessary for her to complete the assigned tasks and monitor her performance frequently.

D. Let her know about the lack of follow-through and give her more time to improve her performance.

Development level _____ Action _____

Situation 3

Because of a new and very important unit project, for the past 3 months you have made sure that your staff members understood their responsibilities and expected level of performance, and you have supervised them closely. Due to some recent project setbacks, your staff members have become somewhat discouraged. Their morale has dropped, and so has their performance.

A. Continue to direct and closely supervise their performance.

B. Give the group members more time to overcome the setbacks but occasionally check their progress.

C. Continue to define group activities but involve the group members more in decision making and incorporate their ideas.

D. Participate in their problem-solving activities and encourage and support their efforts to overcome the project setbacks.

Development level _____ Action _____

Situation 4

As a director of the sales department, you have asked a member of your staff to take charge of a new sales campaign. You have worked with this person on other sales campaigns, and you know he has the job knowledge and experience to be successful at new assignments. However, he seems a little unsure about his ability to do the job.

A. Assign the new sales campaign to him and let him function on his own.

B. Set goals and objectives for this new assignment but consider his suggestions and involve him in decision making.

C. Listen to his concerns but assure him he can do the job and support his efforts.

D. Tell him exactly what the new campaign involves and what you expect of him, and supervise his performance closely.

Development level _____ Action _____

SOURCE: Adapted from *Game Plan for Leadership and the One Minute Manager* (Figure 5.20, Learning Activity, p. 5), by K. Blanchard, P. Zigarmi, and D. Zigarmi, 1992, Escondido, CA: Blanchard Training and Development (phone 760-489-5005). Used with permission.

Scoring Interpretation

A short discussion of the correct answers to the brief questionnaire will help to explain the nature of situational leadership questionnaires.

Situation 1 in the brief questionnaire describes a common problem faced by organizations during downsizing: the need to consolidate. In this particular situation, the leader has identified a person to direct the downsizing project who appears to be highly competent, experienced, and motivated. According to the SLII model, this person is at Developmental Level 4, which calls for a delegative approach. Of the four response alternatives, it is the (A) response, "Assign the project to her and let her determine how to accomplish it," that best represents delegating (S4): low supportive–low directive leadership.

Situation 2 describes a problem familiar to leaders at all levels in nearly all organizations: lack of follow-through by an enthusiastic employee. In the given example, the employee falls in Developmental Level 1 because she lacks the experience to do the job even though she is highly motivated to succeed. The SLII approach prescribes directing (S1) leadership for this type of employee. She needs to be told when and how to do her specific job. After she is given directions, her performance should be supervised closely. The correct response is (C), "Define the steps necessary to complete the assigned tasks and monitor her performance frequently."

Situation 3 describes a very different circumstance. In this situation, the employees seem to have developed some experience and an understanding of what is required of them, but they have lost some of their motivation to complete the task. Their performance and commitment have stalled because of recent setbacks, even though the leader has been directing them closely. According to SLII, the correct response for the leader is to shift to a more supportive coaching style (S2) of leadership. The action response that reflects coaching is (C), "Continue to define group activities but involve the group members more in decision making and incorporate their ideas."

Situation 4 describes some of the concerns that arise for a director attempting to identify the correct person to head a new sales campaign. The person identified for the position obviously has the skills necessary to do a good job with the new sales campaign, but he appears apprehensive about his own abilities. In this context, SLII suggests that the director should use a supportive style (S3), which is consistent with leading employees who are competent but lacking a certain degree of confidence. A supportive style is represented by action response (C), "Listen to his concerns but assure him he can do the job and support his efforts."

Now select two employees. Diagnose their current development level on three different tasks and your style of leadership in each situation. Is there a match? If not, what specifically can you do for them as a leader to ensure that they have what they need to succeed?

SUMMARY

Situational leadership is a prescriptive approach to leadership that suggests how leaders can become effective in many different types of organizational settings involving a wide variety of organizational tasks. This approach provides a model that suggests to leaders how they should behave based on the demands of a particular situation.

Situational leadership classifies leadership into four styles: S1 is high directive–low supportive, S2 is high directive–high supportive, S3 is low directive–high supportive, and S4 is low directive–low supportive. The situational leadership (SLII) model describes how each of the four leadership styles applies to subordinates who work at different levels of development, from D1 (low in competence and high in commitment), to D2 (moderately competent and low in commitment), to D3 (moderately competent but lacking commitment), to D4 (great deal of competence and a high degree of commitment).

Effective leadership occurs when the leader can accurately diagnose the development level of subordinates in a task situation and then exhibit the prescribed leadership style that matches that situation.

Leadership is measured in this approach with questionnaires that ask respondents to assess a series of work-related situations. The questionnaires provide information about the leader's diagnostic ability, flexibility, and effectiveness. They are useful in helping leaders to learn about how they can change their leadership style to become more effective across different situations.

There are four major strengths to the situational approach. First, it is recognized by many as a standard for training leaders. Second, it is a practical approach, which is easily understood and easily applied. Third, this approach sets forth a clear set of prescriptions for how leaders should act if they want to enhance their leadership effectiveness. Fourth, situational leadership recognizes and stresses that there is not one best style of leadership; instead, leaders need to be flexible and adapt their style to the requirements of the situation.

Criticisms of situational leadership suggest that it also has limitations. Unlike many other leadership theories, this approach does not have a strong body of research findings to justify and support the theoretical underpinnings on which it stands. As a result, there is ambiguity regarding how the approach conceptualizes certain aspects of leadership. It is not clear in explaining how subordinates move from low development levels to high development levels, nor is it clear on how commitment changes over time for subordinates. Without the basic research findings, the validity of the basic prescriptions for matching leader styles to subordinates' development levels must be questioned. In addition, the model does not address how demographic characteristics affect employees' preferences for leadership. Finally, the model does not provide guidelines for how leaders can use this approach in group settings as opposed to one-to-one contexts.

> Visit the Student Study Site at **www.sagepub.com/northouse6e** for web quizzes, leadership questionnaires, and media links represented by the icons.

REFERENCES

Blanchard, K. H. (1985). *SLII: A situational approach to managing people*. Escondido, CA: Blanchard Training and Development.

Blanchard, K., Zigarmi, D., & Nelson, R. (1993). Situational leadership after 25 years: A retrospective. *Journal of Leadership Studies, 1*(1), 22–36.

Blanchard, K., Zigarmi, P., & Zigarmi, D. (1985). *Leadership and the one minute manager: Increasing effectiveness through situational leadership*. New York: William Morrow.

Blanchard, K., Zigarmi, P., & Zigarmi, D. (1992). *Game plan for leadership and the one-minute manager*. Escondido, CA: Blanchard Training and Development.

Carew, P., Parisi-Carew, E., & Blanchard, K. H. (1990). *Group development and situational leadership II*. Escondido, CA: Blanchard Training and Development.

Fernandez, C. F., & Vecchio, R. P. (1997). Situational leadership theory revisited: A test of an across-jobs perspective. *Leadership Quarterly, 8*(1), 67–84.

Graeff, C. L. (1983). The situational leadership theory: A critical view. *Academy of Management Review, 8*, 285–291.

Graeff, C. L. (1997). Evolution of situational leadership theory: A critical review. *Leadership Quarterly, 8*(2), 153–170.

Hersey, P., & Blanchard, K. H. (1969a). Life-cycle theory of leadership. *Training and Development Journal, 23*, 26–34.

Hersey, P., & Blanchard, K. H. (1969b). *Management of organizational behavior: Utilizing human resources*. Englewood Cliffs, NJ: Prentice Hall.

Hersey, P., & Blanchard, K. H. (1977). *Management of organizational behavior: Utilizing human resources* (3rd ed.). Englewood Cliffs, NJ: Prentice Hall.

5.3 Chapter Summary

Hersey, P., & Blanchard, K. H. (1988). *Management of organizational behavior: Utilizing human resources* (5th ed.). Englewood Cliffs, NJ: Prentice Hall.

Hersey, P., & Blanchard, K. H. (1993). *Management of organizational behavior: Utilizing human resources* (6th ed.). Englewood Cliffs, NJ: Prentice Hall.

Reddin, W. J. (1967, April). The 3-D management style theory. *Training and Development Journal*, pp. 8–17.

Vecchio, R. P. (1987). Situational leadership theory: An examination of a prescriptive theory. *Journal of Applied Psychology, 72*(3), 444–451.

Vecchio, R. P., & Boatwright, K. J. (2002). Preferences for idealized style of supervision. *Leadership Quarterly, 13*, 327–342.

Vecchio, R. P., Bullis, R. C., & Brazil, D. M. (2006). The utility of situational leadership theory: A replication in a military setting. *Small Group Leadership, 37*, 407–424.

Vroom, V. H., & Yetton, P. W. (1973). *Leadership and decision-making*. Pittsburgh, PA: University of Pittsburgh Press.

Yukl, G. A. (1989). *Leadership in organizations* (2nd ed.). Englewood Cliffs, NJ: Prentice Hall.

Yukl, G. A. (1998). *Leadership in organizations* (4th ed.). Upper Saddle River, NJ: Prentice Hall.

Contingency Theory

DESCRIPTION

Although several approaches to leadership could be called contingency theories, the most widely recognized is Fiedler's (1964, 1967; Fiedler & Garcia, 1987). Contingency theory is a *leader–match* theory (Fiedler & Chemers, 1974), which means it tries to match leaders to appropriate situations. It is called *contingency* because it suggests that a leader's effectiveness depends on how well the leader's style fits the context. To understand the performance of leaders, it is essential to understand the situations in which they lead. Effective leadership is *contingent* on matching a leader's style to the right setting.

Fiedler developed contingency theory by studying the styles of many different leaders who worked in different contexts, primarily military organizations. He assessed leaders' styles, the situations in which they worked, and whether they were effective. After analyzing the styles of hundreds of leaders who were both good and bad, Fiedler and his colleagues were able to make empirically grounded generalizations about which styles of leadership were best and which styles were worst for a given organizational context.

In short, contingency theory is concerned with *styles* and *situations*. It provides the framework for effectively matching the leader and the situation.

Leadership Styles

Within the framework of contingency theory, leadership styles are described as *task motivated* or *relationship motivated*. Task-motivated leaders are concerned primarily with reaching a goal, whereas relationship-motivated leaders are concerned with developing close interpersonal relationships. To measure leader styles, Fiedler developed the Least Preferred Coworker (LPC) scale. Leaders who score high on this scale are described as relationship motivated, and those who score low on the scale are identified as task motivated.

Situational Variables

Contingency theory suggests that situations can be characterized in terms of three factors: *leader–member relations, task structure,* and *position power* (Figure 6.1). Leader–member relations consist of the group atmosphere and the degree of confidence, loyalty, and attraction that followers feel for their leader. If group atmosphere is positive and subordinates trust, like, and get along with their leader, the leader–member relations are defined as good. On the other hand, if the atmosphere is unfriendly and friction exists within the group, the leader–member relations are defined as poor.

The second situational variable, task structure, is the degree to which the requirements of a task are clear and spelled out. Tasks that are completely structured tend to give more control to the leader, whereas vague and unclear tasks lessen the leader's control and influence. A task is considered structured when (a) the requirements of the task are clearly stated

Figure 6.1   Contingency Model

Leader–Member Relations	Good				Poor			
Task Structure	High Structure		Low Structure		High Structure		Low Structure	
Position Power	Strong Power	Weak Power	Strong Power	Weak Power	Strong Power	Weak Power	Strong Power	Weak Power
	1	2	3	4	5	6	7	8
Preferred Leadership Style	Low LPCs Middle LPCs				High LPCs			Low LPCs

SOURCE: Adapted from *A Theory of Leadership Effectiveness,* by F. E. Fiedler, 1967, New York: McGraw-Hill. Used by permission.

6.1 Theory Study   6.1 Characteristics of Contingency Theory

and known by the people required to perform them, (b) the path to accomplishing the task has few alternatives, (c) completion of the task can be clearly demonstrated, and (d) only a limited number of correct solutions to the task exist. An example of a highly structured task is cleaning the milk-shake machine at McDonald's. The rules for doing it are clearly stated to the employees, there is only one way to do it, whether it has been done can be verified, and whether it has been done correctly can also be determined easily. An example of a highly unstructured task is the task of running a fund-raiser for a local volunteer organization. Running a fund-raiser does not have a clear set of rules to follow, there are many alternative ways of doing it, one cannot verify the correctness of the way it has been done, and no single best way exists to do it.

Position power, the third characteristic of situations, is the amount of authority a leader has to reward or to punish followers. It includes the legitimate power individuals acquire as a result of the position they hold in an organization. Position power is strong if a person has the authority to hire and fire or give raises in rank or pay; it is weak if a person does not have the authority to do these things.

Together, these three situational factors determine the favorableness of various situations in organizations. Situations that are rated most favorable are those having good leader–follower relations, defined tasks, and strong leader–position power. Situations that are rated least favorable have poor leader–follower relations, unstructured tasks, and weak leader–position power. Situations that are rated moderately favorable fall between these two extremes.

Based on research findings, contingency theory posits that certain styles are effective in certain situations. People who are task motivated (low LPC score) will be effective in both very favorable and very unfavorable situations—that is, in situations that are going along very smoothly or situations that are out of control. People who are relationship motivated (high LPC score) are effective in moderately favorable situations—that is, in situations in which there is some degree of certainty but things are neither completely under their control nor completely out of their control.

It is not entirely clear why leaders with high LPC scores are effective in moderately favorable situations or why leaders with low LPC scores are effective in both very favorable and very unfavorable situations. Fiedler's (1995) interpretation of the theory adds a degree of clarity to this issue.

6.2 Least Preferred Coworker Theory |  **6.2** Role of Leaders

He provides the following line of reasoning for why leaders who are working in the "wrong" (i.e., mismatched) situation are ineffective:

(a) A leader whose LPC style does not match a particular situation experiences stress and anxiety;

(b) under stress, the leader reverts to less mature ways of coping that were learned in early development; and

(c) the leader's less mature coping style results in poor decision making, which results in negative work outcomes.

Although various interpretations of contingency theory can be made, researchers are still unclear regarding the inner workings of the theory.

HOW DOES CONTINGENCY THEORY WORK? ————————

By measuring a leader's LPC score and the three situational variables, one can predict whether the leader is going to be effective in a particular setting. The relationship between a leader's style and various types of situations is illustrated in Figure 6.1. The figure is best understood by interpreting the rows from top to bottom. For example, a situation that has good leader–member relations, a structured task, and strong position power would fall in Category 1 of preferred leadership style. Alternatively, a situation that has poor leader–member relations, a structured task, and weak position power would fall in Category 6 of leadership style. By assessing the three situational variables, one can place any organizational context in one of the eight categories represented in Figure 6.1.

Once the nature of the situation is determined, the fit between the leader's style and the situation can be evaluated. The figure indicates that low LPCs (low LPC score) are effective in Categories 1, 2, 3, and 8, whereas high LPCs (high LPC score) are effective in Categories 4, 5, 6, and 7. Middle LPCs are effective in Categories 1, 2, and 3. If a leader's style matches the appropriate category in the model, that leader will be effective; if a leader's style does not match the category, that leader will not be effective.

It is important to point out that contingency theory stresses that leaders are not effective in all situations. If your style is a good match for the situation in which you work, you will succeed at your job. If your style does not match the situation, you probably will fail.

 6.2 Follower Self-Leadership | **6.3** Power Poisoning

STRENGTHS

Contingency theory has several major strengths. First, it is supported by a great deal of empirical research (see Peters, Hartke, & Pohlman, 1985; Strube & Garcia, 1981). In an era in which print and electronic media abound with accounts of "how to be a successful leader," contingency theory offers an approach to leadership that has a long tradition. Many researchers have tested it and found it to be a valid and reliable approach to explaining how effective leadership can be achieved. Contingency theory is grounded in research.

Second, contingency theory has broadened our understanding of leadership by forcing us to consider the impact of situations on leaders. Before contingency theory was developed, leadership theories focused on whether there was a single, best type of leadership (e.g., trait approach). However, contingency theory emphasized the importance of focusing on the relationship between the leader's style and the demands of various situations. In essence, contingency theory shifted the emphasis to leadership contexts, particularly the link between the leader and the situations.

Third, contingency theory is predictive and therefore provides useful information about the type of leadership that is most likely to be effective in certain contexts. From the data provided by the LPC scale and the descriptions of three aspects of a situation (i.e., leader–member relations, task structure, and position power), it is possible to determine the probability of success for a given person in a given situation. This gives contingency theory predictive power that other leadership theories do not have.

Fourth, this theory does not require that people be effective in all situations. So often leaders in organizations feel the need to be all things to all people, which may be asking too much of them. Contingency theory argues that leaders should not expect to be able to lead in every situation. Companies should try to place leaders in optimal situations, in situations that are ideal for their leadership style. When it is obvious that leaders are in the wrong situation, efforts should be made to change the work variables or move the leader to another context. Contingency theory matches the leader and the situation, but does not demand that the leader fit every situation.

Fifth, contingency theory provides data on leaders' styles that could be useful to organizations in developing leadership profiles. The LPC score is

6.3 Healthcare Providers   **6.3** Global Mindset

one piece of information that could be used, along with other assessments in human resource planning, to develop profiles on individuals to determine how and where they would best serve an organization.

CRITICISMS

Although many studies support the validity of contingency theory, it has also received much criticism in the research literature. A brief discussion of these criticisms will help to clarify the overall value of contingency theory as a leadership theory.

First, contingency theory has been criticized because it fails to explain fully why people with certain leadership styles are more effective in some situations than in others. Fiedler (1993) called this a "black box problem" because a level of mystery remains about why task-motivated leaders are good in extreme settings and relationship-motivated leaders are good in moderately favorable settings.

The answer provided by the theory for why leaders with low LPC scores are effective in extremes is that these people feel more certain in contexts where they have a lot of control and are comfortable strongly exerting themselves. On the other hand, high LPCs are not effective in extreme situations because when they have a lot of control, they tend to overreact; when they have little control, they tend to focus so much on relationships that they fail to do the task. In moderate situations, high LPCs are effective because they are allowed to focus on relationship issues, whereas low LPCs feel frustrated because of the lack of certainty. Because critics find these explanations somewhat inadequate, contingency theory is often challenged.

A second major criticism of this theory concerns the LPC scale. The LPC scale has been questioned because it does not seem valid on the surface, it does not correlate well with other standard leadership measures (Fiedler, 1993), and it is not easy to complete correctly.

The LPC scale measures a person's leadership style by asking the person to characterize another person's behavior. Because projection is involved in the measure, it is difficult for respondents to understand how their descriptions of another person on the scale reflect their own leadership style. It does not make sense, on the surface, to measure your style through your evaluations of another person's style.

▶ 6.2 Fiedler's Contingency Theory

Although it may not be adequate for many people, the answer to this criticism is that the LPC scale is a measure of a person's motivational hierarchy. Those who are highly task motivated see their least preferred coworker in a very negative light because that person gets in the way of their own accomplishment of a task. The primary need for these people is to get the job done, and only their secondary needs shift toward people issues. On the other hand, those who are relationship motivated see their least preferred coworker in terms that are more positive because their primary need is to get along with people, and only their secondary needs revolve around tasks. In short, the LPC scale measures a respondent's style by assessing the degree to which the respondent sees another person getting in the way of his or her own goal accomplishment.

Although it takes only a few minutes to complete, the instructions on the LPC scale are not clear; they do not fully explain how the respondent is to select his or her least preferred coworker. Some respondents may get confused between a person who is their least *liked* coworker and one who is their least *preferred* coworker. Because their final LPC score is based on whom they choose as a least preferred coworker, the lack of clear directions on whom to choose as a least preferred coworker makes the LPC measure problematic.

Although Fiedler and his colleagues have research to back up the test–retest reliability of the LPC scale (Fiedler & Garcia, 1987), the scale remains suspect for many practitioners because it lacks face validity. Another criticism of contingency theory is that it is cumbersome to use in real-world settings. It is cumbersome because it entails assessing the leader's style and three complex situational variables (leader–member relations, task structure, and position power), each of which requires a different instrument. Administering a battery of questionnaires in ongoing organizations can be difficult because it breaks up the normal flow of organizational communication and operations.

A final criticism of contingency theory is that it fails to explain adequately what organizations should do when there is a mismatch between the leader and the situation in the workplace. Because it is a personality theory, contingency theory does not advocate teaching leaders how to adapt their styles to various situations as a means to improve leadership in an organization. Rather, this approach advocates that leaders engage in situational engineering, which means, in essence, changing situations to fit the leader. Although Fiedler and his colleagues argue that most situations can be changed in one respect or another to fit the leader's style, the

6.4 Leader Behavior Diagnostics

prescriptions for how one engages in situational engineering are not clearly set forth in the theory.

In fact, situations are not always easily changed to match the leader's style. For example, if a leader's style does not match an unstructured, low-power situation, it may be impossible to make the task more structured and increase the position power to fit the leader's style. Similarly, progression up the management ladder in organizations may mean that a leader moves into a new situation in which her or his style does not fit. For example, a manager with a high LPC (relationship-motivated) score might receive a promotion that places her in a context that has good leader–member relations, task structure, and position power, thus rendering her ineffective according to contingency theory. Certainly, it would be questionable for a company to change this situation, which otherwise would be considered nearly ideal in most ways. Overall, changing the situation can result in positive outcomes, but this does present significant workability problems for organizations.

APPLICATION

Contingency theory has many applications in the organizational world: It can be used to answer a host of questions about the leadership of individuals in various types of organizations. For example, it can be used to explain why a person is ineffective in a particular position even though the person is a conscientious, loyal, and hardworking manager. In addition, the theory can be used to predict whether a person who has worked well in one position in an organization will be equally effective if moved into a quite different position in the same company. Furthermore, contingency theory can point to changes that upper management might like to make in a lower-level position in order to guarantee a good fit between an existing manager and a particular work context. These are just a few of the ways in which this theory could be applied in organizational settings.

CASE STUDIES

The following three case studies (Cases 6.1, 6.2, and 6.3) provide leadership situations that can be analyzed and evaluated from the perspective of contingency theory. As you read the cases, try to diagnose them using the

6.5 Contingency Approach   6.4 Leadership Effectiveness

principles of contingency theory. It will be helpful to try to categorize each case using information provided in Figure 6.1. At the end of each case, a series of questions will help you analyze the case.

CASE 6.1

No Control Over the Student Council

Tamara Popovich has been elected president of the student council at the local college she attends. She likes the other council members, and they seem to like her. Her first job as president of the council is to develop a new policy for student computer fees. This is the first year that computer fees are being assessed, so there are no specific guidelines for what should be included in this policy. Because the council members are elected by the student body, Tamara has no control over how they work, and has no way of rewarding or punishing them. In a leadership course Tamara took, she filled out the LPC questionnaire, and her score was 98.

Questions

1. How will Tamara do as president of the student council?

2. According to her LPC score, what are her primary needs?

3. How will these needs affect her ability to develop the new policy for computer fees?

4. How can Tamara change the situation to match her management style?

CASE 6.2

Giving Him a Hard Time

Bill Smith has been the high school band teacher for 15 years. Every year, he is in charge of planning and conducting a different type of concert for the holidays. This year, his plan is to present a special jazz program in conjunction with the senior choir. For some reason, the band and choir members have it in for Bill and are constantly giving him trouble. Band and choir are extracurricular activities in which students volunteer to participate. While taking a management class at a local university, Bill took the LPC scale, and his score was 44.

(Continued)

(Continued)

Questions

1. According to Figure 6.1, what category does this situation fall into?

2. Will Bill be successful in his efforts to run the holiday program?

3. Should the school administration make any changes regarding Bill's position?

CASE 6.3

What's the Best Leader Match?

Universal Drugs is a family-owned pharmaceutical company that manufactures generic drugs such as aspirin and vitamin pills. The owners of the company have expressed a strong interest in making the management of the company, which traditionally has been very authoritarian, more teamwork oriented.

To design and implement the new management structure, the owners have decided to create a new position. The person in this position would report directly to the owners and have complete freedom to conduct performance reviews of all managers directly involved in the new system. Two employees from within the company have applied for the new position.

Martha Lee has been with Universal for 15 years and has been voted by her peers "most outstanding manager" on three different occasions. She is friendly, honest, and extremely conscientious about reaching short-term and long-term goals. When given the LPC scale by the personnel department, Martha received a score of 52.

Bill Washington came to Universal 5 years ago with an advanced degree in organizational development. He is director of training, where all of his subordinates say he is the most caring manager they have ever had. While at Universal, Bill has built a reputation for being a real people person. Reflecting his reputation is his score on the LPC scale, an 89.

Questions

1. According to contingency theory, which of the two applicants should the new owner choose to head the new management structure? Why?

2. Could the owner define the new position according to contingency theory in such a way that it would qualify one of the applicants more than the other?

3. Will Universal Drugs benefit by using contingency theory in its decision making regarding its new management structure?

LEADERSHIP INSTRUMENT

The LPC scale is used in contingency theory to measure a person's leadership style. For example, it measures your style by having you describe a coworker with whom you had difficulty completing a job. This need not be a coworker you disliked a great deal but rather someone with whom you least liked to work. After you have selected this person, the LPC instrument asks you to describe your coworker on 18 sets of adjectives.

Low LPCs are task motivated. Their primary needs are to accomplish tasks, and their secondary needs are focused on getting along with people. In a work setting, they are concerned with achieving success on assigned tasks, even at the cost of poor interpersonal relationships with coworkers. Low LPCs gain self-esteem by achieving their goals. They may attend to interpersonal relationships, but only after they first have directed themselves toward the tasks of the group.

Middle LPCs are socioindependent. In the context of work, they are self-directed and not overly concerned with the task or with how others view them. They are more removed from the situation and act more independently than low or high LPCs.

High LPCs are motivated by relationships. These people derive their major satisfaction in an organization from interpersonal relationships. A high LPC sees positive qualities even in the coworker she or he least prefers, and even if the high LPC does not work well with that person. In an organizational setting, the high LPC attends to tasks, but only after she or he is certain that the relationships between people are in good shape.

Least Preferred Coworker (LPC) Measure

Instructions: Think of the person with whom you can work least well. He or she may be someone you work with now or someone you knew in the past. That person does not have to be the person you like the least but should be the person with whom you had the most difficulty in getting a job done. Describe this person as he or she appears to you by circling the appropriate number for each of the following items.

1.	Pleasant	8	7	6	5	4	3	2	1	Unpleasant
2.	Friendly	8	7	6	5	4	3	2	1	Unfriendly
3.	Rejecting	1	2	3	4	5	6	7	8	Accepting
4.	Tense	1	2	3	4	5	6	7	8	Relaxed
5.	Distant	1	2	3	4	5	6	7	8	Close
6.	Cold	1	2	3	4	5	6	7	8	Warm
7.	Supportive	8	7	6	5	4	3	2	1	Hostile
8.	Boring	1	2	3	4	5	6	7	8	Interesting
9.	Quarrelsome	1	2	3	4	5	6	7	8	Harmonious
10.	Gloomy	1	2	3	4	5	6	7	8	Cheerful
11.	Open	8	7	6	5	4	3	2	1	Closed
12.	Backbiting	1	2	3	4	5	6	7	8	Loyal
13.	Untrustworthy	1	2	3	4	5	6	7	8	Trustworthy
14.	Considerate	8	7	6	5	4	3	2	1	Inconsiderate
15.	Nasty	1	2	3	4	5	6	7	8	Nice
16.	Agreeable	8	7	6	5	4	3	2	1	Disagreeable
17.	Insincere	1	2	3	4	5	6	7	8	Sincere
18.	Kind	8	7	6	5	4	3	2	1	Unkind

SOURCE: Adapted from "The LPC Questionnaire," in *Improving Leadership Effectiveness* by Fiedler, F. E., & Chemers, M. M. Copyright © 1984. Reprinted with permission.

Scoring Interpretation

Your final LPC score is the sum of the numbers you circled on the 18 scales. If your score is 57 or below, you are a low LPC, which suggests that you are task motivated. If your score is within the range of 58 to 63, you are a middle LPC, which means you are independent. People who score 64 or above are called high LPCs, and they are thought to be more relationship motivated.

Because the LPC is a personality measure, the score you get on the LPC scale is believed to be quite stable over time and not easily changed. Low LPCs tend to remain low, moderate LPCs tend to remain moderate, and high LPCs tend to remain high. As was pointed out earlier in the chapter, research shows that the test–retest reliability of the LPC is very strong (Fiedler & Garcia, 1987).

SUMMARY

Contingency theory represents a shift in leadership research from focusing on only the leader to focusing on the leader in conjunction with the situation in which the leader works. It is a leader–match theory that emphasizes the importance of matching a leader's style with the demands of a situation.

To measure leadership style, a personality-like measure called the Least Preferred Coworker (LPC) scale is used. It delineates people who are highly task motivated (low LPCs), those who are socioindependent (middle LPCs), and those who are relationship motivated (high LPCs).

To measure situations, three variables are assessed: leader–member relations, task structure, and position power. Taken together, these variables point to the style of leadership that has the best chance of being successful. In general, contingency theory suggests that low LPCs are effective in extremes and that high LPCs are effective in moderately favorable situations.

The strengths of contingency theory include these: It is backed by a large amount of research, it is the first leadership theory to emphasize the impact of situations on leaders, it is predictive of leadership effectiveness, it allows leaders not to be effective in all situations, and it can provide useful leadership profile data.

On the negative side, contingency theory can be criticized because it has not adequately explained the link between styles and situations, and it relies heavily on the LPC scale, which has been questioned for its face validity and workability. Contingency theory is not easily used in ongoing organizations. Finally, it does not fully explain how organizations can use the results of this theory in situational engineering. Regardless of these criticisms, contingency theory has made a substantial contribution to our understanding of the leadership process.

> Visit the Student Study Site at **www.sagepub.com/northouse6e** for web quizzes, leadership questionnaires, and media links represented by the icons.

6.3 Chapter Summary

REFERENCES

Fiedler, F. E. (1964). A contingency model of leadership effectiveness. In L. Berkowitz (Ed.), *Advances in experimental social psychology* (Vol. 1, pp. 149–190). New York: Academic Press.

Fiedler, F. E. (1967). *A theory of leadership effectiveness*. New York: McGraw-Hill.

Fiedler, F. E. (1993). The leadership situation and the black box in contingency theories. In M. M. Chemers & R. Ayman (Eds.), *Leadership, theory, and research: Perspectives and directions* (pp. 1–28). New York: Academic Press.

Fiedler, F. E. (1995). Reflections by an accidental theorist. *Leadership Quarterly, 6*(4), 453–461.

Fiedler, F. E., & Chemers, M. M. (1974). *Leadership and effective management.* Glenview, IL: Scott, Foresman.

Fiedler, F. E., & Chemers, M. M. (1984). *Improving leadership effectiveness: The leader match concept* (2nd ed.). New York: Wiley.

Fiedler, F. E., & Garcia, J. E. (1987). *New approaches to leadership: Cognitive resources and organizational performance.* New York: Wiley.

Peters, L. H., Hartke, D. D., & Pohlman, J. T. (1985). Fiedler's contingency theory of leadership: An application of the meta-analysis procedures of Schmidt and Hunter. *Psychological Bulletin, 97,* 274–285.

Strube, M. J., & Garcia, J. E. (1981). A meta-analytic investigation of Fiedler's contingency model of leadership effectiveness. *Psychological Bulletin, 90,* 307–321.

7

Path–Goal Theory

DESCRIPTION

Path–goal theory is about how leaders motivate subordinates to accomplish designated goals. Drawing heavily from research on what motivates employees, path–goal theory first appeared in the leadership literature in the early 1970s in the works of Evans (1970), House (1971), House and Dessler (1974), and House and Mitchell (1974). The stated goal of this leadership theory is to enhance employee performance and employee satisfaction by focusing on employee motivation.

In contrast to the situational approach, which suggests that a leader must adapt to the development level of subordinates (see Chapter 5), and unlike contingency theory, which emphasizes the match between the leader's style and specific situational variables (see Chapter 6), path–goal theory emphasizes the relationship between the leader's style and the characteristics of the subordinates and the work setting. The underlying assumption of path–goal theory is derived from expectancy theory, which suggests that subordinates will be motivated if they think they are capable of performing their work, if they believe their efforts will result in a certain outcome, and if they believe that the payoffs for doing their work are worthwhile.

For the leader, the challenge is to use a leadership style that best meets subordinates' motivational needs. This is done by choosing behaviors that complement or supplement what is missing in the work setting. Leaders try to enhance subordinates' goal attainment by providing information or rewards in the work environment (Indvik, 1986); leaders provide subordinates with the elements they think subordinates need to reach their goals.

According to House and Mitchell (1974), leadership generates motivation when it increases the number and kinds of payoffs that subordinates receive from their work. Leadership also motivates when it makes the path to the goal clear and easy to travel through coaching and direction, removing obstacles and roadblocks to attaining the goal, and making the work itself more personally satisfying (Figure 7.1).

Figure 7.1   The Basic Idea Behind Path–Goal Theory

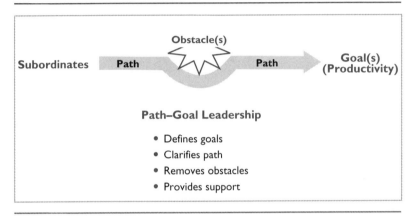

In brief, path–goal theory is designed to explain how leaders can help subordinates along the path to their goals by selecting specific behaviors that are best suited to subordinates' needs and to the situation in which subordinates are working. By choosing the appropriate style, leaders increase subordinates' expectations for success and satisfaction.

Conceptually, path–goal theory is complex. It is useful to break it down into smaller units so we can better understand the complexities of this approach.

Figure 7.2 illustrates the different components of path–goal theory, including leader behaviors, subordinate characteristics, task characteristics, and motivation. Path–goal theory suggests that each type of leader behavior has a different kind of impact on subordinates' motivation. Whether a particular leader behavior is motivating to subordinates is contingent on the subordinates' characteristics and the characteristics of the task.

7.1 Motivation Theories

Figure 7.2   Major Components of Path–Goal Theory

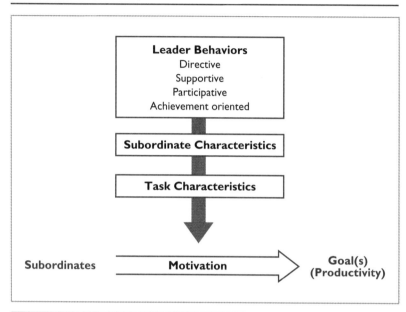

Leader Behaviors

Although many different leadership behaviors could have been selected to be a part of path–goal theory, this approach has so far examined *directive, supportive, participative,* and *achievement-oriented* leadership behaviors (House & Mitchell, 1974, p. 83). Path–goal theory is explicitly left open to the inclusion of other variables.

Directive Leadership

Directive leadership is similar to the "initiating structure" concept described in the Ohio State studies (Halpin & Winer, 1957) and the "telling" style described in situational leadership. It characterizes a leader who gives subordinates instructions about their task, including what is expected of them, how it is to be done, and the time line for when it should be completed. A directive leader sets clear standards of performance and makes the rules and regulations clear to subordinates.

7.1 Directive Leadership

Supportive Leadership

Supportive leadership resembles the consideration behavior construct that was identified by the Ohio State studies discussed in Chapter 4. Supportive leadership consists of being friendly and approachable as a leader and includes attending to the well-being and human needs of subordinates. Leaders using supportive behaviors go out of their way to make work pleasant for subordinates. In addition, supportive leaders treat subordinates as equals and give them respect for their status.

Participative Leadership

Participative leadership consists of inviting subordinates to share in the decision making. A participative leader consults with subordinates, obtains their ideas and opinions, and integrates their suggestions into the decisions about how the group or organization will proceed.

Achievement-Oriented Leadership

Achievement-oriented leadership is characterized by a leader who challenges subordinates to perform work at the highest level possible. This leader establishes a high standard of excellence for subordinates and seeks continuous improvement. In addition to expecting a lot from subordinates, achievement-oriented leaders show a high degree of confidence that subordinates are capable of establishing and accomplishing challenging goals.

House and Mitchell (1974) suggested that leaders might exhibit any or all of these four styles with various subordinates and in different situations. Path–goal theory is not a trait approach that locks leaders into only one kind of leadership. Leaders should adapt their styles to the situation or to the motivational needs of their subordinates. For example, if subordinates need participative leadership at one point in a task and directive leadership at another, the leader can change her or his style as needed. Different situations may call for different types of leadership behavior. Furthermore, there may be instances when it is appropriate for a leader to use more than one style at the same time.

In addition to leader behaviors, Figure 7.2 illustrates two other major components of path–goal theory: subordinate characteristics and task characteristics. Each of these two sets of characteristics influences the way

▶ 7.2 Steve Jobs

leaders' behaviors affect subordinate motivation. In other words, the impact of leadership is *contingent* on the characteristics of both subordinates and their task.

Subordinate Characteristics

Subordinate characteristics determine how a leader's behavior is interpreted by subordinates in a given work context. Researchers have focused on subordinates' *needs for affiliation, preferences for structure, desires for control,* and *self-perceived level of task ability.* These characteristics and many others determine the degree to which subordinates find the behavior of a leader an immediate source of satisfaction or instrumental to some future satisfaction.

Path–goal theory predicts that subordinates who have strong *needs for affiliation* prefer supportive leadership because friendly and concerned leadership is a source of satisfaction. For subordinates who are dogmatic and authoritarian and have to work in uncertain situations, path–goal theory suggests directive leadership because that provides psychological *structure* and task clarity. Directive leadership helps these subordinates by clarifying the path to the goal, making it less ambiguous. The authoritarian type of subordinate feels more comfortable when the leader provides a greater sense of certainty in the work setting.

Subordinates' *desires for control* have received special attention in path–goal research through studies of a personality construct locus of control that can be subdivided into internal and external dimensions. Subordinates with an *internal locus of control* believe that they are in charge of the events that occur in their life, whereas those with an *external locus of control* believe that chance, fate, or outside forces determine life events. Path–goal theory suggests that for subordinates with an internal locus of control participative leadership is most satisfying because it allows them to feel in charge of their work and to be an integral part of decision making. For subordinates with an external locus of control, path–goal theory suggests that directive leadership is best because it parallels subordinates' feelings that outside forces control their circumstances.

Another way in which leadership affects subordinates' motivation is the *subordinates' perception of their own ability* to perform a specific task. As subordinates' perception of their own abilities and competence goes up, the need for directive leadership goes down. In effect, directive leadership

 7.1 Hope and Leadership | **7.1** Subordinates as Individuals

becomes redundant and perhaps excessively controlling when subordinates feel competent to complete their own work.

Task Characteristics

In addition to subordinate characteristics, task characteristics also have a major impact on the way a leader's behavior influences subordinates' motivation (see Figure 7.2). Task characteristics include the design of the *subordinate's task*, the *formal authority system* of the organization, and the *primary work group* of subordinates. Collectively, these characteristics in themselves can provide motivation for subordinates. When a situation provides a clearly structured task, strong group norms, and an established authority system, subordinates will find the paths to desired goals apparent and will not need a leader to clarify goals or coach them in how to reach these goals. Subordinates will feel as if they can accomplish their work and that their work is of value. Leadership in these types of contexts could be seen as unnecessary, unempathic, and excessively controlling.

In some situations, however, the *task characteristics* may call for leadership involvement. Tasks that are unclear and ambiguous call for leadership input that provides structure. In addition, highly repetitive tasks call for leadership that gives support in order to maintain subordinates' motivation. In work settings where the *formal authority* system is weak, leadership becomes a tool that helps subordinates by making the rules and work requirements clear. In contexts where the *group norms* are weak or nonsupportive, leadership assists in building cohesiveness and role responsibility.

A special focus of path–goal theory is helping subordinates overcome obstacles. Obstacles could be just about anything in the work setting that gets in the way of subordinates. Specifically, obstacles create excessive uncertainties, frustrations, or threats for subordinates. In these settings, path–goal theory suggests that it is the leader's responsibility to help subordinates by removing these obstacles or helping them around them. Helping subordinates around these obstacles will increase subordinates' expectations that they can complete the task and increase their sense of job satisfaction.

In 1996, House published a reformulated path–goal theory that extends his original work to include eight classes of leadership behaviors. Besides the four leadership behaviors discussed previously in this chapter— (a) directive, (b) supportive, (c) participative, and (d) achievement-oriented

7.3 Path-Goal Leadership

behavior—the new theory adds (e) work facilitation, (f) group-oriented decision process, (g) work-group representation and networking, and (h) value-based leadership behavior. The essence of the new theory is the same as the original: To be effective, leaders need to help subordinates by giving them what is missing in their environment and by helping them compensate for deficiencies in their abilities.

HOW DOES PATH–GOAL THEORY WORK?

Path–goal theory is an approach to leadership that is not only theoretically complex, but also pragmatic. In theory, it provides a set of assumptions about how various leadership styles interact with characteristics of subordinates and the work setting to affect the motivation of subordinates. In practice, the theory provides direction about how leaders can help subordinates to accomplish their work in a satisfactory manner. Table 7.1 illustrates how leadership behaviors are related to subordinate and task characteristics in path–goal theory.

Theoretically, the path–goal approach suggests that leaders need to choose a leadership style that best fits the needs of subordinates and the

Table 7.1   Path–Goal Theory: How It Works

Leadership Behavior	Subordinate Characteristics	Task Characteristics
Directive	Dogmatic	Ambiguous
Provides guidance and psychological structure	Authoritarian	Unclear rules
		Complex
Supportive	Unsatisfied	Repetitive
Provides nurturance	Need affiliation	Unchallenging
	Need human touch	Mundane
Participative	Autonomous	Ambiguous
Provides involvement	Need for control	Unclear
	Need for clarity	Unstructured
Achievement Oriented	High expectations	Ambiguous
Provides challenges	Need to excel	Challenging
		Complex

7.2 Goal Orientation

work they are doing. The theory predicts that a directive style of leadership is best in situations in which subordinates are dogmatic and authoritarian, the task demands are ambiguous, the organizational rules are unclear, and the task is complex. In these situations, directive leadership complements the work by providing guidance and psychological structure for subordinates (House & Mitchell, 1974, p. 90).

For tasks that are structured, unsatisfying, or frustrating, path–goal theory suggests that leaders should use a supportive style. The supportive style provides what is missing by nurturing subordinates when they are engaged in tasks that are repetitive and unchallenging. Supportive leadership offers a sense of human touch for subordinates engaged in mundane, mechanized activity.

Participative leadership is considered best when a task is ambiguous: Participation gives greater clarity to how certain paths lead to certain goals, and helps subordinates learn what leads to what (House & Mitchell, 1974, p. 92). In addition, participative leadership has a positive impact when subordinates are autonomous and have a strong need for control because this kind of subordinate responds favorably to being involved in decision making and in the structuring of work.

Furthermore, path–goal theory predicts that achievement-oriented leadership is most effective in settings in which subordinates are required to perform ambiguous tasks. In settings such as these, leaders who challenge and set high standards for subordinates raise subordinates' confidence that they have the ability to reach their goals. In effect, achievement-oriented leadership helps subordinates feel that their efforts will result in effective performance. In settings where the task is more structured and less ambiguous, however, achievement-oriented leadership appears to be unrelated to subordinates' expectations about their work efforts.

Pragmatically, path–goal theory is straightforward. An effective leader has to attend to the needs of subordinates. The leader should help subordinates to define their goals and the paths they want to take in reaching those goals. When obstacles arise, the leader needs to help subordinates confront them. This may mean helping the subordinate around the obstacle, or it may mean removing the obstacle. The leader's job is to help subordinates reach their goals by directing, guiding, and coaching them along the way.

7.3 Empowerment

STRENGTHS

Path–goal theory has several positive features. First, path–goal theory provides a useful theoretical framework for understanding how various leadership behaviors affect subordinates' satisfaction and work performance. It was one of the first theories to specify four conceptually distinct varieties of leadership (e.g., directive, supportive, participative, and achievement oriented), expanding the focus of prior research, which dealt exclusively with task- and relationship-oriented behaviors (Jermier, 1996). The path–goal approach was also one of the first situational contingency theories of leadership to explain how task and subordinate characteristics affect the impact of leadership on subordinate performance. The framework provided in path–goal theory informs leaders about how to choose an appropriate leadership style based on the various demands of the task and the type of subordinates being asked to do the task.

A second positive feature of path–goal theory is that it attempts to integrate the motivation principles of expectancy theory into a theory of leadership. This makes path–goal theory unique because no other leadership approach deals directly with motivation in this way. Path–goal theory forces us continually to ask questions such as these about subordinate motivation: How can I motivate subordinates to feel that they have the ability to do the work? How can I help them feel that if they successfully do their work, they will be rewarded? What can I do to improve the payoffs that subordinates expect from their work? Path–goal theory is designed to keep these kinds of questions, which address issues of motivation, at the forefront of the leader's mind.

A third strength, and perhaps its greatest, is that path–goal theory provides a model that in certain ways is very practical. The representation of the model (see Figure 7.1) underscores and highlights the important ways leaders help subordinates. It shouts out for leaders to clarify the paths to the goals and remove or help subordinates around the obstacles to the goals. In its simplest form, the theory reminds leaders that the overarching purpose of leadership is to guide and coach subordinates as they move along the path to achieve a goal.

CRITICISMS

Although path–goal theory has various strengths, it also has several identifiable weaknesses. First, path–goal theory is so complex and incorporates so many different aspects of leadership that interpreting the theory can be confusing. For example, path–goal theory makes predictions about which of four different leadership styles is appropriate for tasks with different degrees of structure, for goals with different levels of clarity, for workers at different levels of ability, and for organizations with different degrees of formal authority. To say the least, it is a daunting task to incorporate all of these factors simultaneously into one's selection of a preferred leadership style. Because the scope of path–goal theory is so broad and encompasses so many different interrelated sets of assumptions, it is difficult to use this theory fully in trying to improve the leadership process in a given organizational context.

A second limitation of path–goal theory is that it has received only partial support from the many empirical research studies that have been conducted to test its validity (House & Mitchell, 1974; Indvik, 1986; Schriesheim, Castro, Zhou, & DeChurch, 2006; Schriesheim & Kerr, 1977; Schriesheim & Schriesheim, 1980; Stinson & Johnson, 1975; Wofford & Liska, 1993). For example, some research supports the prediction that leader directiveness is positively related to worker satisfaction when tasks are ambiguous, but other research has failed to confirm this relationship. Furthermore, not all aspects of the theory have been given equal attention. A great deal of research has been designed to study directive and supportive leadership, but fewer studies address participative and achievement-oriented leadership. The claims of path–goal theory remain tentative because the research findings to date do not provide a full and consistent picture of the basic assumptions and corollaries of path–goal theory (Evans, 1996; Jermier, 1996; Schriesheim & Neider, 1996).

Another criticism of path–goal theory is that it fails to explain adequately the relationship between leadership behavior and worker motivation. Path–goal theory is unique in that it incorporates the tenets of expectancy theory; however, it does not go far enough in explicating how leadership is related to these tenets. The principles of expectancy theory suggest that subordinates will be motivated if they feel competent and trust that their efforts will get results, but path–goal theory does not describe how a leader could use various styles directly to help subordinates feel competent or assured of success. For example, path–goal theory does not explain how directive leadership during ambiguous tasks increases subordinate motivation. Similarly, it does not explain how supportive leadership during tedious work relates to subordinate motivation. The result is that the practitioner is left with an inadequate understanding of how her or his leadership will affect subordinates' expectations about their work.

🎙 **7.2 Rewards**

A final criticism that can be made of path–goal theory concerns a practical outcome of the theory. Path–goal theory suggests that it is important for leaders to provide coaching, guidance, and direction for subordinates, to help subordinates define and clarify goals, and to help subordinates around obstacles as they attempt to reach their goals. In effect, this approach treats leadership as a one-way event: The leader affects the subordinate. The potential difficulty in this type of "helping" leadership is that subordinates may easily become dependent on the leader to accomplish their work. Path–goal theory places a great deal of responsibility on leaders and much less on subordinates. Over time, this kind of leadership could be counterproductive because it promotes dependency and fails to recognize the full abilities of subordinates.

APPLICATION

Path–goal theory is not an approach to leadership for which many management training programs have been developed. You will not find many seminars with titles such as "Improving Your Path–Goal Leadership" or "Assessing Your Skills in Path–Goal Leadership," either. Nevertheless, path–goal theory does offer significant insights that can be applied in ongoing settings to improve one's leadership.

Path–goal theory provides a set of general recommendations based on the characteristics of subordinates and tasks for how leaders should act in various situations if they want to be effective. It informs us about when to be directive, supportive, participative, or achievement oriented. For instance, the theory suggests that leaders should be directive when tasks are complex, and the leader should give support when tasks are dull. Similarly, it suggests that leaders should be participative when subordinates need control and that leaders should be achievement oriented when subordinates need to excel. In a general way, path–goal theory offers leaders a road map that gives directions about ways to improve subordinate satisfaction and performance.

The principles of path–goal theory can be used by leaders at all levels in the organization and for all types of tasks. To apply path–goal theory, a leader must carefully assess the subordinates and their tasks, and then choose an appropriate leadership style to match those characteristics. If subordinates are feeling insecure about doing a task, the leader needs to

7.4 Role-Play Exercise

adopt a style that builds subordinate confidence. For example, in a university setting where a junior faculty member feels apprehensive about his or her teaching and research, a department chair should give supportive leadership. By giving care and support, the chair helps the junior faculty member gain a sense of confidence about his or her ability to perform the work (Bess & Goldman, 2001). If subordinates are uncertain whether their efforts will result in reaching their goals, the leader needs to prove to them that their efforts will be rewarded. As discussed earlier in the chapter, path–goal theory is useful because it continually reminds leaders that their central purpose is to help subordinates define their goals and then to help subordinates reach their goals in the most efficient manner.

CASE STUDIES

The following cases provide descriptions of various situations in which a leader is attempting to apply path–goal theory. Two of the cases, Cases 7.1 and 7.2, are from traditional business contexts; the third, Case 7.3, is from an informal social organization. As you read the cases, try to apply the principles of path–goal theory to determine the degree to which you think the leaders in the cases have done a good job of using this theory.

CASE 7.1

Three Shifts, Three Supervisors

Brako is a small manufacturing company that produces parts for the automobile industry. The company has several patents on parts that fit in the brake assembly of nearly all domestic and foreign cars. Each year, the company produces 3 million parts that it ships to assembly plants throughout the world. To produce the parts, Brako runs three shifts with about 40 workers on each shift.

The supervisors for the three shifts (Art, Bob, and Carol) are experienced employees, and each has been with the company for more than 20 years. The supervisors appear satisfied with their work and have reported no major difficulty in supervising employees at Brako.

Art supervises the first shift. Employees describe him as being a very hands-on type of leader. He gets very involved in the day-to-day operations of the facility. Workers joke that Art knows to the milligram the amount of raw materials the company has on hand at any given time. Art often can be found walking through the plant and reminding people of the correct procedures to follow in doing their work. Even for those working on the production line, Art always has some directions and reminders.

Workers on the first shift have few negative comments to make about Art's leadership. However, they are negative about many other aspects of their work. Most of the work on this shift is very straightforward and repetitive; as a result, it is monotonous. The rules for working on the production line or in the packaging area are all clearly spelled out and require no independent decision making on the part of workers. Workers simply need to show up and go through the motions. On lunch breaks, workers often are heard complaining about how bored they are doing the same old thing over and over. Workers do not criticize Art, but they do not think he really understands their situation.

Bob supervises the second shift. He really enjoys working at Brako and wants all the workers on the afternoon shift to enjoy their work as well. Bob is a people-oriented supervisor whom workers describe as very genuine and caring. Hardly a day goes by that Bob does not post a message about someone's birthday or someone's personal accomplishment. Bob works hard at creating camaraderie, including sponsoring a company softball team, taking people out to lunch, and having people over to his house for social events.

Despite Bob's personableness, absenteeism and turnover are highest on the second shift. The second shift is responsible for setting up the machines and equipment when changes are made from making one part to making another. In addition, the second shift is responsible for the complex computer programs that monitor the machines. Workers on the second shift take a lot of heat from others at Brako for not doing a good job.

Workers on the second shift feel pressure because it is not always easy to figure out how to do their tasks. Each setup is different and entails different procedures. Although the computer is extremely helpful when it is calibrated appropriately to the task, it can be extremely problematic when the software it uses is off the mark. Workers have complained to Bob and upper management many times about the difficulty of their jobs.

Carol supervises the third shift. Her style is different from that of the others at Brako. Carol routinely has meetings, which she labels troubleshooting sessions, for the purpose of identifying problems workers are

(Continued)

(Continued)

experiencing. Any time there is a glitch on the production line, Carol wants to know about it so she can help workers find a solution. If workers cannot do a particular job, she shows them how. For those who are uncertain of their competencies, Carol gives reassurance. Carol tries to spend time with each worker and help the workers focus on their personal goals. In addition, she stresses company goals and the rewards that are available if workers are able to make the grade.

People on the third shift like to work for Carol. They find she is good at helping them do their job. They say she has a wonderful knack for making everything fall into place. When there are problems, she addresses them. When workers feel down, she builds them up. Carol was described by one worker as an interesting mixture of part parent, part coach, and part manufacturing expert. Upper management at Brako is pleased with Carol's leadership, but they have experienced problems repeatedly when workers from Carol's shift have been rotated to other shifts at Brako.

Questions

1. Based on the principles of path–goal theory, describe why Art and Bob appear to be less effective than Carol.

2. How does the leadership of each of the three supervisors affect the motivation of their respective subordinates?

3. If you were consulting with Brako about leadership, what changes and recommendations would you make regarding the supervision of Art, Bob, and Carol?

CASE 7.2

Direction for Some, Support for Others

Daniel Shivitz is the manager of a small business called The Copy Center, which is located near a large university. The Copy Center employs about 18 people, most of whom work part-time while going to school full-time. The store caters to the university community by specializing in course packs, but it also provides desktop publishing and standard copying services. It has three large, state-of-the-art copy machines and several computer workstations.

There are two other national chain copy stores in the immediate vicinity of The Copy Center, yet this store does more business than both of the other stores combined. A major factor contributing to the success of this store is Daniel's leadership style.

One of the things that stand out about Daniel is the way he works with his part-time staff. Most of them are students, who have to schedule their work hours around their class schedules, and Daniel has a reputation of being really helpful with working out schedule conflicts. No conflict is too small for Daniel, who is always willing to juggle schedules to meet the needs of everyone. Students talk about how much they feel included and like the spirit at The Copy Center. It is as if Daniel makes the store like a second family for them.

Work at The Copy Center divides itself into two main areas: duplicating services and desktop publishing. In both areas, Daniel's leadership is effective.

Duplicating is a straightforward operation that entails taking a customer's originals and making copies of them. Because this job is tedious, Daniel goes out of his way to help the staff make it tolerable. He promotes a friendly work atmosphere by doing such things as letting the staff wear casual attire, letting them choose their own tapes for background music, and letting them be a bit wild on the job. Daniel spends a lot of time each day conversing informally with each employee; he also welcomes staff talking with each other. Daniel has a knack for making each worker feel significant even when the work is insignificant. He promotes camaraderie among his staff, and he is not afraid to become involved in their activities.

The desktop publishing area is more complex than duplicating. It involves creating business forms, advertising pieces, and résumés for customers. Working in desktop publishing requires skills in writing, editing, design, and layout. It is challenging work because it is not always easy to satisfy customers' needs. Most of the employees in this area are full-time workers.

Through the years, Daniel has found that employees who work best in desktop publishing are a unique type of person, very different from those who work in duplicating. They are usually quite independent, self-assured, and self-motivated. In supervising them, Daniel gives them a lot of space, is available when they need help, but otherwise leaves them alone.

Daniel likes the role of being the resource person for these employees. For example, if an employee is having difficulty on a customer's project, he

(Continued)

(Continued)

willingly joins the employee in troubleshooting the problem. Similarly, if one of the staff is having problems with a software program, Daniel is quick to offer his technical expertise. Because the employees in desktop publishing are self-directed, Daniel spends far less time with them than with those who work in duplicating.

Overall, Daniel feels successful with his leadership at The Copy Center. Profits for the store continue to grow each year, and its reputation for high-quality service is widespread.

Questions

1. According to path–goal theory, why is Daniel an effective leader?

2. How does his leadership style affect the motivation of employees at The Copy Center?

3. How do characteristics of the task and the subordinates influence Daniel's leadership?

4. One of the principles of path–goal theory is to make the end goal valuable to workers. What could Daniel do to improve subordinate motivation in this area?

CASE 7.3

Marathon Runners at Different Levels

David Abruzzo is the newly elected president of the Metrocity Striders Track Club (MSTC). One of his duties is to serve as the coach for runners who hope to complete the New York City Marathon. Because David has run many marathons and ultramarathons successfully, he feels quite comfortable assuming the role and responsibilities of coach for the marathon runners.

The training period for runners intending to run New York is 16 weeks. During the first couple of weeks of training, David was pleased with the progress of the runners and had little difficulty in his role as coach. However, when the runners reached Week 8, the halfway mark, some things began to occur that raised questions in David's mind regarding how best to help his runners. The issues of concern seemed quite different from those that David had expected to hear from runners in a marathon training program. All in all, the runners and their concerns could be divided into three different groups.

One group of runners, most of whom had never run a marathon, peppered the coach with all kinds of questions. They were very concerned about how to do the marathon and whether they had the ability to complete such a challenging event successfully. They asked questions about how far to run in training, what to eat, how much to drink, and what kind of shoes to wear. One runner wanted to know what to eat the night before the marathon, and another wanted to know whether it was likely that he would pass out when he crossed the finish line. For David the questions were never-ending and rather basic.

Another set of runners seemed most concerned about the effects of training on their running. For example, they wanted to know precisely how their per-week running mileage related to their possible marathon finishing time. Would running long practice runs help them through the wall at the 20-mile mark? Would carbo-loading improve their performance during the marathon? Would taking a rest day during training actually help their overall conditioning? Basically, all the runners in this group seemed to want assurances from David that they were training in the right way for New York.

A third group was made up of seasoned runners, most of whom had run several marathons and many of whom had finished in the top 10 of their respective age divisions. Regardless of their experience, these runners still seemed to be having trouble. They complained of feeling flat and acted a bit moody and down about training. Even though they had confidence in their ability to compete and finish well, they lacked excitement about running in the New York event. The occasional questions they raised usually concerned such things as whether their overall training strategy was appropriate or whether their training would help them in other races besides the New York City Marathon.

Questions

1. Based on the principles described in path–goal theory, what kind of leadership should David exhibit with each of the three running groups?

2. What does David have to do to help the runners accomplish their goals?

3. Are there obstacles that David can remove or help runners to confront?

4. In general, how can David motivate each of the three groups?

LEADERSHIP INSTRUMENT ─────────────────────

Because the path–goal theory was developed as a complex set of theoretical assumptions to direct researchers in developing new leadership theory, it has used many different instruments to measure the leadership process. The Path–Goal Leadership Questionnaire has been useful in measuring and learning about important aspects of path–goal leadership (Indvik, 1985, 1988). This questionnaire provides information for respondents about four different leadership styles: directive, supportive, participative, and achievement oriented. Respondents' scores on each of the different styles provide them with information on their strong and weak styles and the relative importance they place on each of the styles.

To understand the path–goal questionnaire better, it may be useful to analyze a hypothetical set of scores. For example, hypothesize that your scores on the questionnaire were 29 for directive, which is high; 22 for supportive, which is low; 21 for participative, which is average; and 25 for achievement, which is high. These scores suggest that you are a leader who is typically more directive and achievement oriented than most other leaders, less supportive than other leaders, and quite similar to other leaders in the degree to which you act participatively.

According to the principles of path–goal theory, if your scores matched these hypothetical scores, you would be effective in situations where the tasks and procedures are unclear and your subordinates have a need for certainty. You would be less effective in work settings that are structured and unchallenging. In addition, you would be moderately effective in ambiguous situations with subordinates who want control. Last, you would do very well in uncertain situations where you could set high standards, challenge subordinates to meet these standards, and help them feel confident in their abilities.

In addition to the Path–Goal Leadership Questionnaire, leadership researchers have commonly used multiple instruments to study path–goal theory, including measures of task structure, locus of control, employee expectancies, and employee satisfaction. Although the primary use of these instruments has been for theory building, many of the instruments offer valuable information related to practical leadership issues.

Path–Goal Leadership Questionnaire

Instructions: This questionnaire contains questions about different styles of path–goal leadership. Indicate how often each statement is true of your own behavior.

Key: 1 = Never 2 = Hardly ever 3 = Seldom 4 = Occasionally 5 = Often
6 = Usually 7 = Always

1. I let subordinates know what is expected of them.   1 2 3 4 5 6 7

2. I maintain a friendly working relationship with subordinates.   1 2 3 4 5 6 7

3. I consult with subordinates when facing a problem.   1 2 3 4 5 6 7

4. I listen receptively to subordinates' ideas and suggestions.   1 2 3 4 5 6 7

5. I inform subordinates about what needs to be done and how it needs to be done.   1 2 3 4 5 6 7

6. I let subordinates know that I expect them to perform at their highest level.   1 2 3 4 5 6 7

7. I act without consulting my subordinates.   1 2 3 4 5 6 7

8. I do little things to make it pleasant to be a member of the group.   1 2 3 4 5 6 7

9. I ask subordinates to follow standard rules and regulations.   1 2 3 4 5 6 7

10. I set goals for subordinates' performance that are quite challenging.   1 2 3 4 5 6 7

11. I say things that hurt subordinates' personal feelings.   1 2 3 4 5 6 7

12. I ask for suggestions from subordinates concerning how to carry out assignments.   1 2 3 4 5 6 7

13. I encourage continual improvement in subordinates' performance.   1 2 3 4 5 6 7

14. I explain the level of performance that is expected of subordinates.   1 2 3 4 5 6 7

15. I help subordinates overcome problems that stop them from carrying out their tasks.   1 2 3 4 5 6 7

16. I show that I have doubts about subordinates' ability to meet most objectives.   1 2 3 4 5 6 7

17. I ask subordinates for suggestions on what assignments should be made.   1 2 3 4 5 6 7

18. I give vague explanations of what is expected of   1 2 3 4 5 6 7
    subordinates on the job.

19. I consistently set challenging goals for subordinates   1 2 3 4 5 6 7
    to attain.

20. I behave in a manner that is thoughtful of subordinates'   1 2 3 4 5 6 7
    personal needs.

Scoring

1. Reverse the scores for Items 7, 11, 16, and 18.

2. Directive style: Sum of scores on Items 1, 5, 9, 14, and 18.

3. Supportive style: Sum of scores on Items 2, 8, 11, 15, and 20.

4. Participative style: Sum of scores on Items 3, 4, 7, 12, and 17.

5. Achievement-oriented style: Sum of scores on Items 6, 10, 13, 16, and 19.

Scoring Interpretation

- Directive style: A common score is 23, scores above 28 are considered high, and scores below 18 are considered low.
- Supportive style: A common score is 28, scores above 33 are considered high, and scores below 23 are considered low.
- Participative style: A common score is 21, scores above 26 are considered high, and scores below 16 are considered low.
- Achievement-oriented style: A common score is 19, scores above 24 are considered high, and scores below 14 are considered low.

The scores you received on the path–goal questionnaire provide information about which style of leadership you use most often and which you use less often. In addition, you can use these scores to assess your use of each style relative to your use of the other styles.

SOURCES: Adapted from *A Path–Goal Theory Investigation of Superior Subordinate Relationships,* by J. Indvik, unpublished doctoral dissertation, University of Wisconsin–Madison, 1985; and Indvik (1988). Based on the work of House and Dessler (1974) and House (1977) cited in Fulk and Wendler (1982). Used by permission.

SUMMARY

Path–goal theory was developed to explain how leaders motivate subordinates to be productive and satisfied with their work. It is a contingency approach to leadership because effectiveness depends on the fit between the leader's behavior and the characteristics of subordinates and the task.

The basic principles of path–goal theory are derived from expectancy theory, which suggests that employees will be motivated if they feel competent, if they think their efforts will be rewarded, and if they find the payoff for their work valuable. A leader can help subordinates by selecting a style of leadership (directive, supportive, participative, or achievement oriented) that provides what is missing for subordinates in a particular work setting. In simple terms, it is the leader's responsibility to help subordinates reach their goals by directing, guiding, and coaching them along the way.

Path–goal theory offers a large set of predictions for how a leader's style interacts with subordinates' needs and the nature of the task. Among other things, it predicts that directive leadership is effective with ambiguous tasks, that supportive leadership is effective for repetitive tasks, that participative leadership is effective when tasks are unclear and subordinates are autonomous, and that achievement-oriented leadership is effective for challenging tasks.

Path–goal theory has three major strengths. First, it provides a theoretical framework that is useful for understanding how directive, supportive, participative, and achievement-oriented styles of leadership affect the productivity and satisfaction of subordinates. Second, path–goal theory is unique in that it integrates the motivation principles of expectancy theory into a theory of leadership. Third, it provides a practical model that underscores the important ways in which leaders help subordinates.

On the negative side, four criticisms can be leveled at path–goal theory. First, the scope of path–goal theory encompasses so many interrelated sets of assumptions that it is hard to use this theory in a given organizational setting. Second, research findings to date do not support a full and consistent picture of the claims of the theory. Furthermore, path–goal theory does not show in a clear way how leader behaviors directly

7.4 Chapter Summary

affect subordinate motivation levels. Last, path–goal theory is very leader oriented and fails to recognize the transactional nature of leadership. It does not promote subordinate involvement in the leadership process.

Visit the Student Study Site at **www.sagepub.com/northouse6e** for web quizzes, leadership questionnaires, and media links represented by the icons.

REFERENCES

Bess, J. L., & Goldman, P. (2001). Leadership ambiguity in universities and K–12 schools and the limits of contemporary leadership theory. *Leadership Quarterly, 12,* 419–450.

Evans, M. G. (1970). The effects of supervisory behavior on the path–goal relationship. *Organizational Behavior and Human Performance, 5,* 277–298.

Evans, M. G. (1996). R. J. House's "A path–goal theory of leader effectiveness." *Leadership Quarterly, 7*(3), 305–309.

Fulk, J., & Wendler, E. R. (1982). Dimensionality of leader–subordinate interactions: A path–goal investigation. *Organizational Behavior and Human Performance, 30,* 241–264.

Halpin, A. W., & Winer, B. J. (1957). A factorial study of the leader behavior descriptions. In R. M. Stogdill & A. E. Coons (Eds.), *Leader behavior: Its description and measurement.* Columbus: Ohio State University, Bureau of Business Research.

House, R. J. (1971). A path–goal theory of leader effectiveness. *Administrative Science Quarterly, 16,* 321–328.

House, R. J. (1977). A 1976 theory of charismatic leadership. In J. G. Hunt & L. L. Larson (Eds.), *Leadership: The cutting edge* (pp. 189–207). Carbondale: Southern Illinois University Press.

House, R. J. (1996). Path–goal theory of leadership: Lessons, legacy, and a reformulated theory. *Leadership Quarterly, 7*(3), 323–352.

House, R. J., & Dessler, G. (1974). The path–goal theory of leadership: Some post hoc and a priori tests. In J. Hunt & L. Larson (Eds.), *Contingency approaches in leadership* (pp. 29–55). Carbondale: Southern Illinois University Press.

House, R. J., & Mitchell, R. R. (1974). Path–goal theory of leadership. *Journal of Contemporary Business, 3,* 81–97.

Indvik, J. (1985). *A path–goal theory investigation of superior–subordinate relationships.* Unpublished doctoral dissertation, University of Wisconsin–Madison.

Indvik, J. (1986). Path–goal theory of leadership: A meta-analysis. In *Proceedings of the Academy of Management Meeting* (pp. 189–192). Briarcliff Manor, NY: Academy of Management.

Indvik, J. (1988). *A more complete testing of path–goal theory.* Paper presented at the Academy of Management, Anaheim, CA.

Jermier, J. M. (1996). The path–goal theory of leadership: A subtextual analysis. *Leadership Quarterly, 7*(3), 311–316.

Schriesheim, C. A., Castro, S. L., Zhou, X., & DeChurch, L. A. (2006). An investigation of path-goal and transformational leadership theory predictions at the individual level of analysis. *Leadership Quarterly, 17,* 21–38.

Schriesheim, C. A., & Kerr, S. (1977). Theories and measures of leadership: A critical appraisal. In J. G. Hunt & L. L. Larson (Eds.), *Leadership: The cutting edge* (pp. 9–45). Carbondale: Southern Illinois University Press.

Schriesheim, C. A., & Neider, L. L. (1996). Path–goal leadership theory: The long and winding road. *Leadership Quarterly, 7*(3), 317–321.

Schriesheim, J. R., & Schriesheim, C. A. (1980). A test of the path–goal theory of leadership and some suggested directions for future research. *Personnel Psychology, 33,* 349–370.

Stinson, J. E., & Johnson, R. W. (1975). The path–goal theory of leadership: A partial test and suggested refinement. *Academy of Management Journal, 18,* 242–252.

Wofford, J. C., & Liska, L. Z. (1993). Path–goal theories of leadership: A meta-analysis. *Journal of Management, 19*(4), 857–876.

8

Leader–Member Exchange Theory

DESCRIPTION

Most of the leadership theories discussed thus far in this book have emphasized leadership from the point of view of the leader (e.g., trait approach, skills approach, and style approach) or the follower and the context (e.g., situational leadership, contingency theory, and path–goal theory). Leader–member exchange (LMX) theory takes still another approach and conceptualizes leadership as a process that is centered on the *interactions* between leaders and followers. As Figure 8.1 illustrates, LMX theory makes the *dyadic relationship* between leaders and followers the focal point of the leadership process.

Before LMX theory, researchers treated leadership as something leaders did toward all of their followers. This assumption implied that leaders treated followers in a collective way, as a group, using an average leadership style. LMX theory challenged this assumption and directed researchers' attention to the differences that might exist between the leader and each of the leader's followers.

Early Studies

In the first studies of exchange theory, which was then called vertical dyad linkage (VDL) theory, researchers focused on the nature of the *vertical linkages* leaders formed with each of their followers (Figure 8.2). A leader's relationship to the work unit as a whole was viewed as a series of vertical dyads (Figure 8.3). In assessing the characteristics of these vertical dyads,

Figure 8.1   Dimensions of Leadership

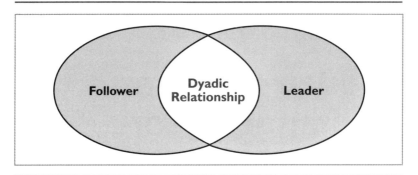

SOURCE: Reprinted from *Leadership Quarterly*, 6(2), G. B. Graen & M. Uhl-Bien, "Relationship-Based Approach to Leadership: Development of Leader–Member Exchange (LMX) Theory of Leadership Over 25 Years: Applying a Multi-Level, Multi-Domain Perspective" (pp. 219–247), Copyright © 1995, with permission from Elsevier.

NOTE: LMX theory was first described 28 years ago in the works of Dansereau, Graen, and Haga (1975), Graen (1976), and Graen and Cashman (1975). Since it first appeared, it has undergone several revisions, and it continues to be of interest to researchers who study the leadership process.

Figure 8.2   The Vertical Dyad

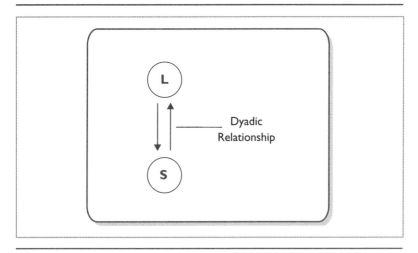

NOTE: The leader (L) forms an individualized working relationship with each of his or her subordinates (S). The exchanges (both content and process) between the leader and subordinate define their dyadic relationship.

8.1 Relationships

Figure 8.3   Vertical Dyads

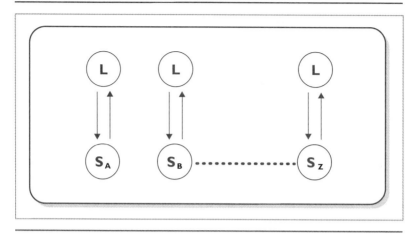

NOTE: The leader (L) forms special relationships with all of his or her subordinates (S). Each of these relationships is special and has its own unique characteristics.

researchers found two general types of linkages (or relationships): those that were based on expanded and negotiated role responsibilities (extra-roles), which were called the *in-group*, and those that were based on the formal employment contract (defined roles), which were called the *out-group* (Figure 8.4).

Within an organizational work unit, subordinates become a part of the in-group or the out-group based on how well they work with the leader and how well the leader works with them. Personality and other personal characteristics are related to this process (Dansereau et al., 1975). In addition, membership in one group or the other is based on how subordinates involve themselves in expanding their role responsibilities with the leader (Graen, 1976). Subordinates who are interested in negotiating with the leader what they are willing to do for the group can become a part of the in group. These negotiations involve exchanges in which subordinates do certain activities that go beyond their formal job descriptions, and the leader, in turn, does more for these subordinates. If subordinates are not interested in taking on new and different job responsibilities, they become a part of the out-group.

Subordinates in the in-group receive more information, influence, confidence, and concern from their leaders than do out-group subordinates (Dansereau et al., 1975). In addition, they are more dependable, more

8.2 Attributional Biases   8.1 In and Out Functions

Figure 8.4 In-Groups and Out-Groups

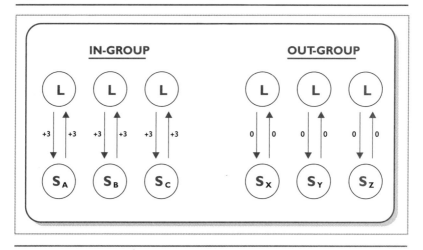

NOTE: A leader (L) and his or her subordinates (S) form unique relationships. Relationships within the in-group are marked by mutual trust, respect, liking, and reciprocal influence. Relationships within the out-group are marked by formal communication based on job descriptions. Plus 3 is a high-quality relationship, and zero is a stranger.

highly involved, and more communicative than out-group subordinates (Dansereau et al., 1975). Whereas in-group members do extra things for the leader and the leader does the same for them, subordinates in the out-group are less compatible with the leader and usually just come to work, do their job, and go home.

Later Studies

After the first set of studies, there was a shift in the focus of LMX theory. Whereas the initial studies of this theory addressed primarily the nature of the differences between in-groups and out-groups, a subsequent line of research addressed how LMX theory was related to organizational effectiveness.

Specifically, these studies focus on how the quality of leader–member exchanges was related to positive outcomes for leaders, followers, groups, and the organization in general (Graen & Uhl-Bien, 1995).

Researchers found that high-quality leader–member exchanges produced less employee turnover, more positive performance evaluations, higher frequency of promotions, greater organizational commitment,

▶ **8.2** In-Groups and Out-Groups

more desirable work assignments, better job attitudes, more attention and support from the leader, greater participation, and faster career progress over 25 years (Graen & Uhl-Bien, 1995; Liden, Wayne, & Stilwell, 1993).

Based on a review of 130 studies of LMX research conducted since 2002, Anand, Hu, Liden, and Vidyarthi (2011) found that interest in studying leader–member exchange has not diminished. A large majority of these studies (70%) examined the antecedents and outcomes of leader–member exchange. The research trends show increased attention to the context surrounding LMX relationships (e.g., group dynamics), analyzing leader–member exchange from individual and group levels, and studying leader–member exchange with non-U.S. samples.

For example, using a sample of employees in a variety of jobs in Israeli organizations, Atwater and Carmeli (2009) examined the connection between employees' perceptions of leader–member exchange and their energy and creativity at work. They found that perceived high-quality leader–member exchange was positively related to feelings of energy in employees, which, in turn, was related to greater involvement in creative work. LMX theory was not directly associated with creativity, but it served as a mechanism to nurture people's feelings, which then enhanced their creativity.

Researchers have also studied how LMX theory is related to empowerment. Harris, Wheeler, and Kacmar (2009) explored how empowerment moderates the impact of leader–member exchange on job outcomes such as job satisfaction, turnover, job performance, and organizational citizenship behaviors. Based on two samples of college alumni, they found that empowerment and leader–member exchange quality had a slight synergistic effect on job outcomes. The quality of leader–member exchange mattered most for employees who felt little empowerment. For these employees, high-quality leader–member exchange appeared to compensate for the drawbacks of not being empowered.

In essence, the aforementioned findings clearly illustrate that organizations stand to gain much from having leaders who can create good working relationships. When leaders and followers have good exchanges, they feel better and accomplish more, and the organization prospers.

Leadership Making

Research of LMX theory has also begun to focus on how exchanges between leaders and subordinates can be used for leadership making (Graen & Uhl-Bien, 1991). Leadership making is a prescriptive approach

 8.1 Supervisor-Subordinate Relationships

to leadership emphasizing that a leader should develop high-quality exchanges with all of the leader's subordinates rather than just a few. It attempts to make every subordinate feel as if he or she is a part of the in-group and, by so doing, avoids the inequities and negative implications of being in an out-group. In general, leadership making promotes partnerships in which the leader tries to build effective dyads with all employees in the work unit (Graen & Uhl-Bien, 1995). In addition, leadership making suggests that leaders can create networks of partnerships throughout the organization, which will benefit the organization's goals and the leader's own career progress.

Graen and Uhl-Bien (1991) suggested that leadership making develops progressively over time in three phases: (1) the stranger phase, (2) the acquaintance phase, and (3) the mature partnership phase (Table 8.1). During Phase 1, the stranger phase, the interactions in the leader–subordinate dyad generally are rule bound, relying heavily on contractual relationships. Leaders and subordinates relate to each other within prescribed organizational roles. They have lower-quality exchanges, similar to those of out-group members discussed earlier in the chapter. The subordinate complies with the formal leader, who has hierarchical status for the purpose of achieving the economic rewards the leader controls. The motives of the subordinate during the stranger phase are directed toward self-interest rather than toward the good of the group (Graen & Uhl-Bien, 1995).

In a study of the early stages of leader-member relationship development, Nahrang, Morgeson, and Ilies (2009) found that leaders look for followers who exhibit enthusiasm, participation, gregariousness, and extraversion. In

Table 8.1 Phases in Leadership Making

	Phase 1 **Stranger**	Phase 2 **Acquaintance**	Phase 3 **Partnership**
Roles	Scripted	Tested	Negotiated
Influences	One way	Mixed	Reciprocal
Exchanges	Low quality	Medium quality	High quality
Interests	Self	Self and other	Group
		Time ⟶	

SOURCE: Adapted from "Relationship-Based Approach to Leadership: Development of Leader–Member Exchange (LMX) Theory of Leadership Over 25 Years: Applying a Multi-Level, Multi-Domain Perspective," by G. B. Graen and M. Uhl-Bien, 1995, *Leadership Quarterly, 6*(2), 231.

8.1 Changing Relationships

contrast, followers look for leaders who are pleasant, trusting, cooperative, and agreeable. Leader extraversion did not influence relationship quality for the followers, and follower agreeableness did not influence relationship quality for the leaders. A key predictor of relationship quality for both leaders and followers was behaviors such as performance.

Phase 2, the acquaintance phase, begins with an offer by the leader or the subordinate for improved career-oriented social exchanges, which involve sharing more resources and personal or work-related information. It is a testing period for both the leader and the subordinate to assess whether the subordinate is interested in taking on more roles and responsibilities and to assess whether the leader is willing to provide new challenges for subordinates. During this time, dyads shift away from interactions that are governed strictly by job descriptions and defined roles and move toward new ways of relating. As measured by LMX theory, it could be said that the quality of their exchanges has improved to medium quality. Successful dyads in the acquaintance phase begin to develop greater trust and respect for each other. They also tend to focus less on their own self-interests and more on the purposes and goals of the group.

Phase 3, mature partnership, is marked by high-quality leader–member exchanges. People who have progressed to this stage in their relationships experience a high degree of mutual trust, respect, and obligation toward each other. They have tested their relationship and found that they can depend on each other. In mature partnerships, there is a high degree of reciprocity between leaders and subordinates: Each affects and is affected by the other. For example, in a study of 75 bank managers and 58 engineering managers, Schriesheim, Castro, Zhou, and Yammarino (2001) found that good leader–member relations were more egalitarian and that influence and control were more evenly balanced between the supervisor and the subordinate. In addition, during Phase 3, members may depend on each other for favors and special assistance. For example, leaders may rely on subordinates to do extra assignments, and subordinates may rely on leaders for needed support or encouragement. The point is that leaders and subordinates are tied together in productive ways that go well beyond a traditional hierarchically defined work relationship. They have developed an extremely effective way of relating that produces positive outcomes for themselves and the organization. In effect, partnerships are transformational in that they assist leaders and followers in moving beyond their own self-interests to accomplish the greater good of the team and organization (see Chapter 9).

8.2 Empowering Employees

The benefits for employees who develop high-quality leader–member relationships include preferential treatment, increased job-related communication, ample access to supervisors, and increased performance-related feedback (Harris et al., 2009). The disadvantages for those with low-quality leader–member relationships include limited trust and support from supervisors and few benefits outside the employment contract (Harris et al., 2009). To evaluate leader–member exchanges, researchers typically use a brief questionnaire that asks leaders and followers to report on the effectiveness of their working relationships. The questionnaire assesses the degree to which respondents express respect, trust, and obligation in their exchanges with others. At the end of this chapter, a version of the LMX questionnaire is provided for you to take for the purpose of analyzing some of your own leader–member relationships.

HOW DOES LMX THEORY WORK?

LMX theory works in two ways: It describes leadership, and it prescribes leadership. In both instances, the central concept is the dyadic relationship that a leader forms with each of the leader's subordinates. Descriptively, LMX theory suggests that it is important to recognize the existence of in-groups and out-groups within a group or an organization.

The differences in how goals are accomplished by in-groups and out-groups are substantial. Working with an in-group allows a leader to accomplish more work in a more effective manner than he or she can accomplish working without one. In-group members are willing to do more than is required in their job description and look for innovative ways to advance the group's goals. In response to their extra effort and devotion, leaders give them more responsibilities and more opportunities. Leaders also give in-group members more of their time and support.

Out-group members act quite differently than in-group members. Rather than trying to do extra work, out-group members operate strictly within their prescribed organizational roles. They do what is required of them but nothing more. Leaders treat out-group members fairly and according to the formal contract, but they do not give them special attention. For their efforts, out-group members receive the standard benefits as defined in the job description.

Prescriptively, LMX theory is best understood within the leadership-making model of Graen and Uhl-Bien (1991). Graen and Uhl-Bien

8.2 NGO Leadership

advocated that leaders should create a special relationship with all subordinates, similar to the relationships described as in-group relationships. Leaders should offer each subordinate the opportunity to take on new roles and responsibilities. Furthermore, leaders should nurture high-quality exchanges with their subordinates. Rather than focusing on the differences between in-group and out-group members, the leadership-making model suggests that leaders should look for ways to build trust and respect with all of their subordinates, thus making the entire work unit an in-group. In addition, leaders should look beyond their own work unit and create high-quality partnerships with people throughout the organization.

Whether descriptive or prescriptive, LMX theory works by focusing our attention on the special, unique relationship that leaders can create with others. When these relationships are of high quality, the goals of the leader, the followers, and the organization are all advanced.

STRENGTHS

LMX theory makes several positive contributions to our understanding of the leadership process. First, it is a strong descriptive theory. Intuitively, it makes sense to describe work units in terms of those who contribute more and those who contribute less (or the bare minimum) to the organization. Anyone who has ever worked in an organization has felt the presence of in-groups and out-groups. Despite the potential harm of out-groups, we all know that leaders have special relationships with certain people who do more and get more. We may not like this because it seems unfair, but it is a reality, and the LMX theory has accurately described this situation. LMX theory validates our experience of how people within organizations relate to each other and the leader. Some contribute more and receive more; others contribute less and get less.

Second, LMX theory is unique because it is the only leadership approach that makes the concept of the dyadic relationship the centerpiece of the leadership process. Other approaches emphasize the characteristics of leaders, followers, contexts, or a combination of these, but none of them addresses the specific relationships between the leader and each subordinate. LMX theory underscores that effective leadership is contingent on effective leader–member exchanges.

Third, LMX theory is noteworthy because it directs our attention to the importance of communication in leadership. The high-quality exchanges advocated in LMX theory are inextricably bound to effective communication.

8.4 Empowerment Through LMX

Communication is the vehicle through which leaders and subordinates create, nurture, and sustain useful exchanges. Effective leadership occurs when the communication of leaders and subordinates is characterized by mutual trust, respect, and commitment.

Fourth, LMX theory provides an important alert for leaders. It warns leaders to avoid letting their conscious or unconscious biases influence who is invited into the in-group (e.g., biases regarding race, gender, ethnicity, religion, or age). The principles outlined in LMX theory serve as a good reminder for leaders to be fair and equal in how they approach each of their subordinates.

Finally, a large body of research substantiates how the practice of LMX theory is related to positive organizational outcomes. In a review of this research, Graen and Uhl-Bien (1995) pointed out that leader–member exchange is related to performance, organizational commitment, job climate, innovation, organizational citizenship behavior, empowerment, procedural and distributive justice, career progress, and many other important organizational variables. By linking the use of LMX theory to real outcomes, researchers have been able to validate the theory and increase its practical value.

CRITICISMS

LMX theory also has some limitations. First, on the surface, leader–member exchange in its initial formulation (vertical dyad linkage theory) runs counter to the basic human value of fairness. Throughout our lives, beginning when we are very young, we are taught to try to get along with everyone and to treat everyone equally. We have been taught that it is wrong to form in-groups or cliques because they are harmful to those who cannot be a part of them. Because LMX theory divides the work unit into two groups and one group receives special attention, it gives the appearance of discrimination against the out-group.

Our culture is replete with examples of people of different genders, ages, cultures, and abilities who have been discriminated against. Although LMX theory was not designed to do so, it supports the development of privileged groups in the workplace. In so doing, it appears unfair and discriminatory. Furthermore, as reported by McClane (1991), the existence of in-groups and out-groups may have undesirable effects on the group as a whole.

Whether LMX theory actually creates inequalities is questionable (cf. Harter & Evanecky, 2002; Scandura, 1999). If a leader does not intentionally keep out-group members "out," and if they are free to become members of the in-group, then LMX theory may not create inequalities. However, the theory does not elaborate on strategies for how one gains access to the in-group if one chooses to do so.

Furthermore, LMX theory does not address other fairness issues, such as subordinates' perceptions of the fairness of pay increases and promotion opportunities (distributive justice), decision-making rules (procedural justice), or communication of issues within the organization (interactional justice) (Scandura, 1999). There is a need for further research on how these types of fairness issues affect the development and maintenance of LMX relationships.

A second criticism of LMX theory is that the basic ideas of the theory are not fully developed. For example, the theory does not fully explain how high-quality leader–member exchanges are created (Anand et al., 2011). In the early studies, it was implied that they were formed when a leader found certain subordinates more compatible in regard to personality, interpersonal skills, or job competencies, but these studies never described the relative importance of these factors or how this process worked (Yukl, 1994). Research has suggested that leaders should work to create high-quality exchanges with all subordinates, but the guidelines for how this is done are not clearly spelled out. For example, the model on leadership making highlights the importance of role making, incremental influence, and type of reciprocity (see Table 8.1), but it does not explain how these concepts function to build mature partnerships. Similarly, the model strongly promotes building trust, respect, and obligation in leader–subordinate relationships, but it does not describe the means by which these factors are developed in relationships.

Based on an examination of 147 studies of leader–member exchange, Schriesheim, Castro, and Cogliser (1999) concluded that improved theorization about leader–member exchange and its basic processes is needed. Similarly, in a review of the research on relational leadership, Uhl-Bien, Maslyn, and Ospina (2012) point to the need for further understanding of how high- and low-quality relationships develop in leader–member exchange. Although many studies have been conducted on leader–member exchange, these studies have not resulted in a clear, refined set of definitions, concepts, and propositions about the theory.

A third criticism of the theory is that researchers have not adequately explained the contextual factors that may have an impact on LMX relationships (Anand et al., 2011). Since leader–member exchange is often studied in isolation, researchers have not examined the potential impact of other variables on LMX dyads. For example, workplace norms and other organizational culture variables are likely to influence leader–member exchange. There is a need to explore how the surrounding constellations of social networks influence specific LMX relationships and the individuals in those relationships.

Finally, questions have been raised about the measurement of leader–member exchanges in LMX theory (Graen & Uhl-Bien, 1995; Schriesheim, Castro, & Cogliser, 1999; Schriesheim, Castro, Zhou, et al., 2001). For example, no empirical studies have used dyadic measures to analyze the LMX process (Schriesheim, Castro, Zhou, et al., 2001). In addition, leader–member exchanges have been measured with different versions of leader–member exchange scales and with different levels of analysis, so the results are not always directly comparable. Furthermore, the content validity and dimensionality of the scales have been questioned (Graen & Uhl-Bien, 1995; Schriesheim, Castro, Zhou, et al., 2001).

APPLICATION

Although LMX theory has not been packaged in a way to be used in standard management training and development programs, it offers many insights that managers could use to improve their own leadership behavior. Foremost, LMX theory directs managers to assess their leadership from a relationship perspective. This assessment will sensitize managers to how in-groups and out-groups develop within their own work unit. In addition, LMX theory suggests ways in which managers can improve their work unit by building strong leader–member exchanges with all of their subordinates.

The ideas set forth in LMX theory can be used by managers at all levels within an organization. For example, LMX theory could be used to explain how chief executive officers develop special relationships with select individuals in upper management to develop new strategic and tactical corporate goals. Likewise, it could be used to explain how line managers in a plant use a select few workers to accomplish the production quotas of their work unit. The point is that the ideas presented in LMX theory are applicable throughout organizations.

In addition, the ideas of LMX theory can be used to explain how individuals create leadership networks throughout an organization to help them accomplish work more effectively (Graen & Scandura, 1987). A person with a network of high-quality partnerships can call on many people to help solve problems and advance the goals of the organization.

LMX theory can also be applied in different types of organizations. It applies in volunteer settings as well as traditional business, education, and government settings. Imagine a community leader who heads a volunteer program that assists older adults. To run the program effectively, the leader depends on a few of the volunteers who are more dependable and committed than the rest of the volunteers. This process of working closely with a small cadre of trusted volunteers is explained by the principles of LMX theory. Similarly, a manager of a traditional business setting might use certain individuals to achieve a major change in the company's policies and procedures. The way the manager goes about this process is explicated in LMX theory.

In summary, LMX theory tells us to be aware of how we relate to our subordinates. It tells us to be sensitive to whether some subordinates receive special attention and some subordinates do not. In addition, it tells us to be fair to all employees and allow each of them to become as involved in the work of the unit as they want to be. LMX theory tells us to be respectful and to build trusting relationships with all of our subordinates, recognizing that each employee is unique and wants to relate to us in a special way.

CASE STUDIES

In the following section, three case studies (Cases 8.1, 8.2, and 8.3) are presented to clarify how LMX theory can be applied to various group settings. The first case is about the creative director at an advertising agency, the second is about a production manager at a mortgage company, and the third is about the leadership of the manager of a district office of the Social Security Administration. After each case, there are questions that will help you analyze it, using the ideas from LMX theory.

▶ **8.3** Motivation at Work

CASE 8.1

His Team Gets the Best Assignments

Carly Peters directs the creative department of the advertising agency of Mills, Smith, & Peters. The agency has about 100 employees, 20 of whom work for Carly in the creative department. Typically, the agency maintains 10 major accounts and a number of smaller accounts. It has a reputation for being one of the best advertising and public relations agencies in the country.

In the creative department, there are four major account teams. Each is led by an associate creative director, who reports directly to Carly. In addition, each team has a copywriter, an art director, and a production artist. These four account teams are headed by Jack, Terri, Julie, and Sarah.

Jack and his team get along really well with Carly, and they have done excellent work for their clients at the agency. Of all the teams, Jack's team is the most creative and talented and the most willing to go the extra mile for Carly. As a result, when Carly has to showcase accounts to upper management, she often uses the work of Jack's team. Jack and his team members are comfortable confiding in Carly and she in them. Carly is not afraid to allocate extra resources to Jack's team or to give them free rein on their accounts because they always come through for her.

Terri's team also performs well for the agency, but Terri is unhappy with how Carly treats her team. She feels that Carly is not fair because she favors Jack's team. For example, Terri's team was counseled out of pursuing an ad campaign because the campaign was too risky, whereas Jack's group was praised for developing a very provocative campaign. Terri feels that Jack's team is Carly's pet: His team gets the best assignments, accounts, and budgets. Terri finds it hard to hold back the animosity she feels toward Carly.

Like Terri, Julie is concerned that her team is not in the inner circle, close to Carly. She has noticed repeatedly that Carly favors the other teams. For example, whenever additional people are assigned to team projects, it is always the other teams who get the best writers and art directors. Julie is mystified as to why Carly doesn't notice her team or try to help it with its work. She feels Carly undervalues her team because Julie knows the quality of her team's work is indisputable.

Although Sarah agrees with some of Terri's and Julie's observations about Carly, she does not feel any antagonism about Carly's leadership. Sarah has worked for the agency for nearly 10 years, and nothing seems to bother her. Her account teams have never been earthshaking, but they have never been problematic either. Sarah views her team and its work more as a nuts-and-bolts operation in which the team is given an assignment and carries it out. Being in Carly's inner circle would entail putting in extra time in the evening or on weekends and would create more headaches for Sarah. Therefore, Sarah is happy with her role as it is, and she has little interest in trying to change the way the department works.

Questions

1. Based on the principles of LMX theory, what observations would you make about Carly's leadership at Mills, Smith, & Peters?

2. Is there an in-group and out-group, and, if so, which are they?

3. In what way is Carly's relationship with the four groups productive or counterproductive to the overall goals of the agency?

4. Do you think Carly should change her approach toward the associate directors? If so, what should she do differently?

CASE 8.2

Working Hard at Being Fair

City Mortgage is a medium-size mortgage company that employs about 25 people. Jenny Hernandez, who has been with the company for 10 years, is the production manager who oversees its day-to-day operations.

Reporting to Jenny are loan originators (salespeople), closing officers, mortgage underwriters, and processing and shipping personnel. Jenny is proud of the company and feels as if she has contributed substantially to its steady growth and expansion.

The climate at City Mortgage is very positive. People like to come to work because the office environment is comfortable. They respect each other at the company and show tolerance for those who are different from themselves.

Whereas at many mortgage companies it is common for resentments to build between people who earn different incomes, this is not the case at City Mortgage.

(Continued)

(Continued)

Jenny's leadership has been instrumental in shaping the success of City Mortgage. Her philosophy stresses listening to employees and then determining how each employee can best contribute to the mission of the company. She makes a point of helping each person explore her or his own talents, and challenges each one to try new things.

At the annual holiday party, Jenny devised an interesting event that symbolizes her leadership style. She bought a large piece of colorful glass and had it cut into 25 pieces and handed out one piece to each person. Then she asked each employee to come forward with the piece of glass and briefly state what he or she liked about City Mortgage and how he or she had contributed to the company in the past year. After the statements were made, the pieces of glass were formed into a cut glass window that hangs in the front lobby of the office. The glass is a reminder of how each individual contributes his or her uniqueness to the overall purpose of the company.

Another characteristic of Jenny's style is her fairness. She does not want to give anyone the impression that certain people have the inside track, and she goes to great lengths to prevent this from happening. For example, she avoids social lunches because she thinks they foster the perception of favoritism. Similarly, even though her best friend is one of the loan originators, she is seldom seen talking with her, and if she is, it is always about business matters.

Jenny also applies her fairness principle to how information is shared in the office. She does not want anyone to feel as if he or she is out of the loop, so she tries very hard to keep her employees informed on all the matters that could affect them. Much of this she does through her open-door office policy. Jenny does not have a special group of employees with whom she confides her concerns; rather, she shares openly with each of them.

Jenny is very committed to her work at City Mortgage. She works long hours and carries a beeper on the weekend. At this point in her career, her only concern is that she could be burning out.

Questions

1. Based on the LMX model, how would you describe Jenny's leadership?

2. How do you think the employees at City Mortgage respond to Jenny?

3. If you were asked to follow in Jenny's footsteps, do you think you could or would want to manage City Mortgage with a similar style?

CASE 8.3

Taking on Additional Responsibilities

Jim Madison is manager of a district office for the Social Security Administration. The office serves a community of 200,000 people and has a staff of 30 employees, most of whom work as claim representatives. The primary work of the office is to provide the public with information about social security benefits and to process retirement, survivor, disability, and Medicare claims.

Jim has been the manager of the office for 6 years; during that time, he has made many improvements in the overall operations of the office. People in the community have a favorable view of the office and have few complaints about the services it provides. On the annual survey of community service organizations, the district office receives consistently high marks for overall effectiveness and customer satisfaction.

Almost all of the employees who work for Jim have been employed at the district office for 6 years or more; one employee has been there for 22 years. Although Jim takes pride in knowing all of them personally, he calls on a few of them more frequently than others to help him accomplish his goals.

When it comes to training staff members about new laws affecting claim procedures, Jim relies heavily on two particular claim representatives, Shirley and Patti, both of whom are very knowledgeable and competent. Shirley and Patti view the additional training responsibilities as a challenge. This helps Jim: He does not need to do the job himself or supervise them closely because they are highly respected people within the office, and they have a history of being mature and conscientious about their work. Shirley and Patti like the additional responsibility because it gives them greater recognition and increased benefits from receiving positive job appraisals.

To showcase the office's services to the community, Jim calls on two other employees, Ted and Jana. Ted and Jana serve as field representatives for the office and give presentations to community organizations about the nature of social security and how it serves the citizens of the district. In addition, they speak on local radio stations, answering call-in questions about the various complexities of social security benefits.

(Continued)

(Continued)

Although many of the claim people in the office could act as field representatives, Jim typically calls on Ted and Jana because of their willingness to take on the public relations challenge and because of their special capabilities in this area. This is advantageous for Jim for two reasons: First, these people do an outstanding job in representing the office to the public. Second, Jim is a reticent person, and he finds it quite threatening to be in the public eye. Ted and Jana like to take on this additional role because it gives them added prestige and greater freedom. Being a field representative has its perks because field staff can function as their own bosses when they are not in the office; they can set their own schedules and come and go as they please.

A third area in which Jim calls on a few representatives for added effort is in helping him supervise the slower claim representatives, who seem to be continually behind in writing up the case reports of their clients. When even a few staff members get behind with their work, it affects the entire office operation. To ameliorate this problem, Jim calls on Glenda and Annie, who are both highly talented, to help the slower staff complete their case reports. Although it means taking on more work themselves, Glenda and Annie do it to be kind and to help the office run more smoothly. Other than personal satisfaction, no additional benefits accrue to them for taking on the additional responsibilities.

Overall, the people who work under Jim's leadership are satisfied with his supervision. There are some who feel that he caters too much to a few special representatives, but most of the staff think Jim is fair and impartial. Even though he depends more on a few, Jim tries very hard to attend to the wants and needs of his entire staff.

Questions

1. From an LMX theory point of view, how would you describe Jim's leadership at the district social security office?

2. Can you identify an in-group and an out-group?

3. Do you think the trust and respect Jim places in some of his staff are productive or counterproductive? Why?

LEADERSHIP INSTRUMENT ────────────────

Researchers have used many different questionnaires to study LMX theory. All of them have been designed to measure the quality of the working relationship between leaders and followers. We have chosen to include in this chapter the LMX 7, a seven-item questionnaire that provides a reliable and valid measure of the quality of leader–member exchanges (Graen & Uhl-Bien, 1995).

The LMX 7 is designed to measure three dimensions of leader–member relationships: respect, trust, and obligation. It assesses the degree to which leaders and followers have mutual respect for each other's capabilities, feel a deepening sense of reciprocal trust, and have a strong sense of obligation to one another. Taken together, these dimensions are the ingredients of strong partnerships.

LMX 7 Questionnaire

Instructions: This questionnaire contains items that ask you to describe your relationship with either your leader or one of your subordinates. For each of the items, indicate the degree to which you think the item is true for you by circling one of the responses that appear below the item.

1. Do you know where you stand with your leader (follower) ... [and] do you usually know how satisfied your leader (follower) is with what you do?

Rarely	Occasionally	Sometimes	Fairly often	Very often
1	2	3	4	5

2. How well does your leader (follower) understand your job problems and needs?

Not a bit	A little	A fair amount	Quite a bit	A great deal
1	2	3	4	5

3. How well does your leader (follower) recognize your potential?

Not at all	A little	Moderately	Mostly	Fully
1	2	3	4	5

4. Regardless of how much formal authority your leader (follower) has built into his or her position, what are the chances that your leader (follower) would use his or her power to help you solve problems in your work?

None	Small	Moderate	High	Very high
1	2	3	4	5

5. Again, regardless of the amount of formal authority your leader (follower) has, what are the chances that he or she would "bail you out" at his or her expense?

None	Small	Moderate	High	Very high
1	2	3	4	5

6. I have enough confidence in my leader (follower) that I would defend and justify his or her decision if he or she were not present to do so.

Strongly disagree	Disagree	Neutral	Agree	Strongly agree
1	2	3	4	5

7. How would you characterize your working relationship with your leader (follower)?

Extremely ineffective	Worse than average	Average	Better than average	Extremely effective
1	2	3	4	5

By completing the LMX 7, you can gain a fuller understanding of how LMX theory works. The score you obtain on the questionnaire reflects the quality of your leader–member relationships, and indicates the degree to which your relationships are characteristic of partnerships, as described in the LMX model.

You can complete the questionnaire both as a leader and as a subordinate. In the leader role, you would complete the questionnaire multiple times, assessing the quality of the relationships you have with each of your subordinates. In the subordinate role, you would complete the questionnaire based on the leaders to whom you report.

Scoring Interpretation

Although the LMX 7 is most commonly used by researchers to explore theoretical questions, you can also use it to analyze your own leadership style. You can interpret your LMX 7 scores using the following guidelines: very high = 30–35, high = 25–29, moderate = 20–24, low = 15–19, and very low = 7–14. Scores in the upper ranges indicate stronger, higher-quality leader–member exchanges (e.g., in-group members), whereas scores in the lower ranges indicate exchanges of lesser quality (e.g., out-group members).

SOURCE: Reprinted from "Relationship-Based Approach to Leadership: Development of Leader–Member Exchange (LMX) Theory of Leadership Over 25 Years: Applying a Multi-Level, Multi-Domain Perspective," by G. B. Graen and M. Uhl-Bien, 1995, *Leadership Quarterly, 6*(2), 219–247. Copyright © 1995. Reprinted with permission from Elsevier Science.

SUMMARY ————————————————————————

Since it first appeared more than 30 years ago under the title "vertical dyad linkage (VDL) theory," LMX theory has been and continues to be a much-studied approach to leadership. LMX theory addresses leadership as a process centered on the interactions between leaders and followers. It makes the leader–member relationship the pivotal concept in the leadership process.

In the early studies of LMX theory, a leader's relationship to the overall work unit was viewed as a series of vertical dyads, categorized as being of two different types: Leader–member dyads based on expanded role relationships were called the leader's in-group, and those based on formal job descriptions were called the leader's out-group. It is believed that subordinates become in-group members based on how well they get along with the leader and whether they are willing to expand their role responsibilities. Subordinates who maintain only formal hierarchical relationships with their leader become out-group members. Whereas in-group members receive extra influence, opportunities, and rewards, out-group members receive standard job benefits.

Subsequent studies of LMX theory were directed toward how leader–member exchanges affect organizational performance. Researchers found that high-quality exchanges between leaders and followers produced multiple positive outcomes (e.g., less employee turnover, greater organizational commitment, and more promotions). In general, researchers determined that good leader–member exchanges result in followers feeling better, accomplishing more, and helping the organization prosper.

The most recent emphasis in LMX research has been on leadership making, which emphasizes that leaders should try to develop high-quality exchanges with all of their subordinates. Leadership making develops over time and includes a stranger phase, an acquaintance phase, and a mature partnership phase. By taking on and fulfilling new role responsibilities, followers move through these three phases to develop mature partnerships with their leaders. These partnerships, which are marked by a high degree of mutual trust, respect, and obligation, have positive payoffs for the individuals themselves, and help the organization run more effectively.

There are several positive features to LMX theory. First, LMX theory is a strong descriptive approach that explains how leaders use some subordinates (in-group members) more than others (out-group members) to

8.5 Future of LMX

accomplish organizational goals effectively. Second, LMX theory is unique in that, unlike other approaches, it makes the leader–member relationship the focal point of the leadership process. Related to this focus, LMX theory is noteworthy because it directs our attention to the importance of effective communication in leader–member relationships. In addition, it reminds us to be evenhanded in how we relate to our subordinates. Last, LMX theory is supported by a multitude of studies that link high-quality leader–member exchanges to positive organizational outcomes.

There are also negative features in LMX theory. First, the early formulation of LMX theory (vertical dyad linkage theory) runs counter to our principles of fairness and justice in the workplace by suggesting that some members of the work unit receive special attention and others do not. The perceived inequalities created by the use of in-groups can have a devastating impact on the feelings, attitudes, and behavior of out-group members. Second, LMX theory emphasizes the importance of leader–member exchanges but fails to explain the intricacies of how one goes about creating high-quality exchanges. Although the model promotes building trust, respect, and commitment in relationships, it does not fully explicate how this takes place. Third, researchers have not adequately explained the contextual factors that influence LMX relationships. Finally, there are questions about whether the measurement procedures used in LMX research are adequate to fully capture the complexities of the leader–member exchange process.

Visit the Student Study Site at **www.sagepub.com/northouse6e** for web quizzes, leadership questionnaires, and media links represented by the icons.

REFERENCES

Anand, S., Hu, J., Liden, R. C., & Vidyarthi, P. R. (2011). Leader-member exchange: Recent research findings and prospects for the future. In A. Bryman, D. Collinson, K. Grint, G. Jackson, B. Uhl-Bien (Eds.), *The SAGE handbook of leadership* (pp. 311–325). London, UK: Sage.

Atwater, L., & Carmeli, A. (2009). Leader-member exchange, feelings of energy, and involvement in creative work. *Leadership Quarterly, 20,* 264–275.

Dansereau, F., Graen, G. B., & Haga, W. (1975). A vertical dyad linkage approach to leadership in formal organizations. *Organizational Behavior and Human Performance, 13,* 46–78.

 **8.4** Chapter Summary

Graen, G. B. (1976). Role-making processes within complex organizations. In M. D. Dunnette (Ed.), *Handbook of industrial and organizational psychology* (pp. 1202–1245). Chicago: Rand McNally.

Graen, G. B., & Cashman, J. (1975). A role-making model of leadership in formal organizations: A developmental approach. In J. G. Hunt & L. L. Larson (Eds.), *Leadership frontiers* (pp. 143–166). Kent, OH: Kent State University Press.

Graen, G. B., & Scandura, T. A. (1987). Toward a psychology of dyadic organizing. In B. Staw & L. L. Cumming (Eds.), *Research in organizational behavior* (Vol. 9, pp. 175–208). Greenwich, CT: JAI.

Graen, G. B., & Uhl-Bien, M. (1991). The transformation of professionals into self-managing and partially self-designing contributions: Toward a theory of leadership making. *Journal of Management Systems, 3*(3), 33–48.

Graen, G. B., & Uhl-Bien, M. (1995). Relationship-based approach to leadership: Development of leader–member exchange (LMX) theory of leadership over 25 years: Applying a multi-level, multi-domain perspective. *Leadership Quarterly, 6*(2), 219–247.

Harris, K. J., Wheeler, A. R., & Kacmar, K. M. (2009). Leader-member exchange and empowerment: Direct and interactive effects on job satisfaction, turnover intentions, and performance. *Leadership Quarterly, 20,* 371–382.

Harter, N., & Evanecky, D. (2002). Fairness in leader–member exchange theory: Do we all belong on the inside? *Leadership Review, 2*(2), 1–7.

Liden, R. C., Wayne, S. J., & Stilwell, D. (1993). A longitudinal study on the early development of leader–member exchange. *Journal of Applied Psychology, 78,* 662–674.

McClane, W. E. (1991). Implications of member role differentiation: Analysis of a key concept in the LMX model of leadership. *Group & Organization Studies, 16*(1), 102–113.

Nahrang, J. D., Morgeson, R. P., & Ilies, R. (2009). The development of leader-member exchanges: Exploring how personality and performance influence leader and member relationships over time. *Organizational Behavior and Human Decision Processes, 108,* 256–266.

Scandura, T. A. (1999). Rethinking leader–member exchange: An organizational justice perspective. *Leadership Quarterly, 10*(1), 25–40.

Schriesheim, C. A., Castro, S. L., & Cogliser, C. C. (1999). Leader–member exchange (LMX) research: A comprehensive review of theory, measurement, and data-analytic practices. *Leadership Quarterly, 10,* 63–113.

Schriesheim, C. A., Castro, S. L., Zhou, X., & Yammarino, F. J. (2001). The folly of theorizing "A" but testing "B": A selective level-of-analysis review of the field and a detailed leader–member exchange illustration. *Leadership Quarterly, 12,* 515–551.

Uhl-Bien, M., Maslyn, J., & Ospina, S. (2012). The nature of relational leadership: A multitheoretical lens on leadership relationships and processes. In D. V. Day & J. Antonakis (Eds.), *The nature of leadership* (2nd ed., pp. 289–330). Thousand Oaks, CA: Sage.

Yukl, G. (1994). *Leadership in organizations* (3rd ed.). Englewood Cliffs, NJ: Prentice Hall.

9

Transformational Leadership

DESCRIPTION

One of the current and most popular approaches to leadership that has been the focus of much research since the early 1980s is the transformational approach. Transformational leadership is part of the "New Leadership" paradigm (Bryman, 1992), which gives more attention to the charismatic and affective elements of leadership. In a content analysis of articles published in *Leadership Quarterly*, Lowe and Gardner (2001) found that one third of the research was about transformational or charismatic leadership. Similarly, Antonakis (2012) found that the number of papers and citations in the field have grown at an increasing rate, not only in traditional fields like management and social psychology, but in other disciplines such as nursing, education, and industrial engineering. Bass and Riggio (2006) suggested that transformational leadership's popularity might be due to its emphasis on intrinsic motivation and follower development, which fits the needs of today's work groups, who want to be inspired and empowered to succeed in times of uncertainty. Clearly, many scholars are studying transformational leadership, and it occupies a central place in leadership research.

As its name implies, transformational leadership is a process that changes and transforms people. It is concerned with emotions, values, ethics, standards, and long-term goals. It includes assessing followers' motives, satisfying their needs, and treating them as full human beings. Transformational leadership involves an exceptional form of influence that moves followers to accomplish more than what is usually expected of them. It is a process that often incorporates charismatic and visionary leadership.

An encompassing approach, transformational leadership can be used to describe a wide range of leadership, from very specific attempts to influence followers on a one-to-one level, to very broad attempts to influence whole organizations and even entire cultures. Although the transformational leader plays a pivotal role in precipitating change, followers and leaders are inextricably bound together in the transformation process.

Transformational Leadership Defined

The term *transformational leadership* was first coined by Downton (1973). Its emergence as an important approach to leadership began with a classic work by political sociologist James MacGregor Burns titled *Leadership* (1978). In his work, Burns attempted to link the roles of leadership and followership. He wrote of leaders as people who tap the motives of followers in order to better reach the goals of leaders and followers (p. 18). For Burns, leadership is quite different from power because it is inseparable from followers' needs.

Burns distinguished between two types of leadership: *transactional* and *transformational.* Transactional leadership refers to the bulk of leadership models, which focus on the exchanges that occur between leaders and their followers. Politicians who win votes by promising "no new taxes" are demonstrating transactional leadership. Similarly, managers who offer promotions to employees who surpass their goals are exhibiting transactional leadership. In the classroom, teachers are being transactional when they give students a grade for work completed. The exchange dimension of transactional leadership is very common and can be observed at many levels throughout all types of organizations.

In contrast to transactional leadership, transformational leadership is the process whereby a person engages with others and creates a connection that raises the level of motivation and morality in both the leader and the follower. This type of leader is attentive to the needs and motives of followers and tries to help followers reach their fullest potential. Burns points to Mohandas Gandhi as a classic example of transformational leadership. Gandhi raised the hopes and demands of millions of his people, and, in the process, was changed himself.

Another good example of transformational leadership can be observed in the life of Ryan White. This teenager raised the American people's awareness about AIDS and in the process became a spokesperson for

9.1 James MacGregor Burns

increasing government support of AIDS research. In the organizational world, an example of transformational leadership would be a manager who attempts to change his or her company's corporate values to reflect a more humane standard of fairness and justice. In the process, both the manager and the followers may emerge with a stronger and higher set of moral values.

Because the conceptualization of transformational leadership set forth by Burns (1978) includes raising the level of morality in others, it is difficult to use this term when describing leaders such as Adolf Hitler and Saddam Hussein, who were transforming but in a negative way. To deal with this problem Bass (1998) coined the term *pseudotransformational leadership*. This term refers to leaders who are self-consumed, exploitive, and power oriented, with warped moral values (Bass & Riggio, 2006). Pseudotransformational leadership is considered personalized leadership, which focuses on the leader's own interests rather than on the interests of others (Bass & Steidlmeier, 1999). Authentic transformational leadership is socialized leadership, which is concerned with the collective good. Socialized transformational leaders transcend their own interests for the sake of others (Howell & Avolio, 1993).

To sort out the complexities related to the "moral uplifting" component of authentic transformational leadership, Zhu, Avolio, Riggio, and Sosik (2011) proposed a theoretical model examining how authentic transformational leadership influences the ethics of individual followers and groups. The authors hypothesize that authentic transformational leadership positively affects followers' moral identities and moral emotions (e.g., empathy and guilt) and this, in turn, leads to moral decision making and moral action by the followers. Furthermore, the authors theorize that authentic transformational leadership is positively associated with group ethical climate, decision making, and moral action. In the future, research is needed to test the validity of the assumptions laid out in this model.

Transformational Leadership and Charisma

At about the same time Burns's book was published, House (1976) published a theory of charismatic leadership. Since its publication, charismatic leadership has received a great deal of attention by researchers (e.g., Conger, 1999; Hunt & Conger, 1999). It is often described in ways that make it similar to, if not synonymous with, transformational leadership.

9.1 Transformational Leadership

The word *charisma* was first used to describe a special gift that certain individuals possess that gives them the capacity to do extraordinary things. Weber (1947) provided the most well-known definition of charisma as a special personality characteristic that gives a person superhuman or exceptional powers and is reserved for a few, is of divine origin, and results in the person being treated as a leader. Despite Weber's emphasis on charisma as a personality characteristic, he also recognized the important role played by followers in validating charisma in these leaders (Bryman, 1992; House, 1976).

In his theory of charismatic leadership, House suggested that charismatic leaders act in unique ways that have specific charismatic effects on their followers (Table 9.1). For House, the personality characteristics of a charismatic leader include being dominant, having a strong desire to influence others, being self-confident, and having a strong sense of one's own moral values.

In addition to displaying certain personality characteristics, charismatic leaders also demonstrate specific types of behaviors. First, they are strong role models for the beliefs and values they want their followers to adopt. For example, Gandhi advocated nonviolence and was an exemplary role model of civil disobedience. Second, charismatic leaders appear competent to followers. Third, they articulate ideological goals that have moral overtones. Martin Luther King, Jr.'s famous "I Have a Dream" speech is an example of this type of charismatic behavior.

Table 9.1   Personality Characteristics, Behaviors, and Effects on Followers of Charismatic Leadership

Personality Characteristics	Behaviors	Effects on Followers
Dominant	Sets strong role model	Trust in leader's ideology
Desire to influence	Shows competence	Belief similarity between leader and follower
Self-confident	Articulates goals	
Strong moral values	Communicates high expectations	Unquestioning acceptance
	Expresses confidence	Affection toward leader
	Arouses motives	Obedience
		Identification with leader
		Emotional involvement
		Heightened goals
		Increased confidence

9.2 Teaching Charisma

Fourth, charismatic leaders communicate high expectations for followers, and they exhibit confidence in followers' abilities to meet these expectations. The impact of this behavior is to increase followers' sense of competence and self-efficacy (Avolio & Gibbons, 1988), which in turn improves their performance.

Fifth, charismatic leaders arouse task-relevant motives in followers that may include affiliation, power, or esteem. For example, former U.S. President John F. Kennedy appealed to the human values of the American people when he stated, "Ask not what your country can do for you; ask what you can do for your country."

According to House's charismatic theory, several effects are the direct result of charismatic leadership. They include follower trust in the leader's ideology, similarity between the followers' beliefs and the leader's beliefs, unquestioning acceptance of the leader, expression of affection toward the leader, follower obedience, identification with the leader, emotional involvement in the leader's goals, heightened goals for followers, and increased follower confidence in goal achievement. Consistent with Weber, House contends that these charismatic effects are more likely to occur in contexts in which followers feel distress because in stressful situations followers look to leaders to deliver them from their difficulties.

House's charismatic theory has been extended and revised through the years (see Conger, 1999; Conger & Kanungo, 1998). One major revision to the theory was made by Shamir, House, and Arthur (1993). They postulated that charismatic leadership transforms followers' self-concepts and tries to link the identity of followers to the collective identity of the organization. Charismatic leaders forge this link by emphasizing the intrinsic rewards of work and deemphasizing the extrinsic rewards. The hope is that followers will view work as an expression of themselves. Throughout the process, leaders express high expectations for followers and help them gain a sense of confidence and self-efficacy. In summary, charismatic leadership works because it ties followers and their self-concepts to the organizational identity.

A Model of Transformational Leadership

In the mid-1980s, Bass (1985) provided a more expanded and refined version of transformational leadership that was based on, but not fully consistent with, the prior works of Burns (1978) and House (1976). In his approach, Bass extended Burns's work by giving more attention to followers' rather than leaders' needs, by suggesting that transformational leadership could apply to situations in which the outcomes were not positive, and by describing transactional and transformational leadership as a single continuum (Figure 9.1) rather than mutually independent continua (Yammarino, 1993). Bass extended House's work by giving more attention to the emotional elements and origins of charisma and by suggesting that charisma is a necessary but not sufficient condition for transformational leadership (Yammarino, 1993).

Figure 9.1   Leadership Continuum From Transformational to Laissez-Faire Leadership

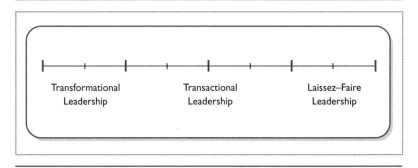

Bass (1985, p. 20) argued that transformational leadership motivates followers to do more than expected by (a) raising followers' levels of consciousness about the importance and value of specified and idealized goals, (b) getting followers to transcend their own self-interest for the sake of the team or organization, and (c) moving followers to address higher-level needs. An elaboration of the dynamics of the transformation process is provided in his model of transformational and transactional leadership (Bass, 1985, 1990; Bass & Avolio, 1993, 1994). Additional clarification of the model is provided by Avolio in his book *Full Leadership Development: Building the Vital Forces in Organizations* (1999).

As can be seen in Table 9.2, the model of transformational and transactional leadership incorporates seven different factors. These factors are also illustrated in the Full Range of Leadership model, which is provided in Figure 9.2 on page 192. A discussion of each of these seven factors will help to clarify Bass's model. This discussion will be divided into three parts: transformational factors (4), transactional factors (2), and the non-leadership, nontransactional factor (1).

9.2 Comparing Leadership Theories

Table 9.2   Leadership Factors

Transformational Leadership	Transactional Leadership	Laissez–Faire Leadership
Factor 1	**Factor 5**	**Factor 7**
Idealized influence	Contingent reward	Laissez–faire
Charisma	Constructive transactions	Nontransactional
Factor 2	**Factor 6**	
Inspirational motivation	Management-by-exception	
Factor 3	Active and passive	
Intellectual stimulation	Corrective transactions	
Factor 4		
Individualized consideration		

Transformational Leadership Factors

Transformational leadership is concerned with improving the performance of followers and developing followers to their fullest potential (Avolio, 1999; Bass & Avolio, 1990a). People who exhibit transformational leadership often have a strong set of internal values and ideals, and they are effective at motivating followers to act in ways that support the greater good rather than their own self-interests (Kuhnert, 1994).

Idealized Influence. Factor 1 is called *charisma* or *idealized influence*. It is the emotional component of leadership (Antonakis, 2012). Idealized influence describes leaders who act as strong role models for followers; followers identify with these leaders and want very much to emulate them. These leaders usually have very high standards of moral and ethical conduct and can be counted on to do the right thing. They are deeply respected by followers, who usually place a great deal of trust in them. They provide followers with a vision and a sense of mission.

The idealized influence factor is measured on two components: an *attributional component* that refers to the attributions of leaders made by followers based on perceptions they have of their leaders, and a *behavioral component* that refers to followers' observations of leader behavior.

▶ **9.1** Transactional vs. Transformational

In essence, the charisma factor describes people who are special and who make others want to follow the vision they put forward. A person whose leadership exemplifies the charisma factor is Nelson Mandela, the first non-White president of South Africa. Mandela is viewed as a leader with high moral standards and a vision for South Africa that resulted in monumental change in how the people of South Africa would be governed. His charismatic qualities and the people's response to them transformed an entire nation.

Figure 9.2   Full Range of Leadership Model

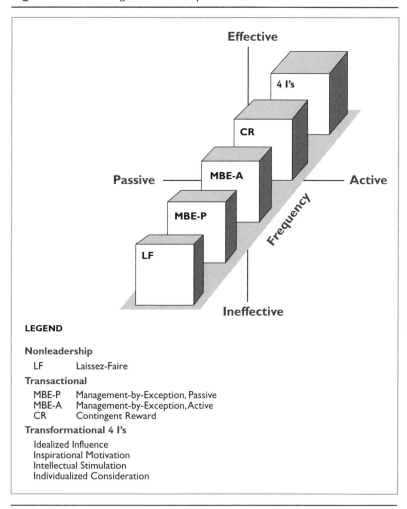

LEGEND

Nonleadership
   LF   Laissez-Faire

Transactional
   MBE-P   Management-by-Exception, Passive
   MBE-A   Management-by-Exception, Active
   CR   Contingent Reward

Transformational 4 I's
   Idealized Influence
   Inspirational Motivation
   Intellectual Stimulation
   Individualized Consideration

SOURCE: From Bass, B. M., & Avolio, B. J., *Improving Organizational Effectiveness Through Transformational Leadership*, © 1994, SAGE Publications, Inc. Reprinted with permission.

9.3 Morals Matter

Inspirational Motivation. Factor 2 is called *inspiration* or *inspirational motivation.* This factor is descriptive of leaders who communicate high expectations to followers, inspiring them through motivation to become committed to and a part of the shared vision in the organization. In practice, leaders use symbols and emotional appeals to focus group members' efforts to achieve more than they would in their own self-interest. Team spirit is enhanced by this type of leadership. An example of this factor would be a sales manager who motivates members of the sales force to excel in their work through encouraging words and pep talks that clearly communicate the integral role they play in the future growth of the company.

Intellectual Stimulation. Factor 3 is *intellectual stimulation.* It includes leadership that stimulates followers to be creative and innovative and to challenge their own beliefs and values as well as those of the leader and the organization.

This type of leadership supports followers as they try new approaches and develop innovative ways of dealing with organizational issues. It encourages followers to think things out on their own and engage in careful problem solving. An example of this type of leadership is a plant manager who promotes workers' individual efforts to develop unique ways to solve problems that have caused slowdowns in production.

Individualized Consideration. Factor 4 of transformational leadership is called *individualized consideration.* This factor is representative of leaders who provide a supportive climate in which they listen carefully to the individual needs of followers. Leaders act as coaches and advisers while trying to assist followers in becoming fully actualized. These leaders may use delegation to help followers grow through personal challenges. An example of this type of leadership is a manager who spends time treating each employee in a caring and unique way. To some employees, the leader may give strong affiliation; to others, the leader may give specific directives with a high degree of structure.

In essence, transformational leadership produces greater effects than transactional leadership (Figure 9.3). Whereas transactional leadership results in expected outcomes, transformational leadership results in performance that goes well beyond what is expected. In a meta-analysis of 39 studies in the transformational literature, for example, Lowe, Kroeck, and Sivasubramaniam (1996) found that people who exhibited transformational leadership were perceived to be more effective leaders with better work outcomes than those who exhibited only transactional leadership. These

9.3 Mother Theresa

Figure 9.3   The Additive Effect of Transformational Leadership

TRANSFORMATIONAL LEADERSHIP

| Idealized Influence | + | Inspirational Motivation | + | Intellectual Stimulation | + | Individualized Consideration |

TRANSACTIONAL LEADERSHIP

Contingent Reward + Management-by-Exception → Expected Outcomes → **Performance Beyond Expectations**

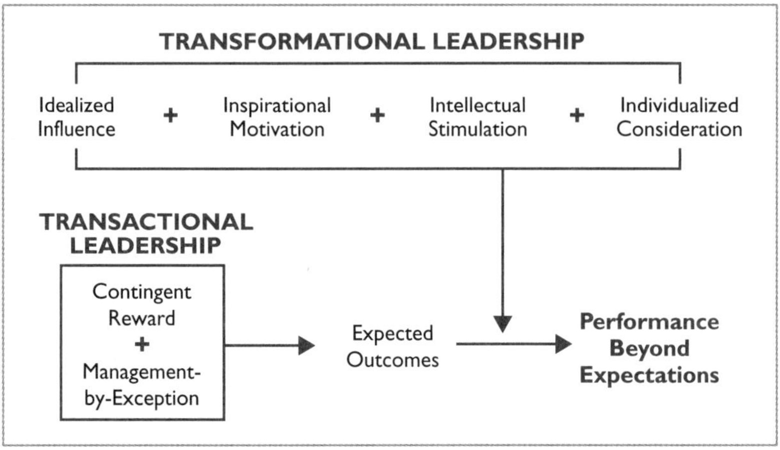

SOURCE: Adapted from "The Implications of Transactional and Transformational Leadership for Individual, Team, and Organizational Development," by B. M. Bass and B. J. Avolio, 1990a, *Research in Organizational Change and Development, 4,* 231–272.

findings were true for higher- and lower-level leaders, and for leaders in both public and private settings. Transformational leadership moves followers to accomplish more than what is usually expected of them. They become motivated to transcend their own self-interests for the good of the group or organization (Bass & Avolio, 1990a).

In a study of 220 employees at a large public transport company in Germany, Rowold and Heinitz (2007) found that transformational leadership augmented the impact of transactional leadership on employees' performance and company profit. In addition, they found that transformational leadership and charismatic leadership were overlapping but unique constructs, and that both were different from transactional leadership.

Similarly, Nemanich and Keller (2007) examined the impact of transformational leadership on 447 employees from a large multinational firm who were going through a merger and being integrated into a new organization. They found that transformational leadership behaviors such as idealized influence, inspirational motivation, individualized consideration, and intellectual stimulation were positively related to acquisition acceptance, job satisfaction, and performance.

9.2 The Additive Effect

More recently, Tims, Bakker, and Xanthopoulou (2011) examined the relationship between transformational leadership and work engagement in 42 employees and their supervisors in two different organizations in The Netherlands. Findings revealed that employees became more engaged in their work (i.e., vigor, dedication, and absorption) when their supervisors were able to boost subordinates' optimism through a transformational leadership style. These findings underscore the important role played by personal characteristics (i.e., optimism) in the transformational leadership-performance process.

Transactional Leadership Factors

Transactional leadership differs from transformational leadership in that the transactional leader does not individualize the needs of subordinates or focus on their personal development. Transactional leaders exchange things of value with subordinates to advance their own and their subordinates' agendas (Kuhnert, 1994). Transactional leaders are influential because it is in the best interest of subordinates for them to do what the leader wants (Kuhnert & Lewis, 1987).

Contingent Reward. Factor 5, *contingent reward*, is the first of two transactional leadership factors (see Figure 9.2). It is an exchange process between leaders and followers in which effort by followers is exchanged for specified rewards. With this kind of leadership, the leader tries to obtain agreement from followers on what must be done and what the payoffs will be for the people doing it. An example of this type of transaction is a parent who negotiates with a child about how much television the child can watch after practicing the piano. Another example often occurs in the academic setting: A dean negotiates with a college professor about the number and quality of publications he or she needs to have written in order to receive tenure and promotion.

Management-by-Exception. Factor 6 is called *management-by-exception*. It is leadership that involves corrective criticism, negative feedback, and negative reinforcement. Management-by-exception takes two forms: active and passive. A leader using the active form of management-by-exception watches followers closely for mistakes or rule violations and then takes corrective action. An example of active management-by-exception can be illustrated in the leadership of a sales supervisor who daily monitors how employees approach customers. She quickly corrects salespeople who are slow to approach customers in the prescribed manner. A leader using the passive form intervenes only after standards have not been met or problems have arisen. An example of passive management-by-exception is illustrated in the leadership of a supervisor who gives an employee a poor performance evaluation without ever talking with the employee about her or his prior work performance. In essence, both the active and passive management types use more negative reinforcement patterns than the positive reinforcement pattern described in Factor 5 under contingent reward.

Nonleadership Factor

In the model, the nonleadership factor diverges farther from transactional leadership and represents behaviors that are nontransactional.

Laissez-Faire. Factor 7 describes leadership that falls at the far right side of the transactional–transformational leadership continuum (see Figure 9.1). This factor represents the absence of leadership. As the French phrase implies, the *laissez-faire* leader takes a "hands-off, let-things-ride" approach. This leader abdicates responsibility, delays decisions, gives no feedback, and makes little effort to help followers satisfy their needs. There is no exchange with followers or attempt to help them grow. An example of a laissez-faire leader is the president of a small manufacturing firm who calls no meetings with plant supervisors, has no long-range plan for the firm, and makes little contact with employees.

Other Transformational Perspectives

In addition to Bass's (1985, 1990; Bass & Avolio, 1994) work, two other lines of research have contributed in unique ways to our understanding of the nature of transformational leadership. They are the research of Bennis and Nanus (1985) and the work of Kouzes and Posner (1987, 2002). These scholars used similar research methods. They identified a number of middle- or senior-level leaders and conducted interviews with them, using open-ended, semistructured questionnaires. From this information, they constructed their models of leadership.

Bennis and Nanus

Bennis and Nanus (1985) asked 90 leaders basic questions such as "What are your strengths and weaknesses?" "What past events most influenced your

9.4 Philanthropic Leadership

leadership approach?" and "What were the critical points in your career?" From the answers leaders provided to these questions, Bennis and Nanus identified four common strategies used by leaders in transforming organizations.

First, transforming leaders had a clear *vision* of the future state of their organizations. It was an image of an attractive, realistic, and believable future (Bennis & Nanus, 1985, p. 89). The vision usually was simple, understandable, beneficial, and energy creating. The compelling nature of the vision touched the experiences of followers and pulled them into supporting the organization. When an organization has a clear vision, it is easier for people within the organization to learn how they fit in with the overall direction of the organization and even the society in general. It empowers them because they feel they are a significant dimension of a worthwhile enterprise (pp. 90–91). Bennis and Nanus found that, to be successful, the vision had to grow out of the needs of the entire organization and to be claimed by those within it. Although leaders play a large role in articulating the vision, the emergence of the vision originates from both the leaders and the followers.

Second, transforming leaders were *social architects* for their organizations. This means they created a shape or form for the shared meanings people maintained within their organizations. These leaders communicated a direction that transformed their organization's values and norms. In many cases, these leaders were able to mobilize people to accept a new group identity or a new philosophy for their organizations.

Third, transforming leaders created *trust* in their organizations by making their own positions clearly known and then standing by them. Trust has to do with being predictable or reliable, even in situations that are uncertain. For organizations, leaders built trust by articulating a direction and then consistently implementing the direction even though the vision may have involved a high degree of uncertainty. Bennis and Nanus (1985) found that when leaders established trust in an organization, it gave the organization a sense of integrity analogous to a healthy identity (p. 48).

Fourth, transforming leaders used *creative deployment of self* through positive self-regard. Leaders knew their strengths and weaknesses, and they emphasized their strengths rather than dwelling on their weaknesses. Based on an awareness of their own competence, effective leaders were able to immerse themselves in their tasks and the overarching goals of their organizations. They were able to fuse a sense of self with the work at hand.

Bennis and Nanus also found that positive self-regard in leaders had a reciprocal impact on followers, creating in them feelings of confidence and high expectations. In addition, leaders in the study were committed to learning and relearning, so in their organizations there was consistent emphasis on education.

Kouzes and Posner

Kouzes and Posner (1987, 2002) developed their model by interviewing leaders about leadership. They interviewed more than 1,300 middle- and senior-level managers in private and public sector organizations and asked them to describe their "personal best" experiences as leaders. Based on a content analysis of these descriptions, Kouzes and Posner constructed a model of leadership.

The Kouzes and Posner model consists of five fundamental *practices* that enable leaders to get extraordinary things accomplished: model the way, inspire a shared vision, challenge the process, enable others to act, and encourage the heart. For each of the five practices of exemplary leadership, Kouzes and Posner also have identified two commitments that serve as strategies for practicing exemplary leadership.

Model the Way. To model the way, leaders need to be clear about their own values and philosophy. They need to find their own voice and express it to others. Exemplary leaders set a personal example for others by their own behaviors. They also follow through on their promises and commitments and affirm the common values they share with others.

Inspire a Shared Vision. Effective leaders create compelling visions that can guide people's behavior. They are able to visualize positive outcomes in the future and communicate them to others. Leaders also listen to the dreams of others and show them how their dreams can be realized. Through inspiring visions, leaders challenge others to transcend the status quo to do something for others.

Challenge the Process. Challenging the process means being willing to change the status quo and step into the unknown. It includes being willing to innovate, grow, and improve. Exemplary leaders are like pioneers: They want to experiment and try new things. They are willing to take risks to make things better. When exemplary leaders take risks, they do it one step at a time, learning from their mistakes as they go.

Enable Others to Act. Outstanding leaders are effective at working with people. They build trust with others and promote collaboration. Teamwork and cooperation are highly valued by these leaders. They listen closely to diverse points of view and treat others with dignity and respect. They also allow others to make choices, and they support the decisions that others make. In short, they create environments where people can feel good about their work and how it contributes to the greater community.

Encourage the Heart. Leaders encourage the heart by rewarding others for their accomplishments. It is natural for people to want support and to be recognized. Effective leaders are attentive to this need and are willing to give praise to workers for jobs well done. They use authentic celebrations and rituals to show appreciation and encouragement to others. The outcome of this kind of support is greater collective identity and community spirit.

Overall, the Kouzes and Posner model emphasizes behaviors and has a prescriptive quality: It recommends what people need to do in order to become effective leaders. The five practices and their accompanying commitments provide a unique set of prescriptions for leaders. Kouzes and Posner (2002, p. 13) stressed that the five practices of exemplary leadership are available to everyone and are not reserved for those with "special" ability. The model is not about personality: It is about practice.

To measure the behaviors described in the model, Kouzes and Posner developed the Leadership Practices Inventory (LPI). The LPI is a 360-degree leadership assessment tool that consists of 30 questions that assess individual leadership competencies. It has been widely used in leadership training and development.

HOW DOES THE TRANSFORMATIONAL APPROACH WORK?

The transformational approach to leadership is a broad-based perspective that encompasses many facets and dimensions of the leadership process. In general, it describes how leaders can initiate, develop, and carry out significant changes in organizations. Although not definitive, the steps followed by transformational leaders usually take the following form.

Transformational leaders set out to empower followers and nurture them in change. They attempt to raise the consciousness in individuals and to get them to transcend their own self-interests for the sake of others.

For example, Jung, Chow, and Wu (2003) studied upper-level leadership in 32 Taiwanese companies and found that transformational leadership was directly related to organizational innovation. Transformational leadership created a culture in which employees felt empowered and encouraged to freely discuss and try new things.

To create change, transformational leaders become strong role models for their followers. They have a highly developed set of moral values and a self-determined sense of identity (Avolio & Gibbons, 1988). They are confident, competent, and articulate, and they express strong ideals. They listen to followers and are not intolerant of opposing viewpoints. A spirit of cooperation often develops between these leaders and their followers. Followers want to emulate transformational leaders because they learn to trust them and believe in the ideas for which they stand.

It is common for transformational leaders to create a vision. The vision emerges from the collective interests of various individuals and units in an organization. The vision is a focal point for transformational leadership. It gives the leader and the organization a conceptual map for where the organization is headed; it gives meaning and clarifies the organization's identity. Furthermore, the vision gives followers a sense of identity within the organization and also a sense of self-efficacy (Shamir et al., 1993).

The transformational approach also requires that leaders become social architects. This means that they make clear the emerging values and norms of the organization. They involve themselves in the culture of the organization and help shape its meaning. People need to know their roles and understand how they contribute to the greater purposes of the organization. Transformational leaders are out front in interpreting and shaping for organizations the shared meanings that exist within them.

Throughout the process, transformational leaders are effective at working with people. They build trust and foster collaboration with others. Transformational leaders encourage others and celebrate their accomplishments. In the end, transformational leadership results in people feeling better about themselves and their contributions to the greater common good.

STRENGTHS

In its present stage of development, the transformational approach has several strengths. First, transformational leadership has been widely researched from many different perspectives, including a series of qualitative studies of prominent leaders and chief executive officers (CEOs) in large, well-known organizations. It has also been the focal point for a large body of leadership research since its introduction in the 1970s. For example, content analysis of all the articles published in *Leadership Quarterly* from 1990 to 2000 showed that 34% of the articles were about transformational or charismatic leadership (Lowe & Gardner, 2001).

Second, transformational leadership has intuitive appeal. The transformational perspective describes how the leader is out front advocating change for others; this concept is consistent with society's popular notion of what leadership means. People are attracted to transformational leadership because it makes sense to them. It is appealing that a leader will provide a vision for the future.

Third, transformational leadership treats leadership as a process that occurs between followers and leaders. Because this process incorporates both the followers' and the leader's needs, leadership is not the sole responsibility of a leader but rather emerges from the interplay between leaders and followers. The needs of others are central to the transformational leader. As a result, followers gain a more prominent position in the leadership process because their attributions are instrumental in the evolving transformational process (Bryman, 1992, p. 176).

Fourth, the transformational approach provides a broader view of leadership that augments other leadership models. Many leadership models focus primarily on how leaders exchange rewards for achieved goals—the transactional process. The transformational approach provides an expanded picture of leadership that includes not only the exchange of rewards, but also leaders' attention to the needs and growth of followers (Avolio, 1999; Bass, 1985).

Fifth, transformational leadership places a strong emphasis on followers' needs, values, and morals. Burns (1978) suggested that transformational leadership involves attempts by leaders to move people to higher standards of moral responsibility. It includes motivating followers to transcend their own self-interests for the good of the team, organization, or community (Howell & Avolio, 1993; Shamir et al., 1993). Transformational leadership is fundamentally morally uplifting (Avolio, 1999). This emphasis sets the transformational approach apart from all other approaches to leadership because it suggests that leadership has a moral dimension. Therefore, the coercive uses of power by people such as Hitler, Jim Jones, and David Koresh can be disregarded as models of leadership.

▶ 9.3 Inspiring Leaders

Finally, there is substantial evidence that transformational leadership is an effective form of leadership (Yukl, 1999). In a critique of transformational and charismatic leadership, Yukl reported that in studies using the Multifactor Leadership Questionnaire (MLQ) to appraise leaders, transformational leadership was positively related to subordinate satisfaction, motivation, and performance. Furthermore, in studies that used interviews and observations, transformational leadership was shown to be effective in a variety of different situations.

CRITICISMS

Transformational leadership has several weaknesses. One criticism is that it lacks conceptual clarity. Because it covers such a wide range of activities and characteristics—including creating a vision, motivating, being a change agent, building trust, giving nurturance, and acting as a social architect, to name a few—it is difficult to define exactly the parameters of transformational leadership. Specifically, research by Tracey and Hinkin (1998) has shown substantial overlap between each of the Four I's (idealized influence, inspirational motivation, intellectual stimulation, and individualized consideration), suggesting that the dimensions are not clearly delimited. Furthermore, the parameters of transformational leadership often overlap with similar conceptualizations of leadership. Bryman (1992), for example, pointed out that transformational and charismatic leadership often are treated synonymously, even though in some models of leadership (e.g., Bass, 1985) charisma is only one component of transformational leadership.

Another criticism revolves around how transformational leadership is measured. Researchers typically have used some version of the MLQ to measure transformational leadership. However, some studies have challenged the validity of the MLQ. In some versions of the MLQ, the four factors of transformational leadership (the Four I's: idealized influence, inspirational motivation, intellectual stimulation, and individualized consideration) correlate highly with each other, which means they are not distinct factors (Tejeda, Scandura, & Pillai, 2001). In addition, some of the transformational factors correlate with the transactional and laissez-faire factors, which means they may not be unique to the transformational model (Tejeda et al., 2001).

A third criticism is that transformational leadership treats leadership as a personality trait or personal predisposition rather than a behavior that people can learn (Bryman, 1992, pp. 100–102). If it is a trait, training people in this approach becomes more problematic because it is difficult to teach people how to change their traits. Even though many scholars, including Weber, House, and Bass, emphasized that transformational leadership is concerned with leader behaviors, such as how leaders involve themselves with followers, there is an inclination to see this approach from a trait perspective. Perhaps this problem is exacerbated because the word *transformational* creates images of one person being the most active component in the leadership process. For example, even though "creating a vision" involves follower input, there is a tendency to see transformational leaders as visionaries. There is also a tendency to see transformational leaders as people who have special qualities that *transform* others. These images accentuate a trait characterization of transformational leadership.

Fourth, researchers have not established that transformational leaders are actually able to transform individuals and organizations (Antonakis, 2012). There is evidence that indicates that transformational leadership is associated with positive outcomes, such as organizational effectiveness; however, studies have not yet clearly established a causal link between transformational leaders and changes in followers or organizations.

A fifth criticism some have made is that transformational leadership is elitist and antidemocratic (Avolio, 1999; Bass & Avolio, 1993). Transformational leaders often play a direct role in creating changes, establishing a vision, and advocating new directions. This gives the strong impression that the leader is acting independently of followers or putting himself or herself above the followers' needs. Although this criticism of elitism has been refuted by Bass and Avolio (1993) and Avolio (1999), who contended that transformational leaders can be directive and participative as well as democratic and authoritarian, the substance of the criticism raises valid questions about transformational leadership.

Related to this criticism, some have argued that transformational leadership suffers from a "heroic leadership" bias (Yukl, 1999). Transformational leadership stresses that it is the *leader* who moves *followers* to do exceptional things. By focusing primarily on the leader, researchers have failed to give attention to shared leadership or reciprocal influence. Followers can influence leaders just as leaders can influence followers. More attention should be directed toward how leaders can encourage followers to challenge the leader's vision and share in the leadership process.

A final criticism of transformational leadership is that it has the potential to be abused. Transformational leadership is concerned with changing people's values and moving them to a new vision. But who is to determine whether the new directions are good and more affirming? Who decides that a new vision is a better vision? If the values to which the leader is moving his or her followers are not better, and if the set of human values is not more redeeming, then the leadership must be challenged. However, the dynamics of how followers challenge leaders or respond to their visions is not fully understood.

There is a need to understand how transformational leaders affect followers psychologically and how leaders respond to followers' reactions. In fact, Burns argued that understanding this area (i.e., charisma and follower worship) is one of the central problems in leadership studies today (Bailey & Axelrod, 2001). The charismatic nature of transformational leadership presents significant risks for organizations because it can be used for destructive purposes (Conger, 1999; Howell & Avolio, 1993).

History is full of examples of charismatic individuals who used coercive power to lead people to evil ends. For this reason, transformational leadership puts a burden on individuals and organizations to be aware of how they are being influenced and in what directions they are being asked to go.

APPLICATION

Rather than being a model that tells leaders what to do, transformational leadership provides a broad set of generalizations of what is typical of leaders who are transforming or who work in transforming contexts. Unlike other leadership approaches, such as contingency theory and situational leadership, transformational leadership does not provide a clearly defined set of assumptions about how leaders should act in a particular situation to be successful. Rather, it provides a general way of thinking about leadership that emphasizes ideals, inspiration, innovations, and individual concerns. Transformational leadership requires that leaders be aware of how their own behavior relates to the needs of their subordinates and the changing dynamics within their organizations.

Bass and Avolio (1990a) suggested that transformational leadership can be taught to people at all levels in an organization and that it can positively affect a firm's performance. It can be used in recruitment, selection and promotion, and training and development. It can also be used in improving team development, decision-making groups, quality initiatives, and reorganizations (Bass & Avolio, 1994).

Programs designed to develop transformational leadership usually require that leaders or their associates take the MLQ (Bass & Avolio, 1990b) or a similar questionnaire to determine the leader's particular strengths and weaknesses in transformational leadership. Taking the MLQ helps leaders pinpoint areas in which they could improve their leadership. For example, leaders might learn that it would be beneficial if they were more confident in expressing their goals, or that they need to spend more time nurturing followers, or that they need to be more tolerant of opposing viewpoints. The MLQ is the springboard to helping leaders improve a whole series of their leadership attributes.

One particular aspect of transformational leadership that has been given special emphasis in training programs is the process of building a vision. For example, it has become quite common for training programs to have leaders write elaborate statements that describe their own five-year career plans and their perceptions of the future directions for their organizations. Working with leaders on vision statements is one way to help them enhance their transformational leadership behavior. Another important aspect of training is teaching leaders to exhibit greater individual consideration and promote intellectual stimulation for their followers. Lowe et al. (1996) found that this is particularly valuable for lower-level leaders in organizations.

The desire to provide effective training in how to be more successful in demonstrating transactional and transformational leadership resulted in the development of a guide by Sosik and Jung (2010). This comprehensive, evidence-based approach includes self-assessments, 360-degree feedback, and leadership development planning. Their work serves as a thorough training guide that explains how, when, and why the full range of leadership behaviors work.

Overall, transformational leadership provides leaders with information about a full range of their behaviors, from nontransactional to transactional to transformational. In the next section, we provide some actual leadership examples to which the principles of transformational leadership can be applied.

CASE STUDIES

In the following section, three brief case studies (Cases 9.1, 9.2, and 9.3) from very different contexts are provided. Each case describes a situation in which transformational leadership is present to some degree. The questions at the end of each case point to some of the unique issues surrounding the use of transformational leadership in ongoing organizations.

CASE 9.1

The Vision Failed

High Tech Engineering (HTE) is a 50-year-old family-owned manufacturing company with 250 employees that produces small parts for the aircraft industry. The president of HTE is Harold Barelli, who came to the company from a smaller business with strong credentials as a leader in advanced aircraft technology. Before Harold, the only other president of HTE was the founder and owner of the company. The organizational structure at HTE was very traditional, and it was supported by a very rich organizational culture.

As the new president, Harold sincerely wanted to transform HTE. He wanted to prove that new technologies and advanced management techniques could make HTE one of the best manufacturing companies in the country. To that end, Harold created a vision statement that was displayed throughout the company. The two-page statement, which had a strong democratic tone, described the overall purposes, directions, and values of the company.

During the first 3 years of Harold's tenure as president, several major reorganizations took place at the company. These were designed by Harold and a select few of his senior managers. The intention of each reorganization was to implement advanced organizational structures to bolster the declared HTE vision.

Yet the major outcome of each of the changes was to dilute the leadership and create a feeling of instability among the employees. Most of the changes were made from the top down, with little input from lower or middle management. Some of the changes gave employees more control in circumstances where they needed less, whereas other changes limited employee input in contexts where employees should have been given more input. There were some situations in which individual workers reported to three different bosses, and other situations in which one manager had far too many workers to oversee. Rather than feeling comfortable in their various roles at HTE, employees began to feel uncertain about their responsibilities and how they contributed to stated goals of the company. The overall effect of the reorganizations was a precipitous drop in worker morale and production.

In the midst of all the changes, the vision that Harold had for the company was lost. The instability that employees felt made it difficult for them to support the company's vision. People at HTE complained that although mission statements were displayed throughout the company, no one understood in which direction they were going.

To the employees at HTE, Harold was an enigma. HTE was an American company that produced U.S. products, but Harold drove a foreign car. Harold claimed to be democratic in his style of leadership, but he was arbitrary in how he treated people. He acted in a nondirective style toward some people, and he showed arbitrary control toward others. He wanted to be seen as a hands-on manager, but he delegated operational control of the company to others while he focused on external customer relations and matters of the board of directors.

At times Harold appeared to be insensitive to employees' concerns. He wanted HTE to be an environment in which everyone could feel empowered, but he often failed to listen closely to what employees were saying.

He seldom engaged in open, two-way communication. HTE had a long, rich history with many unique stories, but the employees felt that Harold either misunderstood or did not care about that history.

Four years after arriving at HTE, Harold stepped down as president after his operations officer ran the company into a large debt and cash-flow crisis. His dream of building HTE into a world-class manufacturing company was never realized.

Questions

1. If you were consulting with the HTE board of directors soon after Harold started making changes, what would you advise them regarding Harold's leadership from a transformational perspective?

2. Did Harold have a clear vision for HTE? Was he able to implement it?

3. How effective was Harold as a change agent and social architect for HTE?

4. What would you advise Harold to do differently if he had the chance to return as president of HTE?

CASE 9.2

An Exploration in Leadership

Every year, Dr. Cook, a college professor, leads a group of 25 college students to the Middle East on an archaeological dig that usually lasts about 8 weeks. The participants, who come from big and small colleges

(Continued)

(Continued)

throughout the country, usually have little prior knowledge or background in what takes place during an excavation. Dr. Cook enjoys leading these expeditions because he likes teaching students about archaeology and because the outcomes of the digs actually advance his own scholarly work.

While planning for his annual summer excavation, Dr. Cook told the following story:

This summer will be interesting because I have 10 people returning from last year. Last year was quite a dig. During the first couple of weeks everything was very disjointed. Team members seemed unmotivated and tired. In fact, there was one time early on when it seemed as if nearly half the students were either physically ill or mentally exhausted. Students seemed lost and uncertain about the meaning of the entire project.

For example, it is our tradition to get up every morning at 4:30 a.m. to depart for the excavation site at 5:00 a.m. However, during the first weeks of the dig, few people were ever ready at 5, even after several reminders.

Every year it takes some time for people to learn where they fit with each other and with the purposes of the dig. The students all come from such different backgrounds. Some are from small, private, religious schools, and others are from large state universities. Each comes with a different agenda, different skills, and different work habits. One person may be a good photographer, another a good artist, and another a good surveyor. It is my job to complete the excavation with the resources available to us.

At the end of Week 2, I called a meeting to assess how things were going. We talked about a lot of things including personal things, how our work was progressing, and what we needed to change. The students seemed to appreciate the chance to talk at this meeting. Each of them described his or her special circumstances and hopes for the summer.

I told the students several stories about past digs; some were humorous, and others highlighted accomplishments. I shared my particular interests in this project and how I thought we as a group could accomplish the work that needed to be done at this important historical site. In particular, I stressed two points: (a) that they shared the responsibility for the successful outcome of the venture, and (b) that they had independent authority to design, schedule, and carry out the details of their respective assignments, with the director and other senior staff available at all times as advisers and resource persons. In regard to the departure time issue, I told the participants that the standard departure time on digs was 5:00 a.m.

Well, shortly after our meeting I observed a real shift in the group attitude and atmosphere. People seemed to become more involved in the work, there was less sickness, and there was more camaraderie. All assignments were completed without constant prodding and in a spirit of mutual support. Each morning at 5:00 a.m. everyone was ready to go.

I find that each year my groups are different. It's almost as if each of them has a unique personality. Perhaps that is why I find it so challenging. I try to listen to the students and use their particular strengths. It really is quite amazing how these students can develop in 8 weeks. They really become good at archaeology, and they accomplish a great deal.

This coming year will again be different because of the 10 returning "veterans."

Questions

1. How is this an example of transformational leadership?

2. Where are Dr. Cook's strengths on the Full Range of Leadership model (see Figure 9.2)?

3. What is the vision Dr. Cook has for the archaeology excavations?

CASE 9.3

Her Vision of a Model Research Center

Rachel Adams began as a researcher at a large pharmaceutical company. After several years of observing how clinical drug studies were conducted, she realized that there was a need and an opportunity for a research center not connected with a specific pharmaceutical company. In collaboration with other researchers, she launched a new company that was the first of its kind in the country. Within 5 years, Rachel had become president and CEO of the Independent Center for Clinical Research (ICCR). Under Rachel's leadership, ICCR has grown to a company with revenues of $6 million and profits of $1 million. ICCR employs 100 full-time employees, most of whom are women.

(Continued)

(Continued)

Rachel wants ICCR to continue its pattern of formidable growth. Her vision for the company is to make it a model research center that will blend credible science with efficient and cost-effective clinical trials. To that end, the company, which is situated in a large urban setting, maintains strong links to academia, industry, and the community.

Rachel and her style have a great deal to do with the success of ICCR. She is a freethinker who is always open to new ideas, opportunities, and approaches. She is a positive person who enjoys the nuances of life, and she is not afraid to take risks. Her optimistic approach has had a significant influence on the company's achievements and its organizational climate. People employed at ICCR claim they have never worked at a place that is so progressive and so positive in how it treats its employees and customers. The women employees at ICCR feel particularly strongly about Rachel's leadership, and many of them use Rachel as a role model. It is not by accident that the majority (85%) of the people who work at ICCR are women. Her support for women's concerns is evident in the type of drug studies the company selects to conduct and in her service to national committees on women's health and research issues. Within ICCR, Rachel has designed an on-site day care program, flextime scheduling for mothers with young children, and a benefit package that gives full health coverage to part-time employees. At a time when most companies are searching for ways to include more women in decision making, ICCR has women in established leadership positions at all levels.

Although Rachel has been extremely effective at ICCR, the success of the company has resulted in many changes that have affected Rachel's leadership at the company.

Rapid growth of ICCR has required that Rachel spend a great deal of time traveling throughout the country. Because of her excessive travel, Rachel has begun to feel distant from the day-to-day operations of ICCR. She has begun to feel as if she is losing her handle on what makes the company tick. For example, although she used to give weekly pep talks to supervisors, she finds that she now gives two formal presentations a year. Rachel also complains of feeling estranged from employees at the company. At a recent directors' meeting, she expressed frustration that people no longer called her by her first name, and others did not even know who she was.

Growth at ICCR has also demanded that more planning and decision making be delegated to department heads. This has been problematic for

Rachel, particularly in the area of strategic planning. Rachel finds that the department heads are beginning to shift the focus of ICCR in a direction that contradicts her ideal model of what the company should be and what it is best at doing. Rachel built the company on the idea that ICCR would be a strong blend of credible science and cost-effective clinical trials, and she does not want to give up that model. The directors, on the other hand, would like to see ICCR become similar to a standard pharmaceutical company dedicated primarily to the research and development of new drugs.

Questions

1. What is it about Rachel's leadership that clearly suggests that she is engaged in transformational leadership?

2. In what ways has the growth of ICCR had an impact on Rachel's leadership?

3. Given the problems Rachel is confronting as a result of the growth of the company, what should she do to reestablish herself as a transformational leader at ICCR?

LEADERSHIP INSTRUMENT

The most widely used measure of transformational leadership is the Multifactor Leadership Questionnaire (MLQ). An earlier version of the MLQ was developed by Bass (1985), based on a series of interviews he and his associates conducted with 70 senior executives in South Africa. These executives were asked to recall leaders who had raised their awareness to broader goals, moved them to higher motives, or inspired them to put others' interests ahead of their own. The executives were then asked to describe how these leaders behaved—what they did to effect change. From these descriptions and from numerous other interviews with both junior and senior executives, Bass constructed the questions that make up the MLQ. The questions measure followers' perceptions of a leader's behavior for each of the factors in the Full Range of Leadership model (see Figure 9.2).

Antonakis, Avolio, and Sivasubramaniam (2003) assessed the psychometric properties of the MLQ using a business sample of more than 3,000 raters and found strong support for the validity of the MLQ. They found that the MLQ (Form 5X) clearly distinguished nine factors in the Full

Range of Leadership model. Similarly, Hinkin and Schriesheim (2008) examined the empirical properties of the transactional and the nonleadership factors on the MLQ and identified several ways to use the questionnaire to generate more reliable and valid results. Since the MLQ was first designed, it has gone through many revisions, and it continues to be refined to strengthen its reliability and validity.

Based on a summary analysis of a series of studies that used the MLQ to predict how transformational leadership relates to outcomes such as effectiveness, Bryman (1992) and Bass and Avolio (1994) have suggested that the charisma and motivation factors on the MLQ are the most likely to be related to positive effects. Individualized consideration, intellectual stimulation, and contingent reward are the next most important factors. Management-by-exception in its passive form has been found to be somewhat related to outcomes, and in its active form it has been found to be negatively related to outcomes. Generally, laissez-faire leadership has been found to be negatively related to outcomes such as effectiveness and satisfaction in organizations.

We present sample items from the MLQ (Form 5X-short) in this section so that you can explore your beliefs and perceptions about transformational, transactional, and nontransactional leadership. This questionnaire should give you a clearer picture of your own style and the complexity of transformational leadership itself.

Sample Items From the Multifactor
Leadership Questionnaire (MLQ) Form 5X-Short

These questions provide examples of the items that are used to evaluate leadership style. The MLQ is provided in both Self and Rater forms. The Self form measures self-perception of leadership behaviors. The Rater form is used to measure leadership. By thinking about the leadership styles as exemplified below, you can get a sense of your own belief about your leadership.

Key: 0 = Not   1 = Once in   2 = Sometimes   3 = Fairly   4 = Frequently,
       at all   a while   often   if not always

Transformational Leadership Styles

Idealized Influence (Attributes)	I go beyond self-interest for the good of the group.	0 1 2 3 4
Idealized Influence (Behaviors)	I consider the moral and ethical consequences of decisions.	0 1 2 3 4
Inspirational Motivation	I talk optimistically about the future.	0 1 2 3 4
Intellectual Stimulation	I reexamine critical assumptions to question whether they are appropriate.	0 1 2 3 4
Individualized Consideration	I help others to develop their strengths.	0 1 2 3 4

Transactional Leadership Styles

Contingent Reward	I make clear what one can expect to receive when performance goals are achieved.	0 1 2 3 4
Management by Exception: Active	I keep track of all mistakes.	0 1 2 3 4

Passive/Avoidant Leadership Styles

Management by Exception: Passive	I wait for things to go wrong before taking action.	0 1 2 3 4
Laissez-Faire	I avoid making decisions.	0 1 2 3 4

SUMMARY

One of the most encompassing approaches to leadership—transformational leadership—is concerned with the process of how certain leaders are able to inspire followers to accomplish great things. This approach stresses that leaders need to understand and adapt to the needs and motives of followers. Transformational leaders are recognized as change agents who are good role models, who can create and articulate a clear vision for an organization, who empower followers to meet higher standards, who act in ways that make others want to trust them, and who give meaning to organizational life.

Transformational leadership emerged from and is rooted in the writings of Burns (1978) and Bass (1985). The works of Bennis and Nanus (1985) and Kouzes and Posner (1987) are also representative of transformational leadership.

Transformational leadership can be assessed through use of the Multifactor Leadership Questionnaire (MLQ), which measures a leader's behavior in seven areas: idealized influence (charisma), inspirational motivation, intellectual stimulation, individualized consideration, contingent reward, management-by-exception, and laissez-faire. High scores on individualized consideration and motivation factors are most indicative of strong transformational leadership.

There are several positive features of the transformational approach, including that it is a current model that has received a lot of attention by researchers, it has strong intuitive appeal, it emphasizes the importance of followers in the leadership process, it goes beyond traditional transactional models and broadens leadership to include the growth of followers, and it places strong emphasis on morals and values.

Balancing against the positive features of transformational leadership are several weaknesses. These include that the approach lacks conceptual clarity; it is based on the MLQ, which has been challenged by some research; it creates a framework that implies that transformational leadership has a trait-like quality; it is sometimes seen as elitist and undemocratic; it suffers from a "heroic leadership" bias; and it has the potential to be used counterproductively in negative ways by leaders. Despite the weaknesses, transformational leadership appears to be a valuable and widely used approach.

▶ **9.4** Chapter Summary

Visit the Student Study Site at **www.sagepub.com/northouse6e** for web quizzes, leadership questionnaires, and media links represented by the icons.

REFERENCES

Antonakis, J. (2012). Transformational and charismatic leadership. In D. V. Day & J. Antonakis (Eds.), *The nature of leadership* (2nd ed., pp. 256–288). Thousand Oaks, CA: Sage.

Antonakis, J., Avolio, B. J., & Sivasubramaniam, N. (2003). Context and leadership: An examination of the nine-factor full-range leadership theory using the Multifactor Leadership Questionnaire. *Leadership Quarterly, 14*(3), 261–295.

Avolio, B. J. (1999). *Full leadership development: Building the vital forces in organizations.* Thousand Oaks, CA: Sage.

Avolio, B. J., & Gibbons, T. C. (1988). Developing transformational leaders: A life span approach. In J. A. Conger, R. N. Kanungo, & Associates (Eds.), *Charismatic leadership: The elusive factor in organizational effectiveness* (pp. 276–308). San Francisco: Jossey-Bass.

Bailey, J., & Axelrod, R. H. (2001). Leadership lessons from Mount Rushmore: An interview with James MacGregor Burns. *Leadership Quarterly, 12*, 113–127.

Bass, B. M. (1985). *Leadership and performance beyond expectations.* New York: Free Press.

Bass, B. M. (1990). From transactional to transformational leadership: Learning to share the vision. *Organizational Dynamics, 18*, 19–31.

Bass, B. M. (1998). The ethics of transformational leadership. In J. Ciulla (Ed.), *Ethics: The heart of leadership* (pp. 169–192). Westport, CT: Praeger.

Bass, B. M., & Avolio, B. J. (1990a). The implications of transactional and transformational leadership for individual, team, and organizational development. *Research in Organizational Change and Development, 4*, 231–272.

Bass, B. M., & Avolio, B. J. (1990b). *Multifactor Leadership Questionnaire.* Palo Alto, CA: Consulting Psychologists Press.

Bass, B. M., & Avolio, B. J. (1993). Transformational leadership: A response to critiques. In M. M. Chemers & R. Ayman (Eds.), *Leadership theory and research: Perspectives and directions* (pp. 49–80). San Diego, CA: Academic Press.

Bass, B. M., & Avolio, B. J. (1994). *Improving organizational effectiveness through transformational leadership.* Thousand Oaks, CA: Sage.

Bass, B. M., & Avolio, B. J. (1995). *Multifactor Leadership Questionnaire for research.* Menlo Park, CA: Mind Garden.

Bass, B. M., & Riggio, R. E. (2006). *Transformational leadership* (2nd ed.). Mahwah, NJ: Lawrence Erlbaum.

Bass, B. M., & Steidlmeier, P. (1999). Ethics, character, and authentic transformational leadership. *Leadership Quarterly, 10*, 181–127.

Bennis, W. G., & Nanus, B. (1985). *Leaders: The strategies for taking charge.* New York: Harper & Row.

Bryman, A. (1992). *Charisma and leadership in organizations.* London: Sage.

Burns, J. M. (1978). *Leadership.* New York: Harper & Row.

Conger, J. A. (1999). Charismatic and transformational leadership in organizations: An insider's perspective on these developing streams of research. *Leadership Quarterly, 10*(2), 145–179.

Conger, J. A., & Kanungo, R. N. (1998). *Charismatic leadership in organizations.* Thousand Oaks, CA: Sage.

Downton, J. V. (1973). *Rebel leadership: Commitment and charisma in a revolutionary process.* New York: Free Press.

Hinkin, T. R., & Schriesheim, C. A. (2008). A theoretical and empirical examination of the transactional and non-leadership dimensions of the Multifactor Leadership Questionnaire (MLQ). *Leadership Quarterly, 19,* 501–513.

House, R. J. (1976). A 1976 theory of charismatic leadership. In J. G. Hunt & L. L. Larson (Eds.), *Leadership: The cutting edge* (pp. 189–207). Carbondale: Southern Illinois University Press.

Howell, J. M., & Avolio, B. J. (1993). The ethics of charismatic leadership: Submission or liberation? *Academy of Management Executive, 6*(2), 43–54.

Hunt, J. G., & Conger, J. A. (1999). From where we sit: An assessment of transformational and charismatic leadership research. *Leadership Quarterly, 10*(3), 335–343.

Jung, D. I., Chow, C., & Wu, A. (2003). The role of transformational leadership in enhancing organizational innovation: Hypotheses and some preliminary findings. *Leadership Quarterly, 14*(4–5), 525–544.

Kouzes, J. M., & Posner, B. Z. (1987). *The leadership challenge: How to get extraordinary things done in organizations.* San Francisco: Jossey-Bass.

Kouzes, J. M., & Posner, B. Z. (2002). *The leadership challenge* (3rd ed.). San Francisco: Jossey-Bass.

Kuhnert, K. W. (1994). Transforming leadership: Developing people through delegation. In B. M. Bass & B. J. Avolio (Eds.), *Improving organizational effectiveness through transformational leadership* (pp. 10–25). Thousand Oaks, CA: Sage.

Kuhnert, K. W., & Lewis, P. (1987). Transactional and transformational leadership: A constructive/developmental analysis. *Academy of Management Review, 12*(4), 648–657.

Lowe, K. B., & Gardner, W. L. (2001). Ten years of the *Leadership Quarterly:* Contributions and challenges for the future. *Leadership Quarterly, 11*(4), 459–514.

Lowe, K. B., Kroeck, K. G., & Sivasubramaniam, N. (1996). Effectiveness correlates of transformational and transactional leadership: A meta-analytic review of the MLQ literature. *Leadership Quarterly, 7*(3), 385–425.

Nemanich, L. A., & Keller, R. T. (2007). Transformational leadership in an acquisition: A field study of employees. *Leadership Quarterly, 18,* 49–68.

Rowold, J., & Heinitz, K. (2007). Transformational and charismatic leadership: Assessing the convergent, divergent and criterion validity of the MLQ and the CKS. *Leadership Quarterly, 18,* 121–133.

Shamir, B., House, R. J., & Arthur, M. B. (1993). The motivational effects of charismatic leadership: A self-concept based theory. *Organization Science, 4*(4), 577–594.

Sosik, J. J., & Jung, D. I. (2010). *Full range leadership development: Pathways for people, profit, and planet.* New York: Psychology Press.

Tejeda, M. J., Scandura, T. A., & Pillai, R. (2001). The MLQ revisited: Psychometric properties and recommendations. *Leadership Quarterly, 12,* 31–52.

Tims, M., Bakker, A. B., & Xanthopoulou, D. (2011). Do transformational leaders enhance their followers' daily work engagement? *Leadership Quarterly, 22,* 121–131.

Tracey, J. B., & Hinkin, T. R. (1998). Transformational leadership or effective managerial practices? *Group & Organization Management, 23*(3), 220–236.

Weber, M. (1947). *The theory of social and economic organizations* (T. Parsons, Trans.). New York: Free Press.

Yammarino, F. J. (1993). Transforming leadership studies: Bernard Bass' leadership and performance beyond expectations. *Leadership Quarterly, 4*(3), 379–382.

Yukl, G. A. (1999). An evaluation of conceptual weaknesses in transformational and charismatic leadership theories. *Leadership Quarterly, 10*(2), 285–305.

Zhu, W., Avolio, B. J., Riggio, R. E., & Sosik, J. J. (2011). The effect of authentic transformational leadership on follower and group ethics. *Leadership Quarterly, 22,* 801–817.

10

Servant Leadership

DESCRIPTION

Servant leadership is a paradox—an approach to leadership that runs counter to common sense. Our everyday images of leadership do not coincide with leaders being servants. Leaders influence, and servants follow. How can leadership be both service *and* influence? How can a person be a leader *and* a servant at the same time? Although servant leadership seems contradictory and challenges our traditional beliefs about leadership, it is an approach that offers a unique perspective.

Servant leadership, which originated in the writings of Greenleaf (1970, 1972, 1977), has been of interest to leadership scholars for more than 40 years. Until recently, little empirical research on servant leadership has appeared in established peer-reviewed journals. Most of the academic and nonacademic writing on the topic has been prescriptive, focusing on how servant leadership should ideally be, rather than descriptive, focusing on what servant leadership actually is in practice (van Dierendonck, 2011). However, in the past 10 years, multiple publications have helped to clarify servant leadership and substantiate its basic assumptions.

Similar to earlier leadership theories discussed in this book (e.g., skills approach and styles approach), servant leadership is an approach focusing on leadership from the point of view of the leader and his or her behaviors. Servant leadership emphasizes that leaders be attentive to the concerns of their followers, empathize with them, and nurture them. Servant leaders put followers *first,* empower them, and help them develop their full personal capacities. Furthermore, servant leaders are ethical (see Chapter 16, "Leadership Ethics," for an extended discussion of this topic) and lead in ways that serve the greater good of the organization, community, and society at large.

▶ 10.1 Robert K. Greenleaf

Servant Leadership Defined

What is servant leadership? Scholars have addressed this approach from many different perspectives resulting in a variety of definitions of servant leadership. Greenleaf (1970) provides the most frequently referenced definition:

> [Servant leadership] begins with the natural feeling that one wants to serve, to serve *first*. Then conscious choice brings one to aspire to lead. . . . The difference manifests itself in the care taken by the servant—first to make sure that other people's highest priority needs are being served. The best test . . . is: do those served grow as persons; do they, *while being served*, become healthier, wiser, freer, more autonomous, more likely themselves to become servants? *And*, what is the effect on the least privileged in society; will they benefit, or, at least, will they not be further deprived? (Greenleaf, 1970, p. 15)

Although complex, this definition sets forth the basic ideas of servant leadership that have been highlighted by current scholars. Servant leaders place the good of followers over their own self-interests and emphasize follower development (Hale & Fields, 2007). They demonstrate strong moral behavior toward followers (Graham, 1991; Walumbwa, Hartnell, & Oke, 2010), the organization, and other stakeholders (Ehrhart, 2004). Practicing servant leadership comes more naturally for some than others, but everyone can learn to be a servant leader (Spears, 2010). Although servant leadership is sometimes treated by others as a trait, in our discussion, servant leadership is viewed as a behavior.

Historical Basis of Servant Leadership

Robert K. Greenleaf coined the term *servant leadership* and is the author of the seminal works on the subject. Greenleaf's persona and writings have significantly influenced how servant leadership has developed on the practical and theoretical level. He founded the Center for Applied Ethics in 1964, now the Greenleaf Center for Servant Leadership, which provides a clearinghouse and focal point for research and writing on servant leadership.

Greenleaf worked for 40 years at AT&T and, after retiring, began exploring how institutions function and how they could better serve society. He was intrigued by issues of power and authority and how individuals in organizations could creatively support each other. Decidedly against coercive leadership, Greenleaf advocated using communication to build consensus in groups.

Greenleaf credits his formulation of servant leadership to Herman Hesse's (1956) novel *The Journey to the East*. It tells the story of a group of travelers on a mythical journey who are accompanied by a servant who does menial chores for the travelers but also sustains them with his spirits and song. The servant's presence has an extraordinary impact on the group. When the servant becomes lost and disappears from the group, the travelers fall into disarray and abandon the journey. Without the servant, they are unable to carry on. It was the servant who was ultimately leading the group, emerging as a leader through his selfless care of the travelers.

In addition to serving, Greenleaf states that a servant leader has a social responsibility to be concerned about the "have-nots" and those less privileged. If inequalities and social injustices exist, a servant leader tries to remove them (Graham, 1991). In becoming a servant leader, a leader uses less institutional power and control while shifting authority to those who are being led. Servant leadership values community because it provides a face-to-face opportunity for individuals to experience interdependence, respect, trust, and individual growth (Greenleaf, 1970).

Ten Characteristics of a Servant Leader

In an attempt to clarify servant leadership for practitioners, Spears (2002) identified 10 characteristics in Greenleaf's writings that are central to the development of servant leadership. Together, these characteristics comprise the first model or conceptualization of servant leadership.

1. *Listening*. Communication between leaders and followers is an interactive process that includes sending and receiving messages (i.e., talking and listening). Servant leaders communicate by listening first. They recognize that listening is a learned discipline that involves hearing and being receptive to what others have to say. Through listening, servant leaders acknowledge the viewpoint of followers and validate these perspectives.

2. *Empathy*. Empathy is "standing in the shoes" of another person and attempting to see the world from that person's point of view. Empathetic servant leaders demonstrate that they truly understand what followers are thinking and feeling. When a servant leader shows empathy, it is confirming and validating for the follower. It makes the follower feel unique.

▶ **10.2** Serving on Southwest

3. *Healing.* To heal means to make whole. Servant leaders care about the personal well-being of their followers. They support followers by helping them overcome personal problems. Greenleaf argues that the process of healing is a two-way street—in helping followers become whole, servant leaders themselves are healed.

4. *Awareness.* For Greenleaf, awareness is a quality within servant leaders that makes them acutely attuned and receptive to their physical, social, and political environments. It includes understanding oneself and the impact one has on others. With awareness, servant leaders are able to step aside and view themselves and their own perspectives in the greater context of the situation.

5. *Persuasion.* Persuasion is clear and persistent communication that convinces others to change. As opposed to coercion, which utilizes positional authority to force compliance, persuasion creates change through the use of gentle nonjudgmental argument. According to Spears (2002), Greenleaf's emphasis on persuasion over coercion is perhaps related to his denominational affiliation with the Religious Society of Friends (Quakers).

6. *Conceptualization.* Conceptualization refers to an individual's ability to be a visionary for an organization, providing a clear sense of its goals and direction. This characteristic goes beyond day-to-day operational thinking to focus on the "big picture." Conceptualization also equips servant leaders to respond to complex organizational problems in creative ways, enabling them to deal with the intricacies of the organization in relationship to its long-term goals.

7. *Foresight.* Foresight encompasses a servant leader's ability to know the future. It is an ability to predict what is coming based on what is occurring in the present and what has happened in the past. For Greenleaf, foresight has an ethical dimension because he believes leaders should be held accountable for any failures to anticipate what reasonably could be foreseen and to act on that understanding.

8. *Stewardship.* Stewardship is about taking responsibility for the leadership role entrusted to the leader. Servant leaders accept the responsibility to carefully manage the people and organization they have been given to lead. In addition, they hold the organization in trust for the greater good of society.

9. *Commitment to the growth of people.* Greenleaf's conceptualization of servant leadership places a premium on treating each follower as a unique person with intrinsic value that goes beyond his or her tangible contributions to the organization. Servant leaders are committed to helping each person in the organization grow personally and professionally.

10.1 Community Health Nursing

Commitment can take many forms, including providing followers with opportunities for career development, helping them develop new work skills, taking a personal interest in the their ideas, and involving them in decision making (Spears, 2002).

10. *Building Community.* Servant leadership fosters the development of community. A community is a collection of individuals who have shared interests and pursuits and feel a sense of unity and relatedness. Community allows followers to identify with something greater than themselves that they value. Servant leaders build community to provide a place where people can feel safe and connected with others, but are still allowed to express their own individuality.

These 10 characteristics of servant leadership represent Greenleaf's seminal work on the servant as leader. They provide a creative lens from which to view the complexities of servant leadership.

Building a Theory About Servant Leadership

For more than three decades after Greenleaf's original writings, servant leadership remained a set of loosely defined characteristics and normative principles. In this form it was widely accepted as a leadership approach, rather than a theory, that has strong heuristic and practical value. Praise for servant leadership came from a wide range of well-known leadership writers, including Bennis (2002), Blanchard and Hodges (2003), Covey (2002), DePree (2002), Senge (2002), and Wheatley (2002). At the same time, servant leadership was adopted as a guiding philosophy in many well-known organizations such as The Toro Company, Herman Miller, Synovus Financial Corporation, ServiceMaster Company, Men's Wearhouse, Southwest Airlines, and TDIndustries (Spears, 2002). Although novel and paradoxical, the basic ideas and prescriptions of servant leadership resonated with many as an ideal way to run an organization.

More recently, researchers have begun to examine the conceptual underpinnings of servant leadership in an effort to build a theory about it. These studies have resulted in a wide array of models that describe servant leadership using a multitude of variables. For example, Russell and Stone (2002) developed a practical model of servant leadership that contained 20 attributes, nine functional characteristics (distinctive behaviors observed in the workplace), and 11 accompanying characteristics that augment these behaviors. Similarly, Patterson (2003) created a value-based model of servant leadership that distinguished seven constructs that characterize the virtues and shape the behaviors of servant leaders.

10.2 Dave Ramsey   **10.2** Servant Leadership Framework

Other conceptualizations of servant leadership have emerged from researchers' efforts to develop and validate instruments to measure the core dimensions of the servant leadership process. Table 10.1 provides a summary of some of these studies, illustrating clearly the extensiveness of characteristics related to servant leadership. This table also exhibits the lack of agreement among researchers on what specific characteristics define servant leadership. While some of the studies include common characteristics, such as humility or empowerment, none of the studies conceptualize servant leadership in exactly the same way. In addition, Table 10.1 demonstrates how servant leadership is treated as a trait phenomenon (e.g., courage, humility) in some studies while other researchers regard it as a behavioral process (e.g., serving and developing others). Although scholars are not in agreement regarding the primary attributes of

Table 10.1   Key Characteristics of Servant Leadership

Laub (1999)	Wong & Davey (2007)	Barbuto & Wheeler (2006)	Dennis & Bocarnea (2005)	Sendjaya, Sarros, & Santora (2008)	van Dierendonck & Nuijten (2011)
• Developing people • Sharing leadership • Displaying authenticity • Valuing people • Providing leadership • Building community	• Serving and developing others • Consulting and involving others • Humility and selflessness • Modeling integrity and authenticity • Inspiring and influencing others	• Altruistic calling • Emotional healing • Persuasive mapping • Organizational stewardship • Wisdom	• Empowerment • Trust • Humility • Agapao love • Vision	• Transforming influence • Voluntary subordination • Authentic self • Transcendental spirituality • Covenantal relationship • Responsible morality	• Empowerment • Humility • Standing back • Authenticity • Forgiveness • Courage • Accountability • Stewardship

SOURCE: Adapted from van Dierendonck, D., 2011. Servant leadership: A review and syntheses. *Journal of Management, 37*(4), 1228–1261.

servant leadership, these studies provide the groundwork necessary for the development of a refined model of servant leadership.

Figure 10.1   Model of Servant Leadership

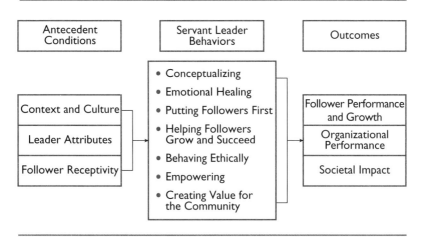

SOURCE: Adapted from Liden, R. C., Panaccio, A., Hu, J., & Meuser, J. D. (in press). Servant leadership: Antecedents, consequences, and contextual moderators. In D. V. Day (Ed.), *The Oxford handbook of leadership and organizations.* Oxford, England: Oxford University Press; and van Dierendonck, D. (2011). Servant leadership: A review and syntheses. *Journal of Management, 37*(4), 1228–1261.

MODEL OF SERVANT LEADERSHIP

This chapter presents a servant leadership model based on Liden, Wayne, Zhao, and Henderson (2008) and Liden, Panaccio, Hu, and Meuser (in press) that has three main components: *antecedent conditions, servant leader behaviors,* and *leadership outcomes* (Figure 10.1). The model is intended to clarify the phenomenon of servant leadership and provide a framework for understanding its complexities.

10.1 Stewardship   10.3 Servant Leadership Review

Antecedent Conditions

As shown on the left side of Figure 10.1, three antecedent, or existing, conditions have an impact on servant leadership: *context and culture, leader attributes,* and *follower receptivity.* These conditions are not inclusive of all the conditions that affect servant leadership, but do represent some factors likely to influence the leadership process.

Context and Culture. Servant leadership does not occur in a vacuum but occurs within a given organizational context and a particular culture. The nature of each of these affects the way servant leadership is carried out. For example, in health care and nonprofit settings, the norm of caring is more prevalent, while for Wall Street corporations it is more common to have competition as an operative norm. Because the norms differ, the ways servant leadership is performed may vary.

Dimensions of culture (see Chapter 15, "Culture and Leadership") will also influence servant leadership. For example, in cultures where power distance is low (e.g., Nordic Europe) and power is shared equally among people at all levels of society, servant leadership may be more common. In cultures with low humane orientation (e.g., Germanic Europe), servant leadership may present more of a challenge. The point is that cultures influence the way servant leadership is able to be achieved.

Leader Attributes. As in any leadership situation, the qualities and disposition of the leader influence the servant leadership process. Individuals bring their own traits and ideas about leading to leadership situations. Some may feel a deep desire to serve or are strongly motivated to lead. Others may be driven by a sense of higher calling (Sendjaya, Sarros, & Santora, 2008). These dispositions shape how individuals demonstrate servant leadership. In addition, people differ in areas such as moral development, emotional intelligence, and self-determinedness, and these traits interact with their ability to engage in servant leadership.

Follower Receptivity. The receptivity of followers is a factor that appears to influence the impact of servant leadership on outcomes such as personal and organizational job performance. Follower receptivity concerns the question "Do all employees show a desire for servant leadership?" Research suggests the answer may be no. Some subordinates do not want to work with servant leaders. They equate servant leadership with micromanagement, and report that they do not want their leader to get to know them or

10.3 Leadership and Performance

try to help, develop, or guide them (Liden, Wayne, et al., 2008). Similarly, Meuser, Liden, Wayne, and Henderson (2011) found empirical evidence showing that when servant leadership was matched with followers who desired it, this type of leadership had a positive impact on performance and organizational citizenship behavior. The opposite was seen when there was no match between servant leadership and the desire of subordinates for it. It appears that for some followers, servant leadership has a positive impact and, for others, servant leadership is not effective.

Servant Leader Behaviors

The middle component of Figure 10.1 identifies seven *servant leader behaviors* that are the core of the servant leadership process. These behaviors emerged from Liden, Wayne, et al.'s (2008) vigorous efforts to develop and validate a measure of servant leadership. The findings from their research provide evidence for the soundness of viewing servant leadership as a multidimensional process. Collectively, these behaviors are the central focus of servant leadership. Individually, each behavior makes a unique contribution.

Conceptualizing. Conceptualizing refers to the servant leader's thorough understanding of the organization—its purposes, complexities, and mission. This capacity allows servant leaders to think through multifaceted problems, to know if something is going wrong, and to address problems creatively in accordance with the overall goals of the organization.

For example, Kate Simpson, a senior nursing supervisor in an emergency room of a large hospital, uses conceptualizing to lead her department. She fully understands the mission of the hospital and, at the same time, knows how to effectively manage staff on a day-to-day basis. Her staff members say Kate has a sixth sense about what is best for people. She is known for her wisdom in dealing with difficult patients and helping staff diagnose complex medical problems. Her abilities, competency, and value as a servant leader earned her the hospital's Caregiver of the Year Award.

Emotional Healing. Emotional healing involves being sensitive to the personal concerns and well-being of others. It includes recognizing others' problems and being willing to take the time to address them. Servant leaders who exhibit emotional healing make themselves available to others, stand by them, and provide them with support.

Emotional healing is apparent in the work of Father John, a much sought-after hospice priest on Chicago's South Side. Father John has a unique approach to hospice patients: He doesn't encourage, give advice, or read Scripture. Instead he simply listens to them. "When you face death, the only important thing in life is relationships," he says. "I practice the art of standing by. I think it is more important to come just to be there than to do anything else."

Putting Followers First. Putting others first is the sine qua non of servant leadership—the defining characteristic. It means using actions and words that clearly demonstrate to followers that their concerns are a priority, including placing followers' interests and success ahead of those of the leader. It may mean a leader breaks from his or her own tasks to assist followers with theirs.

Dr. Autumn Klein, a widely published health education professor at a major research university, is responsible for several ongoing large interdisciplinary public health studies. Although she is the principal investigator on these studies, when multiauthored articles are submitted for publication, Dr. Klein puts the names of other researchers before her own. She chooses to let others be recognized because she knows it will benefit them in their annual performance reviews. She puts the success of her colleagues ahead of her own interests.

Helping Followers Grow and Succeed. This behavior refers to knowing followers' professional or personal goals and helping them to accomplish those aspirations. Servant leaders make subordinates' career development a priority, including mentoring followers and providing them with support. At its core, helping followers grow and succeed is about aiding these individuals to become self-actualized, reaching their fullest human potential.

An example of how a leader helps others grow and succeed is Mr. Yon Kim, a high school orchestra teacher who consistently receives praise from parents for his outstanding work with students. Mr. Kim is a skilled violinist with high musical standards, but he does not let that get in the way of helping each student, from the most highly accomplished to the least capable. Students like Mr. Kim because he listens to them and treats them as adults. He gives feedback without being judgmental. Many of his former students have gone on to become music majors. They often visit Mr. Kim to let him know how important he was to them. Yon Kim is a servant leader who helps students grow through his teaching and guidance.

▶ **10.3** Service Leadership

Behaving Ethically. Behaving ethically is doing the right thing in the right way. It is holding to strong ethical standards, including being open, honest, and fair with followers. Servant leaders do not compromise their ethical principles in order to achieve success.

An example of ethical behavior is how Chief Executive Officer (CEO) Elizabeth Angliss responded when one of her employees brought her a copy of a leaked document from their company's chief competitor, outlining its plans to go after some of Angliss's largest customers. Although she knew the document undoubtedly had valuable information, she shredded it instead of reading it. She then called the rival CEO and told him she had received the document and wanted him to be aware that he might have a security issue within his company. "I didn't know if what I received was real or not," she explains. "But it didn't matter. If it was the real thing, someone on his end did something wrong, and my company wasn't going to capitalize on that."

Empowering. Empowering refers to allowing followers the freedom to be independent, make decisions on their own, and be self-sufficient. It is a way for leaders to share power with followers by allowing them to have control. Empowerment builds followers' confidence in their own capacities to think and act on their own because they are given the freedom to handle difficult situations in the way they feel is best.

For example, a college professor teaching a large lecture class empowers two teaching assistants assigned to him by letting them set their own office hours, independently grade student papers, and practice teaching by giving one of the weekly class lectures. They become confident in their teaching abilities and bring new ideas to the professor to try in the classroom.

Creating Value for the Community. Servant leaders create value for the community by consciously and intentionally giving back to the community. They are involved in local activities and encourage followers to also volunteer for community service. Creating value for the community is one way for leaders to link the purposes and goals of an organization with the broader purposes of the community.

An example of creating value for the community can be seen in the leadership of Mercedes Urbanez, principal of Alger High School. Alger is an alternative high school in a midsize community with three other high schools. Mercedes's care and concern for students at Alger is remarkable. Ten percent of Alger's students have children, so the school provides on-site day care. Fifteen percent of the students are on probation, and Alger is often their last stop before dropping out entirely and resuming criminal activities. While the other schools in town foster competition and push advanced placement courses, Alger focuses on removing the barriers that keep its students from excelling and offers courses that provide what its students need including multimedia skills, reading remediation, and parenting.

Under Mercedes, Alger High School is a model alternative school appreciated at every level in the community. Students, who have failed in other schools, find they have a safe place to go where they are accepted and adults try to help them solve their problems. Law enforcement supports the school's efforts to help these students get back into the mainstream of society and away from crime. The other high schools in the community know that Alger provides services they find difficult to provide. Mercedes Urbanez serves the have-nots in the community, and the whole community reaps the benefits.

Outcomes

Although servant leadership focuses primarily on leader behaviors, it is also important to examine the potential outcomes of servant leadership. The outcomes of servant leadership are *follower performance and growth, organizational performance,* and *societal impact* (see Figure 10.1). As Greenleaf highlighted in his original work (1970), the central goal of servant leadership is to create healthy organizations that nurture individual growth, strengthen organizational performance, and, in the end, produce a positive impact on society.

Follower Performance and Growth. In the model of servant leadership, most of the servant leader behaviors focus directly on recognizing followers' contributions and helping them realize their human potential. The expected outcome for followers is greater self-actualization. That is, followers will realize their full capabilities when leaders nurture them, help them with their personal goals, and give them control.

Another outcome of servant leadership, suggested by Meuser et al. (2011), is that it will have a favorable impact on subordinate in-role performance — the way followers do their assigned work. When servant leaders were matched with subordinates who were open to this type of leadership, the results were positive. Subordinates became more effective at accomplishing their jobs and fulfilling their job descriptions.

Finally, another expected result of servant leadership is that followers themselves may become servant leaders. Greenleaf's conceptualization of servant leadership hypothesizes that when followers receive caring and empowerment from ethical leaders they, in turn, will likely begin treating others in this way. Servant leadership would produce a ripple effect in which servant leaders create more servant leaders. Further research is needed, however, to test this hypothesis.

Organizational Performance. In addition to positively affecting followers and their performance, initial research has shown that servant leadership has an influence on organizational performance. Several studies have found a positive relationship between servant leadership and organizational citizenship behaviors (OCBs), which are subordinate behaviors that go beyond the basic requirements of their duties and help the overall functioning of the organization (Ehrhart, 2004; Liden, Wayne, et al., 2008; Neubert, Kacmar, Carlson, Chonko, & Roberts, 2008; Walumbwa et al., 2010).

Servant leadership also affects the way organizational teams function. Hu and Liden (2011) found that servant leadership enhanced team effectiveness by increasing the members' shared confidence that they could be effective as a work group. Furthermore, their results showed that servant leadership contributed positively to team potency by enhancing group process and clarity. However, when servant leadership was absent, team potency decreased, despite clearer goals. In essence, it frustrates people to know exactly what the goal is, but not get the support needed to accomplish the goal.

Current research on organizational outcomes is in its initial stages. Further study is needed to substantiate the direct and indirect ways that servant leadership is related to organizational performance.

Societal Impact. Another outcome expected of servant leadership is that it is likely to have a positive impact on society. Although societal impact is not commonly measured in studies of servant leadership, there are examples of servant leadership's impact that are highly visible. One example we are all familiar with is the work of Mother Teresa whose years of service for the hungry, homeless, and unwanted resulted in the creation of a new religious order, the Missionaries of Charity. This order now has more than 1 million workers in over 40 countries that operate hospitals, schools, and hospices for the poor. Mother Teresa's servant leadership has had an extraordinary impact on society throughout the world.

10.2 Servant Leader Beginnings

In the business world, an example of the societal impact of servant leadership can be observed at Southwest Airlines (see Case 10.3). Leaders at Southwest instituted an "others first" organizational philosophy in the management of the company, which starts with how it treats its employees. This philosophy is adhered to by those employees who themselves become servant leaders in regards to the airline's customers. Because the company thrives, it impacts society by providing jobs in the communities it serves and, to a lesser extent, by providing the customers who rely on it with transportation.

In his conceptualization of servant leadership, Greenleaf did not frame the process as one that was intended to directly change society. Rather, he visualizes leaders who become servants first and listen to others and help them grow. As a result, their organizations are healthier, ultimately benefiting society. In this way, the long-term outcomes of putting others first include positive social change and helping society flourish.

Summary of the Model of Servant Leadership

In summary, the model of servant leadership consists of three components: antecedent conditions, servant leader behaviors, and outcomes. The central focus of the model is the seven behaviors of leaders that foster servant leadership: conceptualizing, emotional healing, putting followers first, helping followers grow and succeed, behaving ethically, empowering, and creating value for the community. These behaviors are influenced by context and culture, the leader's attributes, and the followers' receptivity to this kind of leadership. When individuals engage in servant leadership, it is likely to improve outcomes at the individual, organizational, and societal levels.

HOW DOES SERVANT LEADERSHIP WORK?

The servant leadership approach works differently than many of the prior theories we have discussed in this book. For example, it is unlike the trait approach (Chapter 2), which emphasizes that leaders should have certain specific traits. It is also unlike path–goal theory (Chapter 7), which lays out principles regarding what style of leadership is needed in various situations. Instead, servant leadership focuses on the behaviors leaders should exhibit to put followers first and to support followers' personal

10.4 Cultural Servant Leadership

development. It is concerned with how leaders treat subordinates and the outcomes that are likely to emerge.

So what is the mechanism that explains how servant leadership works? It begins when leaders commit themselves to putting their subordinates first, being honest with them, and treating them fairly. Servant leaders make it a priority to listen to their followers and develop strong long-term relationships with them. This allows leaders to understand the abilities, needs, and goals of followers, which, in turn, allows these subordinates to achieve their full potential. When many leaders in an organization adopt a servant leadership orientation, a culture of serving others within and outside the organization is created (Liden, Wayne, et al., 2008).

Servant leadership works best when leaders are altruistic and have a strong motivation and deep-seated interest in helping others. In addition, for successful servant leadership to occur, it is important that followers are open and receptive to servant leaders who want to empower them and help them grow.

It should be noted that in much of the writing on servant leadership there is an underlying philosophical position, originally set forth by Greenleaf (1970), that leaders should be altruistic and humanistic. Rather than using their power to dominate others, leaders should make every attempt to share their power and enable others to grow and become autonomous. Leadership framed from this perspective downplays competition in the organization and promotes egalitarianism.

Finally, in an ideal world, servant leadership results in community and societal change. Individuals within an organization who care for each other become committed to developing an organization that cares for the community. Organizations that adopt a servant leadership culture are committed to helping those in need who operate outside of the organization. Servant leadership extends to serving the "have-nots" in society (Graham, 1991). Case 10.2 in this chapter provides a striking example of how one servant leader's work led to positive outcomes for many throughout the world.

STRENGTHS

In its current stage of development, research on servant leadership has made several positive contributions to the field of leadership. First, while there are other leadership approaches such as transformational and

▶ 10.4 Essence of Leadership

authentic leadership that include an ethical dimension, servant leadership is unique in the way it makes altruism the central component of the leadership process. Servant leadership argues unabashedly that leaders should put followers first, share control with followers, and embrace their growth. It is the only leadership approach that frames the leadership process around the principle of caring for others.

Second, servant leadership provides a counterintuitive and provocative approach to the use of influence, or power, in leadership. Nearly all other theories of leadership treat influence as a positive factor in the leadership process, but servant leadership does just the opposite. It argues that leaders should not dominate, direct, or control; but rather, leaders should share control and influence. To give up control rather than seek control is the goal of servant leadership. Servant leadership is an influence process that does not incorporate influence in a traditional way.

Third, rather than imply that servant leadership is a panacea, research on servant leadership has shown there are conditions under which servant leadership is not a preferred kind of leadership. Findings indicate that servant leadership may not be effective in contexts where subordinates are not open to being guided, supported, and empowered. Followers' readiness to receive servant leadership moderates the potential usefulness of leading from this approach (Liden, Wayne, et al., 2008).

Fourth, recent research has resulted in a sound measure of servant leadership. Using a rigorous methodology, Liden, Wayne, et al. (2008) developed and validated the Servant Leadership Questionnaire (SLQ), which appears at the end of the chapter. It comprises 28 items that identify seven distinct dimensions of servant leadership. Studies show that the SLQ is unique and measures aspects of leadership that are different from those measured by the transformational and leader–member exchange theories (Liden, Wayne, et al., 2008; Schaubroeck, Lam, & Peng, 2011). The SLQ has proved to be a suitable instrument for use in future research on servant leadership.

CRITICISMS

In addition to the positive features of servant leadership, this approach has several limitations. First, the paradoxical nature of the title "servant leadership" creates semantic noise that diminishes the potential value of the approach. Because the name appears contradictory, servant leadership is prone to be perceived as fanciful or whimsical. In addition, being a servant leader implies following, and following is viewed as the opposite of leading. Although servant leadership incorporates influence, the mechanism of how influence functions as a part of servant leadership is not fully explicated in the approach.

Second, there is debate among servant leadership scholars regarding the core dimensions of the process. As illustrated in Table 10.1, servant leadership is hypothesized to include a multitude of abilities, traits, and behaviors. To date, researchers have been unable to reach consensus on a common definition or theoretical framework for servant leadership (van Dierendonck, 2011). Until a larger body of findings is published on servant leadership, the robustness of theoretical formulations about it will remain limited.

Third, a large segment of the writing on servant leadership has a prescriptive overtone that implies that good leaders "put others first." While advocating an altruistic approach to leadership is commendable, it has a utopian ring because it conflicts with individual autonomy and other principles of leadership such as directing, concern for production, goal setting, and creating a vision (Gergen, 2006). Furthermore, along with the "value-push" prescriptive quality, there is an almost moralistic nature that seems to surround servant leadership. As a result, many practitioners of servant leadership are not necessarily researchers who want to conduct studies to test the validity of servant leadership theory.

Finally, it is unclear why "conceptualizing" is included as one of the servant leadership behaviors in the model of servant leadership (see Figure 10.1). Is conceptualizing actually a behavior, or is it a cognitive ability? Furthermore, what is the rationale for identifying conceptualizing as a determinant of servant leadership? Being able to conceptualize is undoubtedly an important cognitive capacity in all kinds of leadership, but why is it a defining characteristic of servant leadership? A clearer explanation for its central role in servant leadership needs to be addressed in future research.

APPLICATION

Servant leadership can be applied at all levels of management and in all types of organizations. Within a philosophical framework of caring for others, servant leadership sets forth a list of behaviors that individuals can engage in if they want to be servant leaders. The prescribed behaviors of servant leadership are not esoteric; they are easily understood and generally applicable to a variety of leadership situations.

Unlike leader–member exchange theory (Chapter 8) or authentic leadership (Chapter 11), which are not widely used in training and development, servant leadership has been used extensively in a variety of organizations for more than 30 years. Many organizations in the Fortune 500 (e.g., Starbucks, AT&T, Southwest Airlines, and Vanguard Group) employ ideas from servant leadership. Training in servant leadership typically involves self-assessment exercises, educational sessions, and goal setting. The content of servant leadership is straightforward and accessible to employees at every level within the organization.

Liden, Wayne, et al. (2008) suggest that organizations that want to build a culture of servant leadership should be careful to select people who are interested in and capable of building long-term relationships with followers. Furthermore, because "behaving ethically" is positively related to job performance, organizations should focus on selecting people who have high integrity and strong ethics. In addition, organizations should develop training programs that spend time helping leaders develop their emotional intelligence, ethical decision making, and skills for empowering others. Behaviors such as these will help leaders nurture followers to their full potential.

Servant leadership is taught at many colleges and universities around the world and is the focus of numerous independent coaches, trainers, and consultants. In the United States, Gonzaga University and Regent University are recognized as prominent leaders in this area because of the academic attention they have given to servant leadership. Overall, the most recognized and comprehensive center for training in servant leadership is the Greenleaf Center for Servant Leadership (http://www.greenleaf.org/).

In summary, servant leadership provides a philosophy and set of behaviors that individuals in the organizational setting can learn and develop. The following section features cases illustrating how servant leadership has been manifested in different ways.

CASE STUDIES

This section provides three case studies (Cases 10.1, 10.2, and 10.3) that illustrate different facets of servant leadership. The first case describes the servant leadership of several individuals who anonymously gave a huge amount of money to create college scholarships for a Midwest community. The second case is about Dr. Paul Farmer and his efforts to stop disease in

Haiti and other parts of the world. The third case is about the leaders of Southwest Airlines who created a servant leadership culture that permeates the company. At the end of each case, several questions are provided to help you analyze the case from the perspective of servant leadership.

CASE 10.1

Anonymous Servant Leaders

In November 2005, a small group of Kalamazoo, Michigan, residents anonymously gave a huge amount of money to create the Kalamazoo Promise, a program to provide college scholarships to every graduate of the Kalamazoo Public Schools (KPS) for perpetuity.

The enormity of the gift was staggering (some think it may be as much as $250 million). With more than 500 KPS graduates each year, the Promise was no small gesture. In the excitement that surrounded the program, many people asked first, "Who are these donors?" and then, "Why would they do this?"

The only people with the answers seem to be the donors themselves and Dr. Janice Brown, the superintendent of KPS at the time. While their identities may never be known, the donors' motivations are clear.

In the decade leading up to the Promise, Kalamazoo suffered enormous job losses in its chief industries of paper, automobile, and pharmaceutical manufacturing. Plant closures and mergers had forced many workers to relocate or into unemployment. In addition, KPS, which has a large minority and low-income student population, experienced an exodus of students as families that could afford to moved to adjacent communities to take advantage of better ranked schools. Kalamazoo's poverty rate stood at 17.6%, almost twice the national average.

The donors saw the Promise as a way to revitalize their city by becoming a catalyst for economic, educational, and community change. The donors knew, as downtown Kalamazoo real estate developer William Johnston stated, that "a better economy was going to require a healthier school system" (Boudette, 2006).

The impact was immediate. KPS adopted a new "college-bound" culture, where every student was considered "college material" and conversations about attending college began in kindergarten. The school district

(Continued)

(Continued)

raised expectations for students' progress, eliminated "social promotion," and boosted support services for underachieving students. KPS Superintendent Michael Rice said, "We're not doing kids any favors when we tell them 'Stay in school and you'll get the Promise.' The fact is you have to read well, you have to write well, you have to do math well to succeed in college. That's the dirty little secret" (Mack, 2007).

Beyond the classroom, the implications of the Promise radiated out to the housing market, businesses, the city, and the broader region. KPS experienced enrollment increases, and housing prices in the district went up. Households that no longer had to save for their children's college had more disposable income, generating increased consumer spending. Economic development experts used the Promise as an incentive to bring new business to the area, speculating that an increase in available jobs would attract new residents and provide income for existing residents as well.

The Promise was also a catalyst for bringing together the disparate socioeconomic and ethnic communities within the city. A leader in Kalamazoo's African American community pointed out that the city "is one of the most segregated communities in Michigan" but that the Promise made the city "one community with one vision and one common future" (Miller-Adams, 2009).

Like a pebble dropped into a pond, the Promise caused a ripple in the community through the creation of initiatives to support the program. Some parents volunteered in schools for the first time. Churches and neighborhood associations offered mentoring programs. The local community college and university strengthened their services for first-generation college students while businesses established programs that would help bolster the Promise.

But not all reaction to the Promise was positive. After the program was announced, enrollment in area private schools dropped, even leading to one school's closure. Concerns were raised about the potential gentrification of urban neighborhoods that would price lower-income residents out of the market. Others claimed the Promise's universal approach to tuition meant that middle-class students would ultimately benefit more from the Promise than low-income students who didn't have the financial resources to bear the other costs of college.

The creators of the Promise have never spoken publicly about their intent or the reason for their anonymity. Regardless of their reasons, the donors' gift is a true example of the "pay it forward" philosophy. By ensuring that the children of the city have an educational future, the Kalamazoo Promise has given the community new means to survive and thrive.

Questions

1. How do the donors' behaviors fit into Liden, Wayne, et al.'s (2008) seven characteristics of servant leader behavior?

2. The effectiveness of servant leadership is related to whether followers are open to it. Do you see any aspects of the Kalamazoo Promise that could make it problematic for some people in the Kalamazoo community?

3. Based on the model of servant leadership (Figure 10.1), how would you assess the outcomes of the Kalamazoo Promise? That is, how did the Promise affect follower performance and growth, as well as the organizational performance of the Kalamazoo Public Schools, and what was the impact of the Promise on the greater Kalamazoo community?

CASE 10.2

Doctor to the Poor

"Education wasn't what he wanted to perform on the world... He was after transformation."

—Kidder (2003)

When Paul Farmer graduated from Duke University at 22, he was unsure whether he wanted to be an anthropologist or a doctor. So he went to Haiti. As a student, Paul had become obsessed with the island nation after meeting many Haitians at local migrant camps. Paul was used to the grittier side of life; he had grown up in a family of eight that lived in a converted school bus and later on a houseboat moored in a bayou. But what he observed at the migrant camps and learned from his discussions with Haitian immigrants made his childhood seem idyllic.

In Haiti, he volunteered for a small charity called Eye Care Haiti, which conducted outreach clinics in rural areas. He was drawn in by the deplorable conditions and lives of the Haitian people and determined to use his time

(Continued)

(Continued)

there to learn everything he could about illness and disease afflicting the poor. Before long, Paul realized that he had found his life's purpose: He'd be a doctor to poor people, and he'd start in Haiti.

Paul entered Harvard University in 1984 and, for the first two years, traveled back and forth to Haiti where he conducted a health census in the village of Cange. During that time he conceived of a plan to fight disease in Haiti by developing a public health system that included vaccination programs and clean water and sanitation. The heart of this program, however, would be a cadre of people from the villages who were trained to administer medicines, teach health classes, treat minor ailments, and recognize the symptoms of grave illnesses such as HIV, tuberculosis, and malaria.

His vision became reality in 1987, thanks to a wealthy donor who gave $1 million to help Paul create Partners in Health (PIH). At first it wasn't much of an organization—no staff, a small advisory board, and three committed volunteers. But its work was impressive: PIH began building schools and clinics in and around Cange. Soon PIH established a training program for health outreach workers and organized a mobile unit to screen residents of area villages for preventable diseases.

In 1990, Paul finished his medical studies and became a fellow in infectious diseases at Brigham and Women's Hospital in Boston. He was able to remain in Haiti for most of each year, returning to Boston to work at Brigham for a few months at a time, sleeping in the basement of PIH headquarters.

It wasn't long before PIH's successes started gaining attention outside of Haiti. Because of its success treating the disease in Haiti, the World Health Organization appointed Paul and PIH staffer Jim Yong Kim to spearhead pilot treatment programs for multiple-drug-resistant tuberculosis (MDR-TB). Paul's attention was now diverted to the slums of Peru and Russia where cases of MDR-TB were on the rise. In Peru, Paul and PIH encountered barriers in treating MDR-TB that had nothing to do with the disease. They ran headlong into governmental resistance and had to battle to obtain expensive medications. Paul learned to gently navigate governmental obstacles, while the Bill & Melinda Gates Foundation stepped in with a $44.7 million grant to help fund the program.

In 2005, PIH turned its attention to another part of the world: Africa, the epicenter of the global AIDS pandemic. Beginning its efforts in Rwanda, where few people had been tested or were receiving treatment, PIH tested 30,000 people in 8 months and enrolled nearly 700 in drug therapy to treat the disease. Soon, the organization expanded its efforts to the African nations of Lesotho and Malawi (Partners in Health, 2011).

But Paul's efforts weren't just in far-flung reaches of the world. From his work with patients at Brigham, Paul observed the needs of the impoverished in Boston. The Prevention and Access to Care and Treatment (PACT) project was created to offer drug therapy for HIV and diabetes for the poor residents of the Roxbury and Dorchester districts. PIH has since sent PACT project teams across the United States to provide support to other community health programs.

By 2009, Partners in Health had grown to 11,000 employees working in 49 health centers and hospitals across 11 countries (Partners in Health, 2011). Each year the organization increases the number of facilities and personnel that provide health care to the residents of some of the most impoverished and diseased places in the world. Paul continues to travel around the world, monitoring programs and raising funds for Partners in Health in addition to leading the Department of Global Health and Social Medicine at Harvard Medical School.

Questions

1. Would you characterize Paul Farmer as a servant leader? Explain your answer.

2. Putting others first is the essence of servant leadership. In what way did Paul Farmer put others first?

3. Another characteristic of a servant leader is getting followers to serve. Who were Paul's followers, and how did they become servants to his vision?

4. What role do you think Paul's childhood had in his development as a servant leader?

CASE 10.3

Servant Leadership Takes Flight

A young mother traveling with a toddler on a long cross-country flight approached the flight attendant looking rather frantic. Because of weather and an hour-and-a-half wait on the runway to take off, the plane would arrive at its destination several hours late. The plane had

(Continued)

(Continued)

made an intermediate stop in Denver to pick up passengers but not long enough for travelers to disembark. The mother told the attendant that with the delays and the long flight, her child had already eaten all the food she brought and if she didn't feed him soon he was bound to have a total meltdown. "Can I get off for five minutes just to run and get something for him to eat?" she pleaded.

"I have to recommend strongly that you stay on the plane," the attendant said, sternly. But then, with a smile, she added, "But I can get off. The plane won't leave without me. What can I get your son to eat?"

Turns out that flight attendant not only got the little boy a meal, but brought four other children on board meals as well. Anyone who has traveled in a plane with screaming children knows that this flight attendant not only took care of some hungry children and frantic parents, but also indirectly saw to the comfort of a planeload of other passengers.

This story doesn't surprise anyone familiar with Southwest Airlines. The airline's mission statement is posted every 3 feet at all Southwest locations: Follow the Golden Rule—treat people the way you want to be treated.

It's a philosophy that the company takes to heart and begins with how it treats employees. Colleen Barrett, the former president of Southwest Airlines, says the company's cofounder and her mentor, Herb Kelleher, was adamant that "a happy and motivated workforce will essentially extend that goodwill to Southwest's customers" (Knowledge@Wharton, 2008). If the airline took care of its employees, the employees would take care of the customers, and the shareholders would win, too.

From the first days of Southwest Airlines, Herb resisted establishing traditional hierarchies within the company. He focused on finding employees with substance, willing to say what they thought and committed to doing things differently. Described as "an egalitarian spirit," he employed a collaborative approach to management that involved his associates at every step.

Colleen, who went from working as Herb's legal secretary to being the president of the airline, is living proof of his philosophy. A poor girl from rural Vermont who got the opportunity of a lifetime to work for Herb when he was still just a lawyer, she rose from his aide to become vice president of administration, then executive vice president of customers, and then president and chief operating officer in 2001 (which she stepped down from in 2008). She had no formal training in aviation, but that didn't matter. Herb "always treated me as a complete equal to him," she says.

It was Colleen who instituted the Golden Rule as the company motto and developed a model that focuses on employee satisfaction and issues first, followed by the needs of the passengers. The company hired employees for their touchy-feely attitudes and trained them for skill. Southwest Airlines developed a culture that celebrated and encouraged humor. The example of being themselves on the job started at the top with Herb and Colleen.

This attitude has paid off. Southwest Airlines posted a profit for 35 consecutive years and continues to make money while other airlines' profits are crashing. Colleen says the most important numbers on the balance sheet, however, are those that indicate how many millions of people have become frequent flyers of the airline, a number that grows every year.

Questions

1. What type of servant leader behaviors did Herb Kelleher exhibit in starting the airline? What about Colleen Barrett?

2. How do the leaders of Southwest Airlines serve others? What others are they serving?

3. Southwest Airlines emphasizes the Golden Rule. What role does the Golden Rule play in servant leadership? Is it always a part of servant leadership? Discuss.

4. Based on Figure 10.1, describe the outcomes of servant leadership at Southwest Airlines, and how follower receptivity may have influenced those outcomes.

LEADERSHIP INSTRUMENT

Many questionnaires have been used to measure servant leadership (See Table 10.1). Because of its relevance to the content, the Servant Leadership Questionnaire (SLQ) by Liden, Wayne, et al. (2008) was chosen for inclusion in this chapter. It is a 28-item scale that measures seven major dimensions of servant leadership: conceptualizing, emotional healing, putting followers first, helping followers grow and succeed, behaving ethically, empowering, and creating value for the community. Using exploratory and confirmatory factor analysis, Liden, Wayne, et al. established the multiple dimensions of this scale and described how it is uniquely different from other leadership measures.

By completing the SLQ you will gain an understanding of how servant leadership is measured and explore where you stand on the different dimensions of servant leadership. Servant leadership is a complex process, and taking the SLQ is one way to discover the dynamics of how it works.

Servant Leadership Questionnaire

Instructions: Select two people who know you in a leadership capacity such as a coworker, fellow group member, or subordinate. Make two copies of this questionnaire and give a copy to each individual you have chosen. Using the following 7-point scale, ask them to indicate the extent to which they agree or disagree with the following statements as they pertain to your leadership. In these statements, "He/She" is referring to you in a leadership capacity.

Key: 1 = Strongly disagree   2 = Disagree   3 = Disagree somewhat
      4 = Undecided   5 = Agree Somewhat   6 = Agree   7 = Strongly agree

 1. Others would seek help from him/her if they had   1 2 3 4 5 6 7
    a personal problem.

 2. He/She emphasizes the importance of giving back to   1 2 3 4 5 6 7
    the community.

 3. He/She can tell if something work related is going wrong.   1 2 3 4 5 6 7

 4. He/She gives others the responsibility to make   1 2 3 4 5 6 7
    important decisions about their own jobs.

 5. He/She makes others' career development a priority.   1 2 3 4 5 6 7

 6. He/She cares more about others' success than
    his/her own.   1 2 3 4 5 6 7

 7. He/She holds high ethical standards.   1 2 3 4 5 6 7

 8. He/She cares about others' personal well-being.   1 2 3 4 5 6 7

 9. He/She is always interested in helping people in the   1 2 3 4 5 6 7
    community.

10. He/She is able to think through complex problems.   1 2 3 4 5 6 7

11. He/She encourages others to handle important   1 2 3 4 5 6 7
    work decisions on their own.

12. He/She is interested in making sure others reach   1 2 3 4 5 6 7
    their career goals.

13. He/She puts others' best interests above his/her own.   1 2 3 4 5 6 7

14. He/She is always honest.   1 2 3 4 5 6 7

15. He/She takes time to talk to others on a personal level.   1 2 3 4 5 6 7

16. He/She is involved in community activities.   1 2 3 4 5 6 7

17. He/She has a thorough understanding of the   1 2 3 4 5 6 7
    organization and its goals.

18. He/She gives others the freedom to handle difficult   1 2 3 4 5 6 7
    situations in the way they feel is best.

19. He/She provides others with work experiences that   1 2 3 4 5 6 7
    enable them to develop new skills.

20. He/She sacrifices his/her own interests to meet   1 2 3 4 5 6 7
    others' needs.

21. He/She would not compromise ethical principles   1 2 3 4 5 6 7
    in order to meet success.

22. He/She can recognize when others are feeling   1 2 3 4 5 6 7
    down without asking them.

23. He/She encourages others to volunteer   1 2 3 4 5 6 7
    in the community.

24. He/She can solve work problems with new or   1 2 3 4 5 6 7
    creative ideas.

25. If others need to make important decisions at work,   1 2 3 4 5 6 7
    they do not need to consult him/her.

26. He/She wants to know about others' career goals.   1 2 3 4 5 6 7

27. He/She does what he/she can to make others'   1 2 3 4 5 6 7
    jobs easier.

28. He/She values honesty more than profits.   1 2 3 4 5 6 7

SOURCE: Reprinted (adapted version) from "Servant Leadership: Development of a Multidimensional Measure and Multi-Level Assessment," by R. C. Liden, S. J. Wayne, H. Zhao, and D. Henderson, 2008, *The Leadership Quarterly, 19*, 161–177. Copyright © Reprinted with permission from Elsevier Science.

Scoring

Using the questionnaires on which others assessed your leadership, take the separate scores for each item, add them together, and divide that sum by two. This will give you the average score for that item. For example, if Person A assessed you at 4 for Item 2, and Person B marked you as a 6, your score for Item 2 would be 5.

Once you have averaged each item's scores, use the following steps to complete the scoring of the questionnaire:

1. Add up the scores on 1, 8, 15, and 22. This is your score for emotional healing.

2. Add up the scores for 2, 9, 16, and 23. This is your score for creating value for the community.

3. Add up the scores for 3, 10, 17, and 24. This is your score for conceptual skills.

4. Add up the scores for 4, 11, 18, and 25. This is your score for empowering.

5. Add up the scores for 5, 12, 19, and 26. This is your score for helping subordinates grow and succeed.

6. Add up the scores for 6, 13, 20, and 27. This is your score for putting subordinates first.

7. Add up the scores for 7, 14, 21, and 28. This is your score for behaving ethically.

Scoring Interpretation

- *High range:* A score between 23 and 28 means you strongly exhibit this servant leadership behavior.
- *Moderate range:* A score between 14 and 22 means you tend to exhibit this behavior in an average way.
- *Low range:* A score between 8 and 13 means you exhibit this leadership below the average or expected degree.
- *Extremely low range:* A score between 0 and 7 means you are not inclined to exhibit this leadership behavior at all.

The scores you received on the Servant Leadership Questionnaire indicate the degree to which you exhibit the seven behaviors characteristic of a servant leader. You can use the results to assess areas in which you have strong servant leadership behaviors and areas in which you may strive to improve.

SUMMARY

Originating in the seminal work of Greenleaf (1970), servant leadership is a paradoxical approach to leadership that challenges our traditional beliefs about leadership and influence. Servant leadership emphasizes that leaders should be attentive to the needs of followers, empower them, and help them develop their full human capacities.

Servant leaders make a conscious choice to *serve first*—to place the good of followers over the leaders' self-interests. They build strong relationships with others, are empathic and ethical, and lead in ways that serve the greater good of followers, the organization, the community, and society at large.

Based on an idea from Herman Hesse's (1956) novel *The Journey to the East*, Greenleaf argued that the selfless servant in a group has an extraordinary impact on the other members. Servant leaders attend fully to the needs of followers, are concerned with the less privileged, and aim to remove inequalities and social injustices. Because servant leaders shift authority to those who are being led, they exercise less institutional power and control.

Scholars have conceptualized servant leadership in multiple ways. According to Spears (2002), there are 10 major characteristics of servant leadership: listening, empathy, healing, awareness, persuasion, conceptualization, foresight, stewardship, commitment to the growth of people, and building community. Additional efforts by social science researchers to develop and validate measures of servant leadership have resulted in an extensive list of other servant leadership attributes.

Liden, Panaccio, et al. (in press) have created a promising model of servant leadership that has three main components: antecedent conditions, servant leader behaviors, and leadership outcomes. *Antecedent conditions* that are likely to impact servant leaders include context and culture, leader attributes, and follower receptivity. Central to the servant leader process are the seven *servant leader behaviors*: conceptualizing, emotional healing, putting followers first, helping followers grow and succeed, behaving ethically, empowering, and creating value for the community. The *outcomes* of servant leadership are follower performance and growth, organizational performance, and societal impact.

Research on servant leadership has several strengths. First, it is unique because it makes altruism the main component of the leadership process.

10.5 Chapter Summary

Second, servant leadership provides a counterintuitive and provocative approach to the use of influence wherein leaders give up control rather than seek control. Third, rather than a panacea, research has shown that there are conditions under which servant leadership is not a preferred kind of leadership. Last, recent research has resulted in a sound measure of servant leadership (Servant Leadership Questionnaire) that identifies seven distinct dimensions of the process.

The servant leadership approach also has limitations. First, the paradoxical nature of the title "servant leadership" creates semantic noise that diminishes the potential value of the approach. Second, no consensus exists on a common theoretical framework for servant leadership. Third, servant leadership has a utopian ring that conflicts with traditional approaches to leadership. Last, it is not clear why "conceptualizing" is a defining characteristic of servant leadership.

Despite the limitations, servant leadership continues to be an engaging approach to leadership that holds much promise. As more research is done to test the substance and assumptions of servant leadership, a better understanding of the complexities of the process will emerge.

Visit the Student Study Site at **www.sagepub.com/northouse6e** for web quizzes, leadership questionnaires, and media links represented by the icons.

REFERENCES

Barbuto, J. E., Jr., & Wheeler, D. W. (2006). Scale development and construct clarification of servant leadership. *Group and Organizational Management, 31,* 300–326.

Bennis, W. (2002). Become a tomorrow leader. In L. C. Spears & M. Lawrence (Eds.), *Focus on leadership: Servant-leadership for the twenty-first century,* (pp. 101–110). New York: John Wiley & Sons.

Blanchard, K., & Hodges, P. (2003). *The servant leader: Transforming your hearts, heads, hands, and habits.* Nashville, TN: Thomas Nelson.

Boudette, N. E. (2006, March 10). Kalamazoo, Mich., pegs revitalization on tuition plan. *The Wall Street Journal,* p. A1.

Covey, S. R. (2002). Forward. In R. K. Greenleaf (Ed.), *Servant leadership: A journey into the nature of legitimate power and greatness* (pp. 1–14). New York: Paulist Press.

Dennis, R. S., & Bocarnea, M. (2005). Development of the servant leadership assessment instrument. *Leadership & Organization Development Journal, 26,* 600–615.

DePree, M. (2002). Servant-leadership: Three things necessary. In L. C. Spears & M. Lawrence (Eds.), *Focus on leadership: Servant-leadership for the twenty-first century* (pp. 27–34). New York: John Wiley & Sons.

Ehrhart, M. G. (2004). Leadership and procedural justice climate as antecedents of unit-level organizational citizenship behavior. *Personnel Psychology, 57,* 61–94.

Gergen, D. (2006, June 11). Bad news for bullies. *U.S. News and World Report, 140,* 54.

Graham, J. W. (1991). Servant leadership in organizations: Inspirational and moral. *Leadership Quarterly, 2,* 105–119.

Greenleaf, R. K. (1970). *The servant as leader.* Westfield, IN: The Greenleaf Center for Servant Leadership.

Greenleaf, R. K. (1972). *The institution as servant.* Westfield, IN: The Greenleaf Center for Servant Leadership.

Greenleaf, R. K. (1977). *Servant leadership: A journey into the nature of legitimate power and greatness.* New York: Paulist Press.

Hale, J. R., & Fields, D. L. (2007). Exploring servant leadership across cultures: A study of followers in Ghana and the USA. *Leadership, 3,* 397–417.

Hesse, H. (1956). *The journey to the East.* London: P. Owen.

Hu, J., & Liden, R. C. (2011). Antecedents of team potency and team effectiveness: An examination of goal and process clarity and servant leadership. *Journal of Applied Psychology, 96*(4), 851–862.

Kidder, T. (2003). *Mountains beyond mountains: The quest of Dr. Paul Farmer, a man who would cure the world.* New York: Random House.

Knowledge@Wharton. (2008, July 9). *Southwest Airlines' Colleen Barrett flies high on fuel hedging and "servant leadership."* Retrieved November 13, 2011, from http://knowledge.wharton.upenn.edu/article.cfm?articleid=2006.

Laub, J. A. (1999). Assessing the servant organization: Development of the servant organizational leadership assessment (SOLA) instrument. *Dissertation Abstracts International, 60* (02), 308. (UMI No. 9921922)

Liden, R. C., Panaccio, A., Hu, J., & Meuser, J. D. (in press). Servant leadership: Antecedents, consequences, and contextual moderators. In D. V. Day (Ed.), *The Oxford handbook of leadership and organizations.* Oxford, England: Oxford University Press.

Liden, R. C., Wayne, S. J., Zhao, H., & Henderson, D. (2008). Servant leadership: Development of a multidimensional measure and multi-level assessment. *Leadership Quarterly, 19,* 161–177.

Mack, J. (2007, October 1). Rice stresses "hard work" to boost kids' educations. *Kalamazoo Gazette,* p. A1.

Meuser, J. D, Liden, R. C., Wayne, S. J., & Henderson, D. J. (2011, August). *Is servant leadership always a good thing? The moderating influence of servant leadership prototype.* Paper presented at the meeting of the Academy of Management, San Antonio, TX.

Miller-Adams, M. (2009). *The power of a promise: Education and economic renewal in Kalamazoo.* Kalamazoo, MI: W. E. Upjohn Institute for Employment Research.

Neubert, M. J., Kacmar, K. M., Carlson, D. S., Chonko, L. B., & Roberts, J. A. (2008). Regulatory focus as a mediator of the influence of initiating structure and servant leadership on employee behavior. *Journal of Applied Psychology*, 93, 1220–1233.

Partners in Health. (2011). *History*. Retrieved September 27, 2011, from http://www.pih.org/pages/partners-in-health-history.html

Patterson, K. A. (2003). *Servant leadership: A theoretical model* (Doctoral dissertation, Regent University, ATT 30882719).

Russell, R. F., & Stone, A. G. (2002). A review of servant-leadership attributes: Developing a practical model. *Leadership & Organization Development Journal*, 23, 145–157.

Schaubroeck, J., Lam, S. S. K., & Peng, A. C. (2011). Cognition-based and affect-based trust as mediators of leader behavior influences on team performance. *Journal of Applied Psychology*, 96(4), 863–871.

Sendjaya, S., Sarros, J. C., & Santora, J. C. (2008). Defining and measuring servant leadership behaviour in organizations. *Journal of Management Studies*, 45(2), 402–424.

Senge, P. M. (2002). Afterword. In R. K. Greenleaf (Ed.), *Servant leadership: A journey into the nature of legitimate power and greatness* (pp. 343–360). New York: Paulist Press.

Spears, L. C. (2002). Tracing the past, present, and future of servant-leadership. In L. C. Spears & M. Lawrence (Eds.), *Focus on leadership: Servant-leadership for the 21st century* (pp. 1–16). New York: John Wiley & Sons.

Spears, L. C. (2010). Servant leadership and Robert K. Greenleaf's legacy. In D. van Dierendonck & K. Patterson (Eds.), *Servant leadership: Developments in theory and research* (pp. 11–24). New York: Palgrave Macmillan.

van Dierendonck, D. (2011). Servant leadership: A review and synthesis. *Journal of Management*, 37(4), 1228–1261.

van Dierendonck, D., & Nuijten, I. (2011). The servant leadership survey: Development and validation of a multidimensional measure. *Journal of Business and Psychology*, 26, 249–267.

Walumbwa, F. O., Hartnell, C. A., & Oke, A. (2010). Servant leadership, procedural justice climate, service climate, employee attitudes, and organizational citizenship behavior: A cross-level investigation. *Journal of Applied Psychology*, 95, 517–529.

Wheatley, M. (2002). The work of the servant leader. In L. C. Spears & M. Lawrence (Eds.), *Focus on leadership: Servant-leadership for the twenty-first century* (pp. 349–362). New York: John Wiley & Sons.

Wong, P. T. P., & Davey, D. (2007). *Best practices in servant leadership*. Paper presented at the Servant Leadership Research Roundtable, Regent University, Virginia Beach, VA.

11

Authentic Leadership

DESCRIPTION

Authentic leadership represents one of the newest areas of leadership research. It focuses on whether leadership is genuine and "real." As the title of this approach implies, authentic leadership is about the *authenticity* of leaders and their leadership. Unlike many of the theories that we have discussed in this book, authentic leadership is still in the formative phase of development. As a result, authentic leadership needs to be considered more tentatively: It is likely to change as new research about the theory is published.

In recent times, upheavals in society have energized a tremendous demand for authentic leadership. The destruction on 9/11, corporate scandals at companies like WorldCom and Enron, and massive failures in the banking industry have all created fear and uncertainty. People feel apprehensive and insecure about what is going on around them, and, as a result, they long for bona fide leadership they can trust and for leaders who are honest and good. People's demands for trustworthy leadership make the study of authentic leadership timely and worthwhile.

In addition to the public's interest, authentic leadership has been intriguing to researchers: It was identified earlier in transformational leadership research but never fully articulated (Bass, 1990; Bass & Steidlmeier, 1999; Burns, 1978; Howell & Avolio, 1993). Furthermore, practitioners had developed approaches to authentic leadership that were not evidence based, and so needed further clarification and testing. In attempts to more fully explore authentic leadership, researchers set out to identify the parameters of authentic leadership and more clearly conceptualize it, efforts that continue today.

Authentic Leadership Defined

On the surface, authentic leadership appears easy to define. In actuality, it is a complex process that is difficult to characterize. Among leadership scholars, there is no single accepted definition of authentic leadership. Instead, there are multiple definitions, each written from a different viewpoint and with a different emphasis (Chan, 2005).

One of those viewpoints is the *intrapersonal* perspective, which focuses closely on the leader and what goes on within the leader. It incorporates the leader's self-knowledge, self-regulation, and self-concept. In Shamir and Eilam's (2005) description of the intrapersonal approach, they suggest that authentic leaders exhibit genuine leadership, lead from conviction, and are originals, not copies. This perspective emphasizes a leader's life experiences and the meaning he or she attaches to those experiences as being critical to the development of the authentic leader.

A second way of defining authentic leadership is as an *interpersonal* process. This perspective outlines authentic leadership as relational, created by leaders and followers together (Eagly, 2005). It results not from the leader's efforts alone, but also from the response of followers. Authenticity emerges from the interactions between leaders and followers. It is a reciprocal process because leaders affect followers and followers affect leaders.

Finally, authentic leadership can be defined from a *developmental* perspective, which is exemplified in the work of Avolio and his associates (Avolio & Gardner, 2005; Gardner, Avolio, & Walumbwa, 2005; Walumbwa, Avolio, Gardner, Wernsing, & Peterson, 2008). This perspective, which underpins the approaches to authentic leadership discussed in the following section, views authentic leadership as something that can be nurtured in a leader, rather than as a fixed trait. Authentic leadership develops in people over a lifetime and can be triggered by major life events, such as a severe illness or a new career.

Taking a developmental approach, Walumbwa et al. (2008) conceptualized authentic leadership as a pattern of leader behavior that develops from and is grounded in the leader's positive psychological qualities and strong ethics. They suggest that authentic leadership is composed of four distinct but related components: self-awareness, internalized moral perspective, balanced processing, and relational transparency (Avolio, Walumbwa, & Weber, 2009). Over a lifetime, authentic leaders learn and develop each of these four types of behavior.

11.1 Building Authenticity

Approaches to Authentic Leadership

Formulations about authentic leadership can be differentiated into two areas: (1) the practical approach, which evolved from real-life examples and training and development literature; and (2) the theoretical approach, which is based on findings from social science research. Both approaches offer interesting insights about the complex process of authentic leadership.

Practical Approaches

Books and programs about authentic leadership are popular today; people are interested in the basics of this type of leadership. Specifically, they want to know the "how to" steps to become an authentic leader. In this section, we will discuss two practical approaches to authentic leadership: (1) Robert Terry's authentic leadership approach (1993), and (2) Bill George's authentic leadership approach (2003). Each of these approaches presents a unique perspective on how to practice authentic leadership.

Robert Terry's Authentic Leadership Approach. Terry's approach to authentic leadership is practice oriented. It utilizes a formula or guide for "how to do" leadership. At its core, the Terry approach is action centered: It focuses on the actions of the leader, leadership team, or organization in a particular situation. The moral premise underlying this approach is that leaders should strive to do what is right. The framework of the approach serves as a guide to these actions.

In any given situation where leadership is needed, Terry advocates that two core leadership questions must be addressed. First, what is really, *really* going on? Second, what are we going to do about it? Authentic leadership involves correctly answering these questions. It includes knowing and acting on what is "true" in yourself (authenticity), in your organization, and in the world. The challenge for leaders is to distinguish between authentic and inauthentic actions, and then to commit to authentic actions over the inauthentic. Unless leaders know what truly is going on, their actions will be inappropriate and can have serious consequences.

Terry developed the Authentic Action Wheel (Figure 11.1) to help diagnose and address underlying problems in organizations. The wheel has six components: Around the top of the wheel are *Meaning, Mission,* and *Power;* clockwise around the bottom are *Structure, Resources,* and *Existence.* The center of the wheel is labeled *Fulfillment* and represents

Figure 11.1　Authentic Action Wheel

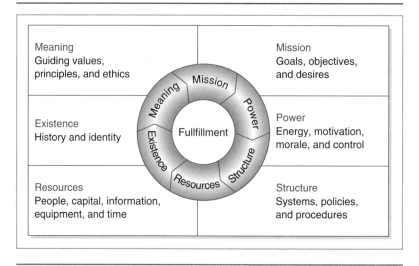

Meaning
Guiding values,
principles, and ethics

Mission
Goals, objectives,
and desires

Existence
History and identity

Power
Energy, motivation,
morale, and control

Resources
People, capital, information,
equipment, and time

Structure
Systems, policies,
and procedures

(Wheel labels: Meaning, Mission, Power, Structure, Resources, Existence, Fullfillment)

SOURCE: Adapted from *Authentic Leadership: Courage in Action,* by Robert W. Terry, 1993, p. 84, and Action Wheel Publishing.

the completion of the process. To answer the questions posed by Terry, two steps are required: (1) Locate the problem on the diagnostic wheel, and (2) strategically select an appropriate response to the problem.

The first step, locating the problem, is accomplished by doing an assessment of employees and their organizational concerns. Based on this assessment, leaders can identify on the action wheel the real concerns of the organization. For example, if employees make comments such as "We seem lost" or "Nobody cares around here," their concerns would be diagnosed as a problem related to *mission.* If employees are saying such things as "We are really stretched thin" or "We can't possibly do what they're asking us to do," their concerns could be diagnosed as *resource* issues on the wheel. Although there are an infinite number of possible issues within a group or an organization, the Authentic Action Wheel provides a structure that allows leaders to categorize various employee concerns into six major areas.

The second step, selecting the appropriate response to the issue, is also accomplished by using the Authentic Action Wheel. However, in this phase of the process the wheel is used prescriptively, to recommend a particular course of action. After a problem is identified, the wheel is used

▶ **11.1** Steve Jobs Commencement Speech

to encourage leaders to explore alternative explanations for the problem and to select a response based on that information. For example, if employees seem to be struggling with issues related to *power* and who is in control, leaders may wish to pay attention to the *mission* of the organization and the goals and objectives of the people involved. Similarly, if employees are raising questions about the *meaning* of a particular program, leaders may want to focus on *existence* because their concerns may be about the history and identity that undergirds the program. In other words, the Authentic Action Wheel is used to explore the various possible responses to a problem and to select the response that comes closest to solving the issue. Authentic leaders try to address the real problem in the most appropriate fashion.

To illustrate how the Authentic Action Wheel is used, consider the following story about problems in a high school baseball program.

Troubles began when leaders of the booster club asked for an investigation of the coach because of alleged improper use of funds, favoritism (i.e., the coach selected his son over others to be on the team), and violations of school policy (i.e., the coach allowed a parent with a DUI on his record to drive players home from practice). The booster club's concerns made the front page of the local newspaper, and local blogs and editorial pages were filled with reactions by parents, former players, and community members.

To analyze the baseball problem, a leader should have asked, "What is really, *really* going on in this situation?" An initial diagnosis might have suggested that the concerns about the coach clustered around issues of *structure* (i.e., school policy). Leaders of the booster club thought the coach violated school policies and wanted something done about it, while the coach thought his decisions were reasonable and that the booster club was overreaching its authority. The leaders of the booster club and the principal had different opinions about the policies governing the coach and the baseball team.

Using the Authentic Action Wheel as a guide, an authentic leader might have surmised that the conflict was about *power*. Who had the power to make decisions about use of funds, the selection of team players, or which parents could give rides to students? Using the wheel, a leader should have explored how issues of *power* were operating in this conflict. In the end, because these questions were not addressed, effective conflict resolution was *not* attained. Power struggles became even more apparent as the principal replaced the disgruntled cochairs of the booster club with different parents.

In summary, the Authentic Action Wheel is a visual diagnostic tool to help leaders frame problems. Leaders, with their followers, locate the problem on the wheel and then strategically respond to the major issues of concern. The Terry approach encourages individuals to see things differently and more clearly. In essence, this approach urges leaders to be authentic or "true" to themselves, their organization, and their world, and to base their actions on what is really going on in the situation.

Bill George's Authentic Leadership Approach. Although the Terry Authentic Action Wheel focuses on problem areas, the authentic leadership approach developed by George (2003; George & Sims, 2007) focuses on the characteristics of authentic leaders. George describes, in a practical way, the essential qualities of authentic leadership and how individuals can develop these qualities if they want to become authentic leaders.

Based on his experience as a corporate executive and through interviews with a diverse sample of 125 successful leaders, George found that authentic leaders have a genuine desire to serve others, they know themselves, and they feel free to lead from their core values. Specifically, authentic leaders demonstrate five basic characteristics: (1) They understand their purpose, (2) they have strong values about the right thing to do, (3) they establish trusting relationships with others, (4) they demonstrate self-discipline and act on their values, and (5) they are passionate about their mission (i.e., act from their heart) (Figure 11.2; George, 2003).

Figure 11.2 illustrates five dimensions of authentic leadership identified by George: purpose, values, relationships, self-discipline, and heart. The figure also illustrates each of the related characteristics—passion, behavior, connectedness, consistency, and compassion—that individuals need to develop to become authentic leaders.

In his interviews, George found that authentic leaders have a real sense of *purpose.* They know what they are about and where they are going. In addition to knowing their purpose, authentic leaders are inspired and intrinsically motivated about their goals. They are *passionate* individuals who have a deep-seated interest in what they are doing and truly care about their work.

A good example of an authentic leader who exhibited passion about his goals was Terry Fox, a cancer survivor, whose leg was amputated after it was overcome by bone cancer. Using a special leg prosthesis, Terry Fox attempted to run across Canada, from the Atlantic to the Pacific, to raise awareness and

11.2 The Authentic Leader

Figure 11.2   Authentic Leadership Characteristics

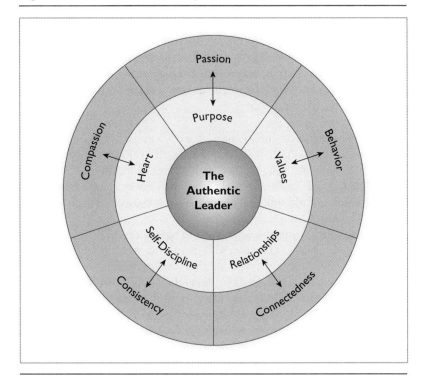

SOURCE: From *Authentic Leadership: Rediscovering the Secrets to Creating Lasting Value* by Bill George, copyright © 2003. Reproduced with permission of John Wiley & Sons, Inc.

money for cancer research. Although Terry died before he finished his run, his courage and passion affected the lives of millions of people. He also accomplished his goals to increase cancer awareness and to raise money for cancer research. Today, the Terry Fox Foundation is going strong and has raised more than $400 million (Canadian) for cancer research (http://www.terryfoxrun.org). Of the dimensions and characteristics in Figure 11.2, Terry Fox clearly demonstrated purpose and passion in his leadership.

Authentic leaders understand their own *values* and *behave* toward others based on these values. Stated another way, George suggests that authentic leaders know their "True North." They have a clear idea of who they are, where they are going, and what the right thing is to do. When tested in difficult situations, authentic leaders do not compromise their values, but rather use those situations to strengthen their values.

11.3 Stock Exchange Leadership

An example of a leader with a strong set of values is Nobel Peace Prize Laureate Nelson Mandela. Mandela is a deeply moral man with a strong conscience. While fighting to abolish apartheid in South Africa, he was unyielding in his pursuit of justice and equality for all. When he was in prison and offered early release in exchange for denouncing his viewpoint, he chose to remain incarcerated rather than compromise his position. Nelson Mandela knew who he was at his core. He knew his values, and his leadership reflected those values.

A third characteristic of authentic leadership in the George approach is strong *relationships*. Authentic leaders have the capacity to open themselves up and establish a *connection* with others. They are willing to share their own story with others and listen to others' stories. Through mutual disclosure, leaders and subordinates develop a sense of trust and closeness.

George argued that people today want to have access to their leaders and they want their leaders to be open with them. In a sense, people are asking leaders to soften the boundary around their leadership role and to be more transparent. People want to have a trusting relationship with their leaders. In exchange, people are willing to give leaders greater loyalty and commitment.

As we discussed in Chapter 8 (leader–member exchange theory), effective leader–follower relationships are marked by high-quality communication in which leaders and followers demonstrate a high degree of mutual trust, respect, and obligation toward each other. Leaders and followers are tied together in productive ways that go beyond the stereotypical leader–subordinate relationship. This results in strong leader–member relationships, greater understanding, and higher productivity.

Self-discipline is another dimension of authentic leadership, and is the quality that helps leaders to reach their goals. Self-discipline gives leaders focus and determination. When leaders establish objectives and standards of excellence, self-discipline helps them to reach these goals and to keep everyone accountable. Furthermore, self-discipline gives authentic leaders the energy to carry out their work in accordance with their values.

Like long-distance runners, authentic leaders with self-discipline are able to stay focused on their goals. They are able to listen to their inner compass and can discipline themselves to move forward, even in challenging circumstances. In stressful times, self-discipline allows authentic leaders to remain cool, calm, and *consistent*. Because disciplined leaders are predictable in their behavior, other people know what to expect and find

▶ **11.2** Vital Leadership

it easier to communicate with them. When the leader is self-directed and "on course," it gives other people a sense of security.

Last, the George approach identifies *compassion* and *heart* as important aspects of authentic leadership. Compassion refers to being sensitive to the plight of others, opening one's self to others, and being willing to help them. George (2003, p. 40) argued that as leaders develop compassion, they learn to be authentic. Leaders can develop compassion by getting to know others' life stories, doing community service projects, being involved with other racial or ethnic groups, or traveling to developing countries (George, 2003). These activities increase the leader's sensitivity to other cultures, backgrounds, and living situations.

In summary, George's authentic leadership approach highlights five important features of authentic leaders. Collectively, these features provide a practical picture of what people need to do to become authentic in their leadership. Authentic leadership is a lifelong developmental process, which is formed and informed by each individual's life story.

Theoretical Approach

Although still in its initial stages of development, a theory of authentic leadership is emerging in social science literature. In this section, we identify the basic components of authentic leadership and describe how these components are related to one another.

Background to the Theoretical Approach. Although people's interest in "authenticity" is probably timeless, research on authentic leadership is very recent, with the first article appearing in 2003. The primary catalyst for this research was a leadership summit at the University of Nebraska. This summit was sponsored by the Gallup Leadership Institute, and focused on the nature of authentic leadership and its development. From the summit, two sets of publications emerged: (1) a special issue of *Leadership Quarterly* in Summer 2005, and (2) *Monographs in Leadership and Management*, titled "Authentic Leadership Theory and Process: Origins, Effects and Development," also published in 2005. Prior to the summit, Luthans and Avolio (2003) published an article on authentic leadership development and positive organizational scholarship. The article also helped to ignite this area of research.

Interest in authentic leadership increased during a time in which there was a great deal of societal upheaval and instability in the United States.

11.1 Authentic Leadership Questionnaire

The attacks of 9/11, widespread corporate corruption, and a troubled economy all created a sense of uncertainty and anxiety in people about leadership. Widespread unethical and ineffective leadership necessitated the need for more humane, constructive leadership that served the common good (Fry & Whittington, 2005; Luthans & Avolio, 2003).

In addition, researchers felt the need to extend the work of Bass (1990) and Bass and Steidlmeier (1999) regarding the meaning of authentic transformational leadership. There was a need to operationalize the meaning of authentic leadership and create a theoretical framework to explain it. To develop a theory of authentic leadership, researchers drew from the fields of leadership, positive organizational scholarship, and ethics (Cooper, Scandura, & Schriesheim, 2005; Gardner et al., 2005).

A major challenge confronting researchers in developing a theory was to define the construct and identify its characteristics. As we discussed earlier in the chapter, authentic leadership has been defined in multiple ways, with each definition emphasizing a different aspect of the process. For this chapter, we have selected the definition set forth in a recent article by Walumbwa et al. (2008), who defined authentic leadership as "a pattern of leader behavior that draws upon and promotes both positive psychological capacities and a positive ethical climate, to foster greater self-awareness, an internalized moral perspective, balanced processing of information, and relational transparency on the part of leaders working with followers, fostering positive self-development" (p. 94). Although complex, this definition captures the current thinking of scholars regarding the phenomenon of authentic leadership and how it works.

In the research literature, different models have been developed to illustrate the process of authentic leadership. Gardner et al. (2005) created a model that frames authentic leadership around the developmental processes of leader and follower self-awareness and self-regulation. Ilies, Morgeson, and Nahrgang (2005) constructed a multicomponent model that discusses the impact of authenticity on leaders' and followers' happiness and well-being. In contrast, Luthans and Avolio (2003) formulated a model that explains authentic leadership as a developmental process. In this chapter, we will present a basic model of authentic leadership that is derived from the research literature that focuses on the core components of authentic leadership. Our discussion will focus on authentic leadership as a process.

Components of Authentic Leadership. In an effort to further our understanding of authentic leadership, Walumbwa and associates (2008) conducted a comprehensive review of the literature and interviewed groups of content experts in the field to determine what components constituted authentic leadership and to develop a valid measure of this construct. Their research identified four components: self-awareness, internalized moral perspective, balanced processing, and relational transparency (Figure 11.3). Together, these four components form the foundation for a theory of authentic leadership.

Self-awareness refers to the personal insights of the leader. It is not an end in itself but a process in which individuals understand themselves, including their strengths and weaknesses, and the impact they have on others. Self-awareness includes reflecting on your core values, identity, emotions, motives, and goals, and coming to grips with who you really are at the deepest level. In addition, it includes being aware of and trusting your own feelings (Kernis, 2003). When leaders know themselves and have a clear sense of who they are and what they stand for, they have a strong

Figure 11.3 Authentic Leadership

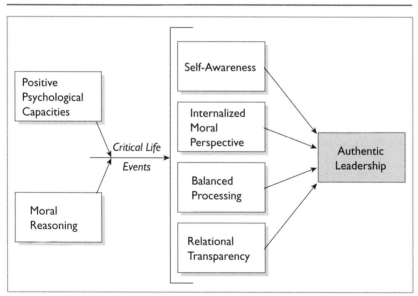

SOURCE: Adapted from Luthans, F., & Avolio, B. J. 2003. Authentic leadership development. In K. S. Cameron, J. E. Dutton, & R. E. Quinn (Eds.), *Positive organizational scholarship* (pp. 241–258). San Francisco: Berrett-Koehler, 2003; and W. L. Gardner, B. J. Avolio, F. Luthans, D. R. May, & F. O. Walumbwa, 2005. "Can you see the real me?" A self-based model of authentic leader and follower development. *Leadership Quarterly, 16,* 343–372.

11.2 Florence Nightingale

anchor for their decisions and actions (Gardner et al., 2005). Other people see leaders who have greater self-awareness as more authentic.

Internalized moral perspective refers to a self-regulatory process whereby individuals use their internal moral standards and values to guide their behavior rather than allow outside pressures to control them (e.g., group or societal pressure). It is a self-regulatory process because people have control over the extent to which they allow others to influence them. Others see leaders with an internalized moral perspective as authentic because their actions are consistent with their expressed beliefs and morals.

Balanced processing is also a self-regulatory behavior. It refers to an individual's ability to analyze information objectively and explore other people's opinions before making a decision. It also means avoiding favoritism about certain issues and remaining unbiased. Balanced processing includes soliciting viewpoints from those who disagree with you and fully considering their positions before taking your own action. Leaders with balanced processing are seen as authentic because they are open about their own perspectives, but are also objective in considering others' perspectives.

Relational transparency refers to being open and honest in presenting one's true self to others. It is self-regulatory because individuals can control their transparency with others. Relational transparency occurs when individuals share their core feelings, motives, and inclinations with others in an appropriate manner (Kernis, 2003). It includes the individuals showing both positive and negative aspects of themselves to others. In short, relational transparency is about communicating openly and being real in relationships with others.

Fundamentally, authentic leadership comprises the above four factors—self-awareness, internalized moral perspective, balanced processing, and relational transparency. These factors form the basis for authentic leadership.

Factors That Influence Authentic Leadership. There are other factors such as positive psychological capacities, moral reasoning, and critical life events that influence authentic leadership (Figure 11.3).

There are four key *positive psychological attributes* that have an impact on authentic leadership: confidence, hope, optimism, and resilience, which have been drawn from the fields of positive psychology and positive organizational behavior (Table 11.1; Luthans & Avolio, 2003). Positive attributes predispose or enhance a leader's capacity to develop the components of

Table 11.1   Related Positive Psychological Capacities

- Confidence

- Hope

- Optimism

- Resilience

SOURCE: Luthans, F., & Avolio, B. J. 2003. Authentic leadership development. In K. S. Cameron, J. E. Dutton, & R. E. Quinn (Eds.), *Positive organizational scholarship* (pp. 241–258). San Francisco: Berrett-Koehler.

authentic leadership discussed in the previous section. Each of these attributes has a trait-like and a state-like quality. They are trait-like because they may characterize a relatively fixed aspect of someone's personality that has been evident throughout his or her life (e.g., extraversion), and they are state-like because, with training or coaching, individuals are capable of developing or changing their characteristics.

Confidence refers to having self-efficacy—the belief that one has the ability to successfully accomplish a specified task. Leaders who have confidence are more likely to be motivated to succeed, to be persistent when obstacles arise, and to welcome a challenge (Bandura, 1997; Luthans & Avolio, 2003). *Hope* is a positive motivational state based on willpower and goal planning (Luthans & Avolio, 2003). Authentic leaders with hope have goals they know can be accomplished; their hope inspires followers to trust them and believe in their goals. *Optimism* refers to the cognitive process of viewing situations from a positive light and having favorable expectations about the future. Leaders with optimism are positive about their capabilities and the outcomes they can achieve. They approach life with a sense of abundance rather than scarcity (Covey, 1990). *Resilience* is the capacity to recover from and adjust to adverse situations. It includes the ability to positively adapt to hardships and suffering. During difficult times, resilient people are able to bounce back from challenging situations and feel strengthened and more resourceful as a result of them (Sutcliffe & Vogus, 2003).

Moral reasoning is another factor that can influence authentic leadership (Figure 11.3). It is the capacity to make ethical decisions about issues of right or wrong and good or bad. Developing the capacity for moral reasoning is a lifelong process. Higher levels of moral reasoning make it possible for the authentic leader to make decisions that transcend individual differences and align individuals toward a common goal. They enable leaders to be selfless and make judgments that serve the greater good of the group, organization, or community. Moral reasoning capacity also enables authentic leaders to use this ability to promote justice and achieve what is right for a community.

A final factor related to authentic leadership is *critical life events* (Figure 11.3). Critical events are major events that shape people's lives. They can be positive events, like receiving an unexpected promotion, having a child, or reading an important book; or they can be negative events, like being diagnosed with cancer, getting a negative year-end evaluation, or having a loved one die. Critical life events act as catalysts for change. Shamir and Eilam (2005) argued that authentic leadership rests heavily on the insights people attach to their life experiences. When leaders tell their life stories, they gain greater self-knowledge, more clarity about who they are, and a better understanding of their role. By understanding their own life experiences, leaders become more authentic.

Critical life events also stimulate growth in individuals and help them become stronger leaders (Luthans & Avolio, 2003). For example, Howard Schultz (founder and CEO of Starbucks) tells a story about when he was little: His father, who was a delivery driver, fell and was hurt on the job. His father did not have health insurance or worker's compensation. Seeing the problems that resulted from his father's difficulties, when Schultz built Starbucks he provided comprehensive health insurance for employees who worked as few as 20 hours a week. Schultz's style of leadership was triggered by his childhood experience.

As the theory of authentic leadership develops further, other antecedent factors that influence the process may be identified. To date, however, it is positive psychological capacities, moral reasoning capacities, and critical life events that have been identified as factors that are influential in a person's ability to become an authentic leader.

HOW DOES AUTHENTIC LEADERSHIP THEORY WORK?

In this chapter, we have discussed authentic leadership from practical and theoretical perspectives. Both perspectives describe authentic leadership as a developmental process that forms in leaders over time; however, both perspectives provide different descriptions for how authentic leadership works.

11.4 Fostering Authenticity

The practical approaches provide prescriptions for how to be authentic and how to develop authentic leadership. For example, the Terry approach (1993) emphasizes that leaders should frame issues by questioning *what is really going* on in a given situation. Authentic leadership works when leaders and followers come together to define their "real" concerns and determine what is the "right thing" to do about them. Authentic leadership tries to determine what is truly good for the leader, followers, and organization.

The process of authentic leadership works differently using the George approach (2003), which focuses on five characteristics leaders should develop to become authentic leaders. More specifically, George advocates that leaders become more *purposeful, value centered, relational, self-disciplined,* and *compassionate*. The essence of authentic leadership is being a leader who strongly demonstrates these five qualities.

Rather than simple prescriptions, the theoretical approach describes what authentic leadership is and what accounts for it. From this perspective, authentic leadership works because leaders demonstrate *self-awareness*, an *internalized moral perspective, balanced processing,* and *relational transparency*. Leaders develop these attributes through a lifelong process that is often influenced by critical life events. In addition, the literature suggests that positive psychological characteristics and moral reasoning have a significant impact on authentic leaders.

To illustrate, in a study of 387 employees and their immediate supervisors, Walumbwa, Wang, Wang, Schaubroeck, and Avolio (2010) examined the impact of the components of authentic leadership on follower behaviors. Overall, their findings indicated that the more leaders were seen as authentic, the more employees identified with them, felt empowered, engaged in work roles, and demonstrated organizational citizenship behaviors.

Authentic leadership is a complex process that emphasizes the development of qualities that help leaders to be perceived as trustworthy and believable by their followers. The leader's job is to learn to develop these qualities and apply them to the common good as he or she serves others.

STRENGTHS

Although it is in its early stages of development, the authentic leadership approach has several strengths. First, it fulfills an expressed need for trustworthy leadership in society. During the past 20 years, failures in public and private leadership have created distrust in people. Authentic leadership helps to fill a void and provides an answer to people who are searching for good and sound leadership in an uncertain world.

Second, authentic leadership provides broad guidelines for individuals who want to become authentic leaders. Both the practical and theoretical approaches clearly point to what leaders should do to become authentic leaders. For example, Terry (1993) argued that to be authentic, leaders need to work with followers to find what is really going on in a given situation and address it. Similarly, the social science literature emphasizes that it is important for leaders to have self-awareness, an internalized moral perspective, balanced processing, and relational transparency to be authentic. Taken together, these approaches provide a map for becoming an authentic leader.

Third, similar to transformational and servant leadership, authentic leadership has an explicit moral dimension. Underlying both the practical and theoretical approaches is the idea that authenticity requires leaders to do what is "right" and "good" for their followers and society. Authentic leaders understand their own values, place followers' needs above their own, and work with followers to align their interests in order to create a greater common good.

Fourth, authentic leadership emphasizes that authentic values and behaviors can be developed in leaders over time. Authentic leadership is not an attribute that only some people exhibit: Everyone can develop authenticity and learn to be more authentic. For example, leaders can learn to become more aware and transparent, or they can learn to be more relational and other-directed. Leaders can also develop moral reasoning capacities. Furthermore, Luthans and Avolio (2003) contended that leaders could learn to develop positive psychological capacities such as confidence, hope, optimism, and resilience, and could use these to create a positive organizational climate. They contended that there are many ways that leaders can learn to become authentic leaders over a lifetime.

Finally, authentic leadership can be measured using the Authentic Leadership Questionnaire (ALQ). The ALQ is a validated, theory-based instrument comprising 16 items that measure four factors of authentic leadership (Avolio et al., 2009; Walumbwa et al., 2008). As research moves forward in refining authentic leadership theory, it is valuable to have an established instrument of this construct that is theory-based and can be used to measure authentic leadership in future research.

▶ **11.3** Finding Authenticity

CRITICISMS

Authentic leadership is still in the formative stages of development, and there are a number of questions that still need to be addressed about the theory. First, the concepts and ideas presented in the practical approaches (i.e., George, 2003; Terry, 1993) are not fully substantiated. Whereas both of these approaches are interesting and offer insights on authentic leadership, neither approach is built on a broad empirical base, and neither approach has been tested for its validity. Without research support, the ideas set forth in the practical approaches should be treated cautiously as explanations of the authentic leadership process.

Second, the moral component of authentic leadership is not fully explained. Whereas authentic leadership implies that leaders are motivated by higher-order end values such as justice and community, the way that these values function to influence authentic leadership is not clear. For example, how are a leader's values related to a leader's self-awareness? Or, what is the path or underlying process through which moral values affect other components of authentic leadership? In its present form, authentic leadership does not offer thorough answers to these questions.

Third, researchers have questioned whether positive psychological capacities should be included as components of authentic leadership. Although there is an interest in the social sciences to study positive human potential and the best of the human condition (Cameron, Dutton, & Quinn, 2003), the rationale for including positive psychological capacities as an inherent part of authentic leadership has not been clearly explained by researchers. In addition, some have argued that the inclusion of positive leader capacities in authentic leadership broadens the construct of authentic leadership too much and makes it difficult to measure (Cooper et al., 2005). At this point in the development of research on authentic leadership, the role of positive psychological capacities in authentic leadership theory needs further clarification.

Finally, it is not clear how authentic leadership results in positive organizational outcomes. Given that it is a new area of research, it is not unexpected that there are few data on outcomes, but these data are necessary to substantiate the value of the theory. Although authentic leadership is intuitively appealing on the surface, questions remain about whether this approach is effective, in what contexts it is effective, and whether authentic leadership results in productive outcomes. Relatedly, it is also not clear in the research whether authentic leadership is sufficient to achieve organizational goals. For

11.4 Authenticity Framework

example, can an authentic leader who is disorganized and lacking in technical competence be an effective leader? Authenticity is important and valuable to good leadership, but how authenticity relates to effective leadership is unknown. Clearly, future research should be conducted to explore how authentic leadership is related to organizational outcomes.

APPLICATION

Because authentic leadership is still in the early phase of its development, there has been little research on strategies that people can use to develop or enhance authentic leadership behaviors. There have been some prescriptions from the practical theories, but there is little evidence-based research on whether these prescriptions or how-to strategies actually increase authentic leadership behavior.

In spite of the lack of intervention research, there are common themes from the authentic leadership literature that may be applicable to organizational or practice settings. One theme common to all of the formulations of authentic leadership is that people have the capacity to learn to be authentic leaders. In their original work on authentic leadership, Luthans and Avolio (2003) constructed a model of authentic leadership development. Conceptualizing it as a lifelong learning process, they argued that authentic leadership is a process that can be developed over time. This suggests that human resource departments may be able to foster authentic leadership behaviors in employees who move into leadership positions. Another theme that can be applied to organizations is the overriding goal of authentic leaders to try to do the "right" thing, to be honest with themselves and others, and to work for the common good. Last, authentic leadership is shaped and reformed by critical life events that act as triggers to growth and greater authenticity. Being sensitive to these events and using them as springboards to growth may be relevant to many people who are interested in becoming leaders who are more authentic.

CASE STUDIES

The following section provides three case studies (Cases 11.1, 11.2, and 11.3) of individuals who demonstrate authentic leadership. The first case is about Sally Helgesen, author of *The Female Advantage: Women's Ways*

▶ **11.4** Teaching Authentic Leadership

of Leadership (1990). The second case is about Greg Mortenson and how his mission to promote schools and peace in Pakistan and Afghanistan came under fire when he was accused of lying and financial impropriety. The final case is about Betty Ford, former First Lady of the United States, and her work in the areas of breast cancer awareness and substance abuse treatment. At the end of each of the cases, questions are provided to help you analyze the case using ideas from authentic leadership.

CASE 11.1

Am I Really a Leader?

Sally Helgesen was born in the small Midwestern town of Saint Cloud, Minnesota. Her mother was a housewife who later taught English, and her father was a college professor of speech. After attending a local state college, where she majored in English and comparative religion, Sally spread her wings and moved to New York, inspired by the classic film *Breakfast at Tiffany's*.

Sally found work as a writer, first in advertising and then as an assistant to a columnist at the then-influential *Village Voice*. She contributed freelance articles to magazines such as *Harper's, Glamour, Vogue, Fortune,* and *Inside Sports*. She also returned to school, completing a degree in classics at Hunter College and taking language courses at the city graduate center in preparation for a PhD in comparative religion. She envisioned herself as a college professor, but also enjoyed freelancing. She felt a strong dichotomy within her, part quiet scholar and part footloose dreamer. The conflict bothered her, and she wondered how she would resolve it. Choosing to be a writer—actually declaring herself to be one—seemed scary, grandiose, and fraudulent.

Then one day, while walking on a New York side street in the rain, Sally saw an adventuresome black cat running beside her. It reminded her of Holly Golightly's cat in *Breakfast at Tiffany's*, an emblem in the movie for Holly's dreamy temperament and rootlessness. It made her realize how much the freedom and independence offered by her "temporary" career as a writer suited her temperament. Sally told the cat she was a writer—she'd never been able to say the words before—and decided she was going to commit to full-time writing, at least for a time. When she saw the opportunity to cover a prominent murder trial in Fort Worth, Texas, she took it.

(Continued)

(Continued)

While covering the trial, Sally became intrigued with the culture of Texas, and decided she wanted to write a book on the role of independent oil producers in shaping the region. Doing so required a huge expenditure of time and money, and for almost a year Sally lived out of the trunk of her car, staying with friends in remote regions all over Texas. It was lonely and hard and exhilarating, but Sally was determined to see the project through. When the book, *Wildcatters* (1981), was published, it achieved little recognition, but Sally felt an enormous increase in confidence and commitment as a result of having finished the book. It strengthened her conviction that, for better or worse, she was a writer.

Sally moved back to New York and continued to write articles and search around for another book. She also began writing speeches for the chief executive officer (CEO) at a Fortune 500 company. She loved the work, and particularly enjoyed being an observer of office politics, even though she did not perceive herself to be a part of them. Sally viewed her role as being an "outsider looking in," an observer of the culture. She sometimes felt like an actor in a play about an office, but this detachment made her feel professional rather than fraudulent.

As a speechwriter, Sally spent a lot of time interviewing people in the companies she worked for. Doing so made her realize that men and women often approach their work in fundamentally different ways. She also became convinced that many of the skills and attitudes women brought to their work were increasingly appropriate for the ways in which organizations were changing, and that women had certain advantages as a result. She also noticed that the unique perspectives of women were seldom valued by CEOs or other organizational leaders, who could have benefited if they had better understood and been more attentive to what women had to offer.

These observations inspired Sally to write another book. In 1988, she signed a contract with a major publisher to write a book on what women had to contribute to organizations. Until then, almost everything written about women at work focused on how they needed to change and adapt. Sally felt strongly that if women were encouraged to emphasize the negative, they would miss an historic opportunity to help lead organizations in a time of change. The time was right for this message, and *The Female Advantage: Women's Ways of Leadership* (1990) became very successful, topping a number of best-seller charts and remaining steadily in print for nearly 20 years. The book's prominence resulted in numerous speaking and consulting opportunities, and Sally began traveling the world delivering seminars and working with a variety of clients.

This acclaim and visibility were somewhat daunting to Sally. While she recognized the value of her book, she also knew that she was not a social scientist with a body of theoretical data on women's issues. She saw herself as an author rather than an expert, and the old questions about fraudulence that she had dealt with in her early years in New York began to reassert themselves in a different form. Was she really being authentic? Could she take on the mantle of leadership and all it entailed? In short, she wondered if she could be the leader that people seemed to expect.

The path Sally took to answer these questions was simply to present herself for who she was. She was Sally Helgesen, an outsider looking in, a skilled and imaginative observer of current issues. For Sally, the path to leadership did not manifest itself in a step-by-step process. Sally's leadership began with her own journey of finding herself and accepting her personal authenticity. Through this self-awareness, she grew to trust her own expertise as a writer with a keen eye for current trends in organizational life.

Sally continues to be an internationally recognized consultant and speaker on contemporary issues, and has published five books. She remains uncertain about whether she will finish her degree in comparative religion and become a college professor, but always keeps in mind the career of I. F. Stone, an influential political writer in the 1950s and 1960s who went back to school and got an advanced degree in classics at the age of 75.

Questions

1. Learning about one's self is an essential step in becoming an authentic leader. What role did self-awareness play in Sally Helgesen's story of leadership?

2. How would you describe the authenticity of Sally Helgesen's leadership?

3. At the end of the case, Sally Helgesen is described as taking on the "mantle of leadership." Was this important for her leadership? How is taking on the mantle of leadership related to a leader's authenticity? Does every leader reach a point in his or her career where embracing the leadership role is essential?

CASE 11.2

A Leader Under Fire

(The previous edition of this book includes a case study outlining Greg Mortenson's creation of the Central Asia Institute and highlighting his authentic leadership qualities in more detail. For an additional perspective on Mortenson, you can access the original case study at www.sagepub. com/northouse6e.)

By 2011, there were few people who had never heard of Greg Mortenson. He was the subject of two best-selling books, *Three Cups of Tea* (2006) and *Stones into Schools* (2009), which told how the former emergency trauma room nurse had become a hero who built schools in rural areas of Afghanistan and Pakistan.

His story was phenomenal: Lost and sick after attempting to scale K2, Greg was nursed back to health by the villagers of remote Korphe, Afghanistan. Greg promised to build the village a school, a monumental effort that took him three years as he learned to raise money, navigate the foreign culture, and build a bridge above a 60-foot-deep chasm. His success led him to create the Central Asia Institute (CAI), a nonprofit organization that "empowers communities of Central Asia through literacy and education, especially for girls, promotes peace through education, and conveys the importance of these activities globally." By 2011, the CAI had successfully established or supported more than 170 schools in Pakistan and Afghanistan, and helped to educate more than 68,000 students (CAI, 2011a).

Greg's story seemed too good to be true. In April 2011, television news show *60 Minutes* and author Jon Krakauer alleged that it was. *60 Minutes* accused Greg of misusing money and benefitting excessively from the CAI. The show's reporter visited schools the CAI had built overseas and claimed that he could not find six of the schools and that others were abandoned. The show featured an interview with Krakauer, who claimed Greg had fabricated parts of his best-selling book, *Three Cups of Tea*. When *60 Minutes* approached Greg for comment at a book signing, he refused to talk to the program.

The next day, Krakauer (*Into Thin Air* [1997] and *Under the Banner of Heaven* [2003]) published a short online book, *Three Cups of Deceit* (2011), in which he claimed Greg lied many times in *Three Cups of Tea*, starting with his initial tale of being in Korphe.

Greg and CAI were caught in a firestorm of media and public scrutiny. An investigation into the alleged financial improprieties was launched by Montana's Attorney General (the CAI is based in Bozeman), and two

Montana legislators filed a $5 million class action lawsuit claiming he fooled 4 million people into buying his books.

Greg withdrew from the public eye. The day the *60 Minutes* program aired, he posted a letter on the CAI website saying he stood by his books and claiming the news show "paints a distorted picture using inaccurate information, innuendo and a microscopic focus on one year's (2009) IRS 990 financial, and a few points in the book *Three Cups of Tea* that occurred almost 18 years ago" (CAI, 2011b). Many criticized the organization's founder for not more aggressively defending himself.

What many people did not know, however, was that two days before the *60 Minutes* segment appeared, Greg had been diagnosed with a hole and a large aneurysm in his heart and was scheduled for open-heart surgery in the next few months. Meanwhile, the CAI worked to ensure its transparency by posting its tax returns and a master list of projects and their status. The report documented 210 schools, with 17 of those receiving "full support" from the CAI, which includes teachers' salaries, supplies, books, and furniture and monitoring by CAI contractors (Flandro, 2011).

The Attorney General investigation was still not concluded by October 1, 2011, and the lawsuit has dropped the CAI as a defendant but continues its claims against Greg and coauthor David Oliver Relin. Greg's legal advisers have advised him not to engage with the media, but he has begun to schedule a small number of public speaking engagements. Until the investigation is concluded, a cloud of suspicion hangs over Greg and the CAI. Former CAI board member Andrew Marcus says that is unfortunate and hopes the public will consider what Greg and the organization have accomplished.

"It's hard to imagine anyone who's done more for education in that part of the world," Marcus has said. "It took a real human being to do that" (Flandro, 2011).

Questions

1. Would you describe Greg Mortenson as an authentic leader? Explain your answer.

2. In the chapter, we discussed moral reasoning and transparency as components of authentic leadership. Do you think Greg exhibited these components as part his leadership?

3. How was Greg's response to the allegations against him characteristic of an authentic leader?

4. In the future, how will the investigations of Greg Mortenson affect the authenticity of his leadership?

CASE 11.3

The Reluctant First Lady

Betty Ford admits that August 9, 1974, the day her husband was sworn in as the 38th President of the United States, was "the saddest day of my life" (Ford, 1978, p. 1).

Elizabeth Bloomer Ford was many things—a former professional dancer and dance teacher, the mother of four nearly grown children, the wife of 13-term U.S. Congressman Gerald "Jerry" R. Ford who was looking forward to their retirement—but she never saw being the country's First Lady as her destiny.

As she held the Bible her husband's hand rested on while he took the oath of office, Betty began a journey in which she would become many more things: a breast cancer survivor, an outspoken advocate of women's rights, a recovering alcoholic and addict, and cofounder and president of the Betty Ford Center, a nonprofit treatment center for substance abuse.

The Fords' path to the White House began in October 1973, when Jerry was tapped to replace then-U.S. Vice President Spiro Agnew who had resigned. After only 9 months in that role, Jerry became the U.S. President after Richard M. Nixon left office amidst the Watergate scandal.

In her first days as the First Lady, Betty became known for her openness and candor. At the time, women were actively fighting for equal rights in the workplace and in society. Less than half of American women were employed outside the home, and women's earnings were only 38% of their male counterparts' (Spraggins, 2005). Betty raised a number of eyebrows in her first press conference, when she spoke out in support of abortion rights, women in politics, and the Equal Rights Amendment.

Betty hadn't even been in the White House a month when she was diagnosed with breast cancer. She again broke with social conventions and spoke openly about the diagnosis and treatment for a disease that was not widely discussed in public. With her cooperation, *Newsweek* magazine printed a complete account of her surgery and treatment, which included a radical mastectomy. This openness helped raise awareness of breast cancer screening and treatment options and created an atmosphere of support and comfort for other women fighting the disease.

"Lying in the hospital, thinking of all those women going for cancer checkups because of me, I'd come to recognize more clearly the power of the woman in the White House," she said in her first autobiography,

The Times of My Life. "Not my power, but the power of the position, a power which could be used to help" (Ford, 1978, p. 194).

After her recuperation, Betty made good use of that newfound power. She openly supported and lobbied for passage of the Equal Rights Amendment, a bill that would ensure that *"equality of rights under the law shall not be denied or abridged by the United States or by any state on account of sex" (Francis, 2009).*

In an interview with the television news show 60 Minutes, Betty drew the ire of many conservatives when she candidly shared her views on the provocative issues of abortion rights, premarital sex, and marijuana use. After the interview aired, public opinion of Betty plummeted, but her popularity quickly rebounded, and within months her approval rating had climbed to 75%.

At the same time, Betty was busy with the duties of First Lady, entertaining dignitaries and heads of state from countries across the globe. In 1975 she began actively campaigning for her husband for the 1976 presidential election, inspiring buttons that read "Vote for Betty's Husband." Ford lost the election to Jimmy Carter and, because he was suffering from laryngitis, Betty stepped into the spotlight to read Jerry's concession speech to the country, congratulating Carter on his victory. Betty's time as First Lady ended in January 1977, and the Fords retired to Rancho Mirage, California, and Vail, Colorado.

A little more than a year later, at the age of 60, Betty began another personal battle: overcoming alcoholism and an addiction to prescription medicine. Betty had a 14-year dependence on painkillers for chronic neck spasms, arthritis, and a pinched nerve, but refused to admit she was addicted to alcohol. After checking into the Long Beach Naval Hospital's Alcohol and Drug Rehabilitation Service, she found the strength to face her demons and, again, went public with her struggles.

"I have found that I am not only addicted to the medications I've been taking for my arthritis, but also to alcohol," she wrote in a statement released to the public. "...I expect this treatment and fellowship to be a solution for my problems and I embrace it not only for me but for all the others who are here to participate" (Ford, 1978, p. 285).

Betty Ford found recovering from addiction was particularly daunting at a time when most treatment centers were geared toward treating men.

(Continued)

(Continued)

"The female alcoholic has more emotional problems, more health problems, more parenting problems, makes more suicide attempts, than the alcoholic man," Betty explained in her second autobiography, *Betty, A Glad Awakening* (Ford, 1987, p. 129).

For this reason, Betty helped to establish the nonprofit Betty Ford Center in 1982 in Rancho Mirage. The center splits its space equally between male and female patients, but the treatment is gender specific with programs for the entire family system affected by addiction. The center's success has attracted celebrities as well as everyday people including middle-class moms, executives, college students, and laborers. Betty's activism in the field of recovery earned her the Presidential Medal of Freedom in 1991 and the Congressional Medal of Honor in 1999.

Speaking at an alumni reunion of Betty Ford Center patients, Betty said, "I'm really proud of this center. And I'm really grateful for my own recovery, because with my recovery, I was able to help some other people come forward and address their own addictions. And I don't think there's anything as wonderful in life as being able to help someone else" (Ford, 1987, p. 217).

Questions

1. How would you describe Betty Ford's leadership? In what ways could her leadership be described as authentic?

2. How did critical life events play a role in the development of her leadership?

3. Is there a clear moral dimension to Betty Ford's leadership? In what way is her leadership about serving the common good? Discuss.

4. As we discussed in the chapter, self-awareness and transparency are associated with authentic leadership. How does Betty Ford exhibit these qualities?

LEADERSHIP INSTRUMENT

Although still in its early phases of development, the Authentic Leadership Questionnaire (ALQ) was created by Walumbwa and associates (2008) to explore and validate the assumptions of authentic leadership. It is a

16-item instrument that measures four factors of authentic leadership: self-awareness, internalized moral perspective, balanced processing, and relational transparency. Based on samples in China, Kenya, and the United States, Walumbwa and associates (2008) validated the dimensions of the instrument and found it positively related to outcomes such as organizational citizenship, organizational commitment, and satisfaction with supervisor and performance. To obtain this instrument, contact Mind Garden, Inc., Menlo Park, California, or www.mindgarden.com.

In this section, we provide an authentic leadership self-assessment to help you determine your own level of authentic leadership. This questionnaire will help you understand how authentic leadership is measured and provide you with your own scores on items that characterize authentic leadership. The questionnaire includes 16 questions that assess the four major components of authentic leadership discussed earlier in this chapter: self-awareness, internalized moral perspective, balanced processing, and relational transparency. Your results on this self-assessment questionnaire will give you information about your level of authentic leadership on these underlying dimensions of authentic leadership. This questionnaire is intended for practical applications to help you understand the complexities of authentic leadership. It is not designed for research purposes.

Authentic Leadership Self-Assessment Questionnaire

Instructions: This questionnaire contains items about different dimensions of authentic leadership. There are no right or wrong responses, so please answer honestly. Use the following scale when responding to each statement by writing the number from the scale below that you feel most accurately characterizes your response to the statement.

Key: 1 = Strongly   2 = Disagree   3 = Neutral   4 = Agree   5 = Strongly
           disagree   agree

1.	I can list my three greatest weaknesses.	1 2 3 4 5
2.	My actions reflect my core values.	1 2 3 4 5
3.	I seek others' opinions before making up my own mind.	1 2 3 4 5
4.	I openly share my feelings with others.	1 2 3 4 5
5.	I can list my three greatest strengths.	1 2 3 4 5
6.	I do *not* allow group pressure to control me.	1 2 3 4 5
7.	I listen closely to the ideas of those who disagree with me.	1 2 3 4 5
8.	I let others know who I truly am as a person.	1 2 3 4 5
9.	I seek feedback as a way of understanding who I really am as a person.	1 2 3 4 5
10.	Other people know where I stand on controversial issues.	1 2 3 4 5
11.	I do not emphasize my own point of view at the expense of others.	1 2 3 4 5
12.	I rarely present a "false" front to others.	1 2 3 4 5
13.	I accept the feelings I have about myself.	1 2 3 4 5
14.	My morals guide what I do as a leader.	1 2 3 4 5
15.	I listen very carefully to the ideas of others before making decisions.	1 2 3 4 5
16.	I admit my mistakes to others.	1 2 3 4 5

Scoring

1. Sum the responses on items 1, 5, 9, and 13 (self-awareness).

2. Sum the responses on items 2, 6, 10, and 14 (internalized moral perspective).

3. Sum the responses on items 3, 7, 11, and 15 (balanced processing).

4. Sum the responses on items 4, 8, 12, and 16 (relational transparency).

Total Scores

Self-Awareness: _____

Internalized Moral Perspective: _____

Balanced Processing: _____

Relational Transparency: _____

Scoring Interpretation

This self-assessment questionnaire is designed to measure your authentic leadership by assessing four components of the process: self-awareness, internalized moral perspective, balanced processing, and relational transparency. By comparing your scores on each of these components, you can determine which are your stronger and which are your weaker components in each category. You can interpret your authentic leadership scores using the following guideline: high = 16–20 and low = 15 and below. Scores in the upper range indicate stronger authentic leadership, whereas scores in the lower range indicate weaker authentic leadership.

SUMMARY

As a result of leadership failures in the public and private sectors, authentic leadership is emerging in response to societal demands for genuine, trust-worthy, and good leadership. Authentic leadership describes leadership that is transparent, morally grounded, and responsive to people's needs and values. Even though authentic leadership is still in the early stages of development, the study of authentic leadership is timely and worthwhile, offering hope to people who long for true leadership.

Although there is no single accepted definition of authentic leadership, it can be conceptualized intrapersonally, developmentally, and interperson-ally. The intrapersonal perspective focuses on the leader and the leader's knowledge, self-regulation, and self-concept. The interpersonal perspec-tive claims that authentic leadership is a collective process, created by leaders and followers together. The developmental perspective emphasizes major components of authentic leadership that develop over a lifetime and are triggered by major life events.

There are two practical approaches to authentic leadership that provide "how to" steps to become an authentic leader. Terry's approach (1993) describes how leaders can utilize the Authentic Action Wheel to address *what is really going on* in a situation and determine what actions are truly good for the leader, followers, and the organization.

George's approach (2003) identifies five basic dimensions of authentic leadership and the corresponding behavioral characteristics individuals need to develop to become authentic leaders.

In the social science literature, a theoretical approach to authentic leadership is emerging. Drawing from the fields of leadership, positive organizational scholarship, and ethics, researchers have identified four major components of authentic leadership: self-awareness, internalized moral perspective, balanced processing, and relational transparency.

In addition, researchers have found that authentic leadership is influ-enced by a leader's positive psychological capacities, moral reasoning, and critical life events.

Authentic leadership has several positive features. First, it provides an answer to people who are searching for good and sound leadership in an uncertain world. Second, authentic leadership is prescriptive and provides a

11.5 Leadership for a New Century

great deal of information about how leaders can learn to become authentic. Third, it has an explicit moral dimension that asserts that leaders need to do what is "right" and "good" for their followers and society. Fourth, it is framed as a process that is developed by leaders over time rather than as a fixed trait. Last, authentic leadership can be measured with a theory-based instrument.

There are also negative features to authentic leadership. First, the ideas set forth in the practical approaches need to be treated cautiously because they have not been fully substantiated by research. Second, the moral component of authentic leadership is not fully explained. For example, it does not describe how values such as justice and community are related to authentic leadership. Third, the rationale for including positive psychological capacities as an inherent part of a model of authentic leadership has not been fully explicated. Finally, there is a lack of evidence regarding the effectiveness of authentic leadership and how it is related to positive organizational outcomes.

In summary, authentic leadership is a new and exciting area of research, which holds a great deal of promise. As more research is conducted on authentic leadership, a clearer picture will emerge about the true nature of the process and the assumptions and principles that it encompasses.

Visit the Student Study Site at **www.sagepub.com/northouse6e** for web quizzes, leadership questionnaires, and media links represented by the icons.

REFERENCES

Avolio, B. J., & Gardner, W. L. (2005). Authentic leadership development: Getting to the root of positive forms of leadership. *Leadership Quarterly, 16,* 315–338.

Avolio, B. J., Walumbwa, F. O., & Weber, T. J. (2009). Leadership: Current theories, research, and future directions. *Annual Review of Psychology, 60,* 421–449.

Bandura, A. (1997). *Self-efficacy: The exercise of control.* New York: Freeman.

Bass, B. M. (1990). *Handbook of leadership.* New York: Free Press.

Bass, B. M., & Steidlmeier, P. (1999). Ethics, character, and authentic transformational leadership. *Leadership Quarterly, 10,* 181–217.

Burns, J. M. (1978). *Leadership.* New York: Harper & Row.

Cameron, K. S., Dutton, J. E., & Quinn, R. E. (2003). Foundations of positive organizational scholarship. In K. S. Cameron, J. E. Dutton, & R. E. Quinn (Eds.), *Positive organizational scholarship* (pp. 3–13). San Francisco: Berrett-Koehler.

Central Asia Institute. (2011a). *Central Asia Institute.* Retrieved September 30, 2011, from https://www.ikat.org

Central Asia Institute. (2011b). *Executive Director Greg Mortenson's Message to Supporters 4/17/11.* Retrieved September 30, 2011, from https://www.ikat.org

Chan, A. (2005). Authentic leadership measurement and development: Challenges and suggestions. In W. L. Gardner, B. J. Avolio, & F. O. Walumbwa (Eds.), *Authentic leadership theory and practice: Origins, effects, and development* (pp. 227–251). Oxford: Elsevier Science.

Cooper, C., Scandura, T. A., & Schriesheim, C. A. (2005). Looking forward but learning from our past: Potential challenges to developing authentic leadership theory and authentic leaders. *Leadership Quarterly, 116,* 474–495.

Covey, S. R. (1990). *Principle-centered leadership.* New York: Fireside.

Eagly, A. H. (2005). Achieving relational authenticity in leadership: Does gender matter? *Leadership Quarterly, 16,* 459–474.

Flandro, C. (2011, September 25). *The rise, fall and future of humanitarian Greg Mortenson and the Central Asia Institute.* Retrieved September 27, 2011, from http://www.bozemandailychronicle.com/news/

Ford, B. (1978). *The times of my life.* New York: Harper & Row.

Ford, B. (1987). *Betty, a glad awakening.* Garden City, NY: Doubleday & Company.

Francis, R. W. (2009). *The history of the equal rights amendment.* Accessed May 29, 2009, from http://www.equalrightsamendment.org/

Fry, L. W., & Whittington, J. L. (2005). In search of authenticity: Spiritual leadership theory as a source for future theory, research, and practice on authentic leadership. In W. L. Gardner, B. J. Avolio, & F. O. Walumbwa (Eds.), *Authentic leadership theory and practice: Origins, effects, and development* (pp. 183–202). Oxford: Elsevier Science.

Gardner, W. L., Avolio, B. J., Luthans, F., May, D. R., & Walumbwa, F. O. (2005). "Can you see the real me?" A self-based model of authentic leader and follower development. *Leadership Quarterly, 16,* 343–372.

Gardner, W. L., Avolio, B. J., & Walumbwa, F. O. (2005). Authentic leadership development: Emergent trends and future directions. In W. L. Gardner, B. J. Avolio, & F. O. Walumbwa (Eds.), *Authentic leadership theory and practice: Origins, effects, and development* (pp. 387–406). Oxford: Elsevier Science.

George, B. (2003). *Authentic leadership: Rediscovering the secrets to creating lasting value.* San Francisco: Jossey-Bass.

George, B., & Sims, P. (2007). *True north: Discover your authentic leadership.* San Francisco: Jossey-Bass.

Helgesen, S. (1981). *Wildcatters: A story of Texans, oil, and money.* New York: Doubleday.

Helgesen, S. (1990). *The female advantage: Women's ways of leadership.* New York: Doubleday.

Howell, J. M., & Avolio, B. J. (1993). The ethics of charismatic leadership: Submission or liberation? *Academy of Management Executive, 6*(2), 43–54.

Ilies, R., Morgeson, F. P., & Nahrgang, J. D. (2005). Authentic leadership and eudaemonic well-being: Understanding leader-follower outcomes. *Leadership Quarterly, 16,* 373–394.

Kernis, M. H. (2003). Toward a conceptualization of optimal self-esteem. *Psychological Inquiry, 14*, 1–26.

Krakauer, J. (1997). *Into thin air: A personal account of the Mount Everest disaster.* New York: Villard Books.

Krakauer, J. (2003). *Under the banner of heaven: A story of violent faith.* New York: Doubleday.

Krakauer, J. (2011). *Three cups of deceit.* New York: Anchor Books.

Luthans, F., & Avolio, B. J. (2003). Authentic leadership development. In K. S. Cameron, J. E. Dutton, & R. E. Quinn (Eds.), *Positive organizational scholarship* (pp. 241–258). San Francisco: Berrett-Koehler.

Mortenson, G. (2009). *Stones into schools: Promoting peace with education in Afghanistan and Pakistan.* New York: Penguin Books.

Mortenson, G., & Relin, D. O. (2006). *Three cups of tea: One man's mission to promote peace . . . one school at a time.* New York: Penguin Books.

Shamir, B., & Eilam, G. (2005). "What's your story?" A life-stories approach to authentic leadership development. *Leadership Quarterly, 16*, 395–417.

Spraggins, R. E. (2005). *We the people: Men and women in the United States.* Accessed May 30, 2009, from http://www.census.gov/prod/2005pubs/censr-20.pdf

Sutcliffe, K. M., & Vogus, T. J. (2003). Organizing for resilience. In K. S. Cameron, J. E. Dutton, & R. E. Quinn (Eds.), *Positive organizational scholarship* (pp. 94–110). San Francisco: Berrett-Koehler.

Terry, R. W. (1993). *Authentic leadership: Courage in action.* San Francisco: Jossey-Bass.

Walumbwa, F. O., Avolio, B. J., Gardner, W. L., Wernsing, T. S., & Peterson, S. J. (2008). Authentic leadership: Development and validation of a theory-based measure. *Journal of Management, 34*(1), 89–126.

Walumbwa, F. O., Wang, P., Wang, H., Schaubroeck, J., & Avolio, B. J. (2010). Psychological processes linking authentic leadership to follower behaviors. *The Leadership Quarterly, 21*, 901–914.

12

Team Leadership

Susan E. Kogler Hill

DESCRIPTION

Leadership in organizational work teams has become one of the most popular and rapidly growing areas of leadership theory and research. A team is a specific type of group composed of members who are interdependent, who share common goals, and who must coordinate their activities to accomplish these goals. Examples of such teams include project management teams, task forces, work units, standing committees, quality teams, and improvement teams. Teams have an applied function within an organizational context. A team has specified roles for its members with requisite knowledge and skills to perform these roles (Levi, 2011).

Reviews of the historical roots of group research provide a clear explanation of the long and diverse study of human groups (Levi, 2011; McGrath, Arrow, & Berdahl, 2000; Porter & Beyerlein, 2000). Porter and Beyerlein (2000) indicate that the study of groups actually began in the 1920s and 1930s, with the focus of the human relations movement on collaborative efforts at work, as opposed to the individual efforts previously advocated by scientific management theorists. In the 1940s, the focus shifted to the study of group dynamics and the development of social science theory. In the 1950s, the focus moved to sensitivity training and T-groups, and the role of leadership in these groups. Much of this early research was based on laboratory studies of experimental groups, frequently ignoring the contexts in which the groups were embedded (McGrath et al., 2000).

In the 1960s and 1970s, the era of organizational development, researchers focused on developing team and leadership effectiveness through interventions in ongoing work teams. In the 1980s, competition from Japan and other countries encouraged the focus on quality teams, benchmarking, and continuous improvement. In the 1990s, the focus on organizational teams, while still focusing on quality, shifted to a global perspective focusing on organizational strategies for maintaining a competitive advantage. Organizations have faster response capability because of their flatter organizational structure, which relies on teams and new technology to enable communication across time and space (Porter & Beyerlein, 2000). Mankin, Cohen, and Bikson (1996, p. 217) referred to this new organization as being "team-based, technology-enabled." The organizational team-based structure is an important way to remain competitive by responding quickly and adapting to constant, rapid changes.

Much research has focused on the problems confronting organizational work teams and on ways to make them more effective (Ilgen, Major, Hollenbeck, & Sego, 1993). Research on the effectiveness of organizational teams has suggested that the use of teams has led to greater productivity, a more effective use of resources, better decisions and problem solving, better-quality products and services, and greater innovation and creativity (Parker, 1990). However, for teams to be successful, the organizational culture needs to support employee involvement. Many teams have failed because they exist in a traditional authority structure that does not promote upward communication or decision making at lower levels. Teams will have great difficulty in organizational cultures that are not supportive of collaborative work and decision making. Changing the organizational culture to one that is more supportive of teams is possible, but it takes time and effort (Levi, 2011).

A review of team research suggests that studies since 1996 have become more complex, focusing on more team variables, and no longer focusing exclusively on the outcome of team performance. Current research is also investigating the role of affective, behavioral, and cognitive processes in team success and viability. The role and impact of mediating processes such as trusting, bonding, planning, adapting, structuring, and learning are also being studied in terms of team performance and viability (Ilgen, Hollenbeck, Johnson, & Jundt, 2005).

It is important to focus on and understand the necessary functions of leadership in teams. Zaccaro, Heinen, and Shuffler (2009) urge the development of conceptual frames or models that differ from traditional leadership theory by focusing on *leader–team interactions* (team-centric) instead of *leader–subordinate (leader-centric) interactions.* Traditional leadership approaches do not explain how leaders develop their teams. "A focus on *team* leadership necessitates attention to the *process* by which teams develop critical capabilities. Contingencies that necessitate shifts in leader action are linked to task and team development *dynamics* that vary within teams and over time" (Kozlowski, Watola, Jensen, Kim, and Botero, 2009, p. 114).

Equally essential is understanding the role of leadership within teams to ensure team success and to avoid team failure. "Not surprisingly, the totality of research evidence supports this assertion; team leadership is critical to achieving both affective and behaviorally based team outcomes" (Stagl, Salas, & Burke, 2007, p. 172). Other researchers have claimed that "effective leadership processes" are the most critical factor in team success (Zaccaro, Rittman, & Marks, 2001, p. 452). Conversely, ineffective leadership often is seen as the primary reason teams fail (Stewart & Manz, 1995).

These leadership functions can be performed by the formal team leader *and/or* shared by team members. Day, Gronn, and Salas (2004) referred to this shared or distributed leadership as *team leadership capacity*, encompassing the leadership repertoire of the entire team. Distributed leadership involves the sharing of influence by team members who step forward when situations warrant providing the leadership necessary and then stepping back to allow others to lead. Such shared leadership has become more and more important in today's organizations to allow faster responses to more complex issues (Pearce, Manz, & Sims, 2009; Solansky, 2008). Much of the early work on teams has focused on the traditional role of the formally appointed leader of the team; future research needs to focus more on the distributed or shared leadership within the team. Leadership is provided by anyone who meets the needs of the team (Morgeson, DeRue, & Karam, 2010).

Team Leadership Model

The team leadership model proposed in this chapter places leadership in the driver's seat of team effectiveness. The model provides a mental road map to help the leader (or any team member who is providing leadership) diagnose team problems and take appropriate action to correct these problems.

Hill's Model for Team Leadership (Figure 12.1) is based on the functional leadership claim that the leader's job is to monitor the team and then take whatever action is necessary to ensure team effectiveness. The

12.1 Nursing Team Leaders

model provides a tool for understanding the very complex phenomenon of team leadership, starting at the top with its initial leadership decisions, then moving to leader actions, and finally focusing on the indicators of team effectiveness. Hill's model attempts to integrate mediation and monitoring concepts (Barge, 1996; Hackman & Walton, 1986) with team effectiveness (Hughes, Ginnett, & Curphey, 1993; Larson & LaFasto, 1989; Nadler, 1998). In addition, the model prescribes specific actions that leaders can perform to improve team effectiveness (LaFasto & Larson, 2001; Zaccaro et al., 2001). Effective team leaders need a wide repertoire of communication skills to monitor and take appropriate action. The model is designed to simplify and clarify the complex nature of team leadership and to provide an easy tool to aid leadership problem solving.

Effective team performance begins with the leader's *mental model* of the situation. This mental model reflects not only the components of the problem confronting the team, but also the environmental and organizational contingencies that define the larger context of team action. The leader develops a model of what the team problem is and what solutions are possible in this context, given the environmental and organizational constraints and resources (Zaccaro et al., 2001).

To respond appropriately to the problem envisioned in the mental model, a good leader needs to be behaviorally flexible and have a wide repertoire of actions or skills to meet the team's diverse needs (Barge, 1996). When the leader's behavior matches the complexity of the situation, he or she is behaving with "requisite variety," or the set of behaviors necessary to meet the group's needs (Drecksel, 1991). Effective team leaders are able to construct accurate mental models of the team's problems by observing team functioning, and can take requisite action to solve these problems.

The leader has special responsibility for functioning in a manner that will help the group achieve effectiveness. Within this perspective, leadership behavior is seen as team-based problem solving, in which the leader attempts to achieve team goals by analyzing the internal and external situation and then selecting and implementing the appropriate behaviors to ensure team effectiveness (Fleishman et al., 1991). In addition, Zaccaro et al. (2001) indicated that leaders must use discretion about which problems need intervention, and make choices about which solutions are the most appropriate. The appropriate solution varies by circumstance and focuses on what should be done to make the team more effective. Effective leaders have the ability to determine what leadership interventions are needed, if any, to solve team problems.

12.2 Team Effectiveness

Figure 12.1   Hill's Model for Team Leadership

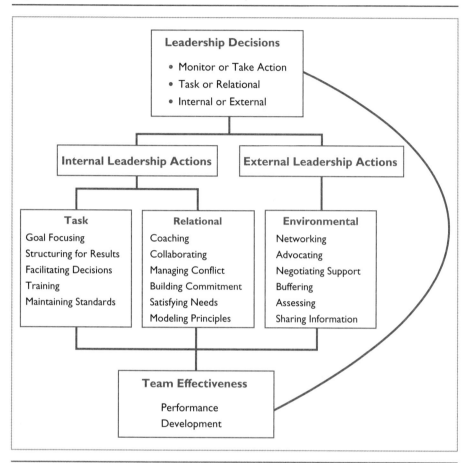

Leadership Decisions

Figure 12.1 outlines the team leadership model. The first box at the top of the model, Leadership Decisions, lists the major decisions a leader needs to make when determining whether and how to intervene to improve team functioning. The first of these decisions is whether it is most appropriate to continue to observe and monitor the team or to intervene in the team's activities and take action. The second decision is to choose whether a task or a relational intervention is needed (i.e., does the team need help in accomplishing its tasks, or does it need help in maintaining relationships?). The final decision is whether to intervene at the internal level (within the team itself) or at the external level (in the team's environment).

Leadership Decision 1: Should I monitor the team or take action? The first decision confronting the leader is whether to keep monitoring the team or to take action to help the team. McGrath (as cited in Hackman & Walton, 1986) outlined the critical leadership functions of group effectiveness, taking into account the analysis of the situation both internally and externally and whether this analysis indicates that the leader should take an immediate action. Figure 12.2, McGrath's Critical Leadership Functions, demonstrates these two dimensions of leadership behavior: *monitoring versus taking action* and *internal group issues versus external group issues*. As leaders, we can diagnose, analyze, or forecast problems (monitoring), or we can take immediate action to solve a problem. We can also focus on the problems within the group (internal) or problems outside the group (external). These two dimensions result in the four types of group leadership functions shown in Figure 12.2.

The first two quadrants in Figure 12.2 focus on the internal operations of the team. In the first quadrant, the leader is diagnosing group deficiencies, and in the second quadrant, the leader is acting to repair or remedy the observed problems. The third and fourth quadrants focus on the external operations of the team. In the third quadrant, the leader is scanning the environment to determine and forecast any external changes that will affect the group. In the fourth quadrant, the leader acts to prevent any negative changes in the environment from hurting the team.

Therefore, the first decision confronting the leader is "Should I continue monitoring these factors, or should I take action based on the information I have already gathered and structured?" To develop an accurate mental model of team functioning, leaders need to monitor both the internal and external environments to gather information, reduce equivocality, provide structure, and overcome barriers. Fleishman et al. (1991) described two phases in this initial process: information search and structuring. A leader must first seek out information to understand the current state of the team's functioning (information search), and then this information must be analyzed, organized, and interpreted so the leader can decide how to act (information structuring). Leaders can also help their information search process by obtaining feedback from team members, networking with others outside the team, conducting team assessment surveys, and evaluating group outcomes. Once

Figure 12.2   McGrath's Critical Leadership Functions

	MONITOR	EXECUTIVE ACTION
INTERNAL	Diagnosing Group Deficiencies 1	Taking Remedial Action 2
EXTERNAL	Forecasting Environmental Changes 3	Preventing Deleterious Changes 4

SOURCE: McGrath's critical leadership functions as cited in "Leading Groups in Organizations," by J. R. Hackman and R. E. Walton, 1986, in P. S. Goodman & Associates (Eds.), *Designing Effective Work Groups* (p. 76). San Francisco: Jossey-Bass.

information on the team is gathered, the leader needs to structure or interpret this information so that he or she can make action plans.

All members of the team can engage in monitoring (information search and structuring) and collectively provide distributed or shared leadership to help the team adapt to changing conditions. In fast-paced, rapidly changing situations, the team leader and members might have to work in concert to assess the situation accurately. The official leader of the team might be too busy processing information from the environment to process information internal to the team. The team members can help the leader by staying on top of internal problems. Together, they can form an accurate mental model of the team's effectiveness.

In addition to gathering and interpreting information, team leaders also must take the right action based on this information. "Action mediation is at the heart of leadership because it involves selecting from among competing courses of action and helping the group create a system of organizing that allows it to make quality decisions" (Barge, 1996, p. 324). Leaders differ in their tendencies to take action quickly or to delay taking action by analyzing the situation at length. Leaders who prefer to take action might prevent problems from getting out of control. However, they might not

12.2 Shared Leadership

make the right intervention because they do not have all the information, and such fast action might undermine the development of shared leadership. Leaders who prefer to carefully analyze the situation might encourage other team members to emerge as leaders, but the problem might become unmanageable. The exact timing of a leadership intervention is as important as the specific type of intervention (Wageman, Fisher, & Hackman, 2009).

Leadership Decision 2: Should I intervene to meet task or relational needs? The second decision confronting the leader is whether the team needs help in dealing with relational issues or task issues. Since the early study of small groups, the focus has been on two critical leadership functions: task and maintenance. Task leadership functions include getting the job done, making decisions, solving problems, adapting to changes, making plans, and achieving goals. Maintenance functions include developing a positive climate, solving interpersonal problems, satisfying members' needs, and developing cohesion. Later scholars studying intact work teams also refer to these functions in terms of performance and development (i.e., how well the team has accomplished its task and how well the team has developed effective relationships).

Superior team leadership focuses constantly on both task and maintenance functions (Kinlaw, 1998); both types of leadership behaviors (task-focused and person-focused) have been found to be related to perceived team effectiveness (Burke et al., 2006).

Task (performance) functions are closely interrelated with maintenance (development) functions. If the team is well maintained and has good relationships, then the members will be able to work together effectively and get their job done. Similarly, if the team is productive and successful in accomplishing its task, it will be easier to maintain a positive climate and good relations. Conversely, failing teams often take their lack of performance out on each other, and fighting teams often accomplish little.

In virtual teams connected across time and space by electronic media, focusing on building team relationships is even more critical than in traditional colocated teams. "Virtual team leaders must be able to 'read' all the personal and contextual nuances in a world of electronic communications. They must be able to understand the possible causes of silence, misunderstanding, and slights without any of the usual signs to guide them. Leaders must be sensitive to the 'flow' of team processes, paying attention to the smallest matters to head off potential troubles that could derail the team's

12.1 Decision Making

task" (Pauleen, 2004, p. 229). Virtual teams place even greater demands on team leaders than the more traditional colocated team demanding 50% more time investment (Dyer, Dyer, & Dyer, 2007). As the prevalence of virtual teams expands, specific leadership issues and interventions related to these virtual teams are increasingly the focus of study (Cordery, Soo, Kirkman, Rosen, & Mathieu, 2009; Zaccaro, Ardison, & Orvis, 2004).

Leadership Decision 3: Should I intervene internally or externally? If a decision was made to take action or intervene, the leader must make the third strategic leadership decision in Figure 12.1 and determine what *level of the team process* needs leadership attention: internal leadership actions or external leadership actions.

Effective team leaders analyze and balance the internal and external demands of the team and react appropriately (Barge, 1996). Is there internal conflict between members of the group? Then perhaps taking an *internal relational action* to maintain the group and improve interpersonal relationships would be most appropriate. Or are the team goals unclear? Then perhaps an *internal task intervention* is needed to focus on goals. Is the organizational environment not providing proper support to the team to do its job? Then perhaps an *external environmental intervention* focusing on obtaining external support for the team might be the most appropriate intervention. The current focus of research is on real-life organizational work teams that exist in a larger organizational environment. In addition to balancing the internal task and relational needs of the team, the leader has to help the team adapt to its external environment. Most teams focus on the internal problems of the team. But it is increasingly important for teams to also be externally oriented to "reach across boundaries to forge dense networks of connection, both inside and outside the organization" so that they can deal effectively with the fast changing environment (Ancona, Bresman, & Caldwell, 2009).

Leadership Actions

The next section of Hill's Model for Team Leadership (Figure 12.1) lists a number of specific leadership actions that can be performed internally (task, relational) or externally (environmental). These lists are not exhaustive but are compiled from research on team excellence and team performance to be discussed later in this chapter. For example, teams that have clear goals and standards and effective structure and decision making will have higher task performance. Teams that can manage conflict, collaborate well together, and build commitment will have good relationships. Teams that are well connected to and protected from their environment will also be more productive. It is up to the leader to assess what action, if any, is needed and then intervene with the specific leadership function to meet the demands of the situation. The leader needs the ability to perform these skills and to make a strategic choice as to the most *appropriate function or skill* for the intervention. For example, if the leader decided that team members were not getting along, he or she might decide to initiate conflict management. *To be an effective leader, one needs to respond with the action that is required of the situation.* Thus, it is the job of the leader to analyze and mediate the situation to make the best decisions for the good of the team.

A team leader needs to recognize and interpret what is getting in the way of the team's goal accomplishment and then make a strategic choice and respond with the appropriate action (Gouran & Hirokawa, 1996). If a problem is diagnosed as a team performance problem, then the leader needs to determine the appropriate action to solve this task problem (e.g., goal focusing, standard setting, or training). If a problem is diagnosed as a team development problem, then the leader needs to determine the appropriate action to solve this relational problem (e.g., managing conflict or building commitment). If a problem is diagnosed as an environmental problem, then the leader needs to determine the appropriate action to solve this context problem (e.g., networking, advocating, or sharing information).

Internal Task Leadership Actions: The task box on Hill's Model for Team Leadership (Figure 12.1) lists the set of skills or actions that the leader might perform to improve task performance.

- Goal focusing (clarifying, gaining agreement)
- Structuring for results (planning, visioning, organizing, clarifying roles, delegating)
- Facilitating decision making (informing, controlling, coordinating, mediating, synthesizing, focusing on issues)
- Training team members in task skills (educating, developing)
- Maintaining standards of excellence (assessing team and individual performance, confronting inadequate performance)

For example, if after monitoring the team's performance the leader observes that the team members do not have the skills necessary for the task, then the leader might choose an intervention to educate the team

12.3 Functional Approach

members or provide them with necessary skills or professional development (*training*). If the leader observes that the team is not clear as to its focus or goals, then he or she might intervene to clarify goals or work with team members to obtain agreement on goals (*goal focusing*). If the leader observes that some team members are coming to work late or not attending important meetings, then the leader might have to take direct action to address this inadequate performance (*standard setting*). If the leader determines that the team is stuck in day-to-day affairs and not looking to or building for the future, then he or she might intervene by helping the team vision and helping to plan for the future (*structuring for results*).

Internal Relational Leadership Actions. The second set of internal leadership actions in Figure 12.1 reflects those that the leader needs to implement to improve team relationships.

- Coaching team members in interpersonal skills
- Collaborating (including, involving)
- Managing conflict and power issues (avoiding confrontation, questioning ideas)
- Building commitment and esprit de corps (being optimistic, innovating, envisioning, socializing, rewarding, recognizing)
- Satisfying individual member needs (trusting, supporting, advocating)
- Modeling ethical and principled practices (fair, consistent, normative)

If, after monitoring the relationships between team members, the leader observes that some of the group members are engaged in interpersonal conflict, then the leader should intervene to manage that conflict (*managing conflict and power issues*). Or if the team seems down in the dumps, the leader should try to build commitment and unity by recognizing past team successes (*building commitment and esprit de corps*). If team members do not seem to be able to communicate effectively, then the leader might intervene by coaching team members in appropriate behaviors (*coaching*).

External Environmental Leadership Actions. The external leadership actions (Figure 12.1) reflect those actions the leader might implement to improve the environmental interface with the team. Real-life teams do not exist in a laboratory—they are subsystems of the larger organizational and societal context. To stay viable, the team needs to monitor this environment closely and determine what actions should be taken to enhance team effectiveness (Barge, 1996; Hyatt & Ruddy, 1997; Zaccaro et al., 2001). If environmental

12.4 Relational Actions

monitoring suggests a leadership intervention, then the leader needs to select from the following functions:

- Networking and forming alliances in environment (gathering information, increasing influence)
- Advocating and representing team to environment
- Negotiating upward to secure necessary resources, support, and recognition for team
- Buffering team members from environmental distractions
- Assessing environmental indicators of team's effectiveness (surveys, evaluations, performance indicators)
- Sharing relevant environmental information with team

If after monitoring the environment the leader learns that the organizational superiors are unaware of the team's successes, she or he might initiate an "FYI" policy, sending information about all successes upward as they happen (*advocating and representing team to environment*). The leader can also initiate a team newsletter that chronicles team efforts to accomplish the same function but to a broader context. Alternatively, the leader might determine that the team does not have enough clerical support to accomplish its goals. The leader then negotiates with upper management to provide the needed support or to alter the goals accordingly (*negotiating upward to secure necessary resources*).

Team leadership is complex; there are no simple recipes for team success. Team leaders must learn to be open and objective in understanding and diagnosing team problems and skillful in selecting the most appropriate actions (or inactions) to help achieve the team's goals. It is important to note that these critical functions need not be carried out only by the leader. Experienced members in a mature team might share these leadership behaviors. As long as the team's critical needs have been met, the leadership behavior, whether enacted by the leader or team members, has been effective. *The key assertion of the functional perspective is that the leader is to do whatever is necessary to take care of unmet needs of the group.* If the group members are taking care of most of the needs, then the leader has to do very little.

Team Effectiveness

The box at the bottom of Hill's Model for Team Leadership (see Figure 12.1) focuses on team effectiveness, or the desired outcome of

12.2 Resourcing

teamwork. Two critical functions of team effectiveness are listed: performance (task accomplishment) and development (maintenance of team). Team performance is the "quality of decision making, the ability to implement decisions, the outcomes of teamwork in terms of problems solved and work completed, and finally the quality of institutional leadership provided by the team" (Nadler, 1998, p. 24). Team development is the cohesiveness of the team and the ability of group members to satisfy their own needs while working effectively with other team members (Nadler, 1998).

Researchers have systematically studied organizational work teams and developed standards of effectiveness or criteria of excellence that can be used to assess a team's health (Hackman, 1990, 2002; Hughes et al., 1993; LaFasto & Larson, 2001; Larson & LaFasto, 1989; Zaccaro et al., 2001). Hackman and Walton (1986) suggested criteria necessary for effectiveness of task-performing teams in organizations. They found that effective groups have a clear, engaging direction; an enabling performance situation that contains structure, support, and coaching; and adequate resources.

Larson and LaFasto (1989) studied real-life successful teams and found that, regardless of the type of team, eight characteristics were consistently associated with team excellence. Table 12.1 demonstrates the similarity of these characteristics to the theoretical components suggested by Hackman and Walton (1986), providing grounded research support for the group effectiveness approach.

Table 12.1 Comparison of Theory and Research Criteria

Conditions of Group Effectiveness (Hackman & Walton, 1986)	Characteristics of Team Excellence (Larson & LaFasto, 1989)
Clear, engaging direction	Clear, elevating goal
Enabling structure	Results-driven structure
	Competent team members
	Unified commitment
	Collaborative climate
Enabling context	Standards of excellence
Adequate material resources	External support and recognition
Expert coaching	Principled leadership

12.1 Future Team Effectiveness

Team leaders need to understand these performance standards and be able to assess their team's level of achievement across them to determine possible areas of ineffectiveness. Assessing how well the team compares to these established indicators of team success is a valuable source of information guiding the leader to take appropriate actions to improve team success.

Clear, Elevating Goal. Team goals must be very clear so that one can tell whether the performance objective has been realized. Groups often fail because they are given a vague task and then asked to work out the details (Hackman, 1990). In addition, the goal must be involving or motivating so that the members believe it to be worthwhile and important. Teams often fail because they let something else replace their goal, such as personal agendas or power issues (Larson & LaFasto, 1989). Research data from numerous teams show that effective leaders keep the team focused on the goal (LaFasto & Larson, 2001).

Results-Driven Structure. Teams need to find the best structure for accomplishing their goals. Structural features that lead to effective teamwork include task design, team composition, and core norms of conduct (Wageman et al., 2009). Top management teams typically deal with power and influence, task forces deal with ideas and plans, customer service teams deal with clients, and production teams deal with technology (Hackman, 1990). Problem resolution teams such as task forces need a structure that emphasizes trust so that all will be willing and able to contribute. Creative teams such as advertising teams need to emphasize autonomy so that all can take risks and be free from undue censorship. Tactical teams such as emergency room teams need to emphasize clarity so that everyone knows what to do and when. In addition, all teams need clear roles for group members, a good communication system, methods of assessing individual performance, and an emphasis on fact-based judgments (Larson & LaFasto, 1989). Appropriate structures enable groups to meet their needs while accomplishing team goals.

Competent Team Members. Groups should be composed of the right number and mix of members to accomplish all the tasks of the group. In addition, members need sufficient information, education, and training to become or remain competent team members (Hackman & Walton, 1986). As a whole, the individual team members need to possess the requisite technical competence to accomplish the team's goals. Members also need to be personally competent in interpersonal and teamwork skills. A common mistake in

12.3 Coaching and Goals   **12.3** Goals

forming teams is to assume that people who have all the technical skills necessary to solve a problem also have the interpersonal skills necessary to collaborate effectively (Hackman, 1990). Team members need certain core competencies that include the ability to do the job and the ability to solve problems. In addition, members need certain teamwork factors such as openness, supportiveness, action orientation, and a positive personal style (LaFasto & Larson, 2001).

Unified Commitment. A common mistake is to call a work group a *team* but treat it as a collection of individuals (Hackman, 1990). Teams do not just happen: They are carefully designed and developed. Excellent teams are those that have developed a sense of unity or identification. Such team spirit often can be developed by involving members in all aspects of the process (Larson & LaFasto, 1989).

Collaborative Climate. The ability of a team to collaborate is essential to team effectiveness. A collaborative climate is one in which members can stay problem focused, listen to and understand one another, feel free to take risks, and be willing to compensate for one another. To build an atmosphere that fosters collaboration, we need to develop trusting relationships based on honesty, openness, consistency, and respect (Larson & LaFasto, 1989). Integration of individual actions is one of the fundamental characteristics of effective teams. Team members "have specific and unique roles, where the performance of each role contributes to collective success. This means that the causes of team failure may reside not only in member inability, but also in their collective failure to coordinate and synchronize their individual contributions" (Zaccaro et al., 2001, p. 451). Research demonstrates that effective team leaders ensure a collaborative climate by making communication safe, demanding and rewarding collaborative behavior, guiding the team's problem-solving efforts, and managing their own control needs (LaFasto & Larson, 2001).

Standards of Excellence. Effective group norms are important for group functioning. Team members' performance should be regulated so that actions can be coordinated and tasks completed (Hackman & Walton, 1986). It is especially important that the organizational context or the team itself set up standards of excellence so that members will feel pressure to perform at their highest levels. The standards must be clear and concrete, and all team members must be required to perform to standard (Larson & LaFasto, 1989). A team leader can facilitate this process by requiring results—making expectations clear; reviewing results—providing feedback

12.4 Collaboration

to resolve performance issues; and rewarding results—acknowledging superior performance (LaFasto & Larson, 2001). With such standards in place and monitored, members will be encouraged to perform at their highest levels.

External Support and Recognition. A supportive organizational context includes material resources, rewards for excellent performance, an educational system to develop necessary team skills, and an information system to provide data needed to accomplish the task (Wageman et al., 2009). A common mistake is to give organizational teams challenging assignments but give them no organizational support to accomplish these assignments (Hackman, 1990). The leader must identify which type of support is needed and intervene as needed to secure this support (Hackman, 2002). The best goals, team members, and commitment will not mean much if you have no money, equipment, or supplies for accomplishing the goals. Also, organizations often ask employees to work on a difficult team assignment but then do not reward them with raises or bonuses for that performance. Hyatt and Ruddy (1997) found that having systems in place to support work groups (clear direction, information, data, resources, rewards, and training) enables the group to become more effective and achieve performance goals. Teams can achieve excellence if they are given the resources needed to do their jobs, are recognized for team accomplishments, and are rewarded for team performance rather than for individual performances (Larson & LaFasto, 1989).

Principled Leadership. Effective team leadership has been found to consistently relate to team effectiveness (Zaccaro et al., 2009). Leadership has been described as the central driver of team effectiveness, influencing the team through four sets of processes: cognitive, motivational, affective, and coordination (Zaccaro et al., 2001). Cognitively, the leader helps the team understand the problems confronting the team. Motivationally, the leader helps the team become cohesive and capable by setting high performance standards and helping the group to achieve them. Affectively, the leader helps the team handle stressful circumstances by providing clear goals, assignments, and strategies. Coordinatively, the leader helps integrate the team's activities by matching members' skills to roles, providing clear performance strategies, monitoring feedback, and adapting to environmental changes.

Effective team leaders are committed to the team's goals and give members autonomy to unleash their talents when possible. Leaders can reduce the effectiveness of their team by being unwilling to confront

12.5 Effective Leadership

inadequate performance, diluting the team's ability to perform by having too many priorities, and overestimating the positive aspects of team performance. Leaders can enhance the effectiveness of their team by keeping the team focused on its goals, maintaining a collaborative climate, building confidence among members, demonstrating technical competence, setting priorities, and managing performance (Larson & LaFasto, 1989). It is essential that the leadership of the team be assessed along with the other criteria of team excellence. Such feedback is essential to the health and effectiveness of the team.

The leadership of the team can use the characteristics of team excellence (Table 12.1) in a normative fashion to assess the health of the teams and to take appropriate action to address any weaknesses. If the team leader assesses that one or more of the eight characteristics of team success are not being achieved, then he or she needs to address these weaknesses. Continually assessing the standards of team effectiveness can also provide feedback, enabling leaders to determine whether past actions and interventions had the desired results. To assess team effectiveness, team leaders need to use whatever tools are at their disposal, such as direct observation, surveys, feedback, and performance indicators. The information gained from the analysis of team effectiveness can provide feedback to the leader and guide future leadership decisions. The line on Hill's Model of Team Leadership (Figure 12.1) that connects the Team Effectiveness box at the bottom to the Leadership Decisions box at the top reflects the ongoing learning process of data gathering, analysis, and decision making. Such feedback loops demonstrate the dynamic and evolving nature of teams (Ilgen et al., 2005). Past leadership decisions and actions are reflected in the team's performance and relational outcomes. In turn, these indicators of team effectiveness shape the future analysis and decisions of the team leadership.

HOW DOES THE TEAM LEADERSHIP MODEL WORK?

Leaders can use the model to help them make decisions about the current state of their team and the specific actions they need to take, if any, to improve the team's functioning. The model portrays leadership as a team oversight function in which the leader's role is to do whatever is necessary to help the group achieve effectiveness. The model provides the leader with a cognitive map for identifying group needs, and offers suggestions about how to take appropriate corrective actions. The model helps the leader make sense of the complexity of groups and offers practical suggestions based on theory and research.

In using the model, the team leader engages in the leader mediation process by deciding which is most appropriate for the team: monitoring or taking action. If the monitoring reveals that all aspects of the team's functioning are satisfactory, then the leader should not take any direct actions but continue to monitor the internal and external environments in terms of team performance and development. If monitoring reveals that action is needed, then the leader decides whether to take an internal-level action or an external-level action or both. Finally, the leader decides which action is appropriate to meet the needs of the team.

Determining the exact intervention is not as easy as it sounds, however, and it clearly reflects the skills necessary for team leadership. For example, a leader monitoring the internal functioning of the team notices infighting for control and power. The leader might see this as an *internal relationship problem* because of the authoritarian and autocratic behavior of one group member. Or perhaps the leader might see it as an *internal task problem* because the structure of the team is not appropriate and the roles and responsibilities of some group members are unclear. Or perhaps the leader sees the problem as an *external environmental problem* because the team is not given sufficient autonomy from the organization; consequently, the members are fighting over what little power and control exist. In any case, the leader can decide to keep monitoring the situation and not take any immediate action. Or the leader can decide at which level to intervene and then decide to enact the most appropriate leadership function at that level. The leader might decide to intervene at all three levels, addressing the authoritarian individual (internal, relational), clarifying group roles (internal, task), and negotiating more team autonomy with those higher up in the organization (external).

The team leadership model helps to point the way for constant team analysis and improvement, much like that of sports teams. In sports, the coach does not stop working just because the team is winning. The coach keeps working to build commitment, develop young players, share expertise, create new methods and strategies, and generally improve team functioning. The effective coach never rests on past successes, but works to improve the team's functioning for the future. Organizational team leaders could learn a great deal from sports team coaches. The team leadership model helps point the way for such constant analysis and improvement. By comparing their own teams with established standards or criteria of team excellence, leaders can determine the areas of greatest weakness that might need critical intervention.

STRENGTHS

One of the strengths of this model is that it is designed to focus on the real-life organizational work group and the leadership needed therein. The model places the ongoing work group or team in an environmental context within the organization, industry, or society. In addition, the real-life focus on performance and team effectiveness enables leaders and members to diagnose and correct team problems. By learning what constitutes excellent teams and applying these criteria to team performance, leaders can learn how to better lead teams to the highest levels of excellence.

A second strength of the model is that it provides a cognitive guide that helps leaders design and maintain effective teams, especially when performance is below standards. Such an approach is consistent with the emerging theoretical notions of the leader as a medium whose job it is to process the complex information inherent in teamwork (Fisher, 1985). Any model or theory that tries to simplify such a complex process would be inappropriate and inadequate. The team leadership model is not simplistic, and it integrates in a manageable and practical form many complex factors that can help a leader be a good medium or processor of information.

Another strength of the model is that it takes into account the changing role of leaders and followers in organizations. The model does not focus on the position power of a leader but instead focuses on the critical functions of leadership as diagnosis and action taking. Any team member can perform the critical leadership functions to assess the current effectiveness of the team and then take appropriate action. This approach is consistent with the current movement in organizations to rethink leadership responsibilities in work groups. The responsibilities or functions of team leadership—such as setting goals, coaching, and rewarding—historically have rested with the group's formal leader, but now, with organizational restructuring, these duties and responsibilities often are distributed across the team.

In addition, this approach to team leadership can help in selection of team leaders. If you have to name a leader for the team, it might be best to select one who is perceptive, open, objective, analytical, and a good listener who has good diagnostic skills. You might want to select a leader who has a wide repertoire of action-taking skills—that is, who is comfortable intervening in the group process in many ways, such as with negotiation, conflict resolution, problem solving, goal focusing, and influencing upward. Good leaders not only can diagnose the team's problems, but also can reach into their bag of tricks and pull out the appropriate action or actions. For example, if I determine that two members of my team are in conflict with one another, I need to be able to determine the root cause of that conflict and select the most appropriate action (or select nonaction).

CRITICISMS

Hill's Model for Team Leadership (Figure 12.1) is a conceptual framework to assist team-based leadership in its decision making. As such, it lists only some of the many skills that leadership might need to employ in making such decisions. Depending on the type of team or situation, additional skills might be needed that focus more on the environment (Cobb, 2012), coaching and training (Zaccaro et al., 2009), or preplanning and timing (Wageman et al., 2009). A team might need to modify the model to include skills that are particularly relevant to its effectiveness.

Even though the model does not include all possible leadership skills, it is still quite complex. Team leaders need to spend time adjusting to the framework so that it comes naturally to them when decisions are needed. This framework also does not provide on-the-spot answers to specific problems facing the team leader, such as "When is the best time to intervene?" "What do you say to a member who is upset and crying?" or "What specific action do you take to deal with an organizational culture that is not supporting teamwork?" The model only points the leader in the right direction and suggests skills needed to solve these complex problems. The model assumes that the leader is skilled in group process, decision making, interpersonal communication, conflict resolution, and other abilities.

To make matters worse, many teams have shared or distributed leadership necessitating that everyone who provides team leadership have a wide range of team-oriented skills. In addition, the roles of leaders and followers can change over time making it very important for the team leader and team members to possess the requisite leadership skills. Increasingly, scholars are providing instruction in diagnosing weaknesses in team leadership skills and offering methods for development and improvement (Cobb, 2012; Levi, 2011; Morgeson et al., 2010; Salas, Burke, & Stagl, 2004). Instruction in teamwork and team leadership needs to focus on team diagnosing and action taking so that team leadership skills can be developed throughout the team and be more easily implemented.

APPLICATION

There are many ways to apply the team leadership model to increase the effectiveness of organizational teams. The model is useful in helping the leader make decisions: Should I act? If so, how should I do so? For example, if the group is not performing effectively (*team effectiveness*), then the leader can make the first strategic choice by monitoring the situation or acting to improve team functioning. If an action seems warranted, then the leader needs to decide whether the action should be directed inward toward team functioning, outward toward the environment, or both. Once the context for the action is determined, then the leader needs to choose from his or her repertoire the most appropriate skill for the situation. It is important to continue monitoring the results of the intervention and adapting accordingly, depending on these results.

The leader might choose to use a survey such as the one included later in this chapter to help conduct the team's diagnosis and set the steps needed for taking action. Team members are asked to fill out the questionnaire, as is the team leader. The results are fed back to the team members and team leader, allowing them to see the areas of greatest strength and weakness. It is particularly important that both team leaders and team members fill out the questionnaire. Research suggests that team leaders overestimate their effectiveness on these dimensions and often score themselves much higher than do group members (LaFasto & Larson, 2001). By comparing the scores by leaders and by members, the leader can determine which dimensions of team or leadership effectiveness need improvement. The team and leader can then prepare action plans to correct the highest-priority problems. Such a team assessment approach is very helpful in monitoring and diagnosing team problems. It aids in determining the complex factors affecting team excellence to build a committed team involved in action planning.

—————————— CASE STUDIES ——————————

To improve your understanding of the team leadership model, refer to the following case studies (Cases 12.1, 12.2, and 12.3). For each case, you will be asked to put yourself in the role of team leader and apply the team leadership model in analyzing and offering solutions to the team problems.

CASE 12.1

Can This Virtual Team Work?

Jim Towne heads a newly formed information technology team for a major international corporation. The team is composed of 20 professionals who live and work in Canada, the United States, Europe, South America, Africa, and Australia. All members of the team report to Jim. The team is a virtual team connected primarily via videoconference, group decision-support software, e-mail, text, and telephone. The team has met twice in a face-to-face setting to set goals and plan. All of the team members are quite competent in their respective technical areas. Some team members have a long and valued history with the company; others have recently joined the company through a corporate merger. The team members have never worked together on any projects.

The task of the team is to develop and implement technology innovations for all global business units. The team members are excited about the importance and the innovative nature of their assignment. They respect each other and enjoy being part of this team. However, the team is having difficulty getting off the ground, and the members report being extremely overloaded. Most team members travel to business sites at least 2 weeks each month. The travel is important, but it causes team members to get farther behind.

The team has one half-time secretary, located in New York. Her primary responsibility is to organize travel and meetings of team members. Team members are working on several projects at once and have great difficulty finishing any of the projects. One team member has 500 unread e-mail messages because each team member sends copies of all messages to everyone on the team. Jim is under great pressure to prove that this team can work and provide a valuable function to the organization.

Questions

1. Which of the eight characteristics (Table 12.1) of team excellence are lacking in this team?

📖 12.5 Making Successful Teams

2. Based on this analysis of team effectiveness, should Jim intervene at this time, or should he just keep monitoring the team? If you think he should take action, at what level should he intervene (internal or external)? If internal, should his action be task or relational?

3. What specific leadership functions should Jim implement to improve the team? Why?

CASE 12.2

They Dominated the Conversation

The local cancer center has a health team designed to coordinate the care of children with cancer. The team is composed of a physician, Dr. Sherif Hidyat (a clinical oncologist); a radiologist, Dr. Wayne Linett; a nurse practitioner, Sharon Whittling; a social worker, Cathy Ing; a physical therapist, Nancy Crosby; and a child life worker, Janet Lewis. The team members meet on a weekly basis to discuss the 18 children under their care and agree on the best course of treatment for each child. Cathy Ing, the social worker, is the head of the team and is responsible for the case management of each child. However, when the team meets, Drs. Hidyat and Linett dominate the conversation. They feel that their medical background gives them greater knowledge and skill in treating cancer in children. They welcome input from the women in the group. When it comes to making a decision, however, they insist on doing it their way for the good of the patient. Cathy Ing (the social worker), Janet Lewis (the child life worker), Nancy Crosby (the physical therapist), and Sharon Whittling (the nurse practitioner) resent this behavior because they are the health care workers who spend the most time with the children and feel that they know best how to handle their long-term care. As a result, the patients feel as if no one cares or understands them. The team is also having trouble working together, and no one on the team is satisfied with the outcome.

Questions

1. How would you assess the effectiveness of this team?

2. In monitoring this team, at what level and function do you see the most serious problems? Internal task? Internal relational? External?

(Continued)

(Continued)

3. Would you take action to improve team functioning? If so, how would you intervene? Why?

4. What specific leadership skill or skills would you use to improve group functioning?

CASE 12.3

Starts With a Bang, Ends With a Whimper

A faculty member, Kim Green from the Management Department, was asked to chair a major university committee to plan the mission of the university for the next 20 years. Three other senior faculty and seven administrators from across the campus were also asked to serve on this committee. The president of the university, Dr. Sulgrave, gave the committee its charge: What should Northcoast University be like in the year 2020? Dr. Sulgrave told the committee that the work of this task force was of utmost importance to the future of the university, and the charge of this committee should take precedence over all other matters. The task force was allowed to meet in the president's conference room and use the president's secretary. The report of the committee was due in 2 months.

The task force members felt very good about being selected for such an important team. The team met on a weekly basis for about 2 hours each time. At first, the members were very interested in the task and participated enthusiastically. They were required to do a great deal of outside research. They came back to the meetings proud to share their research and knowledge. However, after a while the meetings did not go well. The members could not seem to agree on what the charge to the group meant. They argued about what they were supposed to accomplish and resented the time the committee was taking from their regular jobs. Week after week the team met but accomplished nothing. Attendance became a problem, with people skipping several meetings, showing up late, or leaving early. Group members stopped working on their committee assignments. Kim didn't want to admit to the university president that they didn't know what they were doing; instead, she just got more and more frustrated. Meetings became sporadic and eventually stopped altogether. The president was involved in a crisis in the university and seemed to lose interest in the committee. The president never called for the report from the committee, and the report was never completed.

Questions

1. Which characteristics of excellence were lacking in this task force?

2. Which characteristics of excellence were evident in this task force?

3. How would you assess Kim as a leader?

4. What actions would you take (internally or externally) if you were the leader of this task force?

LEADERSHIP INSTRUMENT

Several different instruments have been used to assess team effectiveness and the leadership within those teams. Larson and LaFasto have developed one such survey to assess a team's health after studying many different types of excellent organizational teams (see Larson & LaFasto, 1989). Their research demonstrated eight criteria or factors that are consistently associated with team excellence and high performance. The complete Team Excellence survey contains more than 40 questions across the eight factors that are used to determine a team's performance level and suggest areas that might need corrective action. The eighth factor on this instrument is *principled leadership*. Subsequent research by LaFasto and Larson led to the development of a 42-item questionnaire focusing on this criterion of leadership. The full Collaborative Team Leader instrument and a discussion of its reliability and validity can be found in their latest text (LaFasto & Larson, 2001). The questionnaire included in this chapter provides a sample of questions from these two surveys so that the reader can see how team and team leadership effectiveness can be evaluated.

The team members are given the questionnaire, and their scores are combined and averaged to obtain a group view; the leader fills out the same questionnaire. The responses from the team leader are then compared with the team members' to determine the areas of greatest weakness, if any. Based on these comparisons, the team and its leader can plan the action steps needed to correct and improve the weak areas of team functioning.

The Team Excellence and Collaborative Team Leader surveys are designed as diagnostic tools to help teams sort through the complex problems confronting them and to pinpoint areas for action taking. The Team Excellence and Collaborative Team Leader Questionnaire provided in this chapter contains sample questions from the two instruments developed by

LaFasto and Larson. The first seven questions are taken from the Team Excellence Survey, developed by LaFasto and Larson in 1987 (cited in Larson & LaFasto, 1989) to measure a team's health in terms of the criteria of team excellence (goal, structure, team members, commitment, climate, standards, and external support). Leadership is measured by the next six questions, taken from the Collaborative Team Leader Survey developed by LaFasto and Larson in 1996 (LaFasto & Larson, 2001, pp. 151–154). These six questions assess the effectiveness of the leader in goal focusing, ensuring a collaborative climate, building confidence, demonstrating know-how, setting priorities, and managing performance. All of these team and leadership factors have been found to relate to team effectiveness.

As you fill out the sample questionnaire, think about a group or team to which you belong as a member or as the leader. The items that you score as 1 or 2 (*False* or *More false than true*) are the areas of team weakness from your perspective. To obtain a team assessment, you would compare your scores on this instrument with the scores of the other group members. For example, if almost everyone on the team responds with a 1 or 2 to Item 3 ("Team members possess the essential skills and abilities to accomplish the team's objectives"), then the team leader might need to provide training to increase the competence of team members. Such an instrument that assesses team effectiveness is particularly helpful to the team leader in identifying areas of team or leadership weakness and suggesting solutions for improving team effectiveness.

Team Excellence and Collaborative
Team Leader Questionnaire

Instructions: This questionnaire contains questions about your team and the leadership within this team. Indicate whether you feel each statement is true or not true of your team. Use the following scale:

Key: 1 = False   2 = More false   3 = More true   4 = True
                                    than true   than false

1. There is a clearly defined need—a goal to be achieved   1 2 3 4
   or a purpose to be served—that justifies the existence
   of our team. (team: clear, elevating goal)
2. We have an established method for monitoring   1 2 3 4
   individual performance and providing feedback. (team:
   results-driven structure)
3. Team members possess the essential skills and abilities   1 2 3 4
   to accomplish the team's objectives. (team: competent
   team members)
4. Achieving our team goal is a higher priority than any   1 2 3 4
   individual objective. (team: unified commitment)
5. We trust each other sufficiently to accurately share   1 2 3 4
   information, perceptions, and feedback. (team:
   collaborative climate)
6. Our team exerts pressure on itself to improve performance. 1 2 3 4
   (team: standards of excellence)
7. Our team is given the resources it needs to get the job done. 1 2 3 4
   (team: external support and recognition)
8. If it's necessary to adjust the team's goal, our team leader   1 2 3 4
   makes sure we understand why. (leadership: focus on the goal)
9. Our team leader creates a safe climate for team members   1 2 3 4
   to openly and supportively discuss any issue related to the
   team's success. (leadership: ensure a collaborative climate)
10. Our team leader looks for and acknowledges contributions   1 2 3 4
    by team members. (leadership: build confidence)
11. Our team leader understands the technical issues we must   1 2 3 4
    face in achieving our goal. (leadership: demonstrate sufficient
    technical know-how)
12. Our team leader does not dilute our team's effort with too   1 2 3 4
    many priorities. (leadership: set priorities)
13. Our team leader is willing to confront and resolve issues   1 2 3 4
    associated with inadequate performance by team members.
    (leadership: manage performance)

SOURCES: Questions 1–7: Adapted from the Team Excellence Survey (copyright 1987 LaFasto and Larson; portions reprinted with permission of Profact). Questions 8–13: Adapted from the Collaborative Team Leader Instrument (copyright 1996 LaFasto and Larson; portions reprinted with permission).

Scoring Interpretation

In addition to such targeted questions on each of the criteria of excellence, the complete surveys also ask open-ended questions to allow team members to comment on issues that might not be specifically covered in the directed questions, such as strengths and weaknesses of the team and its leadership, necessary changes, problematic norms, or issues that need to be addressed. The complete version of the survey is given to team members and the team leader, and all are involved in the diagnosis and the resulting action planning. Such a method is clearly consistent with the empowerment movement in organizational teams and helps address the enormous complexity involved in making teams effective.

SUMMARY

The increased importance of organizational teams and the leadership needed for them has produced a growing interest in team leadership theory. The team leadership model provides a framework in which to study the systematic factors that contribute to a group's outcomes or general effectiveness. Within this approach, the critical function of leadership is to help the group accomplish its goals by monitoring and diagnosing the group and taking the requisite action.

A strategic decision model has been developed to reveal the various decisions team leaders must make to improve their group's effectiveness. The model describes the decisions: What type of intervention should be used (monitoring or action taking)? At what level should the intervention be targeted (internal or external)? What leadership function should be implemented to improve group functioning?

Questionnaires filled out by team members and the team leader can aid in diagnosing specific areas of team problems and suggest action steps to be taken by the team.

The strength of this approach is its practical focus on real-life organizational teams and their effectiveness. The model also emphasizes the functions of leadership that can be shared and distributed within the work group. The model offers guidance in selecting leaders and team members with the appropriate diagnostic and action-taking skills. Furthermore, the model is appropriately complex, providing a cognitive model for understanding and improving organizational teams.

> Visit the Student Study Site at **www.sagepub.com/northouse6e** for web quizzes, leadership questionnaires, and media links represented by the icons.

REFERENCES

Ancona, D., Bresman, H., & Caldwell, D. (2009). The x-factor: Six steps to leading high-performing x-teams. *Organizational Dynamics, 38*(3), 217–224.

Barge, J. K. (1996). Leadership skills and the dialectics of leadership in group decision making. In R. Y. Hirokawa & M. S. Poole (Eds.), *Communication and group decision making* (2nd ed., pp. 301–342). Thousand Oaks, CA: Sage.

Burke, C. S., Stagl, K. C., Klein, C., Goodwin, G. F., Salas, E., & Halpin, S. M. (2006). What type of leadership behaviors are functional in teams? A meta-analysis. *Leadership Quarterly, 17*, 288–307.

Cobb, A. T. (2012). *Leading project teams: The basics of project management and team leadership* (2nd ed.). Thousand Oaks, CA: Sage.

Cordery, J., Soo, C., Kirkman, B., Rosen, B., & Mathieu, J. (2009). Leading parallel global virtual teams: Lessons from Alcoa. *Organizational Dynamics, 38*(3), 204–216.

Day, D. V., Gronn, P., & Salas, E. (2004). Leadership capacity in teams. *Leadership Quarterly, 15*, 857–880.

Drecksel, G. L. (1991). Leadership research: Some issues. *Communication Yearbook, 14*, 535–546.

Dyer, W. G., Dyer, W. G., Jr., & Dyer, J. H. (2007). *Team building: Proven strategies for improving team performance* (4th ed.). San Francisco: Jossey-Bass.

Fisher, B. A. (1985, May). Leadership as medium: Treating complexity in group communication research. *Small Group Behavior, 16*(2), 167–196.

Fleishman, E. A., Mumford, M. D., Zaccaro, S. J., Levin, K. Y., Korotkin, A. L., & Hein, M. B. (1991). Taxonomic efforts in the description of leader behavior: A synthesis and functional interpretation. *Leadership Quarterly, 2*(4), 245–287.

Gouran, D. S., & Hirokawa, R. Y. (1996). Functional theory and communication in decision-making and problem-solving groups: An expanded view. In R. Y. Hirokawa & M. D. Poole (Eds.), *Communication and group decision making* (2nd ed., pp. 55–80). Thousand Oaks, CA: Sage.

Hackman, J. R. (1990). Work teams in organizations: An orienting framework. In J. R. Hackman (Ed.), *Groups that work (and those that don't): Creating conditions for effective teamwork* (pp. 1–14). San Francisco: Jossey-Bass.

Hackman, J. R. (2002). *Leading teams: Setting the stage for great performances.* Boston: Harvard Business School Press.

Hackman, J. R., & Walton, R. E. (1986). Leading groups in organizations. In P. S. Goodman & Associates (Eds.), *Designing effective work groups* (pp. 72–119). San Francisco: Jossey-Bass.

Hughes, R. L., Ginnett, R. C., & Curphey, G. J. (1993). *Leadership: Enhancing the lessons of experience.* Homewood, IL: Irwin.

Hyatt, D. E., & Ruddy, T. M. (1997). An examination of the relationship between work group characteristics and performance: Once more into the breach. *Personnel Psychology, 50*, 553–585.

Ilgen, D. R., Hollenbeck, J. R., Johnson, M., & Jundt, D. (2005). Teams in organizations: From input–process–output models to IMOI models. *Annual Review of Psychology, 56*, 517–543.

Ilgen, D. R., Major, D. A., Hollenbeck, J. R., & Sego, D. J. (1993). Team research in the 1990s. In M. M. Chemers & R. Ayman (Eds.), *Leadership theory and research: Perspectives and directions* (pp. 245–270). San Diego, CA: Academic Press.

Kinlaw, D. C. (1998). *Superior teams: What they are and how to develop them.* Hampshire, UK: Grove.

Kozlowski, S. W. J., Watola, D. J., Jensen, J. M., Kim, B. H., & Botero, I. C. (2009). Developing adaptive teams: A theory of dynamic team leadership. In E. Salas,

G. F. Goodwin, & C. S. Burke (Eds.), *Team effectiveness in complex organizations: Cross–disciplinary perspectives and approaches* (pp. 113–155). New York: Taylor & Francis Group.

LaFasto, F. M. J., & Larson, C. E. (1987). *Team excellence survey.* Denver, CO: Author.

LaFasto, F. M. J., & Larson, C. E. (1996). *Collaborative team leader survey.* Denver, CO: Author.

LaFasto, F. M. J., & Larson, C. E. (2001). *When teams work best: 6,000 team members and leaders tell what it takes to succeed.* Thousand Oaks, CA: Sage.

Larson, C. E., & LaFasto, F. M. J. (1989). *Teamwork: What must go right/what can go wrong.* Newbury Park, CA: Sage.

Levi, D. (2011). *Group dynamics for teams.* Thousand Oaks, CA: Sage.

Mankin, D., Cohen, S. G., & Bikson, T. K. (1996). *Teams and technology.* Boston: Harvard Business School Press.

McGrath, J. E., Arrow, H., & Berdahl, J. L. (2000). The study of groups: Past, present, and future. *Personality and Social Psychology Review, 4*(1), 95–105.

Morgeson, F. P., DeRue, D. S., & Karam, E. P. (2010). Leadership in teams: A functional approach to understanding leadership structures and processes. *Journal of Management, 36*(1), 5–39.

Nadler, D. A. (1998). Executive team effectiveness: Teamwork at the top. In D. A. Nadler & J. L. Spencer (Eds.), *Executive teams* (pp. 21–39). San Francisco: Jossey-Bass.

Parker, G. M. (1990). *Team players and teamwork.* San Francisco: Jossey-Bass.

Pauleen, D. J. (2004). An inductively derived model of leader-initiated relationship building with virtual team members. *Journal of Management Information Systems, 20*(3), 227–256.

Pearce, C. L., Manz, C. C., & Sims, H. P. (2009). Where do we go from here? Is shared leadership the key to team success? *Organizational Dynamics, 38*(3), 234–238.

Porter, G., & Beyerlein, M. (2000). Historic roots of team theory and practice. In M. M. Beyerlein (Ed.), *Work teams: Past, present and future* (pp. 3–24). Dordrecht, Netherlands: Kluwer.

Salas, E., Burke, C. S., & Stagl, D. C. (2004). Developing teams and team leaders: Strategies and principles. In D. V. Day, S. J. Zaccaro, & S. M. Halpin (Eds.), *Leader development for transforming organizations: Growing leaders for tomorrow* (pp. 325–355). Mahwah, NJ: Lawrence Erlbaum.

Solansky, S. T. (2008). Leadership style and team processes in self-managed teams. *Journal of Leadership and Organizational Studies, 14*(4), 332–341.

Stagl, K. C., Salas, E., & Burke, C. S. (2007). Best practices in team leadership: What team leaders do to facilitate team effectiveness. In J. A. Conger & R. E. Riggio (Eds.), *The practice of leadership: Developing the next generation of leaders* (pp. 172–197). San Francisco: Jossey-Bass.

Stewart, G. L., & Manz, C. C. (1995). Leadership for self-managing work teams: A typology and integrative model. *Human Relations, 48*(7), 747–770.

Wageman, R., Fisher, C. M., & Hackman, J. R. (2009). Leading teams when the time is right: Finding the best moments to act. *Organizational Dynamics, 38*(3), 192–203.

Zaccaro, S. J., Ardison, S. D., & Orvis, K. L. (2004). Leadership in virtual teams. In D. V. Day, S. J. Zaccaro, & S. M. Halpin (Eds.), *Leader development for transforming organizations: Growing leaders for tomorrow* (pp. 267–292). Mahwah, NJ: Lawrence Erlbaum.

Zaccaro, S. J., Heinen, B., & Shuffler, M. (2009). Team leadership and team effectiveness. In E. Salas, G. F. Goodwin, & C. S. Burke (Eds.), *Team effectiveness in complex organizations: Cross–disciplinary perspectives and approaches* (pp. 83–111). New York: Taylor & Francis Group.

Zaccaro, S. J., Rittman, A. L., & Marks, M. A. (2001). Team leadership. *Leadership Quarterly, 12,* 451–483.

13

Psychodynamic Approach

Ernest L. Stech

DESCRIPTION

The psychodynamic approach consists of several different ways of looking at leadership. There is no single model or theory. One fundamental concept underlies the psychodynamic approach: personality. As used here, the term means a consistent pattern of ways of thinking, feeling, and acting with regard to the environment, including other people. A personality is characterized by a list of tendencies or qualities, such that one person might be shy, intelligent, and rigid in behavior, whereas another is creative, independent, and spontaneous. The list of possible personality traits is large, and psychologists have developed numerous questionnaires that can be used to characterize the personality of an individual. One of those questionnaires, the Myers-Briggs Type Indicator®, is described later in this chapter.

This approach is different from the trait approach in Chapter 2 and the style approach in Chapter 4. In the trait approach, certain characteristics of a person are assumed to be important in attaining leadership status or performing leadership tasks. The style approach suggests that a certain leadership style, particularly the team management (9,9) style, is the best (see Figure 4.1). Situational leadership, discussed in Chapter 5, suggests that the key element is the match between the leader's style or behaviors and the needs of the subordinates. In the psychodynamic approach, personality types are emphasized and evidence is presented that suggests that various personality types are better suited to particular leadership positions or situations.

There have been several efforts to describe leadership from a psychodynamic perspective (Berens et al., 2001; Gabriel, 2011; Kets de Vries, 2006; Kets de Vries and Balazs, 2011; Maccoby, 1981; Zaleznik, 1977), but all emphasize the importance of leaders becoming aware of their own personality type and the personalities of their followers. The psychodynamic approach begins with an examination of the roots of the individual in the family. Our first experience with leadership occurs the day we are born. Mom and Dad, or those who are our primary caregivers, become our leaders, at least for a few years. That is the most basic premise of the psychodynamic approach to leadership. Particularly in the early years of childhood, our primary caregivers (parents, grandparents, et al.) create deep-seated feelings about leadership. The parental image is highlighted in business when we refer to a corporation as paternalistic. Hill (1983) wrote on the law of the father, a psychodynamic examination of leadership. Members of the U.S. Air Force sometimes call their service the Big Blue Mother, referring to the color of the uniforms and the wild blue yonder. The familial metaphor is common in organizations that consider themselves one big happy family, with the natural consequence that the leaders are the parents and the employees the children.

Childhood and adolescent experiences are reflected in reactions to paternalistic, maternalistic, and familial patterns of leadership and management. Some people respect and respond to authority figures in healthy ways. Others may become dependent or rebel and be counterdependent. Most important, however, psychological development produces personality types. The psychodynamic approach makes no assumptions about good traits or a best style and does not attempt to match a style to followers. However, some personality types appear to be better suited to certain conditions, situations, or positions. Instead of beginning with a study of leaders or people in positions of authority, the psychodynamic approach starts with analyses of the human personality and then relates the personality types to leadership levels and types.

In the psychodynamic approach, there is no need to match the personality type of the leader to that of subordinates in order to have an effective work situation. In fact, personality theorists argue that it is difficult to attempt different ways of behaving, particularly under stress. The important point is that the responses of subordinates to a leader are predictable to some extent, and are within some range of behaviors. Some followers resist directions from an authoritarian leader, whereas others are comfortable and even grateful for a strong leader. Although it focuses on the personality of the leader and of followers, the psychodynamic

13.1 Psychological Development

approach ultimately is a way to look at the relationship between leader and follower.

An important underlying assumption in the psychodynamic approach is that the personality characteristics of individuals, being deeply ingrained, are very difficult to change in any significant way. The key is to accept one's own personality characteristics and quirks, understand the effect they have on followers, and accept the features and idiosyncrasies of followers.

A second assumption is that people have motives and feelings that are beneath immediate awareness—that is, in the unconscious. Thus, the behavior of a person results not only from observable actions and responses, but also from the emotional residue of prior experiences.

The emergence of the psychodynamic approach to leadership has its roots in the works of Sigmund Freud (1938) in his development of psychoanalysis. Freud attempted to understand and help patients with problems that did not respond to conventional treatments. He first used hypnosis to treat patients with hysterical paralysis. Later, he discovered that hypnosis was not necessary. Simply having patients talk about their past was enough to effect a cure. Freud thereby created what are known as the talking therapies.

Freud's work spawned many offshoots. One of his well-known disciples was Carl Jung, who eventually developed his own body of psychological writings and whose work is the basis of much of the material in this chapter. Today, Jungian psychology is well accepted, whereas classic Freudian psychoanalysis has found less acceptance in recent years. Yet it is from the works of both Freud and Jung that the psychodynamic approach to leadership has been constructed.

A leading proponent of the psychodynamic approach to leadership was Abraham Zaleznik (1977), a management professor at Harvard. The psychodynamic approach is also behind much of the writing about charismatic leaders (Hummel, 1975; Schiffer, 1973; Winer, Jobe, & Ferrono, 1984–1985). More recently, Michael Maccoby (2003), with a unique combination of anthropological and psychoanalytical training, has written of the productive narcissist as a visionary leader.

One branch of psychodynamic theorizing is called *psychohistory*. It consists of attempts to explain the behavior of historical figures such as Abraham Lincoln and Hitler. These studies review the historical record of the leader and delve into the leader's family background. Some basic ideas underlie the various psychodynamic approaches to leadership. One of those is the concept of the ego state, developed by Eric Berne (1961). It is part of a larger method called transactional analysis.

Eric Berne and Transactional Analysis

A recent addition to the range of psychodynamic models is transactional analysis (TA). Berne (1961) created TA, which he dubbed "a unified system of individual and social psychiatry" (p. 11). The important aspect of that title is the notion of a social psychiatry, one that focuses not only on the individual, but also on one's relationship to others. A few years later, he published a popularized version in *Games People Play* (1964). The TA movement has continued to expand these methods (Stewart & Joines, 1991).

Although TA has not been applied directly to leadership, some of the basic ideas are interesting and can elucidate leader and follower interactions. The most basic concept is that of the ego state, which Berne (1964) defined as "a coherent system of feelings and operationally as a set of coherent behavior patterns" (p. 23). This concept is an effort to link feelings and experiences with how people actually behave.

There are three ego states in TA: parent, adult, and child. When a person thinks, feels, or behaves in ways copied from her or his own parents, that person is said to be in the parent ego state. Similarly, thinking, feeling, or behaving as one did as a child results in being in the child ego state. The adult ego state is characterized by thoughts, feelings, or behaviors that are the direct result of whatever is happening around the person. The adult ego state is one in which an individual is engaging in what is known as reality testing. An important point is that people shift into and out of the three ego states: Anyone can be in any of the three ego states at any time. An assessment of the current state of a person is called structural analysis.

In a further development of TA, the parent and child ego states have been subdivided so that a person can be in either a controlling or a nurturing parent state and can be in either a free child or an adapted child state. The meaning of the adult ego state is self-evident. For the child ego state, the adapted child can be considered the state in which a person conforms and adapts to the demands of others. Conversely, the free child, previously labeled the rebellious child, is the ego state in which one acts and feels like an uninhibited and unsocialized child.

▶ **13.1** Transactional Analysis

In TA, the ego state is not the same as the personality. People shift from one ego state to another depending on the situation, the person with whom they are interacting, and the accessibility of each ego state. The closest TA comes to the idea of personality is in the egogram, developed by Dusay (1980). An egogram is a bar chart created by a person showing the relative frequency with which she or he is in each ego state. An example is shown in Figure 13.1. The ego states are abbreviated as CP for critical parent, NP for nurturing parent, A for adult, FC for free child, and AC for adapted child. A person with an egogram such as that shown in Figure 13.1 operates predominantly in the adult ego state and to a lesser extent in the adapted child and nurturing parent states.

Figure 13.1   A Sample Egogram

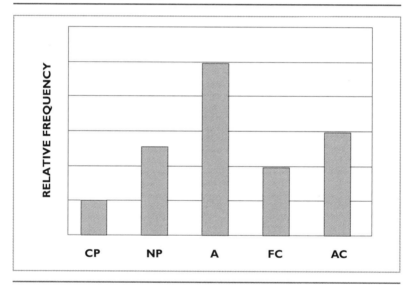

SOURCE: Stewart & Joines, 1987.

TA, as opposed to structural analysis, occurs when the ego states of two people interacting are assessed. For example, one may be in her parent ego state, perhaps the nurturing parent, and the other in his adaptive child ego state. That would be considered a complementary transaction (see Figure 13.2). In technical terms such a transaction is one in which the ego state addressed is the one that responds. A crossed transaction occurs when the vectors or lines connecting the ego states are not parallel, or when the ego state addressed is not the one that responds (see Figure 13.3). An example would be a leader who is in his adult ego state dealing with

Figure 13.2 Ego States of Leader and Subordinate

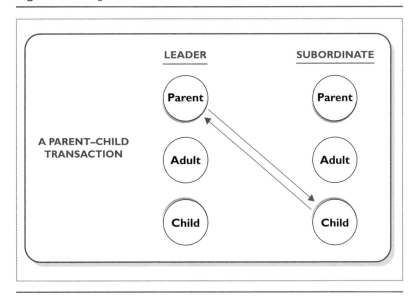

Figure 13.3 Crossed Transaction

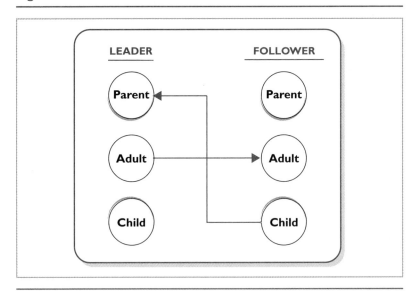

13.2 Transactions

a subordinate who responds from his free child ego state so that the response is somewhat negative, rejecting the input from the leader. If it were a complementary transaction, the adult ego state initiation would be followed by an adult ego state response.

For a leader–follower dyad, the following common complementary transactions could occur:

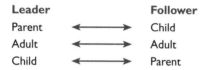

Leader		Follower
Parent	⟷	Child
Adult	⟷	Adult
Child	⟷	Parent

Intuitively, having the leader in the child ego state may not seem reasonable. However, a leader may be in her child ego state and "throw a tantrum" in response to a critical situation. Or a leader may begin a transaction in the adapted child ego state by stressing the importance of following the norms and rules of the organization.

Crossed transactions represent major problems in leader–follower interactions. If a leader initiates an exchange in the adult ego state, describing a situation that requires some action, and the follower responds in the child ego state by asking what could possibly be done, the leader must switch to the parent ego state and help the child by providing guidance and counseling.

From the original work by Berne (1961) to an updated version (Stewart & Joines, 1991), TA focuses entirely on crossed transactions and other unhealthy aspects of human interactions. Effective leadership and followership depend on two or more people operating in the adult ego state, testing reality by acquiring information and assessing possible lines of action and their outcomes. If there are consistent initiations and responses between a leader and a follower, TA could also be used to characterize the nature of the relationship. Some of the ideas behind TA might be useful in analyzing interactions and improving them. A different version of the psychodynamic approach is that of personality types, based on the work of Freud and Jung.

Sigmund Freud and Personality Types

As described earlier, Freud developed the process known as psychoanalysis and wrote extensively on the subject of human beings and their personalities. Most of his work was devoted to psychopathologies—that is, psychological problems such as neuroses and psychoses. However, Freud did use the concept of personality. In one instance, he provided a schema consisting of three personality types. To Freud, personality was a typical or regular way in which human beings relate to the world. There is a core personality, inborn and instinctual, but values, attitudes, and beliefs are overlaid on that core personality.

The three personality types Freud offered were *erotic, obsessive,* and *narcissistic.* Erich Fromm subsequently added a fourth: *marketing* (Maccoby, 2003, pp. 43–44). The following sketches of the four personality types were taken from Maccoby (2003, pp. 45–60).

The *erotic personality* is one in which people seek to love and be loved. They prefer to be liked and accepted over being admired and respected. The erotic personality enjoys talking with others for the simple pleasure of having a conversation and getting to know someone. In work situations, erotics want the group or team to become a close-knit family of nice people who get along. They want to know about the backgrounds of the people with whom they work and even try to delve into personal matters. However, people with an erotic personality are also quite dependent and needy.

In contrast, people with an *obsessive* personality try to live up to standards, follow rules, and obey a strict conscience. Obsessives prefer order and stability rather than acceptance and liking. The most important value is maintaining the status quo, which means following the rules and regulations of society and the organization. Such people have a strong conscience that guides them to do the right thing. This kind of person searches for ways to improve, and particularly to become more knowledgeable and competent. On the negative side, obsessives can be very aggressive and domineering. They believe they are right and do not want to be questioned.

The *marketing* personality is characterized as being highly adaptable; such people conform and align themselves with the right people and situations. Marketers easily adapt to changes in society and in organizations. They usually seek to develop and grow personally, wanting not only to become more competent, but also to grow emotionally. Marketers are good at facilitating and networking, and at using and enjoying the process of collaboration in order to achieve consensus.

Finally, the *narcissistic* personality, the theme of Maccoby's book on visionary leaders, receives no guidance, as do the other three types. Maccoby

13.1 Sigmund Freud

stressed the need to clearly set the narcissist apart from egotistical or egoistic people. The narcissist is not vain and does not attempt to impress, but takes pride in and will talk about actual accomplishments. In fact, Maccoby pointed out that one of the important characteristics of the narcissist is humor, which is most often self-directed. On the positive side, the narcissist has a clear vision of what to do and does not take into account what other people say or do in the pursuit of that vision.

In a further development of the personality types, Maccoby distinguished between productive and unproductive versions of each type. There can be productive erotics, unproductive obsessives, and productive marketing types, or their opposites. Erich Fromm (1947) introduced the idea of productiveness and identified five key elements to define the productive person: The productive person is free and not dependent, is guided by reason, is active or proactive, understands his or her own situation, and has a purpose in life. Maccoby (2003) added perseverance to the list of characteristics of a productive person. At the other end of the spectrum are unproductive people, characterized as limited and averse to risk, irrational, reactive, superficial, aimless, and uncommitted.

In working as a consultant with top executives in many large organizations and across various cultures, Maccoby sensed that the best executives were productive narcissists. They had a vision and were able to motivate others to accept the vision and work toward it. However, there are strengths and weaknesses in the productive narcissist personality, summarized in Table 13.1.

Finally, Maccoby (2003, pp. 204–215) provided advice on how to work with a narcissist. It is important for followers to know their own personality types. A narcissistic leader will not satisfy the needs of any of the other personality types, and followers need to fulfill those needs somewhere else. Second, followers need to develop excellent knowledge of their own field that supplements and does not compete with the narcissist's knowledge. Third, if followers know their own personalities and needs and can support the narcissist, then that kind of leader will more readily accept them as partners. Fourth, followers should avoid getting ego-involved with the leader because she or he will not be able to satisfy those who have their own vision. Finally, followers should do everything they can to protect the image of the productive narcissist.

The productive narcissist is needed in organizations and in work teams, where a vision of the future is important for surviving and coping with chaos and change. Because the narcissist takes risks, the result can be

13.1 Narcissism

Table 13.1   Strengths and Weaknesses of the Productive Narcissist

Strengths	Weaknesses
A vision to change the world and create meaning for people	Unwillingness to listen
Independent thinking and risk taking	Sensitivity to criticism
Passion	Paranoia
Charisma	Anger and put-downs
Voracious learning	Overcompetitive and overcontrolling behavior
Perseverance	Isolation
Alertness to threats	Lack of self-knowledge
Sense of humor	Grandiosity

SOURCE: Adapted from *The Productive Narcissist: The Promise and Peril of Visionary Leadership* (pp. 95 and 132), by M. Maccoby, 2003, New York: Broadway Books.

wonderful or disastrous. Maccoby concentrates on the productive narcissist as the leader of organizations in times of crisis and change. However, the productive versions of the erotic, obsessive, and marketing personality types can also be effective in their own ways. Friendly, empathic, and nurturing people make excellent leaders of organizations and work groups that provide services to human beings. The obsessive personality type is ideal for running an organization that strives to produce goods or services in a consistent, predictable, and routine manner. Finally, the marketing personality works well in an organization or a team that is subject to the whims of other organizations and constituencies.

Social Character and a Shift in Leadership Perspective

Maccoby (2007), using the notion of social character, provided a way of looking at leadership in terms of the psychology of followers. *Social character*, a term introduced by Erich Fromm, is a kind of macro personality based on the emotional attitudes and values shared by people in a certain context (Maccoby, 2007, p. 3). A particular type of social character is created within a specific culture or social class.

The essence of Maccoby's argument is that there has been a shift in social character in recent times reflecting the movement from an industrial to a knowledge-based economy. This resulted from the rapid development of the Information Age. The shift has been from a bureaucratic to an interactive social character. The change has major implications for leadership practice.

The bureaucratic social character was shaped in a time when formal hierarchical organizations were the rule. Every large organization had an organization chart that specified positions in the organization, including "who reported to whom." Managers and leaders created missions, goals, schedules, and budgets; and assigned personnel. Underlings were expected to accept the pronouncements of their leaders without questions. According to Maccoby (2007, p. 65), the ideals of the bureaucratic social character are stability, hierarchy and autonomy, organizational loyalty, and striving for excellence. Managers were expected to demonstrate precision and to be methodical, and they expected the same from others. Followers preferred paternalistic authority, wanting the security that came from having a strong and effective leader.

Modern organizations deal with global markets, rapid changes in technologies, Internet and social media communications, and competition from entrepreneurial companies. There is also employment uncertainty as companies adapt to an ever-changing competitive and technological environment. These factors influence the kind of social character needed to lead and follow, creating a new social character Maccoby dubbed the interactive social character.

There have also been changes in the American family that affect social character. The structure associated with the bureaucratic social structure was the traditional family, common in the 1950s through 1980s, consisting of two parents in a heterosexual relationship with several children. The father, often authoritarian and perhaps somewhat distant, worked, brought home the paycheck, and thereby provided economic security. The wife raised and nurtured the children and provided social and psychological security. When individuals raised in that kind of family structure went to work, they wanted and expected a paternalistic leader, someone who provided the kind of security that had been available in the home. A social and cultural shift has occurred bringing diverse family structures that include single parents, divorced couples with joint custody of the children, blended families, and gay and lesbian couples with children. One outcome of these diverse family structures is that the focus on the paternal authority and maternal nurturer has been replaced by identification with siblings and peers. The importance of parental models has decreased.

The interactive social character is fascinated, in terms of ideals, by the challenge of continual improvement rather than stability, and enjoys creating and using networks as opposed to operating within a hierarchy (Maccoby, 2007, p. 65). Furthermore, individuals operating out of this

▶ 13.3 Michael Maccoby

social character see themselves as free to move from one organization to another rather than to be loyal to a single company. A large part of the social character is the desire to be experimental and innovative and to market ideas.

The net result of the shift from the bureaucratic to the interactive social character is that persons in organizations no longer want to be followers but rather want to be collaborators in a joint effort with their leaders and managers. Maccoby (2007, p. 72) developed a grid consisting of a vertical dimension consisting of the motivation of the leader, ranging from personal power to common good; and a horizontal dimension consisting of motivation of the led, going from have-to-follow to want-to-follow. The preferred combination in the modern organization is the leader who seeks the common good and the follower who wants to follow. This combination results in collaboration between the manager and subordinates, between the leader and what were once followers.

Carl Jung and Personality Types

Human behavior is predictable and understandable, and that became the basis for Carl Jung's way of classifying people and their personalities (Jung, 1923, 1993). He believed that people have preferences for how they think and feel and these preferences become the basis for how people work, relate, and play.

Jung believed there are four dimensions important in assessing personality. The first concerns where a person derives her or his energy (either internally or externally). The second involves the way in which a person gathers information (either in a precise, sequential way or in a more intuitive and random way). The third is the way in which a person makes decisions (either rationally and factually or in a subjective and personal way). The fourth concerns the difference between a person who plans and is organized and one who is more spontaneous and pliant.

These became the basis of the classification of types:

Extraversion versus introversion: Whether a person prefers to derive energy externally or internally

Sensing versus intuiting: Whether a person prefers to gather information in a precise or in an insightful way

🎙 **13.2 Carl Jung**

Thinking versus feeling: Whether a person prefers to make decisions rationally or subjectively

Judging versus perceiving: Whether a person prefers to live in an organized or a spontaneous way

These words have specific meanings in the model of psychological types, and they are explained in detail later in this chapter. A way to assess your own type is also provided.

There are 16 possible combinations of the four dimensions. In this chapter, each combination is considered a type. A pair of terms such as *extraversion and introversion* is a dimension, which is only part of a type. The combinations are coded using the first letters of each word except that *intuition* is abbreviated N to avoid duplicating the *I* from *introversion*. Thus, the 16 combinations are ESTP, ISTP, ESFP, ISFP, ESTJ, ISTJ, ESFJ, ISFJ, ENTJ, INTJ, ENTP, INTP, ENFJ, INFJ, ENFP, and INFP. It is very difficult to try to understand all 16 combinations immediately, and it is not necessary to do so. Instead, a leader should identify his or her own style and concentrate on understanding it. (At this point, it would be helpful to go to the end of the chapter and assess your own psychological type or types.)

It is important eventually to understand and recognize the 16 types because they affect how a leader interacts with subordinates. Some of the types are more compatible than others are; some combinations can result in frustration, misunderstandings, and conflict. However, there are guides to the 16 types (Berens et al., 2001), and they do not need to be learned and memorized in order to be useful.

Functions and Preferences

Labels such as *extravert, sensor, thinker,* and *judger* represent functions of the human personality in Jung's theory of types. Individuals tend to prefer one function of each pair to the other. As noted earlier, combinations of preferences for these functions constitute types.

Extraversion and Introversion

Extraversion is a preference for obtaining information, inspiration, and energy from outside the self. One characteristic of extraverts is that they

13.2 Archetypes

talk a great deal. Such people like to be in contact with other people, and they like action. They are often seen as energetic and well liked in social situations and may be the life of the party. The spelling used here comes from Jung himself, who preferred *extraversion* to *extroversion*.

An introvert uses her or his own ideas and thoughts and does not need external stimulation. Such people would rather listen than talk. They like to acquire information through reading or watching informative television shows. One clue to introversion is the desire to be alone at times in order to be able to think and reenergize. Constant exposure to people and activities can be draining.

According to Kroeger and Theusen (2002, p. 28), there are about three extraverts to every introvert in modern society. That means introverts often need to adapt to an extraverted world. Most people strongly prefer one function to the other, but some people have a weaker preference and are able to use the other function some of the time. Thus, there can be strong extraverts and strong introverts, but also some who are extraverted with a component of introversion, or vice versa.

Sensing and Intuition

The dimensions of sensing and intuition have to do with the way in which people acquire information. Sensors collect data through their senses, and their thinking revolves around facts and practical matters. Such people are quite detail oriented and happy to deal with the "real world." They focus on what they can see, hear, touch, smell, and taste. *Precision* and *accuracy* are the favorite words of a sensor.

Other people are intuitive. They tend to be much more conceptual and theoretical. Common everyday experience bores them. They would prefer to be creative, to fantasize about the future, to apply ingenuity to a problem. In gathering information, intuitors look for possibilities and relationships; they use a theoretical framework to get and understand data. In contrast to the sensor, the intuitor is more likely to use the phrases *approximately* or *as far as I know*.

Thinking and Feeling

After information has been acquired, people need to make decisions based on the data. The two ways of deciding are thinking and feeling.

13.4 Psychological Preferences

Thinkers use logic, strive for objectivity, and are analytical. They often seem to be detached and uninvolved with people, preferring to guide their actions on the basis of possible results. The opposite preference produces feelers. They tend to be more subjective, seek harmony with others, and take into account the feelings of people. Such people are more involved with others at work or elsewhere and are seen as considerate and humane.

Kroeger and Theusen (2002) noted that the distinction between thinking and feeling has been shown to be empirically related to gender differences, in that more men are thinkers and more women feelers. However, this is not absolute. In addition, the difference may be fading as more women are being trained in the sciences, engineering, and management. Furthermore, as discussed later, most managers are thinkers, probably because until recently the field of management was male dominated, and the thinker mode of operation is taught in business schools and rewarded in the organizational world.

Judging and Perceiving

Kroeger and Theusen (2002) suggested that the difference between perceivers and judgers results in some of the most frustrating issues in working and leadership. Judgers prefer structure, plans, schedules, and resolution. They are decisive and deliberate, and quite sure of their way of doing things. Perceivers tend to be much more flexible, adaptable, tentative, and open ended. They are spontaneous. Perceivers often do not take deadlines seriously and may change their minds and decisions without difficulty.

Types and Leadership

There have been efforts to describe leadership in terms of psychological types (Berens et al., 2001; Kroeger & Theusen, 2002). The two sources agree that leadership is intentional, that it entails a vision or an aim, and that people other than the leader must be motivated to move toward a goal or final outcome. Kroeger and Theusen suggested that leadership involves the use of power, including both personal and organizational power. Pearman (in Berens et al., 2001) described a more sophisticated requirement, that of developing processes that promote future leadership activities.

Kroeger and Theusen (2002) related the eight functions to leadership strengths and weaknesses. The results taken from their work are shown in Table 13.2.

13.2 Psychoanalytic Approach

Table 13.2   Psychological Preferences and Leadership

Preference	Leadership Pluses	Leadership Minuses
Thinker	Objective Rational Problem solver	Critical Demanding Insensitive
Feeler	Empathic Cooperative Loyal	Indecisive Changeable
Extravert	Energizing Communicative Open	Communication overload
Introvert	Quiet Reflective Thinking	Slow to decide Hesitant
Intuitor	Strategic thinker Future oriented	Hazy Nonspecific
Sensor	Practical Action oriented	Unimaginative Detail oriented
Judger	Decisive Sticks to plans	Rigid Inflexible
Perceiver	Flexible Curious Informal	Scattered Unfocused

SOURCE: Adapted from *Type Talk at Work,* by O. Kroeger and J. M. Theusen, 2002, New York: Dell.

Table 13.2 is a good example of how the psychological type's schema does not, on the surface, suggest one type as superior to any other in terms of leadership. Each type has its pluses and minuses.

However, there are data showing the preferences of people in management positions. Kroeger and Theusen (2002) provided the results from a database of 20,000 scores on the Myers-Briggs Type Indicator® (MBTI). The people surveyed were from various kinds of organizations, including private industry, government agencies, the military, and accounting firms. One caveat is that the data probably are skewed toward an overrepresentation of men. Furthermore, these were managers and not necessarily leaders. The database was reviewed and information collected on middle managers, upper-level managers, and top executives. The most common

▶ **13.5** MBTI

preference in these three categories was TJ, thinker–judger, with 69.9%, 72.9%, and 85% of the respondents selecting those preferences, respectively, for middle and upper managers and executives. When the thinker preference was combined with all of the other preferences, the results were 86.2%, 92.7%, and 95.4%, respectively, for middle and upper managers and executives. Clearly, management reinforces the need for detached, rational, and analytical ways of thinking. A close second is the preference for the judger (planning, scheduling, organizing, and controlling). In contrast, only 36% of trainers in the same organizations exhibited a preference for thinking and 47% for thinking and judging.

Some kinds of leadership may require different preferences and types. A visionary person is needed to set the long-term mission and direction for an organization. That need would imply a combination of introversion and intuition, someone who is quiet, reflective, and slow to decide. A vision cannot be rushed. Creating a vision may be a solitary activity in

Table 13.3   Psychological Types and Leadership

Type	Value	Appearance
ESTP	Competition	Active, pragmatic, incisive, demanding
ISTP	Efficiency	Active, capable, concrete, proficient
ESFP	Realism	Energetic, inquisitive, encouraging
ISFP	Cooperation	Flexible, synergetic, pragmatic
ESTJ	Organization	Methodical, focused, planned
ISTJ	Productivity	Persistent, logical, practical
ESFJ	Harmony	Helpful, supportive, practical
ISFJ	Consideration	Cooperative, committed, understanding
ENTJ	Command	Analytical, blunt, planned
INTJ	Effectiveness	Analytical, tough minded, systematic
ENTP	Knowledge	Assertive, competitive, resourceful
INTP	Ingenuity	Conceptual, analytical, critical
ENFJ	Collaboration	Warm, supportive, inclusive
INFJ	Creativity	Inventive, idealistic, insightful
ENFP	Innovation	Imaginative, enthusiastic, expressive
INFP	Empathy	Passionate, intuitive, creative

SOURCE: Adapted from *Quick Guide to the 16 Personality Types in Organizations*, by L. V. Berens, S. A. Cooper, L. K. Ernst, C. R. Martin, S. Myers, D. Nardi, R. R. Pearman, S. Segal, and M. A. Smith, 2001, Huntington Beach, CA: Telos.

 13.3 MBTI

which many options are explored. Therefore, the data on the preferences of managers should not be taken as a statement of desired psychological type for all leaders.

Sixteen Types and Leadership

Pearman (in Berens et al., 2001) provided one paragraph on the style of leadership involved in each of the 16 psychological types. Pearman's work is summarized in Table 13.3.

Pearman stressed that there is leadership potential in all 16 types. He also described the potential pitfalls and problems for each type. In looking over the values in Table 13.3, the types including *thinking* (T) tend to be the best descriptors of at least the stereotype of the effective manager. Those values include competition, efficiency, organization, productivity, command, effectiveness, knowledge, and ingenuity.

Dealing With Followers

Kroeger and Theusen (2002, pp. 90–91) provided a matrix showing how a leader operating out of each dimension should deal with a subordinate of the same or a different dimension, a chart too complex to present here. It consists of the eight psychological dimensions (E, I, S, N, T, F, J, and P) for both the leader and subordinates, and results in a 4-by-4 matrix with 16 cells. Following are three examples of how a leader's psychological type can interact with that of a follower.

Suppose the leader is primarily an extravert and is dealing with an introverted follower. The extravert leader likes to talk a great deal and sometimes speaks before really thinking things through. He or she will tend to dominate many conversations. The introvert, on the other hand, needs time to respond, wants to think things through, and likes to explain what he or she means without interruption. The combination of extravert and introvert can cause problems. The extraverted leader may take silence or a slow response on the part of the follower as agreement, when in fact the follower is just thinking over what has been said. If the conversation was about something that should be done, the leader will think that the subordinate will do it, and the subordinate will just be formulating a response. Later the leader will be frustrated by the lack of action, and the follower will be upset that his voice was not heard.

13.3 Leaders and Followers

In such a situation, the leader has to back off during the conversation or maybe even suggest getting back together in an hour or two to go over what needs to be done. This will give the introverted subordinate time to reflect and gather his or her thoughts. If he is also intuitive, the follower may even come up with a better way of doing the assignment.

A common difference in teamwork occurs when there is an intuitor leader and a sensor follower. The intuitor leader is able to and prefers to see the big picture, the overall strategy, and the possibilities in the future. That is a valuable characteristic for a leader. It may be a major factor in moving forward and inducing change. However, the intuitor leader may change goals and strategies while followers are trying to deal with the existing goals and strategies. The intuitor is likely to be bored with the details of implementation. Giving instructions is difficult because the intuitor gives general and vague directions, and the subordinate wants specifics.

A sensor subordinate will be frustrated in dealing with an intuitor leader. The follower wants to know what to do, when to do it, and possibly even how to do it. The leader is not at all concerned with those details. However, the subordinate has to do the work and get results. That is hard to do with nebulous instructions and frequent changes in direction. In such a case, the intuitor leader needs to be made aware of her mode of thinking and make every attempt to satisfy the needs of the subordinate. If that does not happen, the leader may become upset at the lack of progress.

An interesting situation arises in the case of an intuitor leader dealing with an intuitor subordinate. Both will tend to think in conceptual ways. They will be more interested in what comes next, fantasizing or even planning the next project. When it comes to working on the current project, they will do so in a theoretical way without dealing with the realities of the situation. The two intuitors will prefer not to obtain facts and be practical. This is an invitation to disaster. If the leader is aware of the matching preferences, then he will have to make sure that both stay grounded and in the present, working to get through the current situation so that they can move on to the next project.

As can be seen from these examples, an understanding and awareness of psychological preferences and types can be useful in communicating effectively and getting work done. The differences between the types can lead to frustration and perhaps antagonism. One possible solution is to create a team or an organization consisting of only one or two types. They will communicate readily and get along fairly well. However, the resulting team or organization will be limited in its ability to deal with a wide range of programs and issues.

HOW DOES THE PSYCHODYNAMIC APPROACH WORK?

The primary aim of the psychodynamic approach is to raise the awareness of leaders and followers to their own personality types and the implications of those types on work and relationships. For psychological types this is done through an assessment such as the MBTI or a similar method. In the TA model, respondents are given statements describing the various ego states and then asked to identify the existence of those states in their own lives. Whether a personality type or an ego state model is used, the presumed advantage to becoming aware is that one's own behavior and the responses of others to that behavior become more understandable.

In work team or organizational contexts, the psychodynamic approach usually involves the participation of subordinates as well as the leader; it is important to be aware of and understand the differences between various people who must work together. What are first irritants or even conflicts may become understandable when one grasps the psychological types or ego states involved. The presumed ultimate benefit is that leaders and followers are better able to tolerate one another.

This ought to be particularly true when people realize that team or organizational success depends on the existence and application of a diverse set of competencies and interpersonal skills. Some people need to be able to see and create the vision—the big picture—for a group or an organization. Other people need to be able to work diligently to turn the vision into reality. Some people are needed to sell products or services, whereas others are needed to manufacture the products or provide the services. Thus, one application of the psychological type model is to determine the most favorable kind of work for an individual, based on that person's preferences in terms of gathering information, making decisions, structuring the individual's work efforts, and dealing with people.

STRENGTHS

The greatest strength of the psychodynamic approach is that it results in an analysis of the relationship between the leader and the follower. This transactional emphasis is important because of its back-and-forth action and response between two people. In some models of leadership, the leader exhibits certain appropriate behaviors that are intended to create the

13.4 Leadership Development

desired response in the subordinate. In that kind of model, the leader is not an ordinary mortal, but rather someone who can always act in the most appropriate way, and the appropriate way is a function of who is being led and what kind of response is desired. The psychodynamic approach takes the position that both leader and subordinate have a personality type or operate in an ego state, not always consciously understood, and that their relationship is a result of the combination of those types or states.

A second strength is the presumed universality of the psychodynamic approach. Much of the theory underlying this approach has been based on a search for a universal truth in human existence, done through the study of myth. Jung (1923, 1961) and Freud relied heavily on Greek myths to label psychological actions and reactions such as the Oedipus complex.

Another strength of the psychodynamic approach is that it emphasizes the need for awareness on the part of the leader. That awareness is obtained by bringing into consciousness and dealing with ego states or psychological types. By being knowledgeable about these issues, the leader comes to understand his or her reactions to subordinates' actions, and to see why followers react as they do to certain actions by the leader. The ability to understand actions and the responses they produce allows the leader to control these actions.

Finally, the psychodynamic approach, at least in its most modern form, discourages manipulative techniques in leadership. Effective leadership using the psychodynamic approach is based on self-awareness and tolerance for the styles and behaviors of others.

CRITICISMS

One criticism of the psychodynamic approach is that much of the early work was based on clinical observation and treatment of people with serious mental difficulties. This was a psychology of the abnormal rather than the normal. For the most part, psychiatrists work with people who are having problems. This is particularly true for TA. In the most recent works on TA (Stewart & Joines, 1991), the emphasis is on the dysfunctional combinations of ego states. The adult ego state is given almost no attention, even though it is the basis for mature and effective dealings with others. There has been more emphasis on the psychodynamics of the everyday individual in the humanistic and transpersonal psychologies (Maslow, 1998).

The MBTI also represents a limitation. It was developed by Katharine Cook Briggs and Isabel Briggs Myers, based on Jung's functions and preferences. They were not professional test developers. Thus, the MBTI may have reliability or validity problems.

For TA, the limitation is more severe. There is no standardized assessment for describing ego state in an individual. Each person is directed to try to identify her or his ego states from descriptions of them in the literature or in workshops.

The psychodynamic approach is also limited, in that it focuses primarily on the personalities of the leader and followers that dictate the nature of the relationship between them. It does not take into account organizational factors. These could include the culture of the organization, its structure, and the particular kinds of challenges and tasks it faces.

The very nature of the psychodynamic approach also limits its use in practice. Many people simply reject the notion that emotional reactions occur toward leaders, followers, and coworkers, and that those reactions arise from predispositions in individuals and particularly from the unconscious. Organizational leaders, in particular, subscribe to the view that management and leadership ought to be as rational as possible. The very fact that managers tend to be thinkers and judgers may prevent them from accepting the psychodynamic approach. Emotional responses are ignored or rejected, even though many an executive has lain awake at night while replaying an emotional situation from work.

A final limitation is that the psychodynamic approach does not lend itself to training in a conventional sense. There are no clear prescriptions for how an individual can change his or her personality style. Instead, it requires leaders and followers to assess their own ways of acting, to accept those ways, and to tolerate the ways in which others behave.

CASE STUDIES

In this section, we provide three case studies (Cases 13.1, 13.2, and 13.3) of leadership in organizations that can be analyzed using the psychodynamic approach. The questions provided at the end of each case will help you analyze the situations.

CASE 13.1

Not the Type Who Sees the Big Picture

Jenny Folsom is the manager of a group of marketing specialists. She has good relationships with most of her team, except for Connie Perez. Jenny is on the verge of letting Connie go. Connie just cannot seem to work up to Jenny's expectations. Over the past year, Jenny has had four quarterly review sessions with Connie. In each one, Jenny pointed out her expectations and indicated where Connie was falling short. Connie continued to act in much the same way, even though she felt she was trying to improve.

Before going to the drastic step of dismissing an employee, Jenny has gone to the Personnel Department, specifically to the Training and Development Group. She has presented her problem to two training and development specialists. She said, "Connie seems to get bogged down in details. I give her a project to work on and a set of overall objectives. Then, when I talk to her, I find that she is buried in some minor issue, getting all the information she can, talking to other people about that issue. It drives me crazy. I need to get the project completed and have her move on to something else. I want her to see the big picture. We have a lot to do, a whole strategy to implement. I can't afford to have someone getting hung up on minor details."

The training and development specialists sense that there is a big difference in personality types between Jenny and Connie. They invite Jenny to come back the next day, at which time she is given a briefing on types. It quickly becomes evident that Jenny is an intuitive thinker (NT) in the Jungian personality types. She is good at conceptualizing and systematic planning. She can see the underlying principles of organizations and systems.

With each accomplishment of her group, Jenny can see three or four new big challenges. When the training and development specialists talked this way to Jenny, she agreed readily with their description of her.

On the other hand, Connie seems to be a sensor–feeler (SF), based on Jenny's description. Connie is very practical and down to earth. She actually is quite good at problem solving in an immediate way. Also, she is highly resourceful, able to find information and answers. Unfortunately, she simply is not the type to see the big picture.

Jenny asks the training and development specialists, "So what do I do?"

(Continued)

(Continued)

Questions

1. Should Jenny have a session with Connie on her own?

2. Should she have the session with the training and development specialists?

3. Should Connie be given the analysis results for herself and for Jenny?

4. What kinds of issues should the two women discuss?

5. What kinds of tasks should Jenny assign to Connie in the future?

CASE 13.2

Staff Meeting Problems

Stan Williams is the general manager of a division of a small company that provides various kinds of technical services to customers. The division is one of four located in cities away from the main offices. Once a month, Stan holds a staff meeting for all the key people in the division. That includes four technical specialists, three sales and marketing people, and the budget and finance person.

Stan is a very orderly person and creates an agenda for each meeting. He invites participation on each of the agenda items because he believes in developing a team atmosphere in the division. However, there are big differences in the degree and kinds of participation between the technical and marketing people. The budget and finance person does not participate except when asked a direct question. Most of the meetings are dominated by the sales and marketing people. Not only do they do most of the talking, but also they tend to tell jokes and get sidetracked from the agenda. The technical personnel just sit there but occasionally roll their eyes and give off signals that they are frustrated. The result is just the opposite of what Stan wants. Instead of cohesion, there is friction and conflict, although it is not expressed openly.

Stan is considering the possibility of no longer having staff meetings and, instead, meeting with the technical and marketing staffs separately. He has no access to the corporate human resource department. What should Stan do?

Questions

1. Should Stan stop having the meetings?

2. Should Stan be much more directive by asking for participation by specific people when he thinks it is needed on a particular agenda item?

3. Should he devote a meeting to describing what he wants of the team and what he sees happening, inviting everyone to talk about his or her reaction to the meetings and discussing ways to try to become a team?

4. Should he seek out a consultant to help with the problem?

CASE 13.3

Unexpected Reactions

Maxine Simpson is a manager with more than 20 years of experience. She came up through the ranks and obtained her MBA degree 10 years ago. Her approach to supervising is to lay out in the most direct and simple terms what she sees as an issue or a problem. She always seeks to get the best answer she can and is willing to delay a decision if there appears to be a need for it.

Randy Allenberg is a recent transfer into the group Maxine manages. He is an extremely competent person in his specialty, one that is crucial to the operation of the group. He came into the group with high evaluations from his previous manager, who is a somewhat authoritarian person. Randy is used to being told what the problem is, what to do, when it is to be completed, and, in some cases, how to work out a solution. He was comfortable with that kind of situation because it allowed him to apply his skills directly to many fascinating problems.

Since he joined the group, Randy's reactions to Maxine's way of managing have been unpredictable. His most common response is to argue with Maxine about how she has defined the problem or even whether it really represents a problem. Randy does not seem to enjoy this kind of confrontation but appears to be unable to react differently except on a

(Continued)

(Continued)

few occasions. In those situations, Randy becomes very obedient and asks Maxine for more direction. That bothers Maxine, who feels she does not have the time to mother Randy.

Questions

1. Should Maxine just adapt to Randy's way of interacting?

2. Should she try to figure out why his reactions are so unpredictable?

3. Should she ask Randy why he reacts differently in different situations?

4. Should she contact Randy's previous manager to find out whether Randy's reactions were unpredictable in that setting?

5. From a TA perspective, what do you think is going on?

LEADERSHIP INSTRUMENT

The following questionnaire provides a way to assess your preferences for each of the four Myers-Briggs typologies. You can use it to create a profile that shows your preferences for extraversion or introversion, judging or perceiving, thinking or feeling, and sensing or intuiting.

Psychodynamic Approach Survey

Instructions: For each of the following eight sentences, rate the degree to which you believe it describes you on a scale of 1 to 6, as described in the key. The sentences are paired in such a way that your ratings for each pair should add up to 7 (e.g., if you rate one sentence with a 3, then the other sentence in the pair should be rated a 4). For example, you might rate the first two sentences like this:

I am sociable, outgoing, gregarious, a people person, and talkative. 1 2 3 4 5 <u>6</u>

I am reflective, deep, internally focused, an idea person, and quiet. <u>1</u> 2 3 4 5 6

So the total of the two ratings is 6 + 1 = 7.

When you have completed the questionnaire and scoring procedures for yourself, ask someone you know to rate herself or himself. This step is important because the questionnaire is intended to allow you to compare your personality type to that of another person.

Key: 6 = Always 5 = Often 4 = Usually 3 = Sometimes 2 = Rarely 1 = Never
          true   true   true   true   true   true

1. I am sociable, outgoing, gregarious, a people person,   1 2 3 4 5 6
   and talkative.
2. I am reflective, deep, internally focused, an idea person,   1 2 3 4 5 6
   and quiet. (Total ratings for items 1 + 2 = 7)

3. I am practical, realistic, and factual, and I like details.   1 2 3 4 5 6
4. I am conceptual, theoretical, future oriented, and   1 2 3 4 5 6
   a generalist. (Total ratings for items 3 + 4 = 7)

5. I am firm, just, clear, and detached in decision making.   1 2 3 4 5 6
6. I am humane, harmonious, and subjective, and   1 2 3 4 5 6
   I like multiple inputs. (Total ratings for items 5 + 6 = 7)

7. I am structured, scheduled, planned, and in control.   1 2 3 4 5 6
8. I am adaptable, flexible, spontaneous, and open.   1 2 3 4 5 6
   (Total ratings for items 7 + 8 = 7)

Scoring

Circle your ratings for each sentence on the following chart.

Sentence 1: Extravert (E)   1 2 3 4 5 6

Sentence 2: Introvert (I)   1 2 3 4 5 6

Sentence 3: Sensor (S)	1 2 3 4 5 6
Sentence 4: Intuitor (N)	1 2 3 4 5 6
Sentence 5: Thinker (T)	1 2 3 4 5 6
Sentence 6: Feeler (F)	1 2 3 4 5 6
Sentence 7: Judger (J)	1 2 3 4 5 6
Sentence 8: Perceiver (P)	1 2 3 4 5 6

Scoring Interpretation

Your psychological type consists of four out of the eight paired preferences: E or I, S or N, T or F, and J or P. First look at whether your rating for E is higher than for I. If it is higher, then that is part of your type. Based on the scores in the chart above, pick one of the two letters in the following pairs:

Sentences 1 and 2:	E	I
Sentences 3 and 4:	S	N
Sentences 5 and 6:	T	F
Sentences 7 and 8:	J	P

In some of the pairs your ratings probably will be very different. For example, your rating for S might be 6, which makes your score for N 1. That is a strong indication that you prefer the sensor function. In other cases your ratings might be much closer together. For example, you may have given the thinker sentence a rating of 4 and the feeler sentence a rating of 3. That is not a strong preference, so your type could include either T or F. That is fairly common, even in the MBTI (e.g., such a person might be both ENTJ and ENFJ, indicating that the thinker and feeler ratings were close to each other).

The psychological type method is interesting when you apply it to yourself, but is much more useful in comparing your own type with that of another person. Therefore, you should ask someone you know or work with to rate himself or herself on the questionnaire. After you have scored this person's ratings, you can compare his or her type with yours. Although this method is useful, the best way to get an assessment of your personality type is to take the MBTI test under the direction of a counselor or someone else who is qualified to give and interpret the test.

SUMMARY

The psychodynamic approach is based on assessments of the personalities of leaders and followers. It differs from approaches and models that begin by studying and summarizing the traits, behaviors, skills, or styles of leaders. Several ways of identifying personality characteristics are available, including the ego state model from transactional analysis and the personality types of Freud and Jung, as interpreted by Maccoby (2003) and the MBTI, respectively.

Data suggest that some personality types are better suited to management and executive positions, particularly the thinker type in the Jungian schema. Maccoby's extensive work with executives convinced him that the narcissist type is best suited to lead modern organizations. In both cases, however, the other personality types may be more appropriate to certain kinds of positions or organizations.

The psychodynamic approach is used to encourage leaders and followers to become aware of their own personality types and those of the people with whom they work in order to better understand their own behavior and the responses they get from others.

There are pluses and minuses to this approach. An important advantage is that it emphasizes the relationship of leader to follower. Also, ego states and personality types are assumed to be universal. A major strength is that the psychodynamic approach encourages awareness and thereby reduces the degree of manipulation and control by the leader. Because much of the early work in psychodynamics was based on dealing with disturbed people, some of it does not apply to the average or normal person at work. There are also problems associated with the ways in which ego states and personality types are measured and assessed. Perhaps more important is the fact that the approach assumes the existence of unconscious motives and reactions and relies on emotional states that go counter to the ideal of the rational and objective leader. Also, the psychodynamic approach does not lend itself to training because there are no skills or behaviors to learn.

Visit the Student Study Site at **www.sagepub.com/northouse6e** for web quizzes, leadership questionnaires, and media links represented by the icons.

▶ **13.6** Chapter Summary

REFERENCES

Berens, L. V., Cooper, S. A., Ernst, L. K., Martin, C. R., Myers, S., Nardi, D., et al. (2001). *Quick guide to the 16 personality types in organizations.* Huntington Beach, CA: Telos.

Berne, E. (1961). *Transactional analysis in psychotherapy.* New York: Grove.

Berne, E. (1964). *Games people play.* New York: Ballantine.

Dusay, J. (1980). *Egograms.* New York: Bantam.

Freud, S. (1938). *The basic writings of Sigmund Freud* (A. A. Brill, Ed.). New York: Modern Library.

Fromm, E. (1947). *Man for himself.* New York: Holt, Rinehart & Winston.

Gabriel, Y. (2011). Psychoanalytic approaches to leadership. In A. Bryman, D. Collinson, K. Grint, G. Jackson, & M. Uhl-Bien (Eds.), *The SAGE handbook of leadership* (pp. 393–404). London: Sage.

Hill, M. A. (1983). The law of the father. In B. Kellerman (Ed.), *Leadership: Multidisciplinary perspectives.* Englewood Cliffs, NJ: Prentice Hall.

Hummel, R. P. (1975). Psychology of charismatic followers. *Psychological Reports, 37*(3), 759–770.

Jung, C. G. (1923). *Psychological types.* New York: Harcourt Brace.

Jung, C. G. (1961). *Memories, dreams, and reflections.* New York: Vintage.

Jung, C. G. (1993). Psychological types. In V. D. Laszlo (Ed.), *The basic writings of C. G. Jung* (pp. 230–357). New York: Modern Library.

Kets de Vries, M. (2006). *The leader on the couch: A clinical approach to changing people and organizations.* New York: John Wiley and Sons.

Kets de Vries, M., & Balazs, K. (2011). The shadow side of leadership. In A. Bryman, D. Collinson, K. Grint, G. Jackson, & M. Uhl-Bien (Eds.), *The SAGE handbook of leadership* (pp. 380–392). London: Sage.

Kroeger, O., & Theusen, J. M. (2002). *Type talk at work.* New York: Dell.

Maccoby, M. (1981). *The leader: A new face for American management.* New York: Ballantine.

Maccoby, M. (2003). *The productive narcissist: The promise and peril of visionary leadership.* New York: Broadway.

Maccoby, M. (2007). *The leaders we need and what makes us follow.* Boston: Harvard Business School Press.

Maslow, A. (1998). *Maslow on management.* New York: Wiley.

Schiffer, I. (1973). *Charisma: A psychoanalytic look at mass society.* Toronto: Toronto University Press.

Stewart, I., & Joines, V. (1987). *TA today: A new introduction to transactional analysis.* Chapel Hill, NC: Lifespace.

Winer, J. A., Jobe, T., & Ferrono, C. (1984–1985). Toward a psychoanalytic theory of the charismatic relationship. *Annual of Psychoanalysis, 12–13,* 155–175.

Zaleznik, A. (1977, May–June). Managers and leaders: Are they different? *Harvard Business Review, 55,* 67–68.

14

Women and Leadership

Crystal L. Hoyt

DESCRIPTION

When you meet a human being, the first distinction you make is "male or female?" and you are accustomed to make the distinction with unhesitating certainty.

— Sigmund Freud

Writers in the popular press have shown an enduring interest in the topic of gender and leadership, reporting stark and meaningful differences between women and men (Book, 2000; Bowman, Worthy, & Greyser, 1965). These differences turned from a view of women as inferior to men (e.g., some posited that women lacked skills and traits necessary for managerial success; Hennig & Jardin, 1977) to the more modern popular view that extols the superiority of women in leadership positions (Book, 2000; Helgesen, 1990). However, for a variety of reasons, including methodological hindrances, a predominance of male researchers largely uninterested in the topic, and an academic assumption of gender equality in leadership, academic researchers ignored issues related to gender and leadership until the 1970s (Chemers, 1997). The increasing numbers of women in leadership positions and women in academia, brought about by dramatic changes in American society, have fueled the now robust scholarly interest in the study of female leaders.

Scholars started out asking, "Can women lead?" but that is now a moot point. In addition to the increasing presence of women in corporate and political leadership roles, we can point to highly effective female leaders including former prime ministers such as Benazir Bhutto (Pakistan), Margaret Thatcher (UK), Gro Marlem Brundtland (Norway), and Indira Gandhi (India), and current world leaders such as Chancellor Angela Merkel of Germany and President Dilma Rousseff of Brazil. Beyond politics we can point to a number of highly effective female leaders including PepsiCo's CEO Indra Nooyi, Avon's CEO Andrea Jung, Four-Star General Ann E. Dunwoody, and the founder of Teach for America, Wendy Kopp. The primary research question now is "Are there leadership style and effectiveness differences between women and men?" which is often subsumed under a larger question: "Why are women underrepresented in elite leadership roles?" This chapter explores empirical evidence related to these issues of gender and leadership by first examining style and effectiveness differences between men and women, then discussing the gender gap in leadership and prominent explanations for it, and, finally, addressing approaches to promoting women in leadership.

Gender, Leadership Styles, and Leadership Effectiveness

As more women are occupying positions of leadership, questions as to whether they lead in a different manner from men and whether women or men are more effective as leaders have garnered greater attention. Increasingly, writers in the mainstream press are asserting that there are indeed gender differences in leadership styles, and that women's leadership is more effective in contemporary society (Book, 2000; Helgesen, 1990; Rosener, 1995). However, academic researchers have a greater diversity in their views; indeed, many argue that gender has little or no relationship to leadership style and effectiveness (Dobbins & Platz, 1986; van Engen, Leeden, & Willemsen, 2001; Powell, 1990).

Early research examining style differences between women and men compared either interpersonally oriented and task-oriented styles or democratic and autocratic styles. In a meta-analysis, Eagly and Johnson (1990) found that, contrary to stereotypic expectations, women were not found to lead in a more interpersonally oriented and less task-oriented manner than men in organizational studies. These differences were found only in settings where behavior was more regulated by social roles, such as experimental settings. The only robust gender difference found across settings

14.1 Perceived Differences

was that women led in a more democratic, or participative, manner than men. Another meta-analysis examining research between 1987 and 2000 found similar results (van Engen & Willemsen, 2004).

It is important to consider these results in conjunction with findings from a large-scale meta-analysis of the literature on evaluations of female and male leaders who were equated on all characteristics and leadership behaviors (Eagly, Makhijani, & Klonsky, 1992). These studies revealed that women were devalued compared with men when they led in a masculine manner (autocratic or directive; e.g., Bartol & Butterfield, 1976), when they occupied a typically masculine leadership role (e.g., athletic coaches or managers in manufacturing plants; see Knight & Saal, 1984), and when the evaluators were men. These findings indicate that women's greater use of democratic style appears to be adaptive in that they are using the style that produces the most favorable evaluations.

More recent research has examined gender differences in transformational leadership (Bass, 1985; Burns, 1978; see Chapter 9, this volume). A meta-analysis by Eagly, Johannesen-Schmidt, and van Engen (2003) found small but robust differences between female and male leaders on these styles such that women's styles tend to be more transformational than men's, and women tend to engage in more contingent reward behaviors than men. Although these styles predict effectiveness, recent findings suggest that the devaluation of female leaders by male subordinates has been shown to extend to female transformational leaders (Ayman, Korabik, & Morris, 2009).

In addition to leadership style, the relative effectiveness of male and female leaders has been assessed in a number of studies (Jacobson & Effertz, 1974; Tsui & Gutek, 1984). In a meta-analysis comparing the effectiveness of female and male leaders, men and women were equally effective leaders, overall, but there were gender differences such that women and men were more effective in leadership roles that were congruent with their gender (Eagly, Karau, & Makhijani, 1995). Thus, women were less effective to the extent that the leader role was masculinized. For example, women were less effective than men were in military positions, but they were somewhat more effective than men were in education, government, and social service organizations, and substantially more effective than men were in middle management positions, where communal interpersonal skills are highly valued. In addition, women were less effective than men were when they supervised a higher proportion of male subordinates or when a greater proportion of male raters assessed the leaders' performance.

In sum, empirical research supports small differences in leadership style and effectiveness between men and women. Women experience slight effectiveness disadvantages in masculine leader roles, whereas roles that are more feminine offer them some advantages. Additionally, women exceed men in the use of democratic or participatory styles, and they are more likely to use transformational leadership behaviors and contingent reward, styles that are associated with contemporary notions of effective leadership.

The Glass Ceiling Turned Labyrinth

We still think of a powerful man as a born leader and a powerful woman as an anomaly.

—Margaret Atwood

Evidence of the Leadership Labyrinth

Although the predicament of female leaders has improved significantly in recent decades, there is still a long way to go. Women earn 57% of the bachelor's degrees, 60% of the master's degrees, more than half of the doctorate degrees, and nearly half of the first professional degrees awarded in the United States (Catalyst, 2011b), and they make up nearly half of the U.S. labor force (47.2%; U.S. Bureau of Labor Statistics, 2010a). However, women are still underrepresented in the upper echelons of America's corporations and political system. Women are among the leadership ranks in American organizations occupying more than half of all management and professional positions (51.5%; Catalyst, 2011c) and a quarter of all chief executive officer (CEO) positions (25.5%; U.S. Bureau of Labor Statistics, 2010b). However, more elite leadership positions show a different story. For example, women represent less than 3% of Fortune 500 CEOs, and hold only 15.7% of the Fortune 500 board seats and a mere 14.4% of the Fortune 500 executive officer positions (Catalyst, 2011a, 2011c).

On the political front, women currently hold only 90 of the 535 seats in the U.S. Congress (16.8%; 17% in the Senate and 16.8% in the House of Representatives); women of color occupy just 24 seats (Center for American Women and Politics, 2011). Indeed, as of August 2011, the world average of women's representation in national legislatures or parliaments

 14.1 Glass Ceiling   **14.1** Women in Politics

is 19.3%, with the United States ranked 70th out of 187 countries (Inter-Parliamentary Union, 2011). Moreover, women represent just 6.1% of military officers at the level of brigadier general and rear admiral or higher (U.S. Department of Defense, 2008).

The invisible barrier preventing women from ascending into elite leadership positions was initially dubbed the *glass ceiling*, a term introduced into the American vernacular by two *Wall Street Journal* reporters in 1986 (Hymowitz & Schellhardt, 1986). Even in female-dominated occupations, women face the glass ceiling, whereas White men appear to ride a *glass escalator* to the top leadership positions (Maume, 1999; Williams, 1992, 1995). Eagly and Carli (2007) recently identified limitations with the glass ceiling metaphor, including that it implies that everyone has equal access to lower positions until all women hit this single, invisible, and impassable barrier. They put forward an alternative image of a leadership labyrinth conveying the impression of a journey riddled with challenges all along the way, not just near the top, that can and has been successfully navigated by women (Figure 14.1).

Figure 14.1 The Leadership Gap

Educational and Work Attainment	
Women	Men
In Managerial/Professional Positions	
50.8%	49.2%
In U.S. Labor Force	
46.7%	53.3%
Earning Bachelor's Degrees	
57.5%	42.5%
The Leadership Gap	
Women	Men
CEOs in Fortune 500 Companies	
3%	97%
Holding Board Seats in Fortune 500 Companies	
15.2%	84.8%
Members of U.S. Congress	
16.8%	83.2%

14.1 Glass Ceiling

Understanding the Labyrinth

The leadership gap is a global phenomenon whereby women are disproportionately concentrated in lower-level and lower-authority leadership positions than men (Powell & Graves, 2003). Discussions of women's underrepresentation in high-level leadership positions generally revolve around three types of explanations (Figure 14.2). The first set of explanations highlights differences in women's and men's investments in human capital. The next category of explanations considers gender differences between women and men. The final type of explanation focuses on prejudice and discrimination against female leaders.

Human Capital Differences. One prominent set of explanations for the labyrinth is that women have less human capital investment in education, training, and work experience than men (Eagly & Carli, 2004, 2007). This supposed lack of human capital is said to result in a dearth of qualified women, sometimes called a "pipeline problem." However, a closer look at the numbers reveals that women are indeed in the pipeline but that the pipeline is leaking. As already discussed, women are obtaining undergraduate degrees at a far higher rate than men, and women are earning professional and doctorate degrees at a rate greater or nearly equal to that of men, but they are still vastly underrepresented in top leadership positions. In the domain of law, although women earn 45.9% of all law degrees and make up 45.4% of associates, they make up only 19.4% of partners (American Bar Association, 2011). And even though women represent only about one third of those graduating with MBAs from the top 10 business schools (Catalyst, 2011d), their representation in the upper echelons of American business pales in comparison. Finally, there is clear evidence that the lack of women reaching the top is not due to the fact that not enough time has passed for natural career progression to occur (Heilman, 1997).

Women do have somewhat less work experience and employment continuity than men, driven largely by the disproportionate responsibility women assume for child rearing and domestic duties (Bowles & McGinn, 2005; Eagly & Carli, 2007). Although a common explanation for the gender disparity in experience is that women are more likely than men to quit their jobs, there is no consistent research evidence to that effect (Eagly & Carli, 2004). However, there is evidence that women experience greater losses than men do after quitting because women are more likely to quit for family-related reasons (Keith & McWilliams, 1999). Domestic and child-rearing expectations impose an added burden on women climbing the leadership ladder, especially on those women who cannot afford to pay for domestic

Figure 14.2   Understanding the Leadership Labyrinth

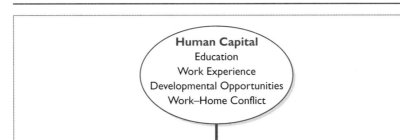

help. Although men's participation in domestic labor has increased significantly in recent years (Galinsky, Aumann, & Bond, 2008), women continue to do the majority of the child care responsibilities and household chores (Belkin, 2008; Craig, 2006; Pailhe & Solaz, 2006). Women respond to these work–home conflicts in a variety of ways (Bowles & McGinn, 2005). Some women choose not to marry or have children, others choose to become "superwomen" and attempt to excel in every role, and others take leaves of absence, take sick days, or choose part-time employment to juggle these work–home conflicts (Hewlett, 2002; Nieva & Gutek, 1981). Antiquated workplace norms make it difficult for women to rise in the leadership ranks: Those who take advantage of workplace leave and flexibility programs are often marginalized, and those who take time off from their careers often find reentry difficult and often enter at a lower level than the level they left (Williams, 2010). A related explanation for the leadership gap is that this culturally prescribed division of labor leads women to self-select themselves out of leadership tracks by choosing "mommy track" positions that do not funnel into leadership positions (Belkin, 2003); however, research does not support this argument (Eagly & Carli, 2004; Williams, 2010).

Although women occupy more than half of all management and professional positions (Catalyst, 2011c), they have fewer developmental opportunities at work than do men. Many of these gender differences in developmental opportunities may be driven in part by the prejudice women experience in the domain of leadership. In addition to having fewer responsibilities in the same jobs as men, women are less likely to receive encouragement, be included in key networks, and receive formal job training than their male counterparts (Knoke & Ishio, 1998; Morrison & Von Glinow, 1990; Ohlott, Ruderman, & McCauley, 1994; Powell & Graves, 2003). One important developmental experience that affects career success is effective mentor relationships (Ensher & Murphy, 2005), and women confront greater barriers to establishing informal mentor relationships than men do (Powell & Graves, 2003). Additionally, women are disproportionately represented in business positions that are less visible, have less responsibility, and do not lead to top leadership positions. For example, women are clustered in the fields of accounting, education, and the velvet ghetto of human resource management (Bowles & McGinn, 2005). Relatedly, when women are promoted to leadership positions they are more likely than men are to be placed on a "glass cliff": They are more likely to be appointed to precarious leadership situations associated with greater risk and criticism (Ryan, Haslam, Hersby, & Bongiorno, 2011).

In sum, there is scant support for the notions that women receive less education than men, that they quit their jobs more often than men do, or that they opt out of the leadership track for the mommy track. There is support for the notion that women have less work experience and more career interruptions than men, largely because women assume significantly more domestic responsibility. Finally, women receive less formal training and have fewer developmental opportunities at work than men, both of which likely are related to prejudice against female leaders.

Gender Differences. Other arguments attempting to explain the leadership gap revolve around the notion that women are just different from men. One argument in this vein is that women's underrepresentation in elite leadership positions is a result of differences in leadership style and effectiveness. As discussed earlier in this chapter, any substantial leadership style differences between women and men should not disadvantage women and can even offer a female advantage (Eagly & Carli, 2007; Vecchio, 2002). Another oft-cited barrier to women's advancement is the presumed gender difference in commitment to employment and motivation to lead. However, research indicates that women show the same level of identification with and commitment to

⑤ 14.2 Gender Differences

paid employment roles as men do, and both women and men view their roles as workers to be secondary to their roles as parents and partners (Bielby & Bielby, 1988; Thoits, 1992). Empirical research does indicate that women are less likely than men are to promote themselves for leadership positions (Bowles & McGinn, 2005). For example, women are more likely to take on informal, as opposed to official, leadership roles, and use terms such as *facilitator* or *organizer* instead of *leader* (Andrews, 1992; Fletcher, 2001). A meta-analytic review of the research literature on leader emergence revealed that although women were less likely than men were to emerge as group leaders, they were more likely to serve as social facilitators than men were (Eagly & Karau, 1991). This research must be interpreted in light of the social costs, or backlash, women experience when they promote themselves or are competent in positions of authority (Rudman & Glick, 2001). Women face significant gender biases and social disincentives when they self-promote. Unlike men, for example, self-promoting women are seen as less socially attractive and less hirable (Rudman, 1998). Thus, women who want to pursue leadership positions may choose not to do so because they have internalized these expectations or are simply aware of the social costs of ambition (Bowles & McGinn, 2005; Powell & Graves, 2003).

Another claim is that men are more likely than women to have the traits necessary for effective leadership. Effective leadership, however, is marked by an androgynous mixture of traits including intelligence, social skills, initiative, and the ability to persuade (Eagly & Carli, 2007). Social science research has shown some small sex differences in traits related to effective leadership, such as integrity, assertiveness, gregariousness, and risk taking; however, these differences favor women as much as they do men (Eagly & Carli, 2007; Feingold, 1994; Franke, Crown, & Spake, 1997). One gender difference that advantages men in leadership is that men are more likely than women to ask for what they want (Babcock & Laschever, 2003). Reaching elite leadership positions is not done in a vacuum: People must negotiate with others to access the right positions, experiences, opportunities, resources, and assistance in both the professional and domestic spheres. Not only are women less likely to negotiate than men are (Small, Gelfand, Babcock, & Gettman, 2007), the negotiations needed to ascend the leadership hierarchy often are unstructured, ambiguous, and rife with gender triggers—exactly the type of situation that particularly disadvantages women (Bowles & McGinn, 2005). Moreover, women face greater social costs for initiating negotiation than men do, so their lower levels of negotiation may represent an adaptive response to social disincentives (Bowles, Babcock, & Lai, 2007).

14.2 Nontraditional Roles

In sum, women are no less effective at leadership, committed to their jobs, or motivated for leadership roles than men. However, women are less likely to self-promote and negotiate than men. Furthermore, research shows a few small sex differences in traits associated with effective leadership, although these differences equally advantage women and men.

Prejudice. One prominent explanation for the leadership gap revolves around gender biases stemming from stereotyped expectations that women take care and men take charge (Hoyt & Chemers, 2008). Stereotypes are cognitive shortcuts that influence the way people process information regarding groups and group members. People assign characteristics to groups, or individual members of groups, regardless of the actual variation in characteristics between the members (Hamilton, Stroessner, & Driscoll, 1994). Gender stereotypes are pervasive, well documented, and highly resistant to change (Dodge, Gilroy, & Fenzel, 1995; Heilman, 2001). Gender stereotypes both describe stereotypic beliefs about the attributes of women and men, and prescribe how men and women ought to be (Burgess & Borgida, 1999; Glick & Fiske, 1999). Men are stereotyped with agentic characteristics such as confidence, assertiveness, independence, rationality, and decisiveness, whereas women are stereotyped with communal characteristics such as concern for others, sensitivity, warmth, helpfulness, and nurturance (Deaux & Kite, 1993; Heilman, 2001).

Gender stereotypes are easily and automatically activated, and they often lead to biased judgments (Fiske, 1998; Kunda & Spencer, 2003). In addition to facing gender-based prejudice, women of color often also confront racial or ethnic prejudice (Bell & Nkomo, 2001). A vivid illustration of gender-based prejudice can be seen in the evaluation of men and women auditioning for symphony orchestras. In the 1970s and 1980s, male-dominated symphony orchestras made one simple change: All applicants were asked to audition while hidden behind a screen. This small change greatly increased the proportion of women in symphony orchestras (Goldin & Rouse, 2000). Merely seeing the applicant's sex evoked stereotype-based expectations in the judges' minds that resulted in a significant bias toward selecting men.

In leadership roles, gender stereotypes are particularly damaging for women because agentic, as opposed to communal, tendencies often are indispensable (Chemers & Murphy, 1995). According to role congruity theory, the agentic qualities thought necessary in the leadership role are incompatible with the predominantly communal qualities stereotypically associated with women, thus resulting in prejudice against female leaders

14.3 Barriers   **14.3 Stereotype**

(Eagly & Karau, 2002). Although the masculine construal of leadership has decreased somewhat over time, it remains pervasive and robust (Koenig, Eagly, Mitchell, & Ristikari, 2011). Thus, in the leadership role, women are confronted with cross-pressures: As leaders, they should be masculine and tough, but as women, they should not be "too manly." These opposing expectations for women often result in the perception that women are less qualified for elite leadership positions than men, and in harsh evaluations of effective female leaders for not being "female enough."

This prejudice against female leaders helps explain the numerous findings indicating less favorable attitudes toward female than male leaders, greater difficulty for women to attain top leadership roles, and greater difficulty for women to be viewed as effective in these roles (Eagly & Karau, 2002). The penalties for violating one's gender stereotypes are clearly illustrated in the classic 1989 Supreme Court case *Price Waterhouse v. Ann Hopkins*. Price Waterhouse told Hopkins that she would not make partner because she was too masculine, going as far as advising her to go to charm school, wear jewelry and makeup, and be less aggressive. In the end, the Court ruled that Price Waterhouse was discriminating based on gender stereotypes (Fiske, Bersoff, Borgida, Deaux, & Heilman, 1991). Gender bias was also evident in the media coverage of the 2008 U.S. presidential primaries involving Hillary Clinton. As Katie Couric noted after Clinton bowed out of contention, "One of the great lessons of that campaign is the continued and accepted role of sexism in American life, particularly the media . . . if Senator Obama had to confront the racist equivalent of an 'Iron My Shirt' poster at campaign rallies or a Hillary nutcracker sold at airports . . . the outrage would not be a footnote, it would be front page news" (Couric & Co., 2008).

Gender biases can be particularly detrimental in the decision-making processes for selecting elite leaders, given that the generally unstructured nature of those decisions allows biased decisions without accountability (Powell & Graves, 2003). Not only are the decision makers influenced by the stereotypes that disadvantage women in the leadership role, but also they may succumb to homosocial reproduction, a tendency for a group to reproduce itself in its own image (Kanter, 1977). People prefer similar others and report the most positive decisions about and evaluations of people who are most similar to them, biases that can clearly disadvantage women when male leaders are looking for replacements.

These stereotypic expectations not only affect others' perceptions and evaluations of female leaders, but also can directly affect the women themselves. Women who make up a very small minority of a male-dominated group are seen as tokens representing all women; they experience significant pressure as their highly visible performance is scrutinized and they are perceived through gender-stereotyped lenses (Kanter, 1977). Women often are very aware of their gender and the accompanying stereotypes (Sekaquaptewa & Thompson, 2003). Research shows that women respond in one of two ways to the gender-based leadership stereotype: Either they demonstrate vulnerability by assimilating to the stereotype, or they react against it by engaging in stereotype-countering behaviors (Hoyt, 2010). Whether the threat of the gender-leader stereotype is met with vulnerability or reactance responses depends on factors such as the leader's self-efficacy, the explicitness of the stereotype, the type of task, the group sex-composition, and the power that the leader holds (Bergeron, Block, & Echtenkamp, 2006; Davies, Spencer, & Steele, 2005; Hoyt & Blascovich, 2007, 2010; Kray, Reb, Galinsky, & Thompson, 2004; Kray, Thompson, & Galinsky, 2001). Furthermore, although female leaders may demonstrate reactance to certain solitary gender stereotype threats, when such threats are combined women are likely to demonstrate deleterious vulnerability responses (Hoyt, Johnson, Murphy, & Skinnell, 2010). In sum, substantial empirical evidence reveals that gender stereotypes can significantly alter the perception and evaluation of female leaders and directly affect women in or aspiring to leadership roles.

Navigating the Labyrinth

The number of women who successfully navigate the labyrinth is on the rise (Eagly & Carli, 2007). A confluence of factors contributes to this increase in effective female leaders (Figure 14.3). Changes in organizations are beginning to make it easier for women to reach top positions. The culture of many organizations is changing; gendered work assumptions such as the male model of work, the notion of uninterrupted full-time careers, and the separation of work and family are being challenged (Cooper & Lewis, 1999; Williams, 2010). Moreover, many organizations are valuing flexible workers and diversity in their top echelons. These organizations can augment women's career development by involving them in career development programs and formal networks, and offering work–life support. In addition, assigning more women to high-visibility positions and developing effective and supportive mentoring relationships for women are key strategies for reducing the leadership gap (Bell & Nkomo, 2001; Ensher & Murphy, 2005; Ragins, Townsend, & Mattis, 1998).

🌐 **14.2** Effectiveness

Figure 14.3   Leadership Effectiveness

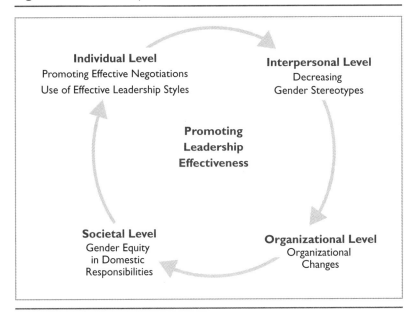

Although the gendered division of labor contributes to the leadership gap, there is recent evidence of increasing parity in the involvement of women and men in child care and housework (Eagly & Carli, 2007). In balancing work and home life, an appealing approach for women is structural role redefinition (Hall, 1972). This approach involves negotiating with both family and colleagues to renegotiate role expectations both at work and at home. For example, at home women can negotiate workload between spouses, team up with friends and family members, and, if able, hire help when necessary (Bowles & McGinn, 2005). At work, women can work for family-friendly reforms such as job-protected maternity leaves. Beyond work–home issues, negotiations for valued positions, experiences, and resources are important social interactions on the road to top leadership positions. Thus, another approach to reducing the leadership gap is to enhance women's negotiation power and restructure negotiations to their advantage (Bowles & McGinn, 2005). For example, research has shown that the term *negotiation* is laden with gendered connotations, so one approach would be to reframe negotiation situations in nongendered terms such as "asking" situations.

Women who are aware of the labyrinth may circumvent barriers by starting their own ventures (Wirth, 2001). Women-owned businesses

14.3 Military Leaders

account for 40% of all privately owned businesses, employ more than 13 million people, and generate $1.9 trillion in sales; businesses owned by women of color grew faster than all privately held businesses between 2002 and 2008 (Center for Women's Business Research, 2008). Women's successful foray into entrepreneurship is working to change the face of business, and by extension leadership, as we know it.

Many of the impediments women face in the leadership domain stem from the incongruity between the female gender role and the leadership role. Women face a double standard in the leadership role: They must come across as extremely competent but also as appropriately "feminine," a set of standards men are not held to (Eagly & Carli, 2003). One way women can increase their perceived warmth and their influence is by combining communal qualities such as warmth and friendliness with agentic qualities such as exceptional competence and assertiveness (Carli, 2001; Rudman & Glick, 2001). Additionally, the transformational leadership style is particularly beneficial for women because it is not a markedly masculine style. This style encompasses traditionally feminine behaviors such as being considerate and supportive, and is strongly associated with leadership effectiveness (see Chapter 9, this volume). Recent research suggests that blending individualized consideration with inspirational motivation is prudent for women seeking leadership advancement (Vinkenburg, van Engen, Eagly, & Johannesen-Schmidt, 2011). The incongruity between the leadership role and the female gender role does appear to be decreasing (Eagly & Carli, 2007). Recent research indicates that women have become significantly more masculine—for example, becoming more assertive and valuing leadership and power more as job attributes, without losing their femininity (Konrad, Ritchie, Lieb, & Corrigall, 2000; Twenge, 2001). In addition, evidence suggests that the leadership role is starting to be seen as less masculine and more androgynous (Koenig et al., 2011; Schein, 2001).

Motives for Removing the Barriers

While the barriers discussed in the previous sections are generally conceived to be against women, the labyrinth can be generalized to encompass other nondominant groups such as ethnic, racial, and sexual minorities as well. There are a number of important motivations for removing these barriers into the upper echelons of leadership.

First, doing so will fulfill the promise of equal opportunity by allowing everyone the possibility of taking on leadership roles, from the boardroom

▶ **14.2** Removing Barriers

to the Senate floor. This larger and more demographically diverse pool of candidates not only makes it easier to find talented people, but it also facilitates greater levels of organizational success.

Second, promoting a richly diverse group of women into leadership roles will not only help make societal institutions, businesses, and governments more representative, but it can also contribute to more ethical, productive, innovative, and financially successful organizations that demonstrate higher levels of collective intelligence and are less rife with conflict (Bernardi, Bosco, & Columb, 2009; Catalyst, 2004; Forsyth, 2010; Miller & Del Carmen Triana, 2009; Nielsen & Huse, 2010; Woolley, Chabris, Pentland, Hashmi, & Malone, 2010).

Despite these barriers, women are showing a greater presence in top leadership positions. With changes in workplace norms and developmental opportunities for women; greater gender equity in domestic responsibilities; greater negotiation power of women, especially regarding the work–home balance; the effectiveness and predominance of women-owned businesses; and changes in the incongruity between women and leadership, we likely will see more women in elite leadership roles.

STRENGTHS

A consideration of the effects of gender on leadership has important implications for a comprehensive understanding of leadership. Contemporary approaches to gender and leadership involve questions that directly affect leadership success, such as style and effectiveness differences between men and women, and the varied barriers confronting women. Gender is integral to contemporary notions of effective leadership styles that have morphed from a traditional masculine, autocratic style to the more feminine or androgynous styles of democratic and transformational leadership. Developing a more androgynous conception of leadership will enhance leadership effectiveness by giving people the opportunity to engage in the best leadership practices, and not by restricting people to those behaviors that are most appropriate for their gender.

Research on gender and leadership is productive in both dispelling myths about the gender gap and shining a light on aspects of the gender barriers that are difficult to see and therefore are often overlooked. For example, gender biases generally are no longer overt but more often take

14.4 Gender Research

the form of subtle and implicit preconceptions and discrimination, making them particularly potent and pernicious. These biases have a detrimental impact on the perception and evaluation of women, and they limit the range of leadership behavior deemed appropriate for women. In addition, awareness of these biases can threaten women in the leadership role. The changes needed to overcome these problems within organizations and society can occur only when we are aware of these often subtle and disguised prejudices.

Understanding the many components of the labyrinth will give us the tools necessary to combat this inequality from many perspectives, including individual, interpersonal, organizational, and societal approaches. In addition, this research addresses larger, more significant considerations about gender and social systems. For example, it acknowledges the profound power division between men and women, and it opens up dialogue on structural questions such as the gendered division of work in society. By not ignoring issues of gender and leadership but rather avidly attempting to understand them, we can help ensure that women have equal opportunity in attaining influential leadership positions, that organizations and constituents have access to the greatest talent pool when selecting leaders, and that there is greater gender diversity in the ranks of leadership, which has been linked to organizational success.

CRITICISMS

Issues of gender and leadership can be subsumed under a more general topic of leadership and diversity. This perspective involves an understanding of the impact of various demographic characteristics on leadership, including—but not limited to—gender, race, ethnicity, and sexual orientation (Chemers & Murphy, 1995; Hoyt & Chemers, 2008). However, unlike the research examining gender and leadership, research into minority leaders is scant (Hoyt & Chemers, 2008). Although some of the issues surrounding minorities in leadership may bear similarities to those surrounding women (e.g., minorities also face negative stereotypes and resulting difficulties ascending the leadership hierarchy), the underlying dynamics and mechanisms are no doubt distinct (Gurin, 1985; Stangor, Lynch, Duan, & Glass, 1992). Leadership researchers should put a greater emphasis on understanding the role of race, ethnicity, sexual orientation and other types of diversity, as well as important interactive effects between, for example, race and gender (Smith & Stewart, 1983), in leadership processes.

▶ 14.3 Diversity

Much of the research examining gender in leadership has taken place in Western contexts; research on gender and leadership in other contexts is sparse. Because most of the findings regarding female leaders stem from the culturally defined role of women in society, many of the findings discussed in this chapter will not generalize well across cultures in which the roles of women and men differ. Therefore, we must realize the limited generalizability of the extant literature on gender and leadership, and researchers should expand their purview to address gender and leadership from a cross-cultural perspective. A final criticism concerns the dearth of essential, complementary research agendas on the domestic sphere. Research on gender and leadership focuses on decreasing the gender gap in leadership positions, thereby lessening gender segregation at work; however, the leadership gap will not be closed without a concurrent focus on closing the gender gap at home.

APPLICATION

Although the gender gap in influential leadership positions remains clearly visible, there is evidence that it is starting to close. Understanding the obstacles that make up the labyrinth and tactics to eradicate the inequality will make it easier for women to reach top positions. The labyrinth has many barriers, and the necessary changes occur at many levels, ranging from individual and interpersonal levels to organizational and societal levels. Prejudice plays an important role in the interpersonal and individual levels; the first step in dealing with these biases is to become aware of them in others and in ourselves. Women are faced with the problem of needing to bolster their leadership competence with appropriate "femaleness": Adopting behaviors such as individualized consideration and inspirational motivation is a promising approach to overcome these biased expectations. In addition, women's use of effective negotiation techniques can aid them in procuring the resources they need at work and at home to augment their leadership advancement.

Changes are also taking place at more macro-organizational and societal levels that will contribute to greater gender equality in leadership. For example, changes in organizational culture, women's career development, mentoring opportunities for women, and increased numbers of women in strategic positions will increase the presence of women in prominent leadership roles. At the societal level, structural changes regarding a more equitable distribution of child rearing and domestic duties are also contributing to the influx of women into elite positions.

—————————— **CASE STUDIES** ——————————

In the following section, three case studies (Cases 14.1, 14.2, and 14.3) are presented to provide practice in diagnosing and making recommendations on situations confronting female leaders in organizations. The first case is about a market analyst in a Wall Street firm, the second case is about a meeting of probation managers, and the third case is about a senior managing director at a manufacturing company. After each case, questions are provided to assist your analysis of the case. All cases were adapted from Blank and Slipp (1994).[1]

CASE 14.1

The "Glass Ceiling"

Lisa Weber never doubted that she would be a partner in her Wall Street firm. A graduate of a prestigious business school with a doctorate in economics, she had taught briefly at a major university. She was the first woman hired as a market analyst in her well-regarded firm. Within 2 years, she has become one of four senior portfolio managers reporting directly to a senior partner. Her clients give her the highest commendations for her outstanding performance; over the past 2 years, she has brought in the largest number of new accounts to the firm.

Despite the admiration of her colleagues and their seeming acceptance of her, there is a disturbing, if flattering, aspect to her job. Most of her peers and some of the partners visit her office during the day to discuss in private her opinions on market performance and financial projections. She enjoys these private sessions but is dismayed that at the weekly staff meetings the CEO, Michael Breyer, usually says something like, "Okay, let's get started and bring Lisa up to date on some of the trouble spots." None of her peers or the partners mention that Lisa knows as much as they do about what's going on in the firm. She never protests this slight to her competence and knowledge of firm business, nor does she mention the almost-daily private meetings where her advice is sought. As the only woman on the executive level, she prefers to be considered a team player and one of the boys.

In the past year, one of her peers has been promoted to partner, although Lisa's performance clearly surpassed his, as measured by the success of her accounts and the amount of new business she brought to the firm. Having heard no mention of partnership for herself, she approached her boss, one of the partners, and asked about the path to a partnership. He replied, "You're doing great, Lisa, but professors do not partners make. What happens if you are a partner and you make a huge mistake? How would you take it? And what about our clients? There's never been a female partner in the 103 years of our firm."

Shortly thereafter, another woman, Pamela Tobias, was hired as a marketing analyst. Once, when the CEO saw Lisa and Pamela together, he called out to the men, "Hey, guys, two women in one room. That's scary."

In the next 6 months, Lisa meets several times with the CEO to make her case for a partnership on the basis of her performance. She finally realizes that there is no possibility of change in the foreseeable future and decides to leave and form her own investment firm.

SOURCE: Adapted from Blank and Slipp (1994).

Questions

1. What advancement barriers did Lisa encounter?

2. What should the firm's top executives, including Michael, have done differently to retain Lisa?

3. What type of organizational policies and opportunities might have benefited Lisa and Pamela?

4. What could the organization do to raise the gender consciousness of Michael and Lisa's male colleagues?

CASE 14.2

Lack of Inclusion and Credibility

Lori Bradley, an experienced probation officer, is meeting with Ted Stolze and Ian Bateson, two other probation officers, and their supervisor, Len Duggan, the assistant chief of probation. They are planning an orientation session for new probation officers on how to prepare investigative reports for the court.

As Lori enters the room, Ted and Ian are throwing paper clips at each other and laughing about a major play in the previous night's NFL

(Continued)

(Continued)

championship game. They continue talking as she enters the room, ignoring her. When Len enters, the two men include him in their talk about the game.

After a few minutes, Len says, "Okay, let's get down to business and start planning the orientation session. Any ideas?"

Lori says, "I looked again at the session prepared by Columbia County, which was described at our last meeting, and I think we should use that. It worked well for them and seems to fit our county." No one looks at Lori or responds to her, but Ted begins making some suggestions for a different idea and the others follow up with questions to him. After problems arise with Ted's suggestion, Ian says, "My idea would be to go for the Columbia County plan. That would work best here." Len, the assistant chief, says, "Ian, I'll go with your judgment." Ted says, "Me, too. Great idea, Ian."

Lori breaks in, "But that's what I proposed initially, and you just ignored me." Ian says, "Stop being so sensitive, Lori. We're supposed to be a team here."

SOURCE: Adapted from Blank and Slipp (1994).

Questions

1. What advancement barriers is Lori encountering?

2. What should Lori's male coworkers have done when Lori entered the room?

3. How should Len have behaved to provide a role model for Lori's male colleagues? What should Len have said after Ian made the same recommendation that Lori did?

4. What could the organization do to foster the effectiveness of all four managers?

CASE 14.3

Pregnancy as a Barrier to Job Status

Marina Soslow is a senior managing director at a manufacturing company. She has worked at the company for 10 years, gradually working her way up to a responsible position. She would like to win promotion to a top executive position and has recently finished an MBA, which supplements her master's degree in chemical engineering.

Several months ago, she found out she was pregnant. She is reluctant to tell her boss, Roy Bond, the division head, because she knows several other women who were eased out of their positions before they gave birth or shortly thereafter.

After a meeting with Roy about a new product, Marina mentions her pregnancy and says that she plans to take a 3-month leave of absence after her delivery. She begins describing the plans she has carefully worked out for distributing her work. Roy cuts her short and says, "I knew this was going to happen sooner or later; it always does." He said this as if a disaster were about to occur. "There's no point in talking about this now. We'll think about it later."

Marina can tell that he's very annoyed about what he thinks is going to happen. She can see his wheels spinning and worries about the implications for her. She thinks, "Doesn't Roy know about the Family and Medical Leave Act of 1993? Legally, this company has to guarantee my job, but I know he can make it very rough for me."

SOURCE: Adapted from Blank and Slipp (1994).

Questions

1. What advancement barriers is Marina encountering?

2. What should Roy have said when Marina told him she was pregnant?

3. What could Roy do to ensure that Marina's work will be covered during her absence and that taking this time off will not hurt her advancement?

4. What type of organizational changes can be made to benefit Marina and other pregnant women in this organization?

LEADERSHIP INSTRUMENT

The Implicit Association Test (IAT) was developed by Anthony Greenwald, Mahzarin Banaji, and Brian Nosek to measure automatic associations by examining reaction times when people classify pictures or words (see Greenwald, McGhee, & Schwartz, 1998). This gender IAT was modified from a version developed by Dasgupta and Asgari (2004) to examine the gender stereotypical associations that contribute to the bias against women as leaders (Eagly & Karau, 2002).

The Gender–Leader Implicit Association Test

Instructions: This exercise begins with a practice trial. Using a pencil, classify each of the words in the middle column into one of the two categories indicated, *Flower* or *Insect,* by putting a check mark in the column to the left or the right. Please do this task as quickly as possible, taking care not to skip over any words.

Practice Trial

Flower		Insect
O	Rose	O
O	Lily	O
O	Dragonfly	O
O	Beetle	O
O	Gnat	O
O	Daffodil	O
O	Mosquito	O
O	Daisy	O
O	Roach	O
O	Tulip	O

   You will now complete the two test trials; you will need a stopwatch for this portion of the test. For these test trials, the categories are Male or Female and Leader or Supporter, and the categories will be combined. If the word you read belongs to the Male or the Leader category, put a check in the left column; if it belongs to the Female or the Supporter category, put a check in the right column. You will record how long it takes you to complete this task by starting your stopwatch when you begin and stopping it after you make your final classification. Remember to work as quickly as possible, without skipping any words.

Test Trial A

Male or Leader		Female or Supporter
O	Emily	O
O	Josh	O
O	Supporter	O
O	Leader	O
O	Brandon	O
O	Ambitious	O
O	Peter	O
O	Determined	O
O	Donna	O
O	Debbie	O
O	Helpful	O
O	Dynamic	O
O	Understanding	O
O	Katherine	O
O	Ian	O
O	Sympathetic	O
O	Compassionate	O
O	Jane	O
O	Andrew	O
O	Assertive	O

Time to complete Test Trial A: _____

You will do this same task a second time, but this time the combination of categories has been switched. If the word you read belongs to the *Male* or the *Supporter* category, put a check in the left column; if it belongs to the *Female* or the *Leader* category, put a check in the right column. Again, use your stopwatch to time how long it takes you to complete the task.

Test Trial B

Male or Supporter		Female or Leader
O	Supporter	O
O	Emily	O
O	Josh	O
O	Leader	O
O	Ambitious	O
O	Brandon	O
O	Peter	O
O	Donna	O
O	Helpful	O
O	Determined	O
O	Dynamic	O
O	Assertive	O
O	Debbie	O
O	Katherine	O
O	Understanding	O
O	Ian	O
O	Sympathetic	O
O	Andrew	O
O	Compassionate	O
O	Jane	O

Time to complete Test Trial B: _____

Scoring

The logic behind the IAT is that the longer it takes to categorize the words when the categories have counterstereotypical pairings (i.e., *Female* and *Leader, Male* and *Supporter*) compared with stereotypical pairings, the more one automatically associates women with supportive qualities as opposed to leadership qualities.

The gender bias effect is computed by subtracting the time it took to complete Trial A (the stereotype congruent task) from the time to complete

Trial B (the stereotype incongruent task). Positive scores reflect automatic associations between *Female* and *Supportive* and between *Male* and *Leadership*. Many people are surprised to find out that they have a biased association favoring males and leadership, especially when it is incompatible with their stated egalitarian values. This test is designed to show people that they might hold associations that they are unaware of and to make people aware of the broad reach of these stereotypes. Please see the IAT website at Harvard University (https://implicit.harvard.edu) for more information on the IAT and a more detailed understanding of the results.

SUMMARY

Beginning in the 1970s, researchers started investigating gender differences in leadership. Investigations into leadership style have revealed that women are somewhat more likely to use democratic and transformational styles than men are. Research looking at leadership effectiveness indicates a slight disadvantage for women in masculine domains, a slight effectiveness advantage for women in feminine domains, and a greater use by women of effective transformational and contingent reward behaviors.

Women are significantly underrepresented in major leadership positions. The barriers women encounter on their leadership journey have been dubbed the *leadership labyrinth*. Removing these barriers will help ensure equal opportunity, access to the greatest talent pool, and diversity, which have been linked to organizational success. There are a number of explanations for the leadership gender gap. One set of explanations focuses on women's lack of human capital investment in education, training, and work experience. There is no empirical support for the argument that women are less educated than men are or that they are more likely to quit their jobs or choose the mommy track. There is evidence that women assume significantly more domestic responsibility, which contributes to less work experience and more career interruptions. Additionally, women receive less formal training and have fewer developmental opportunities at work than men.

Another set of explanations for the gender gap focuses on differences between women and men. Women are no less effective at leadership, committed to their work, or motivated to attain leadership roles than men. However, women are less likely to self-promote than men are, and they are less likely to initiate negotiation, an important tool all leaders need in order to access the right opportunities and resources both in the professional and domestic spheres. Finally, although there are some trait differences between men and women, they equally advantage men and women in leadership.

The prejudice explanation for the leadership gap is strongly supported. Gender stereotypes of women as communal and men as agentic are particularly damaging to women in leadership. The incongruity between the female gender role and the leadership role leads to prejudice against female leaders, who are evaluated and perceived more negatively than their male counterparts. These biases are particularly detrimental during unstructured decision-making processes that often occur when elite leaders are selected. Gender-based leader stereotypes can threaten women eliciting either a vulnerability or a reactance response. There is evidence that this discrepancy is on the decline as the leader role becomes more androgynous and women become more agentic.

Finally, there are a number of approaches to navigating the labyrinth. Significant organizational reform will make it easier for women to reach top positions—including changes in workplace norms, changes in organizational culture, increases in career development for women, increases in effective mentoring opportunities, and women taking more strategic positions leading to higher leadership roles. Effective negotiations will help decrease the gender gap, especially negotiations regarding role expectations at work and at home. Additionally, the combination of warmth with agentic qualities and in particular the melding of individualized consideration with inspirational motivation can be effective for developing female leaders.

Visit the Student Study Site at **www.sagepub.com/northouse6e** for web quizzes, leadership questionnaires, and media links represented by the icons.

NOTE

1. Adapted from *Voices of Diversity*. Copyright 1994 by Renee Blank and Sandra Slipp. Reprinted by permission of AMACOM, a division of American Management Association International, New York, NY. All rights reserved. http://www.amanet.org.

REFERENCES

American Bar Association. (2011). *Commission on women in the profession: A current glance at women in the law 2011.* Retrieved September 23, 2011, from http://www.americanbar.org/content/dam/aba/uncategorized/2011/cwp_current_glance_statistics_2011.authcheckdam.pdf

Andrews, P. H. (1992). Sex and gender differences in group communication: Impact on the facilitation process. *Small Group Research, 23*(1), 74–94.

Ayman, R., Korabik, K., & Morris, S. (2009). Is transformational leadership always perceived as effective? Male subordinates' devaluation of female transformational leaders. *Journal of Applied Social Psychology, 39,* 852–879.

Babcock, L., & Laschever, S. (2003). *Women don't ask: Negotiation and the gender divide*. Princeton, NJ: Princeton University Press.

Bartol, K. M., & Butterfield, D. A. (1976). Sex effects in evaluating leaders. *Journal of Applied Psychology, 61*, 446–454.

Bass, B. M. (1985). Leadership: Good, better, best. *Organizational Dynamics, 13*, 26–40.

Belkin, L. (2003, October 26). The opt-out revolution. *The New York Times*, p. 42.

Belkin, L. (2008, June 15). When mom and dad share it all. *The New York Times*. Retrieved June 15, 2008, from http://www.nytimes.com/2008/06/15/magazine/15parenting-t.html?ref=jobs&pagewanted=all

Bell, E., & Nkomo, S. (2001). *Our separate ways: Black and white women and the struggle for professional identity*. Boston: Harvard Business School Press.

Bergeron, D. M., Block, C. J., & Echtenkamp, B. A. (2006). Disabling the able: Stereotype threat and women's work performance. *Human Performance, 19*(2), 133–158.

Bernardi, R. A., Bosco, S. M., & Columb, V. L. (2009). Does female representation on boards of directors associate with the "Most Ethical Companies" list? *Corporate Reputation Review, 12*, 270–280.

Bielby, D. D., & Bielby, W. T. (1988). She works hard for the money: Household responsibilities and the allocation of work effort. *American Journal of Sociology, 93*, 1031–1059.

Blank, R., & Slipp, S. (1994). *Voices of diversity*. New York: AMACOM.

Book, E. W. (2000). *Why the best man for the job is a woman*. New York: Harper-Collins.

Bowles, H. R., Babcock, L., & Lai, L. (2007). Social incentives for gender differences in the propensity to initiate negotiations: Sometimes it does hurt to ask. *Organizational Behavior and Human Decision Processes, 103*, 84–103.

Bowles, H. R., & McGinn, K. L. (2005). Claiming authority: Negotiating challenges for women leaders. In D. M. Messick & R. M. Kramer (Eds.), *The psychology of leadership: New perspectives and research* (pp. 191–208). Mahwah, NJ: Lawrence Erlbaum.

Bowman, G., Worthy, N., & Greyser, S. (1965). Are women executives people? *Harvard Business Review, 43*(4), 14–28, 164–178.

Burgess, D., & Borgida, E. (1999). Who women are, who women should be: Descriptive and prescriptive gender stereotyping in sex discrimination. *Psychology, Public Policy, & Law, 5*, 665–692.

Burns, J. M. (1978). *Leadership*. New York: Plenum.

Carli, L. L. (2001). Gender and social influence. *Journal of Social Issues, 57*, 725–741.

Catalyst. (2004). *The bottom line: Connecting corporate performance and gender diversity*. New York: Author.

Catalyst. (2011a). *Statistical overview of women in the workplace*. Retrieved September 30, 2011, from http://www.catalyst.org/publication/219/statistical-overview-of-women-in-the-workplace

Catalyst. (2011b). *U.S. labor force, population, and education*. Retrieved October 2, 2011, from http://www.catalyst.org/publication/202/us-labor-force-population-and-education

Catalyst. (2011c). *U.S. women in business.* Retrieved September 21, 2011, from http://www.catalyst.org/publication/132/us-women-in-business

Catalyst. (2011d). *Women MBAs.* Retrieved November 15, 2011, from http://www.catalyst.org/publication/250/women-mbas

Center for American Women and Politics. (2011). *Women in elective office 2011.* Retrieved September 21, 2011, from http://www.cawp.rutgers.edu/fast_facts/levels_of_office/documents/elective.pdf

Center for Women's Business Research. (2008). *Key facts about women owned businesses 2008.* Retrieved May 28, 2009, from http://www.nfwbo.org/facts/index.php

Chemers, M. M. (1997). *An integrative theory of leadership.* Mahwah, NJ: Lawrence Erlbaum.

Chemers, M. M., & Murphy, S. E. (1995). Leadership and diversity in groups and organizations. In M. M. Chemers, S. Oskamp, & M. A. Constanzo (Eds.), *Diversity in organizations: New perspectives for a changing workplace* (pp. 157–190). Thousand Oaks, CA: Sage.

Cooper, C. L., & Lewis, S. (1999). Gender and the changing nature of work. In G. N. Powell (Ed.), *Handbook of gender and work* (pp. 37–46). Thousand Oaks, CA: Sage.

Couric & Co. (2008). *Katie Couric's notebook: Sexism and politics.* Retrieved May 29, 2009, from http://www.cbsnews.com/blogs/2008/06/11/couricandco/entry4174429.shtml

Craig, L. (2006). Does father care mean fathers share? A comparison of how mothers and fathers in intact families spend time with children. *Gender and Society, 20,* 259–281.

Dasgupta, N., & Asgari, S. (2004). Seeing is believing: Exposure to counterstereotypic women leaders and its effect on automatic gender stereotyping. *Journal of Experimental Social Psychology, 40,* 642–658.

Davies, P. G., Spencer, S. J., & Steele, C. M. (2005). Clearing the air: Identity safety moderates the effects of stereotype threat on women's leadership aspirations. *Journal of Personality and Social Psychology, 88,* 276–287.

Deaux, K., & Kite, M. (1993). Gender stereotypes. In F. L. Denmark & M. Paludi (Eds.), *Psychology of women: A handbook of theory and issues* (pp. 107–139). Westport, CT: Greenwood.

Dobbins, G. H., & Platz, S. J. (1986). Sex differences in leadership: How real are they? *Academy of Management Review, 11,* 118–127.

Dodge, K. A., Gilroy, F. D., & Fenzcl, L. M. (1995). Requisite management characteristics revisited: Two decades later. *Journal of Social Behavior and Personality, 10,* 253–264.

Eagly, A. H., & Carli, L. L. (2003). The female leadership advantage: An evaluation of the evidence. *Leadership Quarterly, 14,* 807–834.

Eagly, A. H., & Carli, L. L. (2004). Women and men as leaders. In J. Antonakis, R. J. Sternberg, & A. T. Cianciolo (Eds.), *The nature of leadership* (pp. 279–301). Thousand Oaks, CA: Sage.

Eagly, A. H., & Carli, L. L. (2007). *Through the labyrinth: The truth about how women become leaders.* Boston: Harvard Business School Press.

Eagly, A. H., Johannesen-Schmidt, M. C., & van Engen, M. (2003). Transformational, transactional, and laissez-faire leadership styles: A meta-analysis comparing women and men. *Psychological Bulletin, 129,* 569–591.

Eagly, A. H., & Johnson, B. T. (1990). Gender and leadership style: A meta-analysis. *Psychological Bulletin, 108*(2), 233–256.

Eagly, A. H., & Karau, S. J. (1991). Gender and the emergence of leaders: A meta-analysis. *Journal of Personality and Social Psychology, 60,* 685–710.

Eagly, A. H., & Karau, S. J. (2002). Role congruity theory of prejudice toward female leaders. *Psychological Review, 109,* 573–598.

Eagly, A. H., Karau, S. J., & Makhijani, M. G. (1995). Gender and the effectiveness of leaders: A meta-analysis. *Psychological Bulletin, 117,* 125–145.

Eagly, A. H., Makhijani, M., & Klonsky, B. (1992). Gender and the evaluation of leaders: A meta-analysis. *Psychological Bulletin, 111,* 3–22.

Ensher, E. A., & Murphy, S. E. (2005). *Power mentoring: How successful mentors and protégés get the most out of their relationships.* San Francisco: Jossey-Bass.

Feingold, A. (1994). Gender differences in personality: A meta-analysis. *Psychological Bulletin, 116,* 429–456.

Fiske, S. (1998). Stereotyping, prejudice, and discrimination. In D. T. Gilbert, S. T. Fiske, & G. Lindzey (Eds.), *The handbook of social psychology* (4th ed., Vol. 2, pp. 982–1026). Boston: McGraw-Hill.

Fiske, S., Bersoff, D. N., Borgida, E., Deaux, K., & Heilman, M. E. (1991). Social science research on trial: Use of sex stereotyping research in *Price Waterhouse v. Hopkins. American Psychologist, 46*(10), 1049–1060.

Fletcher, J. K. (2001). *Disappearing acts: Gender, power, and relational practice at work.* Boston: MIT Press.

Forsyth, D. R. (2010). *Group dynamics* (5th ed.). Belmont, CA: Wadsworth.

Franke, G. R., Crown, D. F., & Spake, D. F. (1997). Gender differences in ethical perceptions of business practices: A social role theory perspective. *Journal of Applied Psychology, 82,* 920–934.

Freud, S. (1965). *New introductory lectures on psychoanalysis: Femininity.* New York: W. W. Norton.

Galinsky, E., Aumann, K., & Bond, J. (2008). *Times are changing: Gender and generation at work and at home.* Retrieved November 14, 2011, from http://familiesandwork.org/site/research/reports/Times_Are_Changing.pdf

Glick, P., & Fiske, S. T. (1999). Sexism and other "isms": Independence, status, and the ambivalent content of stereotypes. In W. B. Swann, Jr., & J. H. Langlois (Eds.), *Sexism and stereotypes in modern society: The gender science of Janet Taylor Spence* (pp. 193–221). Washington, DC: American Psychological Association.

Goldin, C., & Rouse, C. (2000). Orchestrating impartiality: The impact of "blind" auditions on female musicians. *American Economic Review, 90*(4), 715–741.

Greenwald, A. G., McGhee, D. E., & Schwartz, J. L. K. (1998). Measuring individual differences in implicit cognition: The implicit association test. *Journal of Personality and Social Psychology, 74,* 1464–1480.

Gurin, P. (1985). Women's gender consciousness. *Public Opinion Quarterly, 49,* 143–163.

Hall, D. T. (1972). A model of coping with role conflict: The role behavior of college-educated women. *Administrative Science Quarterly, 17*(4), 471–486.

Hamilton, D. L., Stroessner, S. J., & Driscoll, D. M. (1994). Social cognition and the study of stereotyping. In P. G. Devine, D. L. Hamilton, & T. M. Ostrom (Eds.), *Social cognition: Impact on social psychology* (pp. 291–321). New York: Academic Press.

Heilman, M. E. (1997). Sex discrimination and the affirmative action remedy: The role of sex stereotypes. *Journal of Business Ethics, 16*, 877–889.

Heilman, M. E. (2001). Description and prescription: How gender stereotypes prevent women's ascent up the organizational ladder. *Journal of Social Issues, 57*, 657–674.

Helgesen, S. (1990). *The female advantage: Women's ways of leadership.* New York: Doubleday.

Hennig, M., & Jardin, A. (1977). *The managerial woman.* Garden City, NY: Anchor.

Hewlett, S. A. (2002). *Creating a life: Professional women and the quest for children.* New York: Talk Miramax.

Hoyt, C. L. (2010). Women, men, and leadership: Exploring the gender gap at the top. *Social and Personality Psychology Compass, 4*, 484–498.

Hoyt, C., & Blascovich, J. (2007). Leadership efficacy and women leaders' responses to stereotype activation. *Group Processes and Intergroup Relations, 10*, 595–616.

Hoyt, C., & Blascovich, J. (2010). The role of self-efficacy and stereotype activation on cardiovascular, behavioral and self-report responses in the leadership domain. *Leadership Quarterly, 21*, 89–103.

Hoyt, C. L., & Chemers, M. M. (2008). Social stigma and leadership: A long climb up a slippery ladder. In C. L. Hoyt, G. R. Goethals, & D. R. Forsyth (Eds.), *Leadership at the crossroads: Leadership and psychology* (Vol. 1, pp. 165–180). Westport, CT: Praeger.

Hoyt, C., Johnson, S., Murphy, S., & Skinnell, K. (2010). The impact of blatant stereotype activation and group sex-composition on female leaders. *Leadership Quarterly, 21*, 716–732.

Hymowitz, C., & Schellhardt, T. D. (1986, March 24). The glass ceiling: Why women can't seem to break the invisible barrier that blocks them from the top jobs. *The Wall Street Journal*, pp. D1, D4–D5.

Inter-Parliamentary Union. (2011). *Women in national parliaments.* Retrieved September 21, 2011, from http://www.ipu.org/wmn-e/classif.htm

Jacobson, M. B., & Effertz, J. (1974). Sex roles and leadership perceptions of the leaders and the led. *Organizational Behavior and Human Performance, 12*, 383–396.

Kanter, R. (1977). *Men and women of the corporation.* New York: Basic Books.

Keith, K., & McWilliams, A. (1999). The returns to mobility and job search by gender: Additional evidence from the NLSY. *Industrial & Labor Relations Review, 52*(3), 460–477.

Knight, P. A., & Saal, F. E. (1984). Effects of gender differences and selection agent expertise on leader influence and performance evaluations. *Organizational Behavior and Human Performance, 34*, 225–243.

Knoke, D., & Ishio, Y. (1998). The gender gap in company job training. *Work and Occupations*, 25(2), 141–167.

Koenig, A. M., Eagly, A. H., Mitchell, A. A., & Ristikari, T. (2011). Are leader stereotypes masculine? A meta-analysis of three research paradigms. *Psychological Bulletin*, 137, 616–642.

Konrad, A. M., Ritchie, J. E., Jr., Lieb, P., & Corrigall, E. (2000). Sex differences and similarities in job attribute preferences: A meta-analysis. *Psychological Bulletin*, 126, 593–641.

Kray, L., Reb, J., Galinsky, A., & Thompson, L. (2004). Stereotype reactance at the bargaining table: The effect of stereotype activation and power on claiming and creating value. *Personality and Social Psychology Bulletin*, 30, 399–411.

Kray, L. J., Thompson, L., & Galinsky, A. (2001). Battle of the sexes: Gender stereotype confirmation and reactance in negotiations. *Journal of Personality & Social Psychology*, 80, 942–958.

Kunda, Z., & Spencer, S. J. (2003). When do stereotypes come to mind and when do they color judgment? A goal-based theory of stereotype activation and application. *Psychological Bulletin*, 129, 522–544.

Maume, D. J., Jr. (1999). Glass ceilings and glass escalators. *Work & Occupations*, 26(4), 483.

Miller, T., & Del Carmen Triana, M. (2009). Demographic diversity in the boardroom: Mediators of the board diversity-firm performance relationship. *Journal of Management Studies*, 46, 755–786.

Morrison, A., & Von Glinow, M. A. (1990). Women and minorities in management. *American Psychologist*, 45, 200–208.

National Center for Education Statistics (NCES). (2008). *The condition of education 2008*. Retrieved November 15, 2011, from http://nces.ed.gov/pubs2008/2008031.pdf

Nielsen, S., & Huse, M. (2010). The contribution of women on boards of directors: Going beyond the surface. *Corporate Governance—An International Review*, 18, 136–148.

Nieva, V. E., & Gutek, B. A. (1981). *Women and work: A psychological perspective*. New York: Praeger.

Ohlott, P. J., Ruderman, M. N., & McCauley, C. D. (1994). Gender differences in managers' developmental job experiences. *Academy of Management Journal*, 37, 46–67.

Pailhe, A., & Solaz, A. (2006). Time with children: Do fathers and mothers replace each other when one parent is unemployed? *European Journal of Population*, 24, 211–236. doi: 10.1007/s10680–007–9143–5

Powell, G. N. (1990). One more time: Do female and male managers differ? *Academy of Management Executive*, 4, 68–75.

Powell, G. N., & Graves, L. M. (2003). *Women and men in management* (3rd ed.). Thousand Oaks, CA: Sage.

Ragins, B. R., Townsend, B., & Mattis, M. (1998). Gender gap in the executive suite: CEOs and female executives report on breaking the glass ceiling. *Academy of Management Executive*, 12, 28–42.

Rosener, J. (1995). *America's competitive secret: Utilizing women as a management strategy*. New York: Oxford University Press.

Rudman, L. A. (1998). Self-promotion as a risk factor for women: The costs and benefits of counter-stereotypical impression management. *Journal of Personality and Social Psychology, 74,* 629–645.

Rudman, L. A., & Glick, P. (2001). Prescriptive gender stereotypes and backlash toward agentic women. *Journal of Social Issues, 57,* 743–762.

Ryan, M. K., Haslam, S. A., Hersby, M. D., & Bongiorno, R. (2011). Think crisis–think female: The glass cliff and contextual variation in the think manager–think male stereotype. *Journal of Applied Psychology, 96,* 470–484.

Schein, V. E. (2001). A global look at psychological barriers to women's progress in management. *Journal of Social Issues, 57,* 675–688.

Sekaquaptewa, D., & Thompson, M. (2003). Solo status, stereotype threat, and performance expectancies: Their effects on women's performance. *Journal of Experimental Social Psychology, 39,* 68–74.

Small, D. A., Gelfand, M., Babcock, L., & Gettman, H. (2007). Who goes to the bargaining table? The influence of gender and framing on the initiation of negotiation. *Journal of Personality and Social Psychology, 93,* 600–613.

Smith, A., & Stewart, A. J. (1983). Approaches to studying racism and sexism in black women's lives. *Journal of Social Issues, 39,* 1–15.

Stangor, C., Lynch, L., Duan, C., & Glass, B. (1992). Categorization of individuals on the basis of multiple social features. *Journal of Personality and Social Psychology, 62,* 207–218.

Thoits, P. A. (1992). Identity structures and psychological well-being: Gender and marital status comparisons. *Social Psychology Quarterly, 55,* 236–256.

Tsui, A. S., & Gutek, B. A. (1984). A role set analysis of gender differences in performance, affective relationship, and career success of industrial middle managers. *Academy of Management Journal, 27,* 619–635.

Twenge, J. M. (2001). Change in women's assertiveness in response to status and roles: A cross-temporal meta-analysis, 1931–1993. *Journal of Personality and Social Psychology, 81,* 133–145.

U.S. Bureau of Labor Statistics. (2010a). *Current population survey, annual averages: Household data.* (Characteristics of the employed, Table 9: Employed persons by occupation, sex, and age). Retrieved September 21, 2011, from http://www.bls.gov/cps/cpsaat9.pdf

U.S. Bureau of Labor Statistics. (2010b). *Current population survey, annual averages: Household data.* (Table 11: Employed persons by detailed occupation, sex, race, and Hispanic or Latino ethnicity). Retrieved September 21, 2011, from http://www.bls.gov/cps/cpsaat11.pdf

U.S. Department of Defense. (2008). *Active duty military personnel by service by rank/grade* (for September 30, 2008). Retrieved April 30, 2009, from http://siadapp.dmdc.osd.mil/personnel/MILITARY/rg0809f.pdf and http://siadapp.dmdc.osd.mil/personnel/MILITARY/rg0809.pdf

van Engen, M. L., Leeden, R. van der, & Willemsen, T. M. (2001). Gender, context and leadership styles: A field study. *Journal of Occupational and Organizational Psychology, 74,* 581–598.

van Engen, M. L., & Willemsen, T. M. (2004). Sex and leadership styles: A meta-analysis of research published in the 1990s. *Psychological Reports, 94,* 3–18.

Vecchio, R. P. (2002). Leadership and gender advantage. *Leadership Quarterly, 13*, 643–671.

Vinkenburg, C. J., van Engen, M. L., Eagly, A. H., & Johannesen-Schmidt, M. C. (2011). An exploration of stereotypical beliefs about leadership styles: Is transformational leadership a route to women's promotion? *The Leadership Quarterly, 22*, 10–21.

Williams, C. L. (1992). The glass escalator: Hidden advantages for men in the "female" professions. *Social Problems, 39*, 253–267.

Williams, C. L. (1995). *Still a man's world: Men who do "women's work."* Berkeley: University of California Press.

Williams, J. (2010). *Reshaping the work-family debate: Why men and class matter.* Cambridge, MA: Harvard University Press.

Wirth, L. (2001). *Breaking through the glass ceiling: Women in management.* Geneva: International Labour Office.

Woolley, A. W., Chabris, C. F., Pentland, A., Hashmi, N., & Malone, T. M. (2010). Evidence for a collective intelligence factor in the performance of human groups. *Science, 330*, 686–688.

15

Culture and Leadership

DESCRIPTION

As the title suggests, this chapter is about culture *and* leadership. Like the previous chapter, this one is multifaceted and focuses on a collection of related ideas rather than on a single unified theory. Our discussion in this chapter will center on research that describes culture, its dimensions, and the effects of culture on the leadership process.

Since World War II, globalization has been advancing throughout the world. Globalization is the increased interdependence (economic, social, technical, and political) between nations. People are becoming more interconnected. There is more international trade, cultural exchange, and use of worldwide telecommunication systems. In the past 10 years, our schools, organizations, and communities have become far more global than in the past. Increased globalization has created many challenges, including the need to design effective multinational organizations, to identify and select appropriate leaders for these entities, and to manage organizations with culturally diverse employees (House & Javidan, 2004). Globalization has created a need to understand how cultural differences affect leadership performance.

Globalization has also created the need for leaders to become competent in cross-cultural awareness and practice. Adler and Bartholomew (1992) contended that global leaders need to develop five cross-cultural competencies: First, leaders need to understand business, political, and cultural environments worldwide. Second, they need to learn the perspectives, tastes, trends, and technologies of many other cultures. Third, they need to be able to work simultaneously with people from many cultures.

▶ **15.1** Globalization   🎙 **15.1** Global vs. Local   383

Fourth, leaders must be able to adapt to living and communicating in other cultures. Fifth, they need to learn to relate to people from other cultures from a position of equality rather than cultural superiority (Adler & Bartholomew, 1992, p. 53). Additionally, Ting-Toomey (1999) said that global leaders need to be skilled in creating transcultural visions. They need to develop communication competencies that will enable them to articulate and implement their vision in a diverse workplace. In sum, today's leaders need to acquire a challenging set of competencies if they intend to be effective in present-day global societies.

Culture Defined

Anthropologists, sociologists, and many others have debated the meaning of the word *culture*. Because it is an abstract term, it is hard to define, and different people often define it in dissimilar ways. For our purposes, *culture* is defined as the learned beliefs, values, rules, norms, symbols, and traditions that are common to a group of people. It is these *shared* qualities of a group that make them unique. Culture is dynamic and transmitted to others. In short, culture is the way of life, customs, and script of a group of people (Gudykunst & Ting-Toomey, 1988).

Related to culture are the terms *multicultural* and *diversity*. *Multicultural* implies an approach or a system that takes more than one culture into account. It refers to the existence of multiple cultures such as African, American, Asian, European, and Middle Eastern. *Multicultural* can also refer to a set of subcultures defined by race, gender, ethnicity, sexual orientation, or age. *Diversity* refers to the existence of different cultures or ethnicities within a group or an organization.

Related Concepts

Before beginning our discussion of the various facets of culture, this section describes two concepts that are closely related to culture and leadership: ethnocentrism and prejudice. Both of these concepts can have impacts on how leaders influence others.

Ethnocentrism

As the word suggests, *ethnocentrism* is the tendency for individuals to place their own group (ethnic, racial, or cultural) at the center of their observations of others and the world. People tend to give priority and value to their own beliefs, attitudes, and values, over and above those of other groups. Ethnocentrism is the perception that one's own culture is better or more natural than the culture of others. It may include the failure to recognize the unique perspectives of others. Ethnocentrism is a universal tendency, and each of us is ethnocentric to some degree.

Ethnocentrism is like a perceptual window through which people from one culture make subjective or critical evaluations of people from another culture (Porter & Samovar, 1997). For example, some Americans think that the democratic principles of the United States are superior to the political beliefs of other cultures; they often fail to understand the complexities of other cultures. Ethnocentrism accounts for our tendency to think our own cultural values and ways of doing things are right and natural (Gudykunst & Kim, 1997).

Ethnocentrism can be a major obstacle to effective leadership because it prevents people from fully understanding or respecting the viewpoints of others. For example, if one person's culture values individual achievement, it may be difficult for that person to understand another person whose culture emphasizes collectivity (i.e., people working together as a whole). Similarly, if one person believes strongly in respecting authority, that person may find it difficult to understand someone who challenges authority or does not easily defer to authority figures. The more ethnocentric we are, the less open or tolerant we are of other people's cultural traditions or practices.

A skilled leader cannot avoid issues related to ethnocentrism. Even though she recognizes her own ethnocentrism, a leader also needs to understand—and to a degree tolerate—the ethnocentrism of others. In reality, it is a balancing act for leaders. On the one hand, they need to promote and be confident in their own ways of doing things; on the other hand, they need to be sensitive to the legitimacy of the ways of other cultures. Skilled leaders are able to negotiate the fine line between trying to overcome ethnocentrism and knowing when to remain grounded in their own cultural values.

Prejudice

Closely related to ethnocentrism is prejudice. *Prejudice* is a largely fixed attitude, belief, or emotion held by an individual about another individual or group that is based on faulty or unsubstantiated data. It refers to judgments about others based on previous decisions or experiences. Prejudice

▶ **15.2** Reducing Ethnocentrism

involves inflexible generalizations that are resistant to change or evidence to the contrary (Ponterotto & Pedersen, 1993). Prejudice often is thought of in the context of race (e.g., European American vs. African American), but it also applies in areas such as gender, age, sexual orientation, and other independent contexts. Although prejudice can be positive (e.g., thinking highly of another culture without sufficient evidence), it is usually negative.

As with ethnocentrism, we all hold prejudices to some degree. Sometimes our prejudices allow us to keep our partially fixed attitudes undisturbed and constant. Sometimes prejudice can reduce our anxiety because it gives us a familiar way to structure our observations of others. One of the main problems with prejudice is that it is self-oriented rather than other-oriented. It helps us to achieve balance for ourselves at the expense of others. Moreover, attitudes of prejudice inhibit understanding by creating a screen that filters and limits our ability to see multiple aspects and qualities of other people. Prejudice often shows itself in crude or demeaning comments that people make about others. Both ethnocentrism and prejudice interfere with our ability to understand and appreciate the human experience of others.

In addition to fighting their own prejudice, leaders also face the challenge of dealing with the prejudice of followers. These prejudices can be toward the leader or the leader's culture. Furthermore, it is not uncommon for the leader to face followers who represent several culturally different groups, and these groups have their own prejudices toward each other. A skilled leader needs to find ways to negotiate with followers from various cultural backgrounds.

Dimensions of Culture

Culture has been the focus of many studies across a variety of disciplines. In the past 30 years, a substantial number of studies have focused specifically on ways to identify and classify the various *dimensions* of culture. Determining the basic dimensions or characteristics of different cultures is the first step in being able to understand the relationships between them.

Several well-known studies have addressed the question of how to characterize cultures. For example, Hall (1976) reported that a primary characteristic of cultures is the degree to which they are focused on the individual (individualistic cultures) or on the group (collectivistic cultures). Taking a different approach, Trompenaars (1994) surveyed more than 15,000 people in 47 different countries and determined that organizational cultures could be classified effectively into two dimensions: egalitarian versus hierarchical, and person versus task orientation. The egalitarian–hierarchical dimension refers to the degree to which cultures exhibit shared power as opposed to hierarchical power. Person–task orientation refers to the extent to which cultures emphasize human interaction and not tasks to accomplish.

Of all the research on *dimensions of culture*, perhaps the most referenced is the research of Hofstede (1980, 2001). Based on an analysis of questionnaires obtained from more than 100,000 respondents in more than 50 countries, Hofstede identified five major dimensions on which cultures differ: power distance, uncertainty avoidance, individualism–collectivism, masculinity–femininity, and long-term–short-term orientation. Hofstede's work has been the benchmark for much of the research on world cultures.

In the specific area of *culture and leadership*, the studies by House, Hanges, Javidan, Dorfman, and Gupta (2004) offer the strongest body of findings to date, as published in the 800-page *Culture, Leadership, and Organizations: The GLOBE Study of 62 Societies*. These studies are called the GLOBE studies, named for the Global Leadership and Organizational Behavior Effectiveness research program. The GLOBE studies have generated a very large number of findings on the relationship between culture and leadership.

The GLOBE research program, which was initiated by Robert House in 1991, is an ongoing program that has involved more than 160 investigators to date. The primary purpose of the project is to increase our understanding of cross-cultural interactions and the impact of culture on leadership effectiveness. GLOBE researchers have used quantitative methods to study the responses of 17,000 managers in more than 950 organizations, representing 62 different cultures throughout the world. GLOBE researchers have collected data in a variety of ways, including questionnaires, interviews, focus groups, and content analysis of printed media. The findings of the GLOBE studies will be provided in more detail throughout this chapter.

As a part of their study of culture and leadership, GLOBE researchers developed their own classification of cultural dimensions. Based on their research and the work of others (e.g., Hofstede, 1980, 2001; Kluckhohn & Strodtbeck, 1961; McClelland, 1961; Triandis, 1995), GLOBE researchers identified nine cultural dimensions: uncertainty avoidance, power distance, institutional collectivism, in-group collectivism, gender egalitarianism,

15.1 Cross-Cultural Leadership

assertiveness, future orientation, performance orientation, and humane orientation. In the following section, each of the dimensions is described.

Uncertainty Avoidance

This dimension refers to the extent to which a society, an organization, or a group relies on established social norms, rituals, and procedures to avoid uncertainty. Uncertainty avoidance is concerned with the way cultures use rules, structures, and laws to make things more predictable and less uncertain.

Power Distance

This dimension refers to the degree to which members of a group expect and agree that power should be shared unequally. Power distance is concerned with the way cultures are stratified, thus creating levels between people based on power, authority, prestige, status, wealth, and material possessions.

Institutional Collectivism

This dimension describes the degree to which an organization or a society encourages institutional or societal collective action. Institutional collectivism is concerned with whether cultures identify with broader societal interests rather than with individual goals and accomplishments.

In-Group Collectivism

This dimension refers to the degree to which people express pride, loyalty, and cohesiveness in their organizations or families. In-group collectivism is concerned with the extent to which people are devoted to their organizations or families.

Gender Egalitarianism

This dimension measures the degree to which an organization or a society minimizes gender role differences and promotes gender equality.

▶ 15.3 Leader and Gender Egalitarianism

Gender egalitarianism is concerned with how much societies deemphasize members' biological sex in determining the roles that members play in their homes, organizations, and communities.

Assertiveness

This dimension refers to the degree to which people in a culture are determined, assertive, confrontational, and aggressive in their social relationships. Assertiveness is concerned with how much a culture or society encourages people to be forceful, aggressive, and tough, as opposed to encouraging them to be timid, submissive, and tender in social relationships.

Future Orientation

This concept refers to the extent to which people engage in future-oriented behaviors such as planning, investing in the future, and delaying gratification. Future orientation emphasizes that people in a culture prepare for the future as opposed to enjoying the present and being spontaneous.

Performance Orientation

This dimension describes the extent to which an organization or a society encourages and rewards group members for improved performance and excellence. Performance orientation is concerned with whether people in a culture are rewarded for setting and meeting challenging goals.

Humane Orientation

The ninth dimension refers to the degree to which a culture encourages and rewards people for being fair, altruistic, generous, caring, and kind to others. Humane orientation is concerned with how much a society or an organization emphasizes sensitivity to others, social support, and community values.

GLOBE researchers used these nine cultural dimensions to analyze the attributes of the 62 different countries in the study. These cultural dimensions formed the basis for studying how the countries varied in their approach to leadership.

15.1 Cross-Cultural Management **15.2** Interpreting GLOBE Dimensions

Clusters of World Cultures

GLOBE researchers divided the data from the 62 countries they studied into regional clusters.[1] These clusters provided a convenient way to analyze the similarities and differences between cultural groups (clusters), and to make meaningful generalizations about culture and leadership.

To create regional clusters, GLOBE researchers used prior research (e.g., Ronen & Shenkar, 1985), common language, geography, religion, and historical accounts. Based on these factors, they grouped countries into 10 distinct clusters: Anglo, Germanic Europe, Latin Europe, Sub-Saharan Africa, Eastern Europe, Middle East, Confucian Asia, Southern Asia, Latin America, and Nordic Europe (Figure 15.1). These 10 regional clusters are the groupings that were used in all of the GLOBE studies.

Figure 15.1   Country Clusters According to GLOBE

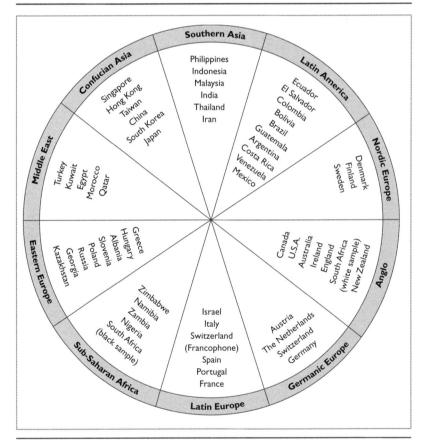

SOURCE: Adapted from House, R.J., Hanges, P.J., Javidan, M., Dorfman, P. W., & Gupta, V., *Culture, Leadership, and Organizations: The GLOBE Study of 62 Societies,* copyright © 2004, Sage Publications, Inc. Reprinted with permission.

15.2 Leadership and Culture

To test whether the clusters, or groups of countries, were valid, research-ers did a statistical analysis of questionnaire data collected from individuals in each of the clusters. Their results indicated that the scores of respon-dents *within a cluster* correlated with one another but were unrelated to the scores of respondents *in different clusters*. From these findings, they concluded that each cluster was unique. In sum, these regional clusters represented a valid and reliable way to differentiate countries of the world into 10 distinct groups.

Characteristics of Clusters

In an effort to characterize the regional clusters, GLOBE researchers analyzed data from each of the regions using the dimensions of culture described earlier. Table 15.1 provides a classification of the cultural clus-ters in regard to how they scored on each cultural dimension. In the table, the nine cultural dimensions are listed in the left-hand column; the high-score and low-score regional clusters are provided in the next two columns. These are the regional clusters that were significantly higher or lower on particular dimensions than other regions. From these data, several observa-tions can be made about the characteristics of these regional cultures.

Anglo

The Anglo cluster consists of Canada, the United States, Australia, Ire-land, England, South Africa (White sample), and New Zealand. These countries or populations were *high* in performance orientation and *low* in in-group collectivism. This means it is characteristic of these countries to be competitive and results oriented, but less attached to their families or similar groups than other countries.

Confucian Asia

This cluster, which includes Singapore, Hong Kong, Taiwan, China, South Korea, and Japan, exhibited *high* scores in performance orienta-tion, institutional collectivism, and in-group collectivism. These coun-tries are results driven, and they encourage the group working together over individual goals. People in these countries are devoted and loyal to their families.

 15.2 Leadership and Cultural Diversity

Table 15.1 Cultural Clusters Classified on Cultural Dimensions

Cultural Dimension	High-Score Clusters	Low-Score Clusters
Assertiveness orientation	Eastern Europe Germanic Europe	Nordic Europe
Future orientation	Germanic Europe Nordic Europe	Eastern Europe Latin America Middle East
Gender egalitarianism	Eastern Europe Nordic Europe	Middle East
Humane orientation	Southern Asia Sub-Saharan Africa	Germanic Europe Latin Europe
In-group collectivism	Confucian Asia Eastern Europe Latin America Middle East Southern Asia	Anglo Germanic Europe Nordic Europe
Institutional collectivism	Nordic Europe Confucian Asia	Germanic Europe Latin America Latin Europe
Performance orientation	Anglo Confucian Asia Germanic Europe	Eastern Europe Latin America
Power distance	No clusters	Nordic Europe
Uncertainty avoidance	Germanic Europe Nordic Europe	Eastern Europe Latin America Middle East

SOURCE: Adapted from House, R. J., Hanges, P. J., Javidan, M., Dorfman, P. W., & Gupta, V. (Eds.), *Culture, Leadership, and Organizations: The GLOBE Study of 62 Societies,* © 2004, SAGE Publications, Inc. Reprinted with permission.

Eastern Europe

Included in this cluster are Greece, Hungary, Albania, Slovenia, Poland, Russia, Georgia, and Kazakhstan. These countries scored *high* on assertiveness, in-group collectivism, and gender egalitarianism. They scored *low* on performance orientation, future orientation, and uncertainty avoidance. People in this cluster tend to be forceful and supportive of their coworkers and to treat men and women equally. They are less likely to be achievement driven, to emphasize strategic planning, and to stress rules and laws as a way to maintain order.

Germanic Europe

The Germanic Europe countries, which include Austria, The Netherlands, Switzerland, and Germany, scored *high* in performance orientation, assertiveness, future orientation, and uncertainty avoidance. They were *low* in humane orientation, institutional collectivism, and in-group collectivism. These countries value competition and aggressiveness and are more results oriented than people oriented. They enjoy planning and investing in the future and using rules and laws to give them control over their environment. At the same time, these countries are more likely to be individualistic and less group oriented. They tend not to emphasize broad societal groups.

Latin America

The Latin America cluster is made up of Ecuador, El Salvador, Colombia, Bolivia, Brazil, Guatemala, Argentina, Costa Rica, Venezuela, and Mexico. People in these countries scored *high* on in-group collectivism and *low* on performance orientation, future orientation, institutional collectivism, and uncertainty avoidance. People in these countries tend to be loyal and devoted to their families and similar groups but less interested in overall institutional and societal groups.

Latin Europe

Comprising Israel, Italy, Francophone Switzerland, Spain, Portugal, and France, the Latin Europe cluster exhibited *more moderate* and *fewer high scores* on any of the cultural dimensions, but they scored *low* on humane orientation and institutional collectivism. It is characteristic of these countries to value individual autonomy and to place less value on the greater societal collective. Individuals are encouraged to watch out for themselves and to pursue individual rather than societal goals.

Middle East

This cluster was made up of Qatar, Morocco, Egypt, Kuwait, and Turkey. These countries scored *high* on in-group collectivism and *low* on future orientation, gender egalitarianism, and uncertainty avoidance. People in these countries tend to show great pride in their families and organizations. They are devoted and loyal to their own people. Furthermore, it is common for these countries to treat people of different genders in distinctly different ways. Women often are afforded less status than men, and fewer women are in positions of authority than men. In the Middle East, orderliness and consistency are not stressed, and people do not place heavy reliance on policies and procedures. There is a tendency to focus on current issues as opposed to attempting to control the future.

Nordic Europe

The Nordic Europe cluster, which includes Denmark, Finland, and Sweden, exhibited several distinctive characteristics. This cluster scored *high* on future orientation, gender egalitarianism, institutional collectivism, and uncertainty avoidance, and *low* on assertiveness, in-group collectivism, and power distance. The Nordic people place a high priority on long-term success. Women are treated with greater equality. The Nordic people identify with the broader society and far less with family groups. In Nordic Europe, rules, orderliness, and consistency are stressed. Assertiveness is downplayed in favor of modesty and tenderness, and power is shared equally among people at all levels of society. Cooperation and societal-level group identity are highly valued by the Nordic people.

Southern Asia

The Philippines, Indonesia, Malaysia, India, Thailand, and Iran form the Southern Asia cluster. These countries exhibited *high* scores on humane orientation and in-group collectivism. Southern Asia could be characterized as countries that demonstrate strong family loyalty and deep concern for their communities.

Sub-Saharan Africa

The Sub-Saharan Africa cluster consisted of Zimbabwe, Namibia, Zambia, Nigeria, and South Africa (Black sample). These countries or populations expressed *high* scores on humane orientation. In Sub-Saharan Africa, people generally are very concerned for and sensitive to others. Concern for family and friends is more important than concern for self.

Leadership Behavior and Culture Clusters

The overall purpose of the GLOBE project was to determine how people from different cultures viewed leadership. In addition, researchers wanted to determine the ways in which cultural characteristics were related to culturally endorsed leadership behaviors. In short, they wanted to find out how differences in cultures were related to differences in approaches to leadership.

The conceptualization of leadership used by GLOBE researchers was derived in part from the work of Lord and Maher (1991) on implicit leadership theory. According to implicit leadership theory, individuals have implicit beliefs and convictions about the attributes and beliefs that distinguish leaders from nonleaders and effective leaders from ineffective leaders. From the perspective of this theory, leadership is in the eye of the beholder (Dorfman, Hanges, & Brodbeck, 2004). Leadership refers to what people see in others when they are exhibiting leadership behaviors.

To describe how different cultures view leadership behaviors in others, GLOBE researchers identified six global leadership behaviors: charismatic/value based, team oriented, participative, humane oriented, autonomous, and self-protective (House & Javidan, 2004). These global leadership behaviors were defined in these studies as follows:

Charismatic/value-based leadership reflects the ability to inspire, to motivate, and to expect high performance from others based on strongly held core values. This kind of leadership includes being visionary, inspirational, self-sacrificing, trustworthy, decisive, and performance oriented.

Team-oriented leadership emphasizes team building and a common purpose among team members. This kind of leadership includes being collaborative, integrative, diplomatic, nonmalevolent, and administratively competent.

Participative leadership reflects the degree to which leaders involve others in making and implementing decisions. It includes being participative and nonautocratic.

Humane-oriented leadership emphasizes being supportive, considerate, compassionate, and generous. This type of leadership includes modesty and sensitivity to other people.

Autonomous leadership refers to independent and individualistic leadership, which includes being autonomous and unique.

 15.2 Global Leaders

Self-protective leadership reflects behaviors that ensure the safety and security of the leader and the group. It includes leadership that is self-centered, status conscious, conflict inducing, face saving, and procedural.

These six global leadership behaviors emerged from the GLOBE research and were used to assess the different ways in which various cultural clusters viewed leadership. From this analysis, the researchers were able to identify a leadership profile for each cluster. Each profile describes the relative importance and desirability that different cultures ascribe to different leadership behaviors. The leadership profiles for each of the 10 culture clusters follow.

Eastern Europe Leadership Profile

For the Eastern European countries, an ideal example of a leader would be a person who was first and foremost independent while maintaining a strong interest in protecting his or her position as a leader (Figure 15.2). In addition, the leader would be moderately charismatic/value based, team oriented, and humane oriented, yet largely uninterested in involving others in the decision-making process. To sum up, this culture describes a leader as one who is highly autonomous, makes decisions independently, and is to a certain degree inspiring, team oriented, and attentive to human needs.

Figure 15.2   Culture Clusters and Desired Leadership Behaviors: Eastern Europe

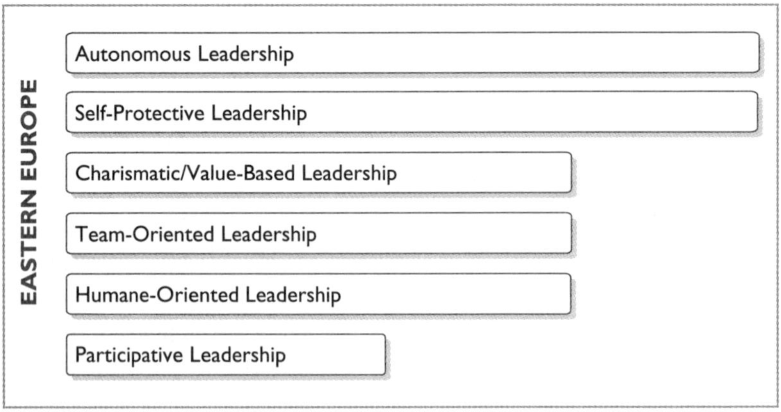

SOURCE: Adapted from House et al. (2004).

Latin America Leadership Profile

Quite different from the Eastern European countries, the Latin American countries place the most importance on charismatic/value-based, team-oriented, and self-protective leadership, and the least importance on autonomous leadership (Figure 15.3). In addition, this cluster is moderately interested in leadership that is participative and humane oriented. The profile for the Latin America cluster is of a leader who is charismatic/value based but somewhat self-serving, collaborative, and inspiring. These leaders tend to be moderately interested in people and their participation in decision making.

Figure 15.3 Culture Clusters and Desired Leadership Behaviors: Latin America

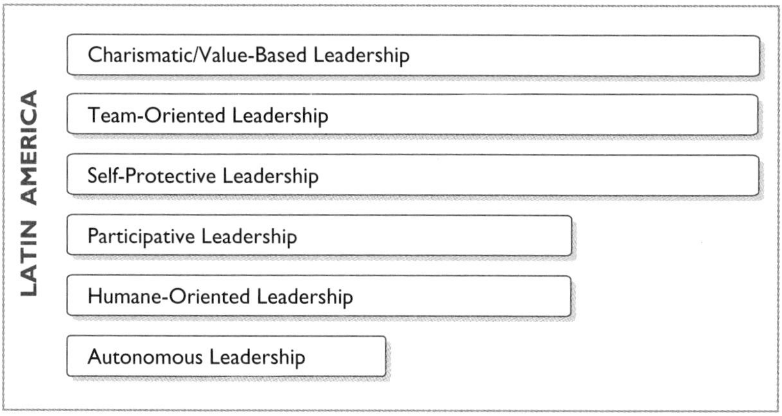

SOURCE: Adapted from House et al. (2004).

Latin Europe Leadership Profile

The Latin Europe cluster values leadership that is charismatic/value based, team oriented, participative, and self-protective (Figure 15.4). Independent leadership and the human side of leadership are downplayed in this cluster. In short, the profile of the Latin Europe cluster centers on leadership that is inspiring, collaborative, participative, and self-oriented, but not highly compassionate.

Figure 15.4 Culture Clusters and Desired Leadership Behaviors:
Latin Europe

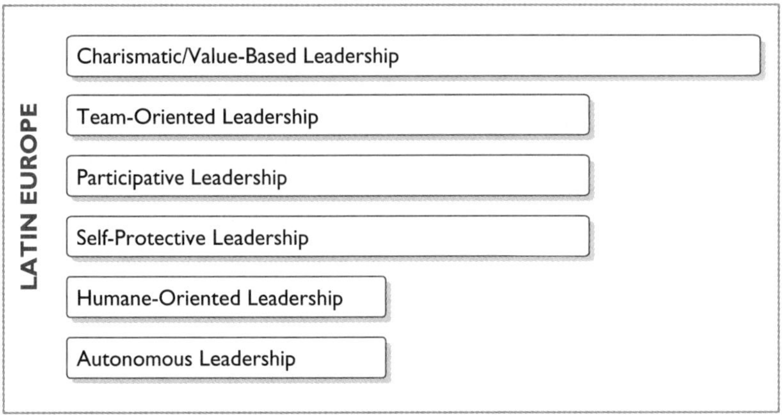

SOURCE: Adapted from House et al. (2004).

Confucian Asia Leadership Profile

The leadership profile of the Confucian Asia countries describes a leader who is self-protective, team oriented, and humane oriented (Figure 15.5). Though independent and to some extent inspiring, this type of leader typically does not invite others to be involved in goal setting or decision making. In sum, the Confucian Asia profile describes a leader who works and cares about others but who uses status and position to make independent decisions without the input of others.

Nordic Europe Leadership Profile

An ideal example of leadership for the Nordic European countries is leadership that is highly visionary and participative, while being somewhat independent and diplomatic (Figure 15.6). For these countries, it is of less importance that their leaders be humane oriented or self-protective. Nordic Europeans prefer leaders who are inspiring, and who involve others in decision making. They do not expect their leaders to be exceedingly compassionate, nor do they expect them to be concerned with status and other self-centered attributes.

15.3 Chinese Culture and Leadership

Figure 15.5   Culture Clusters and Desired Leadership Behaviors: Confucian Asia

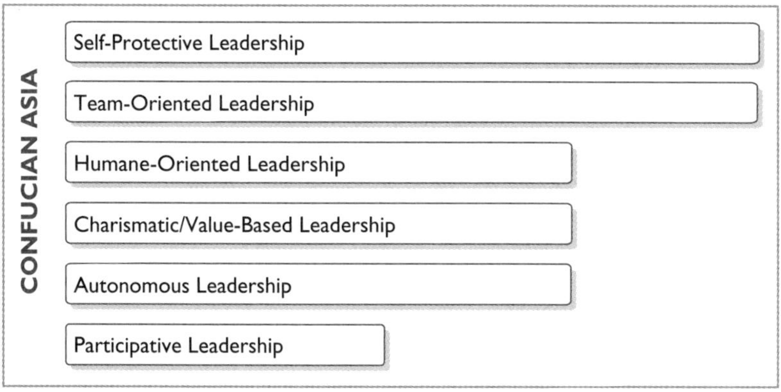

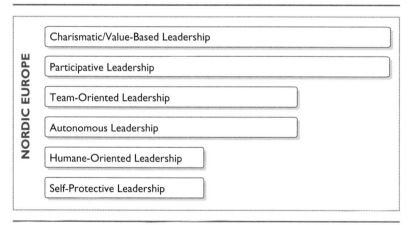

CONFUCIAN ASIA

Self-Protective Leadership

Team-Oriented Leadership

Humane-Oriented Leadership

Charismatic/Value-Based Leadership

Autonomous Leadership

Participative Leadership

SOURCE: Adapted from House et al. (2004).

Figure 15.6   Culture Clusters and Desired Leadership Behaviors: Nordic Europe

NORDIC EUROPE

Charismatic/Value-Based Leadership

Participative Leadership

Team-Oriented Leadership

Autonomous Leadership

Humane-Oriented Leadership

Self-Protective Leadership

SOURCE: Adapted from House et al. (2004).

Anglo Leadership Profile

The profile of leadership for the Anglo countries emphasizes that leaders are especially charismatic/value based, participative, and sensitive to people (Figure 15.7). Stated another way, Anglo countries want leaders to be exceedingly motivating and visionary, not autocratic, and considerate of others. Furthermore, they report that leaders should be team oriented and autonomous. The least important characteristic for Anglo countries is self-protective leadership. They believe it is ineffective if leaders are status conscious or prone to face saving.

Figure 15.7 Culture Clusters and Desired Leadership Behaviors: Anglo

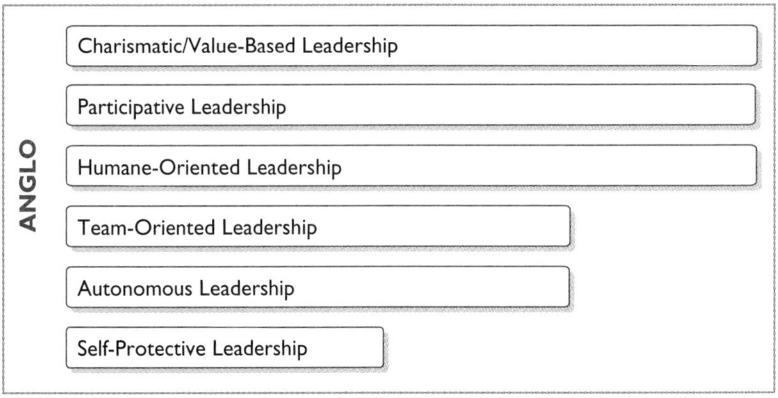

SOURCE: Adapted from House et al. (2004).

Sub-Saharan Africa Leadership Profile

For countries in Sub-Saharan Africa, an ideal leader is modest, compassionate, and sensitive to the people (Figure 15.8). In addition, they believe a leader should be relatively charismatic/value based, team oriented, participative, and self-protective. Leaders who act independently or act alone are viewed as less effective in these countries. In short, the Sub-Saharan Africa profile characterizes effective leadership as caring leadership. Like many other countries, these countries or populations believe leaders should be inspirational, collaborative, and not excessively self-centered. Leaders who act autonomously are seen as ineffective in Sub-Saharan Africa countries.

Southern Asia Leadership Profile

The Southern Asia leadership profile is similar to the profile of Confucian Asia. They both place importance on self-protective, charismatic/value-based, humane-oriented, and team-oriented leadership, and they both find participative leadership ineffective (Figure 15.9). Southern Asia

Figure 15.8   Culture Clusters and Desired Leadership Behaviors:
Sub-Saharan Africa

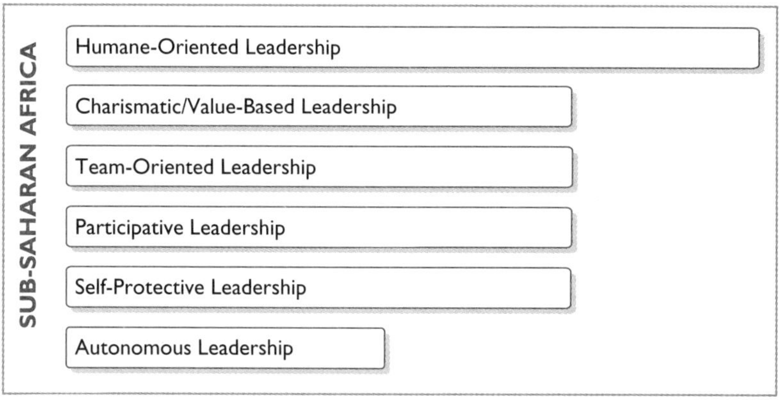

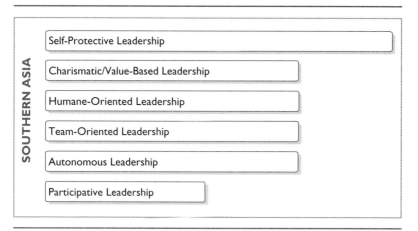

SOURCE: Adapted from House et al. (2004).

Figure 15.9   Culture Clusters and Desired Leadership Behaviors:
Southern Asia

SOURCE: Adapted from House et al. (2004).

countries differ from Confucian Asia countries in believing that charisma is an important leader attribute. The Southern Asia countries characterize effective leadership as especially collaborative, inspirational, sensitive to people's needs, and concerned with status and face saving. Furthermore, they believe leaders who tend to be autocratic are more effective than those who lead by inviting others into the decision-making process.

Germanic Europe Leadership Profile

The ideal leader in the Germanic Europe cluster has a style that is very participative while also being inspirational and independent (Figure 15.10). The ideal leader would be a unique, visionary person who is autonomous, charismatic/value based, participative, humane oriented, and team oriented, but not status conscious or concerned with face saving. In short, the Germanic European countries think effective leadership is based on participation, charisma, and autonomy but not on face saving and other self-centered attributes.

Figure 15.10   Culture Clusters and Desired Leadership Behaviors: Germanic Europe

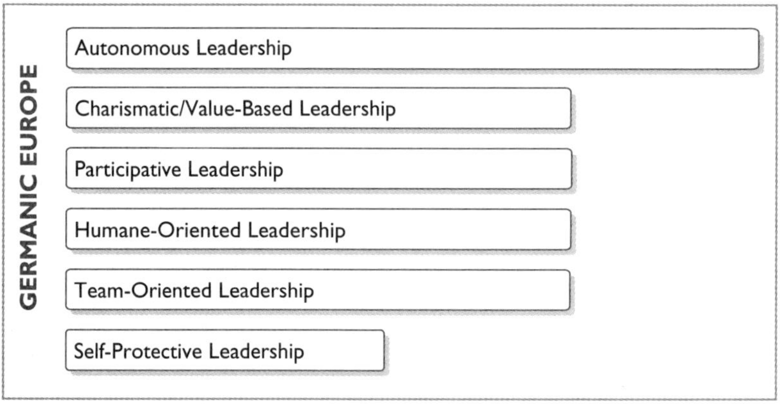

GERMANIC EUROPE

Autonomous Leadership

Charismatic/Value-Based Leadership

Participative Leadership

Humane-Oriented Leadership

Team-Oriented Leadership

Self-Protective Leadership

SOURCE: Adapted from House et al. (2004).

Middle East Leadership Profile

The leadership profile for the Middle Eastern countries differs significantly from the profiles of the other cultural clusters (Figure 15.11). Middle Eastern countries find self-attributes such as face saving and status are important characteristics of effective leadership. They also value being independent and familial. However, they find charismatic/value-based, team-oriented, and participative decision making less essential for effective leadership. To sum up, the Middle Eastern profile of leadership emphasizes status and face saving, and deemphasizes charismatic/value-based and team-oriented leadership.

Figure 15.11   Culture Clusters and Desired Leadership Behaviors:
Middle East

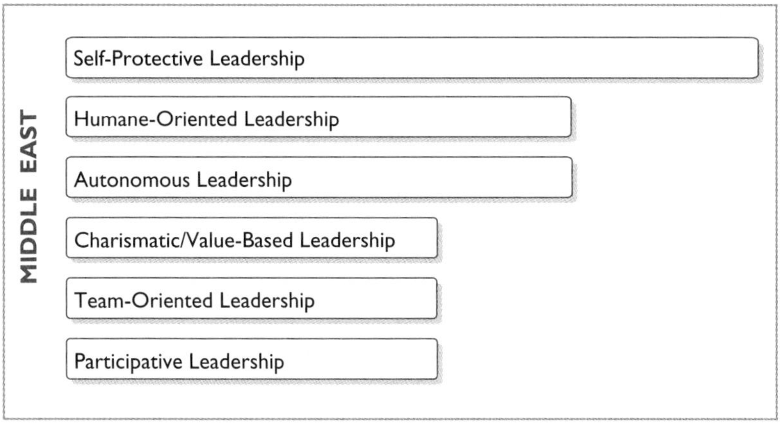

SOURCE: Adapted from House et al. (2004).

Universally Desirable and Undesirable Leadership Attributes

One of the most interesting outcomes of the GLOBE project was the identification of a list of leadership attributes that were universally endorsed by 17,000 people in 62 countries as positive aspects of effective leadership. Respondents in the GLOBE studies identified 22 *valued* leadership attributes (Table 15.2). These attributes were universally endorsed as characteristics that facilitate outstanding leadership.

Based on the list of endorsed attributes, a portrait can be drawn of a leader whom almost everyone would see as exceptional. That portrait is of a leader who is high in integrity, is charismatic/value based, and has interpersonal skills (Dorfman et al., 2004).

The GLOBE project also identified a list of leadership attributes that were universally viewed as *obstacles* to effective leadership (Table 15.3). These characteristics suggest that the portrait of an ineffective leader is someone who is asocial, malevolent, and self-focused. Clearly, people from all cultures find these characteristics to hinder effective leadership.

Table 15.2 Universally Desirable Leadership Attributes

Positive Leader Attributes		
Trustworthy	Just	Honest
Has foresight	Plans ahead	Encouraging
Positive	Dynamic	Motive arouser
Confidence builder	Motivational	Dependable
Intelligent	Decisive	Effective bargainer
Win–win problem solver	Communicative	Informed
Administratively skilled	Coordinative	Team builder
Excellence oriented		

SOURCE: Adapted from House et al. (2004).

Table 15.3 Universally Undesirable Leadership Attributes

Negative Leader Attributes		
Loner	Asocial	Noncooperative
Irritable	Nonexplicit	Egocentric
Ruthless	Dictatorial	

STRENGTHS

Although this chapter on culture and leadership does not represent a single unified theory of leadership, it does present findings that have several strengths. First, the scope of this study is a major strength. For this study, data were collected by 170 social scientists, representing 62 countries from all regions of the world, and included responses from 17,300 managers in 951 organizations. The GLOBE project has been a massive undertaking; the findings that have emerged from this work make a powerful statement about how cultures around the world view leadership.

Second, the findings from GLOBE are valuable because they emerge from a well-developed quantitative research design. In the leadership literature, there are many qualitative studies that focus more narrowly on how people in certain countries view a small number of leadership concepts. Although these studies have contributed to our understanding of culture and leadership, they are limited in scope and generalizability. In contrast, the strength of the GLOBE project is that researchers used a quantitative design and administered standardized instruments to assess leadership and cultural dimensions in 62 countries. Thus, the results from the GLOBE studies about leadership are generalizable between cultures and within cultures around the world.

Third, the GLOBE studies provide a classification of cultural dimensions that is more expansive than the commonly used Hofstede classification system. Whereas Hofstede distinguishes between cultures based on five dimensions (power distance, uncertainty avoidance, individualism–collectivism, masculinity–femininity, and long-term–short-term orientation), the GLOBE studies identify nine cultural dimensions (uncertainty avoidance, power distance, institutional collectivism, in-group collectivism, gender egalitarianism, assertiveness, future orientation, performance orientation, and humane orientation). Although seven of the nine dimensions identified in the GLOBE studies have their origins in the dimensions identified by Hofstede, by expanding the classification system the GLOBE studies provide a broader and more elaborate way of describing dimensions of culture.

Fourth, the GLOBE studies provide useful information about what is universally accepted as good and bad leadership. Clearly, people from most cultures view good leadership as based on integrity, charisma, and interpersonal ability. Conversely, they see bad leadership emerging from leaders who are self-focused, dictatorial, and asocial. These lists of positive and negative attributes provide a useful portrait of how people around the world conceptualize leadership.

Last, the study of culture and leadership underscores the complexity of the leadership process and how it is influenced by culture. Data from the GLOBE studies highlight the need for each of us to expand our ethnocentric tendencies to view leadership from only our own perspective, and instead to "open our window" to the diverse ways in which leadership is viewed by people from different regions around the world. There are many ways to view leadership and the integration of culture; studies of leadership help us to expand and develop a richer understanding of the leadership process.

CRITICISMS

The body of research on culture and leadership also has several weaknesses. First, although the GLOBE research has resulted in a multitude of findings about perceptions of leadership in different cultures, this research does not provide a clear set of assumptions and propositions that can form a single theory about the way culture relates to leadership or influences the leadership process.

A second criticism, more narrow in scope, concerns the way researchers have labeled and defined certain cultural dimensions and leadership behaviors. For example, it is not easy to understand what *power distance* means, nor is the meaning of *self-protective leadership* clear. Because the meanings of these terms are somewhat vague, it is difficult at times to interpret or fully comprehend the findings about culture and leadership.

Another criticism concerns the way in which leadership was conceptualized in the GLOBE studies. In these studies, researchers used a conceptualization of leadership that was based on the ideas set forth by Lord and Maher (1991) in their work on implicit leadership theory. This approach frames leadership from an information-processing perspective, as the implicit beliefs and convictions that individuals have about leaders. In other words, according to this theory, leadership is the process of being perceived by others as being a leader. However, conceptualizing leadership in this way is limited: It focuses on what people perceive to be leadership and ignores a large body of research that frames leadership in terms of what leaders do (e.g., transformational leadership, path–goal theory, skills approach). Research on how people from different cultures view leadership is valuable, but there is a need for further research on how leadership functions in different cultures.[2]

A related criticism concerns the way in which researchers in the GLOBE studies measured leadership. They selected six global leadership behaviors (i.e., charismatic/value-based, team-oriented, participative, humane-oriented, autonomous, and self-protective leadership) that were derived from an analysis of subjects' responses to hundreds of other attributes believed to be related to outstanding leadership. Each of the six global leadership behaviors was measured by a series of subscales. However, the subscales represented a very broad range of behaviors, and as a result compromised the precision and validity of the leadership measures.

Finally, the GLOBE studies provide a provocative list of universally endorsed desirable and undesirable leadership attributes. The attributes identified in the GLOBE studies are comparable to the list of traits we discussed in Chapter 2. As with the trait approach, however, it is difficult to identify a set of universal attributes in isolation from the context in which the leadership occurs. The GLOBE studies tend to isolate a set of attributes that are characteristic of effective leaders without considering the influence of the situational effects.

APPLICATION

Training programs about culture and diversity have been popular for many years. For example, in the training and development field, a wide variety of programs teach cultural sensitivity and address issues related to cultural differences. At the core of these programs, people are taught about the nuances and characteristics of different cultures, and how to be sensitive to people in other countries and cultures.

The findings in this chapter have implications for leadership training. Understanding issues about culture is useful in several ways (Bing, 2004). First, the findings about culture can help leaders understand their own cultural biases and preferences. Understanding their own preferences is the first step in understanding that people in other cultures might have different preferences.

Second, the findings help leaders to understand what it means to be a good leader. Different cultures have different ideas about what they want from their leaders. These findings help our leaders adapt their style to be more effective in different cultural settings.

Third, this chapter's findings can help global leaders communicate more effectively across cultural and geographic boundaries. By understanding cultural differences, leaders can become more empathic and accurate in their communication with others.

Information on culture and leadership has also been applied in very practical ways (Bing, 2004). It has been used to build culturally sensitive websites, design new employee orientation programs, conduct programs in relocation training, improve global team effectiveness, and facilitate multinational merger implementation, to name a few. These examples clearly indicate the wide range of applications for research on culture and leadership in the workplace.

CASE STUDIES

This section provides three case studies (Cases 15.1, 15.2, and 15.3) that describe leadership in various cultural contexts. The first case is about a college student who takes an internship at a Japanese-based automotive company. The second case describes how a small Midwestern bank developed a unique Islamic financing program. The final case describes how two board members from a nonprofit organization developed a capital campaign to renovate a fire station for a Hispanic community. After each of the cases, questions are provided to help you think about how cultural issues are related to the leadership process.

CASE 15.1

A Challenging Workplace

As a leader in campus organizations, Samira Tanaka, a student, often led projects and took deadlines very seriously. Her strong work ethic led to an internship offer at a Japanese automotive company.

At orientation for her internship, Samira learned that Japanese companies historically had little diversity in terms of race and gender. Women in Japan were not as prevalent in the workforce as in North America. In an effort to adapt to North American norms, Japanese subsidiaries had well-developed diversity policies. For example, Samira tracked the usage of minority-owned businesses in the company's supply base. This ensured that the company invested in local businesses that operated in traditionally economically disadvantaged areas. Investing in the local community was already an important business value in Japan, so this was a simple adaptation for Samira's company.

The company culture was a unique blend of Japanese and North American work styles. The employees in North America worked fewer hours than the employees in Japan. Around the office, it was common for employees to hear Japanese and English. However, management still had some internal conflict. Japanese advisers were perceived as focusing on the creation of consensus in teams, often leading to slow decision making. North American workers were seen as rushing into projects without enough planning. Feedback was indirect from both Japanese and North American managers.

Samira successfully completed two internship rotations and was about to graduate from college. Her new manager often asked her to follow up with other team members to complete late tasks. As she had been taught in school, she was proactive with team members about completing their work. Samira thought she was great at consistently inviting others to participate in the decision-making process. She always offered her opinion on how things could be done better, and sometimes even initiated tasks to improve processes on her own. Although she saw herself as an emerging take-charge leader, Samira always downplayed her ambitions. In school, she was often stereotyped in negative ways for being an assertive female leader, and she didn't want to be seen in that way at work.

Some of her peers at work advised her that it was important to consider working at a plant near her hometown because it would be closer to her family. However, she was not interested in following that advice. Samira thought it was more exciting to work near a large city or to take a job that involved travel. She didn't think it was appropriate to discuss with her peers her family concerns in relation to her future job needs.

Toward the end of her final internship, Samira received a performance evaluation from a senior manager. Her manager praised her as being very dependable, as planning deadlines well, and as being very competent at her tasks overall. However, he also told her she was increasingly perceived as too pushy, not a team player, and often speaking out of turn. This often irritated her peers.

Samira had never seen herself this way at work and did not understand why she was not seen as aligning with the company's core value of working with others. Good grades and campus leadership activities had gotten her this far, but this evaluation led her to question whether she could work for this company after graduation.

Samira ultimately realized that her workplace was different from the campus atmosphere she was used to. If she wanted to be an emerging leader in the workplace, she had to better adapt to her new environment.

Questions

1. What similarities and differences can you identify between North American and Japanese working styles?

2. In what way did this company reflect the characteristics of other Confucian Asia countries?

3. Why do you think Samira was not seen as a team player?

4. What universal leadership attributes did Samira exhibit?

5. What other suggestions would you have for Samira in this situation?

CASE 15.2

A Special Kind of Financing

Central Bank is a small Midwestern savings and loan institution that manages $3 billion in assets. It competes with 16 other financial institutions for customers; most of those other institutions have substantially larger holdings. To better serve its customers and attract a larger customer base, Central Bank conducted a financial-need survey of the people who lived in the area.

The survey revealed some interesting and culturally relevant information. Muslims represented a sizable minority in the community, making up about 8% of the overall population. However, a review of the bank registry revealed that few Muslims, if any, banked at Central Bank. The results of the survey were puzzling. Given the large numbers of Muslims in the community, the management wondered why there were no Muslim customers at Central Bank.

To answer this question, Central Bank invited a group of local Muslims to meet and discuss their thoughts about financing and how their ideas related to the financial services offered by the bank. The meeting was a real eye-opener for the bank management. The Muslims' ideas about banking were very different from the traditional Western beliefs about banking.

During the discussion, the management learned that the principles of Islam strongly influence the banking attitudes and behaviors of Muslims. The principles of Islamic finance were set forth in the Koran more than 14 centuries ago. For instance, Koranic law forbids paying or receiving interest. These principles stress that money is only a medium of exchange and should not be used to make more money. From the Islamic point of view, the *human element* in a business venture is more important than the money used to finance the venture. Furthermore, according to Islamic finance, the provider of capital and the user of capital should share equally in the risk of a business venture.

These ideas about finance were different from the way Central Bank thought about them. Central Bank was not accustomed to the way Muslims viewed money as a medium of exchange. Having been enlightened through these discussions, the management at Central Bank felt challenged to develop a financing program that was more in line with the attitudes and values of Islamic finance principles.

In order to attract the business of Muslim customers, Central Bank created and began offering two new types of mortgage financing, called *ijara* and *murabaha*. Ijara is a finance plan in which the bank buys a home for a customer and leases it to the customer, who pays rent plus a portion of the property purchase. Murabaha is a transaction in which the bank buys the home and sells it to the customer at an agreed-upon markup, and the customer pays for the home in installments over 15 to 30 years. Both ijara and murabaha are consistent with Islamic beliefs that prohibit Muslims from paying or receiving interest. In these two types of transactions, money is used to purchase something tangible, but money is not used to make money. Central Bank received favorable legal rulings (*fatwas*) from some of the leading Islamic legal scholars in the United States and the world to validate these types of financing.

Central Bank's Islamic finance plans have become quite popular. Although Central Bank has been successful with these plans, it has also met resistance. Some people have expressed strong disapproval of special finance programs specifically geared to the Muslim population. Others are against it because it mixes issues of faith and public finance. However, the resistance has not stopped Central Bank. Central Bank is very proud to be the only bank in the country to serve the needs of the Muslim community in this way.

Questions

1. Why do you think banks in the United States have been slow to offer financing expressly for Muslims?

2. Do you think it is fair to offer one minority group a special banking opportunity?

3. How does ethnocentrism come into play in this case?

4. How does in-group collectivism relate to Central Bank's finance plans?

5. How do you think the other banks in the community will react to Central Bank?

CASE 15.3

Whose Hispanic Center Is It?

River City is a rapidly growing city in the Midwest with a population of 200,000 people, growing at about 5% annually. It is a diverse community with a racial composition that is 65% White, 20% African American, 13% Hispanic, and 2% Native American. The Hispanic population in River City is one of the fastest growing of all segments, growing at about 10% annually.

(Continued)

(Continued)

The Hispanic community is represented by the Hispanic Center, a nonprofit organization that serves the needs of the Hispanic community and broader River City community through a variety of programs and services. A board of directors and an executive director manage the Hispanic Center. Two newly appointed board members have led a transformation of the center, including renovating the physical facilities and shifting the focus of program services. The new members are Mary Davis, who has experience in neighborhood development, and José Reyna, who has experience in city government. The board of directors is made up of 15 people, 10 of whom identify themselves as Hispanic and 5 of whom identify themselves as non-Hispanic.

The Hispanic Center owned an old building that was slated for renovation so the center could have more space for offices and community programs (e.g., educational programming, cultural competence and leadership training, and legal services). The need for the building was validated by what people expressed at a series of community forums. The building was an old fire station that had been mothballed for 15 years, and the Hispanic Center bought the building from River City for $1. Although the fire station needed a lot of renovation, it was located in a perfect place, at the center of the Hispanic community. However, a complete renovation of the building was needed.

To raise funds for the renovation, the board of directors initiated a citywide capital campaign. The goal of the campaign was to raise $1.4 million, the estimated amount for a complete, first-class renovation of the building.

Along with their regular jobs, Mary and José tackled the fund-raising campaign with a full head of steam. In just 6 months, using their wide array of skills, they successfully raised $1.3 million for the project (most of which came from private foundations and corporations). With just $100,000 still to be raised, the leaders and some board members were getting excited about the possibility of the new community center. This excitement was heightened because the renovated building was going to be constructed using the latest green building techniques. These techniques were environmentally sound and incorporated healthful and highly efficient models of construction.

In order to raise the final $100,000, Mary and José proposed a new series of fund-raising initiatives that would focus on smaller donors (e.g., $10, $20, or $30 donors), primarily from the Hispanic community. To kick off a series of events, a formal event at a local hotel was proposed, with tickets costing $75 per person. Just before this event, Mary and José encountered some resistance and found out that their excitement about the renovation needed to be tempered.

During a scheduled board meeting, several members of the board expressed concern with the latest fund-raising efforts. Some board members questioned the wisdom of targeting the fund-raising to the Hispanic community, believing that Hispanic people tended to give to their churches rather than to public not-for-profit organizations. Others questioned the price of the tickets to fund-raising events that was being sought from small donors, $75. These members argued for a smaller admission fee (e.g., $20) that would allow more members of the community to attend. As the discussion proceeded, other board members expressed discontent with the fancy plans for the new green building. They argued that the renovation was becoming a special interest project and a pet project of a few ambitious visionaries.

Board members also started to question the transformation of the Hispanic Center under Mary and José's leadership. Board members expressed frustrations about the new goals of the center and about how things were proceeding. There was a sense that the request for community-based support was unreasonable and in conflict with cultural norms. In the past, the center moved slowly toward change, keeping the focus on one goal: to provide emergency services to the local community. When change came in the past, it was incremental. People were not aggressive, and they did not make trouble.

Under the leadership of Mary and José, there was a perception that the new center and programs were too grand and refined for the community they were intended to serve. The vision for the new center seemed to take things to a new sophisticated level that was not grounded in the common work or the people-oriented values of the center.

Questions

1. How would you describe the strengths and weaknesses of Mary's and José's leadership on this project?

2. Do you see any problem in targeting part of the fund-raising campaign directly toward the Hispanic community?

3. The Latin America leadership profile stresses the importance of team-oriented leadership and deemphasizes individualistic leadership. How does the leadership of Mary and José compare with the Latin America profile?

4. How do Hispanic cultural dimensions help explain the resistance some people felt and expressed toward the renovation project?

5. If you were Mary or José, how would you temper your excitement about renovating the new fire station?

LEADERSHIP INSTRUMENT ———————————————

Culture and leadership are different concepts; when they are measured, they are measured in different ways using different questionnaires. Currently, there are no measures that assess culture and leadership simultaneously, nor are there measures of cultural leadership. There are questionnaires that measure culture, and, as shown throughout the book, there are many measures of leadership.

Perhaps the best-known measure of culture is Hofstede's Culture in the Workplace™ questionnaire. This questionnaire measures a person's cultural preferences on four dimensions: individualism, power distance, certainty, and achievement. People can use their profiles on these dimensions to learn about themselves and to compare themselves with the profiles of people in other cultures.

The Dimensions of Culture questionnaire that follows is an abbreviated version of the original culture questionnaire used in the GLOBE studies. This questionnaire is included in the chapter for illustrative purposes only and should not be used for research. The scores you receive on the questionnaire are individual-level scores rather than societal- or organization-level scores. People who are interested in using the GLOBE scales for research should use the complete questionnaire, as referenced in House et al. (2004).

The Dimensions of Culture questionnaire will help you examine your perceptions about various characteristics of your culture. This questionnaire is not a personality measure (such as the Myers-Briggs instrument) but rather a measure of your attitudes and perceptions about culture.

Dimensions of Culture Questionnaire

Instructions: Using the following scales, circle the number that most accurately reflects your response to each of the 18 statements. There are no right or wrong answers, so provide your immediate impressions. (The items on this questionnaire are adapted from the items used in the GLOBE studies to assess the dimensions of culture, but the GLOBE studies used five items to analyze each of the cultural dimensions.)

Uncertainty Avoidance

1. In this society, orderliness and consistency are stressed, even at the expense of experimentation and innovation.

   Strongly disagree   Strongly agree

      1   2   3   4   5   6   7

2. In this society, societal requirements and instructions are spelled out in detail so citizens know what they are expected to do.

   Strongly disagree   Strongly agree

      1   2   3   4   5   6   7

Power Distance

1. In this society, followers are expected to:

   Question their leaders   Obey their leaders
   when in disagreement   without question

      1   2   3   4   5   6   7

2. In this society, power is:

   Shared throughout   Concentrated at
   the society   the top

      1   2   3   4   5   6   7

Institutional Collectivism

1. In this society, leaders encourage group loyalty even if individual goals suffer.

   Strongly disagree   Strongly agree

      1   2   3   4   5   6   7

2. The economic system in this society is designed to maximize:

   Individual interests   Collective interests

      1   2   3   4   5   6   7

In-Group Collectivism

1. In this society, children take pride in the individual accomplishments of their parents.

Strongly disagree   Strongly agree

| 1 | 2 | 3 | 4 | 5 | 6 | 7 |

2. In this society, parents take pride in the individual accomplishments of their children.

Strongly disagree   Strongly agree

| 1 | 2 | 3 | 4 | 5 | 6 | 7 |

Gender Egalitarianism

1. In this society, boys are encouraged more than girls to attain a higher education.

Strongly disagree   Strongly agree

| 1 | 2 | 3 | 4 | 5 | 6 | 7 |

2. In this society, who is more likely to serve in a position of high office?

Men   Women

| 1 | 2 | 3 | 4 | 5 | 6 | 7 |

Assertiveness

1. In this society, people are generally:

Nonassertive   Assertive

| 1 | 2 | 3 | 4 | 5 | 6 | 7 |

2. In this society, people are generally:

Tender   Tough

| 1 | 2 | 3 | 4 | 5 | 6 | 7 |

Future Orientation

1. In this society the accepted norm is to:

Accept the status quo   Plan for the future

| 1 | 2 | 3 | 4 | 5 | 6 | 7 |

2. In this society, people place more emphasis on:

Solving current problems   Planning for the future

| 1 | 2 | 3 | 4 | 5 | 6 | 7 |

Performance Orientation

1. In this society, students are encouraged to strive for continuously improved performance.

   Strongly disagree   Strongly agree

   | 1 | 2 | 3 | 4 | 5 | 6 | 7 |

2. In this society, people are rewarded for excellent performance.

   Strongly disagree   Strongly agree

   | 1 | 2 | 3 | 4 | 5 | 6 | 7 |

Humane Orientation

1. In this society, people are generally:

   Not at all   Very concerned
   concerned about others   about others

   | 1 | 2 | 3 | 4 | 5 | 6 | 7 |

2. In this society, people are generally:

   Not at all   Very sensitive
   sensitive to others   toward others

   | 1 | 2 | 3 | 4 | 5 | 6 | 7 |

SOURCE: Adapted from House, R. J., Hanges, P. J., Javidan, M., Dorfman, P. W., & Gupta, V. (Eds.), *Culture, Leadership, and Organizations: The GLOBE Study of 62 Societies,* © 2004, SAGE Publications.

Scoring

The Dimensions of Culture questionnaire is designed to measure your perceptions of the different dimensions of your culture. Score the questionnaire by doing the following. First, sum the two responses you gave for each of the items on each of the dimensions. Second, divide the sum of the responses by two. The result is your mean score for the dimension.

Example. If for power distance you circled 3 in response to Question 1 and 4 in response to Question 2, you would score the dimension as follows:

$$3 + 4 = 7$$
$$7 \div 2 = 3.5$$
Power distance mean score = 3.5

When you are finished scoring, you should have nine mean scores. After you have scored the questionnaire, place your mean scores for each of the dimensions in the table in "Scoring Interpretation."

Scoring Interpretation

Your scores on the Dimensions of Culture questionnaire provide data on how you see the culture in which you live and work. Table 15.4 provides information from the GLOBE project about how subjects from different cultures describe the dimensions of those cultures. The table also provides an *overall* mean for how these dimensions were viewed by people from all of the cultures.

By entering your scores in the last column in Table 15.4, you can get a better understanding of how your perception of your own culture compares to that of others. You can also compare your scores to other specific cultures (e.g., Middle East or Latin America). Do you see your culture as more or less egalitarian than others? Do you think your culture emphasizes the future more than others? Do people from other cultures stress performance less or more than your own culture? Like these questions, the table and your scores can be used to bring to the surface the ways in which your culture and the cultures of others are compatible or incompatible with each other. Understanding how your culture relates to other cultures is the first step to improved understanding between you and people from other cultures.

Table 15.4 Cultural Dimensions and Mean Scores for Selected Cultural Clusters

GLOBE Cultural Dimensions	Mean Scores* of Selected Cultural Clusters						
	Anglo	Latin America	Middle East	Southern Asia	Latin Europe	GLOBE Overall	Your Score
Uncertainty avoidance	4.42	3.62	3.91	4.10	4.18	4.16	____
Power distance	na	na	na	na	na	5.17	____
Institutional collectivism	4.46	3.86	4.28	4.35	4.01	4.25	____
In-group collectivism	4.30	5.52	5.58	5.87	4.80	5.13	____
Gender egalitarianism	3.40	3.41	2.95	3.28	3.36	3.37	____
Assertiveness	4.14	4.15	4.14	3.86	3.99	4.14	____
Future orientation	4.08	3.54	3.58	3.98	3.68	3.85	____
Performance orientation	4.37	3.85	3.90	4.33	3.94	4.10	____
Humane orientation	4.20	4.03	4.36	4.71	3.71	4.09	____

SOURCE: Adapted from House, R. J., Hanges, P. J., Javidan, M., Dorfman, P. W., & Gupta, V. (Eds.), *Culture Leadership, and Organizations: The GLOBE Study of 62 Societies,* © 2004, SAGE Publications, Inc. Reprinted with Permission.

*The mean scores in this table represent societal practice scores for selected cultures on each of the nine cultural dimensions. In the GLOBE studies, mean scores were derived from subjects' responses to five questions for each of the dimensions.

na = not available

SUMMARY

Since World War II, there has been a dramatic increase in globalization throughout the world. Globalization has created a need for leaders with greater understanding of cultural differences and increased competencies in cross-cultural communication and practice. This chapter discusses research on culture, its dimensions, and its effects on the leadership process.

Culture is defined as the commonly shared beliefs, values, and norms of a group of people. Two factors that can inhibit cultural awareness are ethnocentrism and prejudice. Ethnocentrism is the human tendency to place one's own group at the center of one's observations of others and the world. It is problematic for leaders because it prevents them from fully understanding the world of others. Similarly, prejudice consists of judgments about others based on fixed attitudes and unsubstantiated data. Prejudice has a negative impact because it is self-oriented and inhibits leaders from seeing the many facets and qualities of others.

In the past 30 years, many studies have focused on identifying various dimensions of culture. The best known is the work of Hofstede (1980, 2001), who identified five major dimensions: power distance, uncertainty avoidance, individualism–collectivism, masculinity–femininity, and long-term–short-term orientation. Expanding on Hofstede's work, House and his colleagues (2004) delineated additional dimensions of culture, including in-group collectivism, institutional collectivism, future orientation, assertiveness, performance orientation, and humane orientation.

The GLOBE studies offer the strongest body of findings to date on culture and leadership. Using established quantitative research methods, GLOBE researchers studied how 17,000 managers from 62 different countries viewed leadership. They analyzed the similarities and differences between regional clusters of cultural groups by grouping countries into 10 distinct clusters: Anglo, Latin Europe, Nordic Europe, Germanic Europe, Eastern Europe, Latin America, the Middle East, Sub-Saharan Africa, Southern Asia, and Confucian Asia. An analysis of each of the 10 clusters revealed the particular dimensions on which each region was strong or weak and unique from other regions.

In addition, GLOBE researchers identified six global leadership behaviors that could be used to characterize how different cultural groups view leadership: charismatic/value-based, team-oriented, participative, humane-oriented, autonomous, and self-protective leadership. Based on these behaviors, researchers created leadership profiles for each of the 10 cultural clusters that delineate the relative importance and desirability different cultures ascribe to different attributes and characteristics of leadership.

One outcome of the GLOBE project was the identification of a list of leadership attributes that were universally endorsed as positive and negative attributes of leadership. From this list, it appears that the universally endorsed portrait of an exceptional leader has a high degree of integrity, charisma, and interpersonal skill. The portrait of an ineffective leader is someone who is asocial, malevolent, self-focused, and autocratic.

The scope of the GLOBE project is its main strength. The findings from this project make a major statement about how cultures around the world view leadership. Other strengths are its quantitative research design, an expanded classification of cultural dimensions, a list of universally accepted leadership attributes, and the contribution it makes to a richer understanding of the leadership process. On the negative side, the GLOBE studies do not provide findings that form a single theory about the way culture relates to leadership. Furthermore, the definitions of the core cultural dimensions are unclear, the conceptualization of leadership used in the studies is limiting, the leadership measures are not exact, and the list of universally endorsed leadership attributes does not account for the various situations in which leaders operate. Regardless of these limitations, the GLOBE studies stand out because they offer so much valuable information about the unique ways culture influences the leadership process.

> Visit the Student Study Site at **www.sagepub.com/northouse6e** for web quizzes, leadership questionnaires, and media links represented by the icons.

NOTES

1. The Czech Republic was excluded from the analysis because of problems in the data.

2. Researchers from the GLOBE studies (Phase 3) are collecting data from 40 CEOs in 20 countries. These findings may address how the behaviors of leaders (what they do) conform to the beliefs about leadership in various cultures.

REFERENCES

Adler, N. J., & Bartholomew, S. (1992). Managing globally competent people. *Academy of Management Executive, 6,* 52–65.

Bing, J. W. (2004). Hofstede's consequences: The impact of his work on consulting and business practices. *Academy of Management Executive, 18*(1), 80–87.

Dorfman, P. W., Hanges, P. J., & Brodbeck, F. C. (2004). Leadership and cultural variation: The identification of culturally endorsed leadership profiles. In R. J. House, P. J. Hanges, M. Javidan, P. W. Dorfman, V. Gupta, & Associates (Eds.), *Culture, leadership, and organizations: The GLOBE study of 62 societies* (pp. 669–722). Thousand Oaks, CA: Sage.

Gudykunst, W. B., & Kim, Y. Y. (1997). *Communicating with strangers: An approach to intercultural communication* (3rd ed.). New York: McGraw-Hill.

Gudykunst, W. B., & Ting-Toomey, S. (1988). *Culture and interpersonal communication.* Newbury Park, CA: Sage.

Hall, E. T. (1976). *Beyond culture.* New York: Doubleday.

Hofstede, G. (1980). *Culture's consequences: International differences in work-related values.* Beverly Hills, CA: Sage.

Hofstede, G. (2001). *Culture's consequences: Comparing values, behaviors, institutions, and organizations across nations.* Thousand Oaks, CA: Sage.

House, R. J., Hanges, P. J., Javidan, M., Dorfman, P. W., & Gupta, V. (Eds.). (2004). *Culture, leadership, and organizations: The GLOBE study of 62 societies.* Thousand Oaks, CA: Sage.

House, R. J., & Javidan, M. (2004). Overview of GLOBE. In R. J. House, P. J. Hanges, M. Javidan, P. W. Dorfman, V. Gupta, & Associates (Eds.), *Culture, leadership, and organizations: The GLOBE study of 62 societies* (pp. 9–28). Thousand Oaks, CA: Sage.

Kluckhohn, R. R., & Strodtbeck, F. L. (1961). *Variations in value orientations.* New York: HarperCollins.

Lord, R., & Maher, K. J. (1991). *Leadership and information processing: Linking perceptions and performance.* Boston: Unwin-Everyman.

McClelland, D. C. (1961). *The achieving society.* Princeton, NJ: Van Nostrand.

Ponterotto, J. G., & Pedersen, P. B. (1993). *Preventing prejudice: A guide for counselors and educators.* Newbury Park, CA: Sage.

Porter, R. E., & Samovar, L. A. (1997). An introduction to intercultural communication. In L. A. Samovar & R. E. Porter (Eds.), *Intercultural communication: A reader* (8th ed., pp. 5–26). Belmont, CA: Wadsworth.

Ronen, S., & Shenkar, O. (1985). Clustering countries on attitudinal dimensions: A review and synthesis. *Academy of Management Review, 10*(3), 435–454.

Ting-Toomey, S. (1999). *Communicating across cultures.* New York: Guilford.

Triandis, H. C. (1995). *Individualism and collectivism.* Boulder, CO: Westview.

Trompenaars, F. (1994). *Riding the waves of culture.* New York: Irwin.

16

Leadership Ethics

DESCRIPTION

This chapter is different from many of the other chapters in this book. Most of the other chapters focus on one unified leadership theory or approach (e.g., trait approach, path–goal theory, or transformational leadership), whereas this chapter is multifaceted and presents a broad set of ethical viewpoints. The chapter is not intended as an "ethical leadership theory," but rather as a guide to some of the ethical issues that arise in leadership situations.

Probably as long ago as our cave-dwelling days, human beings have been concerned with the ethics of our leaders. Our history books are replete with descriptions of good kings and bad kings, great empires and evil empires, and strong presidents and weak presidents. But despite a wealth of biographical accounts of great leaders and their morals, very little research has been published on the theoretical foundations of leadership ethics. There have been many studies on business ethics in general since the early 1970s, but these studies have been only tangentially related to leadership ethics. Even in the literature of management, written primarily for practitioners, there are very few books on leadership ethics. This suggests that theoretical formulations in this area are still in their infancy.

One of the earliest writings that specifically focused on leadership ethics appeared as recently as 1996. It was a set of working papers generated from a small group of leadership scholars, brought together by the W. K. Kellogg Foundation. These scholars examined how leadership theory and practice could be used to build a more caring and just society. The ideas of the Kellogg group are now published in a volume titled *Ethics, the Heart of Leadership* (Ciulla, 1998).

Interest in the nature of ethical leadership has continued to grow, particularly because of the many recent scandals in corporate America and the political realm. On the academic front, there has also been a strong interest in exploring the nature of ethical leadership (see Aronson, 2001; Ciulla, 2001, 2003; Johnson, 2011; Kanungo, 2001; Price, 2008; Trevino, Brown, & Hartman, 2003).

Ethics Defined

From the perspective of Western tradition, the development of ethical theory dates back to Plato (427–347 B.C.) and Aristotle (384–322 B.C.). The word *ethics* has its roots in the Greek word *ethos*, which translates to customs, conduct, or character. Ethics is concerned with the kinds of values and morals an individual or a society finds desirable or appropriate. Furthermore, ethics is concerned with the virtuousness of individuals and their motives. Ethical theory provides a system of rules or principles that guide us in making decisions about what is right or wrong and good or bad in a particular situation. It provides a basis for understanding what it means to be a morally decent human being.

In regard to leadership, ethics has to do with what leaders do and who leaders are. It is concerned with the nature of leaders' behavior, and with their virtuousness. In any decision-making situation, ethical issues are either implicitly or explicitly involved. The choices leaders make and how they respond in a given circumstance are informed and directed by their ethics.

Ethical Theories

For the purposes of studying ethics and leadership, ethical theories can be thought of as falling within two broad domains: theories about leaders' *conduct* and theories about leaders' *character* (Table 16.1). Stated another way, ethical theories when applied to leadership are about both the actions of leaders and who they are as people. Throughout the chapter, our discussions about ethics and leadership will always fall within one of these two domains: conduct or character.

Ethical theories that deal with the conduct of leaders are in turn divided into two kinds: theories that stress the *consequences* of leaders' actions and those that emphasize the *duty* or *rules* governing leaders' actions (see Table 16.1). Teleological theories, from the Greek word *telos*,

16.1 Practical Ethical Theory

Table 16.1 Domains of Ethical Theories

Conduct	Character
Consequences (telelogical theories)	Virtue-based theories
• Ethical egoism	
• Utilitarianism	
Duty (deontological theories)	

meaning "ends" or "purposes," try to answer questions about right and wrong by focusing on whether a person's conduct will produce desirable consequences. From the teleological perspective, the question "What is right?" is answered by looking at results or outcomes. In effect, the consequences of an individual's actions determine the goodness or badness of a particular behavior.

In assessing consequences, there are three different approaches to making decisions regarding moral conduct (Figure 16.1): *ethical egoism, utilitarianism,* and *altruism.* Ethical egoism states that a person should act so as to create the greatest good for herself or himself. A leader with this orientation would take a job or career that he or she selfishly enjoys (Avolio & Locke, 2002). Self-interest is an ethical stance closely related to transactional leadership theories (Bass & Steidlmeier, 1999). Ethical egoism is common in some business contexts in which a company and its employees make decisions to achieve its goal of maximizing profits. For example, a midlevel, upward-aspiring manager who wants her team to be the best in the company could be described as acting out of ethical egoism.

A second teleological approach, *utilitarianism,* states that we should behave so as to create the greatest good for the greatest number. From this viewpoint, the morally correct action is the action that maximizes social benefits while minimizing social costs (Schumann, 2001). When the U.S. government allocates a large part of the federal budget for preventive health care rather than for catastrophic illnesses, it is acting from a utilitarian perspective, putting money where it will have the best result for the largest number of citizens.

Closely related to utilitarianism, and opposite of ethical egoism, is a third teleological approach, *altruism.* Altruism is an approach that suggests that actions are moral if their primary purpose is to promote the best interests of others. From this perspective, a leader may be called on to act in the

Figure 16.1   Ethical Theories Based on Self-Interest Versus Interest
for Others

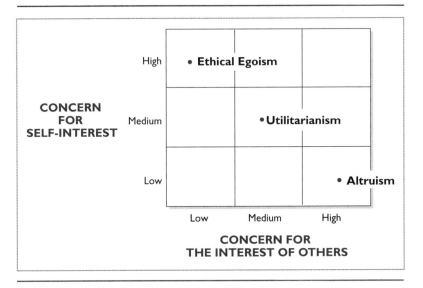

interests of others, even when it runs contrary to his or her own self-interests (Bowie, 1991). Authentic transformational leadership is based on altruistic principles (Bass & Steidlmeier, 1999; Kanungo & Mendonca, 1996). The strongest example of altruist ethics can be found in the work of Mother Teresa, who devoted her life to helping the poor.

Quite different from looking at which actions will produce which outcomes, deontological theory is derived from the Greek word *deos*, which means "duty." Whether a given action is ethical rests not only with its consequences (teleological), but also with whether the action itself is good. Telling the truth, keeping promises, being fair, and respecting others are all examples of actions that are inherently good, independent of the consequences. The deontological perspective focuses on the actions of the leader and his or her moral obligations and responsibilities to do the right thing. A leader's actions are moral if the leader has a moral right to do them, if the actions do not infringe on others' rights, and if the actions further the moral rights of others (Schumann, 2001).

In the late 1990s, the president of the United States, Bill Clinton, was brought before Congress for misrepresenting under oath an affair he had maintained with a White House intern. For his actions, he was impeached by the U.S. House of Representatives, but then was acquitted by the U.S. Senate. At one point during the long ordeal, the president appeared on national television and, in what is now a famous speech, declared his innocence. Because subsequent hearings provided information that suggested that he may have lied during this television speech, many Americans felt President Clinton had violated his duty and responsibility (as a person, leader, and president) to tell the truth. From a deontological perspective, it could be said that he failed his ethical responsibility to do the right thing—to tell the truth.

Whereas teleological and deontological theories approach ethics by looking at the behavior or conduct of a leader, a second set of theories approaches ethics from the viewpoint of a leader's character (see Table 16.1). These theories are called virtue-based theories; they focus on who leaders are as people. In this perspective, virtues are rooted in the heart of the individual and in the individual's disposition (Pojman, 1995). Furthermore, it is believed that virtues and moral abilities are not innate but can be acquired and learned through practice. People can be taught by their families and communities to be morally appropriate human beings.

With their origin traced back in the Western tradition to the ancient Greeks and the works of Plato and Aristotle, virtue theories are experiencing a resurgence in popularity. The Greek term associated with these theories is *aretaic*, which means "excellence" or "virtue." Consistent with Aristotle, current advocates of virtue-based theory stress that more attention should be given to the development and training of moral values (Velasquez, 1992). Rather than telling people what to *do*, attention should be directed toward telling people what to *be*, or helping them to become more virtuous.

What, then, are the virtues of an ethical person? There are many, all of which seem to be important. Based on the writings of Aristotle, a moral person demonstrates the virtues of courage, temperance, generosity, self-control, honesty, sociability, modesty, fairness, and justice (Velasquez, 1992). For Aristotle, virtues allowed people to live well in communities. Applying ethics to leadership and management, Velasquez has suggested that managers should develop virtues such as perseverance, public-spiritedness, integrity, truthfulness, fidelity, benevolence, and humility.

In essence, virtue-based ethics is about being and becoming a good, worthy human being. Although people can learn and develop good values, this theory maintains that virtues are present in one's disposition. When practiced over time, from youth to adulthood, good values become habitual, and part of the people themselves. By telling the truth, people become truthful; by giving to the poor, people become benevolent; by being fair to others, people become just. Our virtues are derived from our actions, and our actions manifest our virtues (Frankena, 1973; Pojman, 1995).

Centrality of Ethics to Leadership

As discussed in Chapter 1, leadership is a process whereby the leader influences others to reach a common goal. The *influence* dimension of leadership requires the leader to have an impact on the lives of those being led. To make a change in other people carries with it an enormous ethical burden and responsibility. Because leaders usually have more power and control than followers, they also have more responsibility to be sensitive to how their leadership affects followers' lives.

Whether in group work, organizational pursuits, or community projects, leaders engage subordinates and utilize them in their efforts to reach common goals. In all these situations, leaders have the ethical responsibility to treat followers with dignity and respect—as human beings with unique identities. This "respect for people" demands that leaders be sensitive to followers' own interests, needs, and conscientious concerns (Beauchamp & Bowie, 1988). Although all of us have an ethical responsibility to treat other people as unique human beings, leaders have a special responsibility, because the nature of their leadership puts them in a special position in which they have a greater opportunity to influence others in significant ways.

Ethics is central to leadership, and leaders help to establish and reinforce organizational values. Every leader has a distinct philosophy and point of view. "All leaders have an agenda, a series of beliefs, proposals, values, ideas, and issues that they wish to 'put on the table'" (Gini, 1998, p. 36). The values promoted by the leader have a significant impact on the values exhibited by the organization (see Carlson & Perrewe, 1995; Schminke, Ambrose, & Noel, 1997; Trevino, 1986). Again, because of their influence, leaders play a major role in establishing the ethical climate of their organizations.

In short, ethics is central to leadership because of the nature of the process of influence, the need to engage followers in accomplishing mutual goals, and the impact leaders have on the organization's values.

16.1 Consequences

The following section provides a discussion of some of the work of prominent leadership scholars who have addressed issues related to ethics and leadership. Although many additional viewpoints exist, those presented are representative of the predominant thinking in the area of ethics and leadership today.

Heifetz's Perspective on Ethical Leadership

Based on his work as a psychiatrist and his observations and analysis of many world leaders (e.g., President Lyndon Johnson, Mohandas Gandhi, and Margaret Sanger), Ronald Heifetz (1994) has formulated a unique approach to ethical leadership. His approach emphasizes how leaders help followers to confront conflict and to address conflict by effecting changes. Heifetz's perspective is related to ethical leadership because it deals with values: the values of workers and the values of the organizations and communities in which they work. According to Heifetz, leadership involves the use of authority to help followers deal with the conflicting values that emerge in rapidly changing work environments and social cultures. It is an ethical perspective because it speaks directly to the values of workers.

For Heifetz (1994), leaders must use authority to mobilize people to face tough issues. The leader provides a "holding environment" in which there is trust, nurturance, and empathy. In a supportive context, followers can feel safe to confront hard problems. Specifically, leaders use authority to get people to pay attention to the issues, to act as a reality test regarding information, to manage and frame issues, to orchestrate conflicting perspectives, and to facilitate decision making (Heifetz, 1994, p. 113). The leader's duties are to assist the follower in struggling with change and personal growth.

Burns's Perspective on Ethical Leadership

As discussed in Chapter 9, Burns's theory of transformational leadership places a strong emphasis on followers' needs, values, and morals. Transformational leadership involves attempts by leaders to move followers to higher standards of moral responsibility. This emphasis sets transformational leadership apart from most other approaches to leadership because it clearly states that leadership has a moral dimension (see Bass & Steidlmeier, 1999).

Similar to that of Heifetz, Burns's (1978) perspective argues that it is important for leaders to engage themselves with followers and help them

▶ **16.1** Ethical Norms

in their personal struggles regarding conflicting values. The resulting connection raises the level of morality in both the leader and the follower.

The origins of Burns's position on leadership ethics are rooted in the works of such writers as Abraham Maslow, Milton Rokeach, and Lawrence Kohlberg (Ciulla, 1998). The influence of these writers can be seen in how Burns emphasizes the leader's role in attending to the personal motivations and moral development of the follower. For Burns, it is the responsibility of the leader to help followers assess their own values and needs in order to raise them to a higher level of functioning, to a level that will stress values such as liberty, justice, and equality (Ciulla, 1998).

Burns's position on leadership as a morally uplifting process has not been without its critics. It has raised many questions: How do you choose what a better set of moral values is? Who is to say that some decisions represent higher moral ground than others? If leadership, by definition, entails raising individual moral functioning, does this mean that the leadership of corrupt leaders is not actually leadership? Notwithstanding these very legitimate questions, Burns's perspective is unique in that it makes ethics the central characteristic of the leadership process. His writing has placed ethics at the forefront of scholarly discussions of what leadership means and how leadership should be carried out.

Principles of Ethical Leadership

In this section, we turn to a discussion of five principles of ethical leadership, the origins of which can be traced back to Aristotle. The importance of these principles has been discussed in a variety of disciplines, including biomedical ethics (Beauchamp & Childress, 1994), business ethics (Beauchamp & Bowie, 1988), counseling psychology (Kitchener, 1984), and leadership education (Komives, Lucas, & McMahon, 1998), to name a few. Although not inclusive, these principles provide a foundation for the development of sound ethical leadership: *respect, service, justice, honesty,* and *community* (Figure 16.2).

Ethical Leaders Respect Others

Philosopher Immanuel Kant (1724–1804) argued that it is our duty to treat others with respect. To do so means always to treat others as ends in themselves and never as means to ends. As Beauchamp and Bowie

16.2 Teaching Ethical Leadership

Figure 16.2   Principles of Ethical Leadership

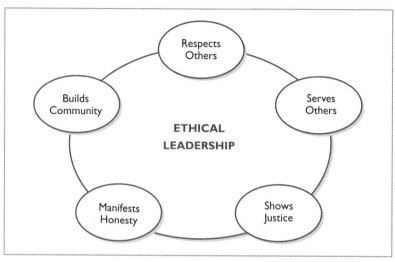

(1988, p. 37) pointed out, "Persons must be treated as having their own autonomously established goals and must never be treated purely as the means to another's personal goals." These writers then suggested that treating others as ends rather than as means requires that we treat other people's decisions and values with respect: Failing to do so would signify that we were treating them as a means to our own ends.

Leaders who respect others also allow them to be themselves, with creative wants and desires. They approach other people with a sense of their unconditional worth and valuable individual differences (Kitchener, 1984). Respect includes giving credence to others' ideas and confirming them as human beings. At times, it may require that leaders defer to others. As Burns (1978) suggested, leaders should nurture followers in becoming aware of their own needs, values, and purposes, and assist followers in integrating these with the leader's needs, values, and purposes.

Respect for others is a complex ethic that is similar to but goes deeper than the kind of respect that parents teach little children. Respect means that a leader listens closely to subordinates, is empathic, and is tolerant of opposing points of view. It means treating subordinates in ways that confirm their beliefs, attitudes, and values. When a leader exhibits respect to

16.1 Ethical Role of Management

subordinates, subordinates can feel competent about their work. In short, leaders who show respect treat others as worthy human beings.

Ethical Leaders Serve Others

Earlier in this chapter, we contrasted two ethical theories, one based on a concern for self (ethical egoism) and another based on the interests of others (ethical altruism). The service principle clearly is an example of altruism. Leaders who serve are altruistic: They place their followers' welfare foremost in their plans. In the workplace, altruistic service behavior can be observed in activities such as mentoring, empowerment behaviors, team building, and citizenship behaviors, to name a few (Kanungo & Mendonca, 1996).

The leader's ethical responsibility to serve others is very similar to the ethical principle in health care of beneficence. Beneficence is derived from the Hippocratic tradition, which holds that health professionals ought to make choices that benefit patients. In a general way, beneficence asserts that providers have a duty to help others pursue their own legitimate interests and goals (Beauchamp & Childress, 1994). Like health professionals, ethical leaders have a responsibility to attend to others, be of service to them, and make decisions pertaining to them that are beneficial and not harmful to their welfare.

In the past decade, the service principle has received a great deal of emphasis in the leadership literature. It is clearly evident in the writings of Block (1993), Covey (1990), De Pree (1989), Gilligan (1982), and Kouzes and Posner (1995), all of whom maintained that attending to others is the primary building block of moral leadership. Further emphasis on service can be observed in the work of Senge (1990) in his well-recognized writing on learning organizations. Senge contended that one of the important tasks of leaders in learning organizations is to be the steward (servant) of the vision within the organization. Being a steward means clarifying and nurturing a vision that is greater than oneself. This means not being self-centered, but rather integrating one's self or vision with that of others in the organization. Effective leaders see their own personal vision as an important part of something larger than themselves—a part of the organization and the community at large.

The idea of leaders serving others was more deeply explored by Robert Greenleaf (1970, 1977), who developed the *servant leadership* approach. Servant leadership, which is explored in depth in Chapter 10, has strong

16.2 Ethical School Leadership

altruistic ethical overtones in how it emphasizes that leaders should be attentive to the concerns of their followers and should take care of them and nurture them. In addition, Greenleaf argues that the servant leader has a social responsibility to be concerned with the have-nots and should strive to remove inequalities and social injustices. Greenleaf places a great deal of emphasis on listening, empathy, and unconditional acceptance of others.

In short, whether it is Greenleaf's notion of waiting on the have-nots or Senge's notion of giving oneself to a larger purpose, the idea behind service is contributing to the greater good of others. Recently, the idea of serving the "greater good" has found an unusual following in the business world. In 2009, 20% of the graduating class of the Harvard Business School, considered to be one of the premier schools producing today's business leaders, took an oath pledging that they will act responsibly and ethically, and refrain from advancing their own ambitions at the expense of others. Similarly, Columbia Business School requires all students to pledge to an honor code requiring they adhere to truth, integrity, and respect (Wayne, 2009). In practicing the principle of service, these and other ethical leaders must be willing to be follower centered, must place others' interests foremost in their work, and must act in ways that will benefit others.

Ethical Leaders Are Just

Ethical leaders are concerned about issues of fairness and justice. They make it a top priority to treat all of their subordinates in an equal manner. Justice demands that leaders place issues of fairness at the center of their decision making. As a rule, no one should receive special treatment or special consideration except when his or her particular situation demands it. When individuals are treated differently, the grounds for different treatment must be clear and reasonable, and must be based on moral values.

For example, many of us can remember being involved with some type of athletic team when we were growing up. The coaches we liked were those we thought were fair with us. No matter what, we did not want the coach to treat anyone differently from the rest. When someone came late to practice with a poor excuse, we wanted that person disciplined just as we would have been disciplined. If a player had a personal problem and needed a break, we wanted the coach to give it, just as we would have been given a break. Without question, the good coaches were those who never had favorites and who made a point of playing everyone on the team. In essence, what we wanted was that our coach be fair and just.

16.2 Ethics in Management

When resources and rewards or punishments are distributed to employees, the leader plays a major role. The rules that are used and how they are applied say a great deal about whether the leader is concerned about justice and how he or she approaches issues of fairness.

Rawls (1971) stated that a concern with issues of fairness is necessary for all people who are cooperating together to promote their common interests. It is similar to the ethic of reciprocity, otherwise known as the Golden Rule—"Do unto others as you would have them do unto you"—variations of which have appeared in many different cultures throughout the ages. If we expect fairness from others in how they treat us, then we should treat others fairly in our dealings with them. Issues of fairness become problematic because there is always a limit on goods and resources, and there is often competition for the limited things available. Because of the real or perceived scarcity of resources, conflicts often occur between individuals about fair methods of distribution. It is important for leaders to clearly establish the rules for distributing rewards. The nature of these rules says a lot about the ethical underpinnings of the leader and the organization.

Beauchamp and Bowie (1988) outlined several of the common principles that serve as guides for leaders in distributing the benefits and burdens fairly in an organization (Table 16.2). Although not inclusive, these principles point to the reasoning behind why leaders choose to distribute things as they do in organizations. In a given situation, a leader may use a single principle or a combination of several principles in treating subordinates.

To illustrate the principles described in Table 16.2, consider the following hypothetical example: You are the owner of a small trucking company that employs 50 drivers. You have just opened a new route, and it

Table 16.2 Principles of Distributive Justice

These principles are applied in different situations.

To each person

- An equal share or opportunity
- According to individual need
- According to that person's rights
- According to individual effort
- According to societal contribution
- According to merit or performance

promises to be one that pays well and has an ideal schedule. Only one driver can be assigned to the route, but seven drivers have applied for it. Each driver wants an *equal opportunity* to get the route. One of the drivers recently lost his wife to breast cancer and is struggling to care for three young children (*individual need*). Two of the drivers are minorities, and one of them feels strongly that he has a *right* to the job. One of the drivers has logged more driving hours for three consecutive years, and she feels her *effort* makes her the logical candidate for the new route. One of the drivers serves on the National Safety Board and has a 20-year accident-free driving record (*societal contribution*). Two drivers have been with the company since its inception, and their *performance* has been meritorious year after year.

As the owner of the company, your challenge is to assign the new route in a fair way. Although many other factors could influence your decision (e.g., seniority, wage rate, or employee health), the principles described in Table 16.2 provide guidelines for deciding who is to get the new route.

Ethical Leaders Are Honest

When we were children, grown-ups often told us we must "never tell a lie." To be good meant we must be truthful. For leaders the lesson is the same: To be a good leader, one must be honest.

The importance of being honest can be understood more clearly when we consider the opposite of honesty: dishonesty (see Jaksa & Pritchard, 1988). Dishonesty is a form of lying, a way of misrepresenting reality. Dishonesty may bring with it many objectionable outcomes; foremost among those outcomes is the distrust it creates. When leaders are not honest, others come to see them as undependable and unreliable. People lose faith in what leaders say and stand for, and their respect for leaders is diminished. As a result, the leader's impact is compromised because others no longer trust and believe in the leader.

When we relate to others, dishonesty also has a negative impact. It puts a strain on how people are connected to each other. When we lie to others, we are in essence saying that we are willing to manipulate the relationship on our own terms. We are saying that we do not trust the other person in the relationship to be able to deal with information we have. In reality, we are putting ourselves ahead of the relationship by saying that we know what is best for the relationship. The long-term effect of this type of behavior is

 16.3 Developing Leadership Character

that it weakens relationships. Even when used with good intentions, dishonesty contributes to the breakdown of relationships.

But being honest is not just about telling the truth. It has to do with being open with others and representing reality as fully and completely as possible. This is not an easy task, however, because there are times when telling the complete truth can be destructive or counterproductive. The challenge for leaders is to strike a balance between being open and candid while monitoring what is appropriate to disclose in a particular situation. Many times, there are organizational constraints that prevent leaders from disclosing information to followers. It is important for leaders to be authentic, but it is also essential that they be sensitive to the attitudes and feelings of others. Honest leadership involves a wide set of behaviors.

Dalla Costa (1998) made the point clearly in his book, *The Ethical Imperative*, that being honest means more than not deceiving. For leaders in organizations, being honest means, "Do not promise what you can't deliver, do not misrepresent, do not hide behind spin-doctored evasions, do not suppress obligations, do not evade accountability, do not accept that the 'survival of the fittest' pressures of business release any of us from the responsibility to respect another's dignity and humanity" (p. 164). In addition, Dalla Costa suggested that it is imperative that organizations recognize and acknowledge the necessity of honesty and reward honest behavior within the organization.

Ethical Leaders Build Community

In Chapter 1, we defined leadership as a process whereby an individual influences a group of individuals to achieve a common goal. This definition has a clear ethical dimension because it refers to a *common* goal. A common goal requires that the leader and followers agree on the direction to be taken by the group. Leaders need to take into account their own and followers' purposes while working toward goals that are suitable for both of them. This factor, concern for others, is the distinctive feature that delineates *authentic* transformational leaders from *pseudo*transformational leaders (Bass & Steidlmeier, 1999). Concern for the common good means that leaders cannot impose their will on others. They need to search for goals that are compatible with everyone.

Burns (1978) placed this idea at the center of his theory on transformational leadership. A transformational leader tries to move the group toward a common good that is beneficial for both the leaders and the followers. In moving toward mutual goals, both the leader and the followers are changed. It is this feature that makes Burns's theory unique. For Burns, leadership has to be grounded in the leader–follower relationship. It cannot be controlled by the leader, such as Hitler's influence in Germany. Hitler coerced people to meet his own agenda and followed goals that did not advance the goodness of humankind.

An ethical leader takes into account the purposes of everyone involved in the group and is attentive to the interests of the community and the culture. Such a leader demonstrates an ethic of caring toward others (Gilligan, 1982) and does not force others or ignore the intentions of others (Bass & Steidlmeier, 1999).

Rost (1991) went a step farther and suggested that ethical leadership demands attention to a civic virtue. By this, he meant that leaders and followers need to attend to more than their own mutually determined goals. They need to attend to the *community's* goals and purpose. As Burns (1978, p. 429) wrote, transformational leaders and followers begin to reach out to wider social collectivities and seek to establish higher and broader moral purposes. Similarly, Greenleaf (1970) argued that building community was a main characteristic of servant leadership. All of our individual and group goals are bound up in the common good and public interest. We need to pay attention to how the changes proposed by a leader and followers will affect the larger organization, the community, and society. An ethical leader is concerned with the common good, in the broadest sense.

STRENGTHS

This chapter discusses a broad set of ideas regarding ethics and leadership. This general field of study has several strengths. First, it provides a body of timely research on ethical issues. There is a high demand for moral leadership in our society today. Beginning with the Nixon administration in the 1970s and continuing through George W. Bush's administration in the last decade, people have been insisting on higher levels of moral responsibility from their leaders. At a time when there seems to be a vacuum in ethical leadership, this research offers us some direction on how to think about and practice ethical leadership.

Second, this body of research suggests that ethics ought to be considered as an integral part of the broader domain of leadership. Except for

 **16.3** Ethical Issues in Nursing    **16.2** Ethical Dilemmas

servant, transformational, and authentic leadership, none of the other leadership theories discussed in this book includes ethics as a dimension of the leadership process. This chapter suggests that leadership is not an amoral phenomenon. Leadership is a process of influencing others; it has a moral dimension that distinguishes it from other types of influence, such as coercion or despotic control. Leadership involves values, including showing respect for followers, being fair to others, and building community. It is not a process that we can demonstrate without showing our values. When we influence, we have an effect on others, which means we need to pay attention to our values and our ethics.

Third, this body of research highlights several principles that are important to the development of ethical leadership. The virtues discussed in this research have been around for more than 2,000 years. They are reviewed in this chapter because of their significance for today's leaders.

CRITICISMS

Although the area of ethics and leadership has many strengths, it also has some weaknesses. First, it is an area of research in its early stage of development, and therefore lacks a strong body of traditional research findings to substantiate it. As was pointed out at the beginning of the chapter, very little research has been published on the theoretical foundations of leadership ethics. Although many studies have been published on business ethics, these studies have not been directly related to ethical leadership. The dearth of research on leadership ethics makes speculation about the nature of ethical leadership difficult. Until more research studies have been conducted that deal directly with the ethical dimensions of leadership, theoretical formulations about the process will remain tentative.

Another criticism is that leadership ethics today relies primarily on the writings of just a few people who have written essays and texts that are strongly influenced by their personal opinions about the nature of leadership ethics and their view of the world. Although these writings, such as Heifetz's and Burns's, have stood the test of time, they have not been tested using traditional quantitative or qualitative research methods. They are primarily descriptive and anecdotal. Therefore, leadership ethics lacks the traditional kind of empirical support that usually accompanies accepted theories of human behavior.

APPLICATION

Although issues of morality and leadership are discussed more often in society today, these discussions have not resulted in a large number of programs in training and development designed to teach ethical leadership. Many new programs are oriented toward helping managers become more effective at work and in life in general, but these programs do not directly target the area of ethics and leadership.

Yet the ethics and leadership research in this chapter can be applied to people at all levels of organizations and in all walks of life. At a very minimum, it is crucial to state that *leadership involves values*, and one cannot be a leader without being aware of and concerned about one's own values. Because leadership has a moral dimension, being a leader demands awareness on our part of the way our ethics defines our leadership.

Managers and leaders can use the information in this research to better understand themselves and strengthen their own leadership. Ethical theories can remind leaders to ask themselves, "What is the right and fair thing to do?" or "What would a good person do?" Leaders can use the ethical principles described in this research as benchmarks for their own behavior. Do I show respect to others? Do I act with a generous spirit? Do I show honesty and faithfulness to others? Do I serve the community? Finally, we can learn from the overriding theme in this research that the leader–follower relationship is central to ethical leadership. To be an ethical leader, we must be sensitive to the needs of others, treat others in ways that are just, and care for others.

—————————— CASE STUDIES ——————————

The following section contains three case studies (Cases 16.1, 16.2, and 16.3) based on actual situations in which ethical leadership was needed. Case 16.1 describes the owner of a small business and the ethical problems he faces during a difficult period of consolidation. Case 16.2 is concerned with one manufacturing company's unique approach to safety standards. Case 16.3 deals with the ethical issues surrounding how a human resource service company established the pricing for its services. At the end of each case, there are questions that point to the intricacies and complexities of practicing ethical leadership.

📖 **16.3** Ethical Case Study

CASE 16.1

A Struggling Company Without Enough Cash

Joe Woodman bought a small, struggling computer company. After several difficult years, revenues started to grow, and it seemed that profits were growing as well, at least according to the financial statements. In reality, though, the business did not have enough cash to function.

The company's key stakeholders, such as the bank, vendors, and investors, were applying pressure on Joe to improve earnings and cash flow. They threatened to take over the business if major changes were not made. About the same time, making matters worse, Joe was notified that several contracts, constituting about 25% of his top-line revenues, would be lost to the competition.

Joe responded by laying off employees, freezing wages, and closing several marginal operations, but these efforts were not enough. Joe was still badly in need of more cash and professional management. To remain viable, he had three options:

- He could negotiate a "capital for control" type of exchange with the investor and the banks. If he did this, the banks could help recruit new talent and offer interim financing to support the company while restructuring occurred. On the downside, with this option his status in the organization would change significantly: Instead of being the owner, Joe would become more of a senior manager.

- Joe could maintain control and hire turnaround management, explaining to new managers that the company was in a critical turnaround phase and that the organization's future depended on their ability to generate credibility and positive performance within a year. He would have to disclose the wage freezes of the past 2 years and explain that he could not initially offer competitive salaries or certain traditional benefits. If he took this option, Joe would have difficulty recruiting skilled managers because they would not want to come into a situation with failing operations, no operating cash, and the prospects of a dramatically dwindling revenue base. If it succeeded, this option would allow Joe to keep control and save his reputation.

- Joe could remain in control and hire turnaround management without fully explaining the serious situation. He might say that the company is one of the fastest-growing companies in the industry, and that it just completed an operational turnaround, had regained profitability, and was upgrading staff to take the company to the next level. He could support this positive picture by representing pro forma financial information as though it were actual. This approach probably would be successful initially in gaining new qualified staff, but the new managers might join only to leave soon afterward. They would probably not develop into loyal, long-term employees because of Joe's dishonesty. This option would give Joe the opportunity to maintain control and keep all his workers employed.

Questions

1. Of the three options available to Joe, which is the most ethical?

2. How does egoism come into play in this case? In which of the three options is altruism most apparent?

3. Which option would provide the greatest good for the greatest number? From an ethical perspective, what is Joe's duty in this situation?

4. What pressures does Joe face regarding honesty and telling the truth about his situation?

CASE 16.2

How Safe Is Safe?

Perfect Plastics Incorporated (PPI) is a small injection molding plastics company that employs 50 people. The company is 10 years old, has a healthy balance sheet, and does about $4 million a year in sales. The company has a good safety record, and the insurance company that has PPI's liability policy has not had to pay any claims to employees for several years. There have been no major injuries of any kind since the company began.

Tom Griffin, the owner, takes great pride in the interior design and working conditions at PPI. He describes the interior of the plant as being like a hospital compared with his competitors. Order, efficiency, and cleanliness are top priorities at PPI. It is a remarkably well-organized manufacturing company.

(Continued)

(Continued)

PPI has a unique approach to guaranteeing safe working conditions. Each year, management brings in outside consultants from the insurance industry and the Occupational Safety and Health Administration (OSHA) to audit the plant for unsafe conditions. Each year, the inspections reveal a variety of concerns, which are then addressed through new equipment, repairs, and changed work-flow designs. Although the inspectors continue to find opportunities for improvement, the overall safety improves each year.

The attorneys for PPI are very opposed to the company's approach to safety. The lawyers are vehemently against the procedure of having outside auditors. If a lawsuit were to be brought against PPI, the attorneys argue that any previous issues could be used as evidence of a historical pattern and knowledge of unsafe conditions. In effect, the audits that PPI conducts voluntarily could be used by plaintiffs to strengthen a case against the company.

The president and management recognize the potential downside of outside audits, but they point out that the periodic reviews are critical to the ongoing improvement of the safety of everyone in the plant. The purpose of the audits is to make the shop a secure place, and that is what has occurred. Management also points out that PPI employees have responded positively to the audits and to the changes that result.

Questions

1. As a company, would you describe PPI as having an identifiable philosophy of moral values? How do its policies contribute to this philosophy?

2. Which ethical perspective best describes PPI's approach to safety issues? Would you say PPI takes a utilitarian-, duty-, or virtue-based approach?

3. Regarding safety issues, how does management see its responsibilities toward its employees? How do the attorneys see their responsibilities toward PPI?

4. Why does it appear that the ethics of PPI and its attorneys are in conflict?

CASE 16.3

Reexamining a Proposal

After working 10 years as the only minority manager in a large printing company, David Jones decided he wanted to set out on his own. Because of his experience and prior connections, David was confident he could survive in the printing business, but he wondered whether he should buy an existing business or start a new one. As part of his planning, David contacted a professional employer organization (PEO), which had a sterling reputation, to obtain an estimate for human resource services for a startup company. The estimate was to include costs for payroll, benefits, workers' compensation, and other traditional human resource services. Because David had not yet started his business, the PEO generated a generic quote applicable to a small company in the printing industry. In addition, because the PEO had nothing tangible to quote, it gave David a quote for human resource services that was unusually high.

In the meantime, David found an existing small company that he liked, and he bought it. Then he contacted the PEO to sign a contract for human resource services at the previously quoted price. David was ready to take ownership and begin his new venture. He signed the original contract as presented.

After David signed the contract, the PEO reviewed the earlier proposal in light of the actual figures of the company he had purchased. This review raised many concerns for management. Although the goals of the PEO were to provide high-quality service, be competitive in the marketplace, and make a reasonable profit, the quote it had provided David appeared to be much too high. It was not comparable in any way with the other service contracts the PEO had with other companies of similar size and function.

During the review, it became apparent that several concerns had to be addressed. First, the original estimate made the PEO appear as if it was gouging the client. Although the client had signed the original contract, was it fair to charge such a high price for the proposed services? Would charging such high fees mean that the PEO would lose this client or similar clients in the future? Another concern was related to the PEO's support of minority businesses. For years, the PEO had prided itself on having strong values about affirmative action and fairness in the workplace, but this contract appeared to actually hurt and to be somewhat

(Continued)

(Continued)

unfair to a minority client. Finally, the PEO was concerned with the implications of the contract for the salesperson who drew up the proposal for David. Changing the estimated costs in the proposal would have a significant impact on the salesperson's commission, which would negatively affect the morale of others in the PEO's sales area.

After a reexamination of the original proposal, a new contract was drawn up for David's company with lower estimated costs. Though lower than the original proposal, the new contract remained much higher than the average contract in the printing industry. David willingly signed the new contract.

Questions

1. What role should ethics play in the writing of a proposal such as this? Did the PEO do the ethical thing for David? How much money should the PEO have tried to make? What would you have done if you were part of management at the PEO?

2. From a deontological (duty) perspective and a teleological (consequences) perspective, how would you describe the ethics of the PEO?

3. Based on what the PEO did for David, how would you evaluate the PEO on the ethical principles of respect, service, justice, honesty, and community?

4. How would you assess the ethics of the PEO if you were David? If you were among the PEO management? If you were the salesperson? If you were a member of the printing community?

LEADERSHIP INSTRUMENT

Ethics and morals often are regarded as very personal, and we resist having others judge us about them. We also resist judging others. Perhaps for this reason, very few questionnaires have been designed to measure ethical leadership. To address this problem, Craig and Gustafson (1998) developed the Perceived Leader Integrity Scale (PLIS), which is based on utilitarian ethical theory. The PLIS attempts to evaluate leaders' ethics by measuring the degree to which coworkers see them as acting in accordance with rules that would produce the greatest good for the greatest number of people. Craig and Gustafson found PLIS ratings to be strongly and positively related to subordinates' job satisfaction, and negatively related to their desire to quit their jobs.

Parry and Proctor-Thomson (2002) used the PLIS in a study of 1,354 managers and found that perceived integrity was positively related to transformational leadership. Leaders who were seen as transformational were also seen as having more integrity. In addition, the researchers found that perceived integrity was positively correlated with leader and organizational effectiveness.

By taking the PLIS, you can try to assess the ethical integrity of a manager you know, such as one of your supervisors. At the same time, the PLIS will allow you to apply the ideas we discussed in the chapter to a real-world setting. By focusing on observers' impressions, the PLIS represents one way to assess the principle of ethical leadership.

In addition, the PLIS can be used for feedback to employees in organizations and as a part of leadership training and development. Finally, if used as part of an organizational climate survey, the PLIS could be useful as a way of identifying areas in an organization that may need an ethics intervention (Craig & Gustafson, 1998).

Perceived Leader Integrity Scale (PLIS)

Instructions: The following items concern your perceptions of another person's behavior. Circle responses to indicate how well each item describes the person you are rating.

Key: 1 = Not at all   2 = Barely   3 = Somewhat   4 = Well

1.	Puts his or her personal interests ahead of the organization	1	2	3	4
2.	Would risk other people to protect himself or herself in work matters	1	2	3	4
3.	Enjoys turning down requests	1	2	3	4
4.	Deliberately fuels conflict between other people	1	2	3	4
5.	Would blackmail an employee if she or he thought she or he could get away with it	1	2	3	4
6.	Would deliberately exaggerate people's mistakes to make them look bad to others	1	2	3	4
7.	Would treat some people better if they were of the other sex or belonged to a different ethnic group	1	2	3	4
8.	Ridicules people for their mistakes	1	2	3	4
9.	Can be trusted with confidential information	1	2	3	4
10.	Would lie to me	1	2	3	4
11.	Is evil	1	2	3	4
12.	Is not interested in tasks that don't bring personal glory or recognition	1	2	3	4
13.	Would do things that violate organizational policy and then expect others to cover for him or her	1	2	3	4
14.	Would allow someone else to be blamed for his or her mistake	1	2	3	4
15.	Would deliberately avoid responding to e-mail, telephone, or other messages to cause problems for someone else	1	2	3	4
16.	Would make trouble for someone who got on his or her bad side	1	2	3	4
17.	Would engage in sabotage against the organization	1	2	3	4
18.	Would deliberately distort what other people say	1	2	3	4
19.	Is a hypocrite	1	2	3	4
20.	Is vindictive	1	2	3	4
21.	Would try to take credit for other people's ideas	1	2	3	4
22.	Likes to bend the rules	1	2	3	4
23.	Would withhold information or constructive feedback because he or she wants someone to fail	1	2	3	4
24.	Would spread rumors or gossip to try to hurt people or the organization	1	2	3	4
25.	Is rude or uncivil to coworkers	1	2	3	4
26.	Would try to hurt someone's career because of a grudge	1	2	3	4
27.	Shows unfair favoritism toward some people	1	2	3	4

28. Would steal from the organization	1 2 3 4
29. Would falsify records if it would help his or her work situation	1 2 3 4
30. Has high moral standards	1 2 3 4

SOURCE: Adapted from a version of the PLIS that appeared in *Leadership Quarterly,* 9(2), S. B. Craig and S. B. Gustafson, "Perceived Leader Integrity Scale: An Instrument for Assessing Employee Perceptions of Leader Integrity," pp. 143–144, 1998. Used with permission of the authors.

Scoring

The PLIS measures your perceptions of another person's integrity in an organizational setting. Your responses on the PLIS indicate the degree to which you see that person's behavior as ethical.

Score the questionnaire by doing the following. First, reverse the scores on items 9 and 30 (i.e., 1 becomes 4, 2 becomes 3, 3 becomes 2, and 4 becomes 1). Next, sum the responses on all 30 items. A low score on the questionnaire indicates that you perceive the person you evaluated to be highly ethical. A high score indicates that you perceive that person to be very unethical. The interpretation of what the score represents follows.

Scoring Interpretation

Your score is a measure of your perceptions of another person's ethical integrity. Based on previous findings (Craig & Gustafson, 1998), the following interpretations can be made about your total score:

- 30–32 High ethical: If your score is in this range, it means that you see the person you evaluated as highly ethical. Your impression is that the person is very trustworthy and principled.
- 33–45 Moderate ethical: Scores in this range mean that you see the person as moderately ethical. Your impression is that the person might engage in some unethical behaviors under certain conditions.
- 46–120 Low ethical: Scores in this range describe people who are seen as very unethical. Your impression is that the person you evaluated does things that are dishonest, unfair, and unprincipled almost any time he or she has the opportunity.

SUMMARY ———————————————————————————

Although there has been an interest in ethics for thousands of years, very little theoretical research exists on the nature of leadership ethics. This chapter has presented an overview of ethical theories as they apply to the leadership process.

Ethical theory provides a set of principles that guide leaders in making decisions about how to act and how to be morally decent. In the Western tradition, ethical theories typically are divided into two kinds: theories about *conduct* and theories about *character*. Theories about conduct emphasize the consequences of leader behavior (teleological approach) or the rules that govern their behavior (deontological approach). Virtue-based theories focus on the character of leaders, and they stress qualities such as courage, honesty, fairness, and fidelity.

Ethics plays a central role in the leadership process. Because leadership involves influence and leaders often have more power than followers, they have an enormous ethical responsibility for how they affect other people. Leaders need to engage followers to accomplish mutual goals; therefore, it is imperative that they treat followers and their ideas with respect and dignity. Leaders also play a major role in establishing the ethical climate in their organization; that role requires leaders to be particularly sensitive to the values and ideals they promote.

Several prominent leadership scholars, including Heifetz, Burns, and Greenleaf, have made unique contributions to our understanding of ethical leadership. The theme common to these authors is an ethic of caring, which pays attention to followers' needs and the importance of leader–follower relationships.

This chapter suggests that sound ethical leadership is rooted in respect, service, justice, honesty, and community. It is the duty of leaders to treat others with *respect*—to listen to them closely and be tolerant of opposing points of view. Ethical leaders *serve* others by being altruistic, placing others' welfare ahead of their own in an effort to contribute to the common good. *Justice* requires that leaders place fairness at the center of their decision making, including the challenging task of being fair to the individual while simultaneously being fair to the common interests of the community. Good leaders are *honest*. They do not lie, nor do they present truth to others in ways that are destructive or counterproductive. Finally, ethical leaders are committed to building *community*, which

▶ **16.4** Chapter Summary

includes searching for goals that are compatible with the goals of followers and with society as a whole.

Research on ethics and leadership has several strengths. At a time when the public is demanding higher levels of moral responsibility from its leaders, this research provides some direction in how to think about ethical leadership and how to practice it. In addition, this research reminds us that leadership is a moral process. Scholars should include ethics as an integral part of the leadership studies and research. Third, this area of research describes basic principles that we can use in developing real-world ethical leadership.

On the negative side, this research area of ethical leadership is still in an early stage of development. Few studies have been done that directly address the nature of ethical leadership. As a result, the theoretical formulations about the process remain tentative. Second, this area of research relies on the writings of a few individuals whose work has been primarily descriptive and anecdotal. As a result, the development of theory on leadership ethics lacks the traditional empirical support that usually accompanies theories of human behavior. Despite these weaknesses, the field of ethical leadership is wide open for future research. There remains a strong need for research that can advance our understanding of the role of ethics in the leadership process.

Visit the Student Study Site at **www.sagepub.com/northouse6e** for web quizzes, leadership questionnaires, and media links represented by the icons.

REFERENCES

Aronson, E. (2001). Integrating leadership styles and ethical perspectives. *Canadian Journal of Administrative Sciences, 18*(4), 244–256.

Avolio, B. J., & Locke, E. E. (2002). Contrasting different philosophies of leader motivation: Altruism versus egoism. *Leadership Quarterly, 13,* 169–191.

Bass, B. M., & Steidlmeier, P. (1999). Ethics, character, and authentic transformational leadership behavior. *Leadership Quarterly, 10*(2), 181–217.

Beauchamp, T. L., & Bowie, N. E. (1988). *Ethical theory and business* (3rd ed.). Englewood Cliffs, NJ: Prentice Hall.

Beauchamp, T. L., & Childress, J. F. (1994). *Principles of biomedical ethics* (4th ed.). New York: Oxford University Press.

Block, P. (1993). *Stewardship: Choosing service over self-interest*. San Francisco: Berrett-Koehler.

Bowie, N. E. (1991). Challenging the egoistic paradigm. *Business Ethics Quarterly, 1*(1), 1–21.

Burns, J. M. (1978). *Leadership*. New York: Harper & Row.

Carlson, D. S., & Perrewe, P. L. (1995). Institutionalization of organizational ethics through transformational leadership. *Journal of Business Ethics, 14*(10), 829–838.

Ciulla, J. B. (1998). *Ethics, the heart of leadership*. Westport, CT: Greenwood.

Ciulla, J. B. (2001). Carving leaders from the warped wood of humanity. *Canadian Journal of Administrative Sciences, 18*(4), 313–319.

Ciulla, J. B. (2003). *The ethics of leadership*. Belmont, CA: Wadsworth/Thomson Learning.

Covey, S. R. (1990). *Principle-centered leadership*. New York: Fireside.

Craig, S. B., & Gustafson, S. B. (1998). Perceived Leader Integrity Scale: An instrument for assessing employee perceptions of leader integrity. *Leadership Quarterly, 9*(2), 127–145.

Dalla Costa, J. (1998). *The ethical imperative: Why moral leadership is good business*. Reading, MA: Addison-Wesley.

De Pree, M. (1989). *Leadership is an art*. New York: Doubleday.

Frankena, W. (1973). *Ethics* (2nd ed.). Englewood Cliffs, NJ: Prentice Hall.

Gilligan, C. (1982). *In a different voice: Psychological theory and women's development*. Cambridge, MA: Harvard University Press.

Gini, A. (1998). Moral leadership and business ethics. In J. B. Ciulla (Ed.), *Ethics, the heart of leadership* (pp. 27–46). Westport, CT: Greenwood.

Greenleaf, R. K. (1970). *The servant as leader*. Newton Centre, MA: Robert K. Greenleaf Center.

Greenleaf, R. K. (1977). *Servant leadership: A journey into the nature of legitimate power and greatness*. New York: Paulist.

Heifetz, R. A. (1994). *Leadership without easy answers*. Cambridge, MA: Harvard University Press.

Jaksa, J. A., & Pritchard, M. S. (1988). *Communication ethics: Methods of analysis*. Belmont, CA: Wadsworth.

Johnson, C. R. (2011). *Meeting the ethical challenges of leadership* (4th ed.). Thousand Oaks, CA: Sage.

Kanungo, R. N. (2001). Ethical values of transactional and transformational leaders. *Canadian Journal of Administrative Sciences, 18*(4), 257–265.

Kanungo, R. N., & Mendonca, M. (1996). *Ethical dimensions of leadership*. Thousand Oaks, CA: Sage.

Kitchener, K. S. (1984). Intuition, critical evaluation, and ethical principles: The foundation for ethical decisions in counseling psychology. *Counseling Psychologist, 12*(3), 43–55.

Komives, S. R., Lucas, N., & McMahon, T. R. (1998). *Exploring leadership: For college students who want to make a difference*. San Francisco: Jossey-Bass.

Kouzes, J. M., & Posner, B. Z. (1995). *The leadership challenge: How to keep getting extraordinary things done in organizations* (2nd ed.). San Francisco: Jossey-Bass.

Parry, K. W., & Proctor-Thomson, S. B. (2002). Perceived integrity of transformational leaders in organisational settings. *Journal of Business Ethics, 35,* 75–96.

Pojman, L. P. (1995). *Ethical theory: Classical and contemporary readings* (2nd ed.). Belmont, CA: Wadsworth.

Price, T. (2008). *Leadership ethics: An introduction.* New York: Cambridge University Press.

Rawls, J. (1971). *A theory of justice.* Boston: Harvard University Press.

Rost, J. C. (1991). *Leadership for the twenty-first century.* New York: Praeger.

Schminke, M., Ambrose, M. L., & Noel, T. W. (1997). The effect of ethical frameworks on perceptions of organizational justice. *Academy of Management Journal, 40*(5), 1190–1207.

Schumann, P. L. (2001). A moral principles framework for human resource management ethics. *Human Resource Management Review, 11,* 93–111.

Senge, P. M. (1990). *The fifth discipline: The art and practice of the learning organization.* New York: Doubleday.

Trevino, L. K. (1986). Ethical decision making in organizations: A person–situation interactionist model. *Academy of Management Review, 11*(3), 601–617.

Trevino, L. K., Brown, M., & Hartman, L. P. (2003). A qualitative investigation of perceived executive ethical leadership: Perceptions from inside and outside the executive suite. *Human Relations, 56*(1), 5–37.

Velasquez, M. G. (1992). *Business ethics: Concepts and cases* (3rd ed.). Englewood Cliffs, NJ: Prentice Hall.

Wayne, L. (2009, May 30). A promise to be ethical in an era of immorality. *The New York Times.* Retrieved on June 15, 2009, from http://www.nytimes.com/2009/05/30/business

Author Index

Subject Index

About the Author

Peter G. Northouse, PhD, is a professor of communication (emeritus) in the School of Communication at Western Michigan University. For more than 25 years, he has taught leadership and interpersonal and organizational communication at both the undergraduate and graduate levels. In addition to publications in professional journals, he is the author of *Introduction to Leadership: Concepts and Practice* and coauthor of *Health Communication: Strategies for Health Professionals* (3rd ed.). His scholarly and curricular interests include models of leadership, leadership assessment, ethical leadership, and leadership and group dynamics. He has worked as a consultant in a variety of areas, including leadership development, leadership education, conflict management, and health communication. He holds a doctorate in speech communication from the University of Denver and master's and bachelor's degrees in communication education from Michigan State University.

About the Contributors

Susan E. Kogler Hill (PhD, University of Denver, 1974) is professor emeritus and former chair of the School of Communication at Cleveland State University. Her research and consulting have been in the areas of interpersonal and organizational communication. She specializes in group leadership, teamwork, empowerment, and mentoring. She is author of a text titled *Improving Interpersonal Competence*. In addition, she has written book chapters and published articles in many professional journals.

Crystal L. Hoyt (PhD, University of California, Santa Barbara, 2003) is an associate professor of leadership studies and psychology at the University of Richmond. As a social psychologist, she brings a psychological perspective to the field of leadership studies. Her primary area of research focuses on understanding the experiences and perceptions of nontraditional leaders, and her secondary area focuses on leader cognitions and ethics. She has published over 35 peer-reviewed articles and book chapters and is the coeditor of two books: *Leadership and Psychology* in the Leadership at the Crossroads series and *For the Greater Good of All: Perspectives on Individualism, Society, and Leadership*.

Ernest L. Stech (PhD, University of Denver, 1969) is an associate member of the Emeritus College at Arizona State University. He is former president and CEO of Frost Engineering Development Corporation and former executive director of the Flagstaff Area National Monuments Foundation. Stech has written numerous articles in professional journals and several textbook chapters. He is author of *The Transformed Leader* and *Leadership Communication*. He is active in lifelong learning programs in the Phoenix, Arizona, area, and his academic interests are in ethics and epistemology.

⑤SAGE research methods online

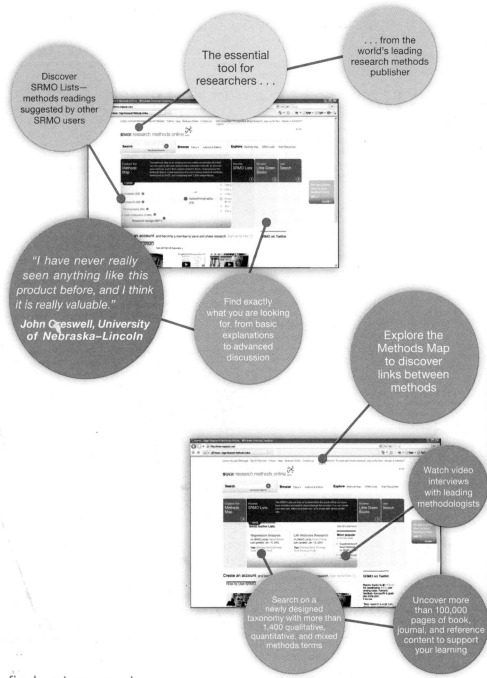

... from the world's leading research methods publisher

The essential tool for researchers ...

Discover SRMO Lists— methods readings suggested by other SRMO users

"I have never really seen anything like this product before, and I think it is really valuable."
John Creswell, University of Nebraska–Lincoln

Find exactly what you are looking for, from basic explanations to advanced discussion

Explore the Methods Map to discover links between methods

Watch video interviews with leading methodologists

Search on a newly designed taxonomy with more than 1,400 qualitative, quantitative, and mixed methods terms

Uncover more than 100,000 pages of book, journal, and reference content to support your learning

find out more at
www.srmo.sagepub.com